T0364889

Ford Transit Custom Diesel
Owners Workshop Manual

Rob Keenan

Models covered

(6423 - 304)

Transit Custom variants with 2.0 litre (1996cc) EcoBlue & 2.2 litre Duratorq (2198cc) turbo-diesel engines

Also covers most mechanical features of Tourneo Custom

Does NOT cover automatic transmission, specialist bodywork/conversions, or technical changes made for 2018 model year (Dec 2017 onward)

Does NOT cover Transit Courier or Connect ranges, or new Transit (full size) range introduced for 2014

© Haynes Group Limited 2018

ABCDE
FGHIJ
KLMNO
PQRS

A book in the **Haynes Owners Workshop Manual Series**

ISBN **978 1 78521 423 3**

British Library Cataloguing in Publication Data
A catalogue record for this book is available from the British Library.

Printed in India

Haynes Group Limited
Sparkford, Yeovil, Somerset BA22 7JJ, England

Haynes North America, Inc
2801 Townsgate Road, Suite 340, Thousand Oaks, CA 91361

Disclaimer

There are risks associated with automotive repairs. The ability to make repairs depends on the individual's skill, experience and proper tools. Individuals should act with due care and acknowledge and assume the risk of performing automotive repairs.

The purpose of this manual is to provide comprehensive, useful and accessible automotive repair information, to help you get the best value from your vehicle. However, this manual is not a substitute for a professional certified technician or mechanic.

This repair manual is produced by a third party and is not associated with an individual vehicle manufacturer. If there is any doubt or discrepancy between this manual and the owner's manual or the factory service manual, please refer to the factory service manual or seek assistance from a professional certified technician or mechanic.

Even though we have prepared this manual with extreme care and every attempt is made to ensure that the information in this manual is correct, neither the publisher nor the author can accept responsibility for loss, damage or injury caused by any errors in, or omissions from, the information given.

Contents

LIVING WITH YOUR FORD TRANSIT CUSTOM

MAINTENANCE

Contents

REPAIRS AND OVERHAUL

Engine and Associated Systems

Transmission

Brakes and suspension

Body equipment

Wiring diagrams

REFERENCE

Index

The Ford Transit covered by this manual was introduced in the UK in December 2012 and continued in production until 2018 when it was replaced by an updated version. Versions are available on a long or short wheelbase chassis.

The Transit is available with 2.0 and 2.2 litre turbocharged diesel engines, in a wide range of power outputs. The engines are DOHC 16-valve units, featuring the latest design of direct injection common rail fuel system. The models covered in this manual are available in front-wheel-drive configuration, with the engine and transmission mounted transversely at the front.

All models are equipped with a 6-speed all synchromesh manual transmission.

Front suspension is fully independent on all models, with a beam axle, supported on semi-elliptic leaf springs employed at the rear.

The dual-circuit, servo-assisted braking system has discs all round. ABS, Electronic Stability Program (ESP) Emergency Brake Assist (EBA) and Electronic Brakeforce Distribution (EBD) are fitted as standard, for extra safety when braking in emergency situations.

A wide range of standard and optional equipment is available within the Transit range, including power steering, air conditioning, remote central locking, electric windows, electronic engine immobiliser and supplemental restraint systems.

For the home mechanic, the Transit is a relatively straightforward vehicle to maintain, and most of the items requiring frequent attention are easily accessible.

Your Ford Transit Manual

The aim of this manual is to help you get the best value from your vehicle. It can do so in several ways. It can help you decide what work must be done (even should you choose to get it done by a garage). It will also provide information on routine maintenance and servicing, and give a logical course of action and diagnosis when random faults occur. However, it is hoped that you will use the manual by tackling the work yourself. On simpler jobs it may even be quicker than booking the vehicle into a garage and going there twice, to leave and collect it. Perhaps most important, a lot of money can be saved by avoiding the costs a garage must charge to cover its labour and overheads.

The manual has drawings and descriptions to show the function of the various components so that their layout can be understood. Tasks are described and photographed in a clear step-by-step sequence.

References to the 'left' and 'right' of the vehicle are in the sense of a person in the driver's seat facing forward.

Project vehicles

The main vehicle used in the preparation of this manual, and which appears in many of the photographic sequences, was a Ford Transit Custom van with a 2.0 litre engine. Additional work was carried out on a Transit Custom van with a 2.2 litre engine.

Acknowledgements

Thanks are due to Draper Tools Limited, who provided some of the workshop tools, and to all those people at Sparkford who helped in the production of this manual.

We take great pride in the accuracy of information given in this manual, but vehicle manufacturers make alterations and design changes during the production run of a particular vehicle of which they do not inform us. No liability can be accepted by the authors or publishers for loss, damage or injury caused by any errors in, or omissions from, the information given.

Working on your car can be dangerous. This page shows just some of the potential risks and hazards, with the aim of creating a safety-conscious attitude.

General hazards

Scalding

• Don't remove the radiator or expansion tank cap while the engine is hot.
• Engine oil, transmission fluid or power steering fluid may also be dangerously hot if the engine has recently been running.

Burning

• Beware of burns from the exhaust system and from any part of the engine. Brake discs and drums can also be extremely hot immediately after use.

Crushing

• When working under or near a raised vehicle, always supplement the jack with axle stands, or use drive-on ramps.
Never venture under a car which is only supported by a jack.
• Take care if loosening or tightening high-torque nuts when the vehicle is on stands. Initial loosening and final tightening should be done with the wheels on the ground.

Fire

• Fuel is highly flammable; fuel vapour is explosive.
• Don't let fuel spill onto a hot engine.
• Do not smoke or allow naked lights (including pilot lights) anywhere near a vehicle being worked on. Also beware of creating sparks (electrically or by use of tools).
• Fuel vapour is heavier than air, so don't work on the fuel system with the vehicle over an inspection pit.
• Another cause of fire is an electrical overload or short-circuit. Take care when repairing or modifying the vehicle wiring.
• Keep a fire extinguisher handy, of a type suitable for use on fuel and electrical fires.

Electric shock

• Ignition HT and Xenon headlight voltages can be dangerous, especially to people with heart problems or a pacemaker. Don't work on or near these systems with the engine running or the ignition switched on.

• Mains voltage is also dangerous. Make sure that any mains-operated equipment is correctly earthed. Mains power points should be protected by a residual current device (RCD) circuit breaker.

Fume or gas intoxication

• Exhaust fumes are poisonous; they can contain carbon monoxide, which is rapidly fatal if inhaled. Never run the engine in a confined space such as a garage with the doors shut.
• Fuel vapour is also poisonous, as are the vapours from some cleaning solvents and paint thinners.

Poisonous or irritant substances

• Avoid skin contact with battery acid and with any fuel, fluid or lubricant, especially antifreeze, brake hydraulic fluid and Diesel fuel. Don't syphon them by mouth. If such a substance is swallowed or gets into the eyes, seek medical advice.
• Prolonged contact with used engine oil can cause skin cancer. Wear gloves or use a barrier cream if necessary. Change out of oil-soaked clothes and do not keep oily rags in your pocket.
• Air conditioning refrigerant forms a poisonous gas if exposed to a naked flame (including a cigarette). It can also cause skin burns on contact.

Asbestos

• Asbestos dust can cause cancer if inhaled or swallowed. Asbestos may be found in gaskets and in brake and clutch linings. When dealing with such components it is safest to assume that they contain asbestos.

Special hazards

Hydrofluoric acid

• This extremely corrosive acid is formed when certain types of synthetic rubber, found in some O-rings, oil seals, fuel hoses etc, are exposed to temperatures above 4000C. The rubber changes into a charred or sticky substance containing the acid. *Once formed, the acid remains dangerous for years. If it gets onto the skin, it may be necessary to amputate the limb concerned.*
• When dealing with a vehicle which has suffered a fire, or with components salvaged from such a vehicle, wear protective gloves and discard them after use.

The battery

• Batteries contain sulphuric acid, which attacks clothing, eyes and skin. Take care when topping-up or carrying the battery.
• The hydrogen gas given off by the battery is highly explosive. Never cause a spark or allow a naked light nearby. Be careful when connecting and disconnecting battery chargers or jump leads.

Air bags

• Air bags can cause injury if they go off accidentally. Take care when removing the steering wheel and trim panels. Special storage instructions may apply.

Diesel injection equipment

• Diesel injection pumps supply fuel at very high pressure. Take care when working on the fuel injectors and fuel pipes.

⚠ *Warning: Never expose the hands, face or any other part of the body to injector spray; the fuel can penetrate the skin with potentially fatal results.*

Remember...

DO

• Do use eye protection when using power tools, and when working under the vehicle.

• Do wear gloves or use barrier cream to protect your hands when necessary.

• Do get someone to check periodically that all is well when working alone on the vehicle.

• Do keep loose clothing and long hair well out of the way of moving mechanical parts.

• Do remove rings, wristwatch etc, before working on the vehicle – especially the electrical system.

• Do ensure that any lifting or jacking equipment has a safe working load rating adequate for the job.

DON'T

• Don't attempt to lift a heavy component which may be beyond your capability – get assistance.

• Don't rush to finish a job, or take unverified short cuts.

• Don't use ill-fitting tools which may slip and cause injury.

• Don't leave tools or parts lying around where someone can trip over them. Mop up oil and fuel spills at once.

• Don't allow children or pets to play in or near a vehicle being worked on.

The following pages are intended to help in dealing with common roadside emergencies and breakdowns. You will find more detailed fault finding information at the back of the manual, and repair information in the main chapters.

If your vehicle won't start and the starter motor doesn't turn

☐ Move the driver's seat fully forward, open the battery box cover and make sure that the battery terminals are clean and tight.
☐ Switch on the headlights and try to start the engine. If the headlights go very dim when you're trying to start, the battery is probably flat. Get out of trouble by jump starting (see next page) using a friend's car.

If your vehicle won't start even though the starter motor turns as normal

☐ Is there fuel in the tank?
☐ Is there moisture on electrical components under the bonnet? Switch off the ignition, then wipe off any obvious dampness with a dry cloth. Spray a water-repellent aerosol product (WD-40 or equivalent) on engine and fuel system electrical connectors like those shown in the photos.

A Check the security and condition of the battery connections (under the driver's seat).

B Check all multi-plugs and wiring connectors for security.

C Check that all fuses are still in good condition and none have blown.

Check that electrical connections are secure (with the ignition switched off) and spray with water dispersant if you suspect a problem due to damp.

Jump starting

When jump-starting a vehicle using a booster battery, observe the following precautions:

✔ Before connecting the booster battery, make sure that the ignition is switched off.

Caution: Remove the key in case the central locking engages when the jump leads are connected

✔ Ensure that all electrical equipment (lights, heater, wipers, etc) is switched off.

✔ Take note of any special precautions printed on the battery case.

✔ Make sure that the booster battery is the same voltage as the discharged one in the vehicle.

✔ If the battery is being jump-started from the battery in another vehicle, the two vehicles MUST NOT TOUCH each other.

✔ Make sure that the transmission is in neutral (or P, in the case of automatic transmission).

HAYNES HINT *Jump starting will get you out of trouble, but you must correct whatever made the battery go flat in the first place. There are three possibilities:*

1 The battery has been drained by repeated attempts to start, or by leaving the lights on.

2 The charging system is not working properly (alternator drivebelt slack or broken, alternator wiring fault or alternator itself faulty).

3 The battery itself is at fault (electrolyte low, or battery worn out).

1 Lift off the cover over the flat battery's positive (+) cable connection point in the engine compartment and connect one end of the red jump lead to the terminal.

2 Connect the other end of the red lead to the positive (+) terminal of the booster battery.

3 Connect one end of the black jump lead to the negative (-) terminal of the booster battery

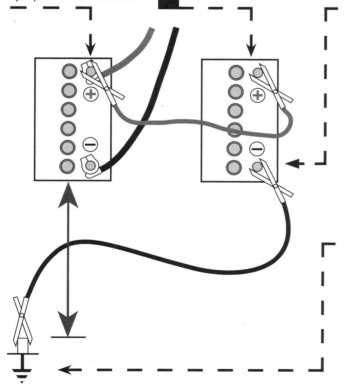

4 Connect the other end of the black jump lead to a bolt or bracket on the engine block on the vehicle to be started.

5 Make sure that the jump leads will not come into contact with the fan, drive-belts or other moving parts of the engine.

6 Start the engine using the booster battery and run it at idle speed. Switch on the lights, rear window demister and heater blower motor, then disconnect the jump leads in the reverse order of connection. Turn off the lights etc.

Wheel changing

 Warning: Do not change a wheel in a situation where you risk being hit by other traffic. On busy roads, try to stop in a lay-by or a gateway. Be wary of passing traffic while changing the wheel – it is easy to become distracted by the job in hand. If you have a passenger, ask them to keep a look out from a safe distance.

Preparation

☐ When a puncture occurs, stop as soon as it is safe to do so.
☐ Park on firm level ground, if possible, and well out of the way of other traffic.
☐ Use hazard warning lights if necessary.

☐ If you have one, use a warning triangle to alert other drivers of your presence.
☐ Apply the handbrake and engage first or reverse gear.
☐ Chock the wheel diagonally opposite the

one being removed – a couple of large stones will do for this.
☐ If the ground is soft, use a flat piece of wood to spread the load under the jack.

Changing the wheel

1 The jack, jack handle and wheelbrace are located in a stowage compartment in the front right-hand stepwell. Release the catches and remove the stowage compartment cover, then unclip the retaining straps and remove the jack, handle and wheelbrace.

2 If fitted in lieu of a puncture repair kit, the spare wheel is located under the rear of the vehicle, held in place by a bracket attached to a steel cable. To access the mechanism that lowers the wheel, locate the guide hole just inside the right-hand rear door, on the floor of the van. Where fitted, unscrew the security bolt located above the guide hole.

3 Insert the flat end of the wheelbrace or the short arm of the jack handle (according to model) into the guide hole and engage the mechanism. Turn the wheelbrace or jack handle anti-clockwise until the spare wheel rests on the ground and there is slack in the cable.

4 Slide the spare wheel out from under the vehicle. First unclip the cable...

5 ...and then disengage the bracket by unscrewing the retaining bolt as shown. The bracket can now be manouevered out from the other side of the wheel

6 Remove any wheel nut covers or wheel trim, using the flat end of the wheelbrace, for access to the wheel nuts. Fit the locking wheel nut adapter, if applicable, and slacken each wheel nut by half a turn.

7 Position the jack under the jacking point nearest the punctured wheel. The front jacking points are the rear bolts for the front subframe which engage with recesses in the flap on top of the jack. Turn the jack handle clockwise until the wheel is raised clear of the ground.

8 The rear jacking points are under the rear eyes of the leaf spring, as near to the wheel as possible. The flap on top of the jack should be rotated through 90° for positive engagement. Turn the jack handle clockwise until the wheel is raised clear of the ground.

9 Unscrew the wheel nuts, noting which way round they fit, and remove the wheel. Fit the spare wheel and screw on the nuts. Lightly tighten the nuts with the wheelbrace.

10 Lower the vehicle to the ground and fully tighten the wheel nuts. On vehicles with 5-stud wheels, tighten the nuts in the sequence shown. On vehicles with 6-stud wheels, tighten the nuts in a diagonal sequence. Refit the wheel nut covers or wheel trim, as applicable.

Finally . . .

- [ ] Remove the wheel chocks.
- [ ] If possible, secure the punctured wheel back under the vehicle using the cable and bracket, then stow the jack and tools in the stowage compartment. However, some alloy wheels cannot be attached to the cable and bracket, and will need to be stored inside the vehicle, while the cables will need to be secured under the vehicle. Note that the Ford handbook states not to lower the winch mechanism without the wheel attached because this can damage the mechanism.
- [ ] Check the tyre pressure on the wheel just fitted. If it is low, or if you don't have a pressure gauge with you, drive slowly to the next garage and inflate the tyre to the correct pressure.
- [ ] Have the damaged tyre or wheel repaired as soon as possible, or another puncture will leave you stranded.
- [ ] Don't leave the spare wheel cradle empty and unsecured – it could drop onto the ground while the vehicle is moving.
- [ ] Have the wheel nuts tightened to the correct torque (see Chapter 10) at the earliest opportunity.

Towing

When all else fails, you may find yourself having to get a tow home – or of course you may be helping somebody else. Long-distance recovery should only be done by a garage or breakdown service. For shorter distances, DIY towing using another car is easy enough, but observe the following points:

- [ ] Use a proper tow-rope – they are not expensive. The vehicle being towed must display an ON TOW sign in its rear window.
- [ ] Always turn the ignition key to the 'On' position when the vehicle is being towed, so that the steering lock is released, and the direction indicator and brake lights work.
- [ ] Only attach the tow-rope to the towing eyes located in the front bumper and below the rear bumper.
- [ ] Before being towed, release the handbrake and select neutral on the transmission.
- [ ] Note that greater-than-usual pedal pressure will be required to operate the brakes, since the vacuum servo unit is only operational with the engine running.
- [ ] Greater-than-usual steering effort will also be required.
- [ ] The driver of the car being towed must keep the tow-rope taut at all times to avoid snatching.
- [ ] Make sure that both drivers know the route before setting off.
- [ ] Only drive at moderate speeds and keep the distance towed to a minimum. Drive smoothly and allow plenty of time for slowing down at junctions.

Identifying leaks

Puddles on the garage floor or drive, or obvious wetness under the bonnet or underneath the car, suggest a leak that needs investigating. It can sometimes be difficult to decide where the leak is coming from, especially if an engine undershield is fitted. Leaking oil or fluid can also be blown rearwards by the passage of air under the car, giving a false impression of where the problem lies.

 Warning: Most automotive oils and fluids are poisonous. Wash them off skin, and change out of contaminated clothing, without delay.

 The smell of a fluid leaking from the car may provide a clue to what's leaking. Some fluids are distinctively coloured. It may help to remove the engine undershield, clean the car carefully and to park it over some clean paper overnight as an aid to locating the source of the leak.
Remember that some leaks may only occur while the engine is running.

Sump oil

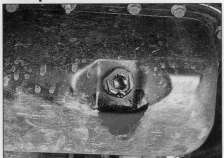

Engine oil may leak from the drain plug...

Oil from filter

...or from the base of the oil filter.

Gearbox oil

Gearbox oil can leak from the seals at the inboard ends of the driveshafts.

Antifreeze

Leaking antifreeze often leaves a crystalline deposit like this.

Brake fluid

A leak occurring at a wheel is almost certainly brake fluid.

Introduction

There are some very simple checks which need only take a few minutes to carry out, but which could save you a lot of inconvenience and expense.

These *Weekly checks* require no great skill or special tools, and the small amount of time they take to perform could prove to be very well spent, for example:

☐ Keeping an eye on tyre condition and pressures, will not only help to stop them wearing out prematurely, but could also save your life.

☐ Many breakdowns are caused by electrical problems. Battery-related faults are particularly common, and a quick check on a regular basis will often prevent the majority of these.

☐ If your car develops a brake fluid leak, the first time you might know about it is when your brakes don't work properly. Checking the level regularly will give advance warning of this kind of problem.

☐ If the oil or coolant levels run low, the cost of repairing any engine damage will be far greater than fixing the leak, for example.

Underbonnet check points

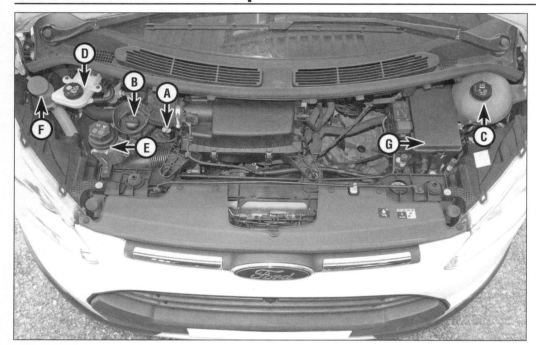

◄ 2.0 litre models

A *Engine oil level dipstick*

B *Engine oil filler cap*

C *Coolant reservoir (expansion tank)*

D *Brake and clutch fluid reservoir*

E *Power steering fluid reservoir*

F *Washer fluid reservoir*

G *Engine compartment fuse/ relay box*

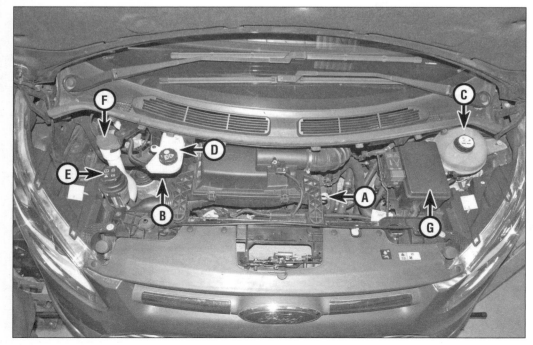

◄ 2.2 litre models

A *Engine oil level dipstick*

B *Engine oil filler cap*

C *Coolant reservoir (expansion tank)*

D *Brake and clutch fluid reservoir*

E *Power steering fluid reservoir*

F *Washer fluid reservoir*

G *Engine compartment fuse/ relay box*

Engine oil level

Before you start

✔ Make sure that the vehicle is on level ground.
✔ The oil level must be checked with the engine at normal operating temperature, however, wait at least 5 minutes after the engine has been switched off.

If the oil is checked immediately after driving the vehicle, some of the oil will remain in the upper engine components, resulting in an inaccurate reading on the dipstick.

The correct oil

Modern engines place great demands on their oil. It is very important that the correct oil for your car is used (see *Lubricants and fluids*).

Vehicle care

● If you have to add oil frequently, you should check whether you have any oil leaks. Place some clean paper under the car overnight, and check for stains in the morning. If there are no leaks, then the engine may be burning oil.
● Always maintain the level between the upper and lower dipstick marks (see photo 3). If the level is too low, severe engine damage may occur. Oil seal failure may result if the engine is overfilled by adding too much oil.

1 The dipstick is brightly coloured for easy identification (see *Underbonnet check points* for exact location). Withdraw the dipstick.

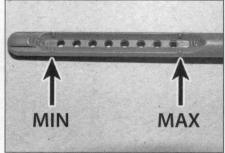

MIN   MAX

3 Note the level on the end of the dipstick, which should be between the upper (MAX) mark and lower (MIN) mark. Approximately 1.5 litres of oil will raise the level from the lower mark to the upper mark.

2 Using a clean rag or paper towel remove all oil from the dipstick. Insert the clean dipstick into the tube as far asit will go, then withdraw it again.

4 Oil is added through the filler cap. Unscrew the cap and top-up the level. A funnel may help to reduce spillage. Add the oil slowly, checking the level on the dipstick frequently. Avoid overfilling (see *Vehicle care*).

Coolant level

Warning: Do not attempt to remove the expansion tank pressure cap when the engine is hot, as there is a very great risk of scalding. Do not leave open containers of coolant about, as it is poisonous.

Vehicle care

● Adding coolant should not be necessary on a regular basis. If frequent topping-up is required, it is likely there is a leak. Check the radiator, all hoses and joint faces for signs of staining or wetness, and rectify as necessary.

● It is important that antifreeze is used in the cooling system all year round, not just during the winter months. Don't top-up with water alone, as the antifreeze will become too diluted.

1 The coolant level varies with the temperature of the engine, and is visible through the expansion tank. When the engine is cold, the coolant level should be between the MAX and MIN marks on the side of the tank. When the engine is hot, the level may rise slightly above the MAX mark.

2 If topping-up is necessary, wait until the engine is cold. Slowly unscrew the expansion tank cap, to release any pressure present in the cooling system, and remove it.

3 Add a mixture of water and antifreeze to the expansion tank until the coolant level is halfway between the level marks. Use only the specified antifreeze – if using Ford antifreeze, make sure it is the same type and colour as that already in the system. Refit the cap and tighten it securely.

Brake and clutch fluid level

Note: *All models have a hydraulically operated clutch, which uses the same fluid as the braking system.*

Warning:
• *Brake fluid can harm your eyes and damage painted surfaces, so use extreme caution when handling and pouring it.*
• *Do not use fluid that has been standing open for some time, as it absorbs moisture from the air, which can cause a dangerous loss of braking effectiveness.*

Safety first!

● If the reservoir requires repeated topping-up this is an indication of a fluid leak somewhere in the system, which should be investigated immediately.

● If a leak is suspected, the car should not be driven until the braking system has been checked. Never take any risks where brakes are concerned.

HAYNES HiNT
• *Make sure that your car is on level ground.*
• *The fluid level in the reservoir will drop slightly as the brake pads and shoes wear down, but the fluid level must never be allowed to drop below the MIN mark.*

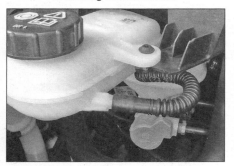

1 The MAX and MIN marks are indicated on the front of the reservoir. The fluid level must be kept between the marks at all times.

2 If topping-up is necessary, first wipe clean the area around the filler cap to prevent dirt entering the hydraulic system. Unscrew the reservoir cap.

3 Carefully add fluid, taking care not to spill it onto the surrounding components. Use only the specified fluid; mixing different types can cause damage to the system. After topping-up to the correct level, securely refit the cap and wipe off any spilt fluid.

Power steering fluid level

Before you start

✔ Park the vehicle on level ground.
✔ Set the steering wheel straight ahead.
✔ The engine should be cold and turned off.

HAYNES HiNT
For the check to be accurate, the steering must not be turned while the level is being checked.

Safety first!

● The need for frequent topping-up indicates a leak, which should be investigated immediately.

1 The reservoir is mounted at the front right-hand side of the engine compartment. The fluid level can be viewed through the reservoir body and should be between the MIN and MAX marks when the engine is cold.

2 If topping-up is necessary, first wipe clean the area around the filler cap to prevent dirt entering the system. Unscrew the reservoir cap.

3 When topping-up, use the specified type of fluid and do not overfill the reservoir. When the level is correct, securely refit the cap.

Tyre condition and pressure

It is very important that tyres are in good condition, and at the correct pressure - having a tyre failure at any speed is highly dangerous. Tyre wear is influenced by driving style - harsh braking and acceleration, or fast cornering, will all produce more rapid tyre wear. As a general rule, the front tyres wear out faster than the rears. Interchanging the tyres from front to rear ("rotating" the tyres) may result in more even wear. However, if this is completely effective, you may have the expense of replacing all four tyres at once!

Remove any nails or stones embedded in the tread before they penetrate the tyre to cause deflation. If removal of a nail does reveal that the tyre has been punctured, refit the nail so that its point of penetration is marked. Then immediately change the wheel, and have the tyre repaired by a tyre dealer.

Regularly check the tyres for damage in the form of cuts or bulges, especially in the sidewalls. Periodically remove the wheels, and clean any dirt or mud from the inside and outside surfaces. Examine the wheel rims for signs of rusting, corrosion or other damage. Light alloy wheels are easily damaged by "kerbing" whilst parking; steel wheels may also become dented or buckled. A new wheel is very often the only way to overcome severe damage.

New tyres should be balanced when they are fitted, but it may become necessary to re-balance them as they wear, or if the balance weights fitted to the wheel rim should fall off. Unbalanced tyres will wear more quickly, as will the steering and suspension components. Wheel imbalance is normally signified by vibration, particularly at a certain speed (typically around 50 mph). If this vibration is felt only through the steering, then it is likely that just the front wheels need balancing. If, however, the vibration is felt through the whole car, the rear wheels could be out of balance. Wheel balancing should be carried out by a tyre dealer or garage.

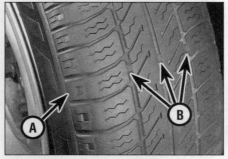

1 *Tread Depth - visual check*
The original tyres have tread wear safety bands (B), which will appear when the tread depth reaches approximately 1.6 mm. The band positions are indicated by a triangular mark on the tyre sidewall (A).

2 *Tread Depth - manual check*
Alternatively, tread wear can be monitored with a simple, inexpensive device known as a tread depth indicator gauge.

3 *Tyre Pressure Check*
Check the tyre pressures regularly with the tyres cold. Do not adjust the tyre pressures immediately after the vehicle has been used, or an inaccurate setting will result.

Tyre tread wear patterns

Shoulder Wear

Underinflation (wear on both sides)
Under-inflation will cause overheating of the tyre, because the tyre will flex too much, and the tread will not sit correctly on the road surface. This will cause a loss of grip and excessive wear, not to mention the danger of sudden tyre failure due to heat build-up.
Check and adjust pressures
Incorrect wheel camber (wear on one side)
Repair or renew suspension parts
Hard cornering
Reduce speed!

Centre Wear

Overinflation
Over-inflation will cause rapid wear of the centre part of the tyre tread, coupled with reduced grip, harsher ride, and the danger of shock damage occurring in the tyre casing.
Check and adjust pressures

If you sometimes have to inflate your car's tyres to the higher pressures specified for maximum load or sustained high speed, don't forget to reduce the pressures to normal afterwards.

Uneven Wear

Front tyres may wear unevenly as a result of wheel misalignment. Most tyre dealers and garages can check and adjust the wheel alignment (or "tracking") for a modest charge.
Incorrect camber or castor
Repair or renew suspension parts
Malfunctioning suspension
Repair or renew suspension parts
Unbalanced wheel
Balance tyres
Incorrect toe setting
Adjust front wheel alignment
Note: *The feathered edge of the tread which typifies toe wear is best checked by feel.*

Washer fluid level

● Screenwash additives not only keep the windscreen clean during bad weather, they also prevent the washer system freezing in cold weather – which is when you are likely to need it most. Don't top-up using plain water, as the screenwash will become diluted, and will freeze in cold weather.

● Check the operation of the windscreen and rear window washers. Adjust the nozzles using a pin if necessary, aiming the spray to a point slightly above the centre of the swept area.

 Warning: On no account use engine coolant antifreeze in the screen washer system – this may damage the paintwork.

1 The reservoir for the washer systems is located on the right-hand side of the engine compartment. If topping-up is necessary, open the filler cap.

2 When topping-up the reservoir a screen-wash additive should be added in the quantities recommended on the bottle.

Wiper blades

● Only fit good-quality wiper blades.
● When removing an old wiper blade, note how it is fitted. Fitting new blades can be a tricky exercise, and noting how the old blade came off can save time.
● While the wiper blade is removed, take care

not to knock the wiper arm from its locked position, or it could strike the glassv.
● Offer the new blade into position the same way round as the old one. Ensure that it clicks home securely, otherwise it may come off in use, damaging the glass.

HAYNES HiNT *If smearing is still a problem despite fitting new wiper blades, try cleaning the glass with neat screenwash additive or methylated spirit.*

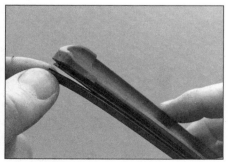

1 Check the condition of the wiper blades; if they are cracked or show any signs of deterioration, or if the glassswept area is smeared, renew them. Wiper blades should be renewed annually.

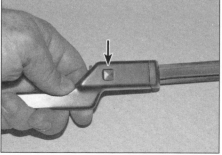

2 To remove a windscreen wiper blade, pull the arm fully away from the windscreen until it locks. Place a thick towel on the glass in case the blade should snap back. Depress the locking button and slide the blade from the arm.

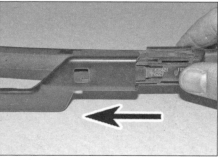

3 When fitting the new blade, make sure that the blade locks securely into the arm, and that the blade is orientated correctly.

Electrical systems

✔ Check all external lights and the horn. Refer to Chapter 12 for details if any of the circuits are found to be inoperative.
✔ Visually check all accessible wiring connectors, harnesses and retaining clips for security, and for signs of chafing or damage.

✔ There are four separate fuse/relay boxes on Transit models. One is located on the left-hand side of the engine compartment, two more are located inside the vehicle behind the glovebox, and another is located under the driver's seat. Refer to Chapter 12 Section 3 for detailed information.

 If you need to check your brake lights and indicators unaided, back up to a wall or garage door and operate the lights. The reflected light should show if they are working properly.

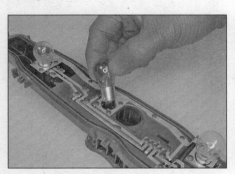

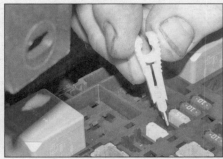

1 If a single indicator light, stop-light or headlight has failed, it is likely that a bulb has blown and will need to be replaced. Refer to Chapter 12, Section 8 for details. If both stop-lights have failed, it is possible that the switch has failed (see Chapter 9, Section 20).

2 If more than one indicator light or headlight has failed, it is likely that either a fuse has blown or that there is a fault in the circuit (see Chapter 12, Section 2). To gain access to the engine compartment fuse/relay box, unclip and remove the cover. Refer to the wiring diagrams at the end of Chapter 12 for details of the fuse locations and circuits protected.

3 To renew a blown fuse, remove it, where applicable, using the plastic tweezers usually provided on the underside of the underbonnet fuse box, or needle-nosed pliers. Fit a new fuse of the same rating, available from car accessory shops. It is important that you find the reason that the fuse blew (see *Electrical fault finding* in Chapter 12, Section 2).

Battery

Caution: Before carrying out any work on the vehicle battery, read the precautions given in 'Safety first!' at the start of this manual. If the battery is to be disconnected, refer to Chapter 5 before proceeding.

✔ Make sure that the battery tray is in good condition, and that the clamp is tight. Corrosion on the tray, retaining clamp and the battery itself can be removed with a solution of water and baking soda. Thoroughly rinse all cleaned areas with water. Any metal parts damaged by corrosion should be covered with a zinc-based primer, and then painted.
✔ Periodically (approximately every three months), check the charge condition of the battery as described in Chapter 5, Section 3.
✔ If the battery is flat, and you need to jump start your vehicle, see *Roadside Repairs*.

 Battery corrosion can be kept to a minimum by applying a layer of petroleum jelly to the clamps and terminals after they are reconnected.

1 The battery is located in a compartment beneath the driver's seat. Move the driver's seat fully forward and open the battery box cover. The exterior of the battery should be inspected periodically for damage such as a cracked case or cover.

2 Check the tightness of battery clamps to ensure good electrical connections. You should not be able to move them. Also check each cable for cracks and frayed conductors.

3 If corrosion (white, fluffy deposits) is evident, remove the cables from the battery terminals, clean them with a small wire brush, then refit them. Automotive stores sell a tool for cleaning the battery post...

4 ...as well as the battery cable clamps

Lubricants and fluids

Engine:

Engine oil...................................	Multigrade engine oil, viscosity SAE 5W/30 to Ford specification WSS-M2C913-C
Alternative specification*......................	Multigrade engine oil, viscosity SAE 5W/30 to specification ACEA A5/B5
Cooling system................................	Antifreeze Super Plus Premium to Ford specification WSS-M97B44-D
Manual transmission	Gear oil to Ford specification WSS-M2C200-D2
Brake and clutch hydraulic system	DOT 4 LV Hydraulic fluid to Ford specification WSS-M6C65-A2

Power steering: **

Vehicles built before 12 March 2013..............	Hydraulic fluid to Ford specification WSS-M2C204-A2
Vehicles built 12 March 2013 onwards	Hydraulic fluid to Ford specification WSA-M2C938-A
Wheel hub bearings	Grease to Ford specification WSD-M1C228-A

Use of the alternative specification engine oils may result in longer cold start cranking time, reduced engine performance, reduced fuel economy and increased emission levels.

**Always top-up with the same colour fluid.*

Tyre pressures

Note: *The pressures in the table below are typical and apply to Van and Kombi models. Refer to the sticker on the driver's door pillar, or to the handbook supplied with the vehicle, for information specific to your model. Pressures are for cold tyres and given in bar (lbf / psi).*

Van and Kombi	Tyre size	Pressures – bar (psi)	
		Front	Rear
250S and 270S...	215/65 R 15 C	3.3 (48)	2.9 (42)
250S and 270S...	215/65 R 16 C	3.5 (51)	3.1 (45)
290S...	215/65 R 15 C	3.3 (48)	3.3 (48)
290S...	215/65 R 16 C	3.5 (51)	3.6 (52)
290L...	215/65 R 15 C	3.5 (51)	3.3 (48)
290L...	215/65 R 16 C	3.8 (55)	3.6 (52)
300S...	215/65 R 15 C	3.4 (49)	3.3 (48)
300L...	215/65 R 15 C	3.7 (54)	3.3 (48)
310S...	215/55 R 15 C	3.4 (49)	3.7 (54)
310L...	215/65 R 15 C	3.9 (57)	4.0 (58)
330S...	215/65 R 16 C	3.6 (52)	4.8 (69)
330L...	215/65 R 16 C	4.0 (58)	4.8 (69)

Chapter 1
Routine maintenance and servicing

Contents

Degrees of difficulty

Easy, suitable for novice with little experience

Fairly easy, suitable for beginner with some experience

Fairly difficult, suitable for competent DIY mechanic

Difficult, suitable for experienced DIY mechanic

Very difficult, suitable for expert DIY or professional

1 Servicing specifications

Capacities

Engine oil

2.0 litre engines with grey dipstick end:

With filter.	8.3 litres
Without filter	8.1 litres
Difference between dipstick minimum and maximum marks.	1.5 litres

2.0 litre engines with yellow dipstick end:

With filter.	9.8 litres
Without filter	9.2 litres
Difference between dipstick minimum and maximum marks.	1.5 litres

2.2 litre engines:

With filter.	6.5 litres
Without filter	6.3 litres
Difference between dipstick minimum and maximum	1.5 litres

Cooling system

2.0 litre engine	11.2 litres
2.2 litre engine	9.3 litres

Fuel tank

Standard fuel tank	80.0 litres
Increased capacity fuel tank.	95.0 litres

Transmission

All models.	2.1 litres

Cooling system

Coolant protection at 40% antifreeze/water mixture ratio:

Slush point	-25°C (-13°F)
Solidifying point	-30°C (-22°F)

Braking system

Minimum brake pad lining thickness	1.5 mm

Torque wrench settings

	Nm	lbf ft
Air conditioning compressor retaining bolts.	25	18
Auxiliary drivebelt cover retaining bolts	10	7
Auxiliary drivebelt tensioner retaining bolts	25	18
Engine oil drain plug.	39	29
Engine oil filter	20	15
Roadwheel nuts	200	148
Transmission filler/level plug.	35	26

2 Maintenance schedule

1 The maintenance intervals in this manual are provided with the assumption that you, not the dealer, will be carrying out the work. These are the minimum maintenance intervals recommended by us for vehicles driven daily. If you wish to keep your vehicle in peak condition at all times, you may wish to perform some of these procedures more often. We encourage frequent maintenance, because it enhances the efficiency, performance and resale value of your vehicle.
2 If the vehicle is driven in dusty areas, used to tow a trailer, or driven frequently at slow speeds (idling in traffic) or on short journeys, more frequent maintenance intervals are recommended.
3 When the vehicle is new, it should be serviced by a dealer service department (or other workshop recognised by the vehicle manufacturer as providing the same standard of service) in order to preserve the warranty. The vehicle manufacturer may reject warranty claims if you are unable to prove that servicing has been carried out as and when specified, using only original equipment parts or parts certified to be of equivalent quality.

Every 250 miles (400 km) or weekly
☐ Refer to *Weekly checks*

Every 7500 miles or 6 months, whichever occurs first
☐ Renew the engine oil and filter (Section 6)*

Note: *The manufacturers recommend that the engine oil and filter are changed every 36,000 miles or 24 months if the vehicle is being operated under normal conditions. However, oil and filter changes are good for the engine and we recommend that the oil and filter are renewed more frequently, especially if the vehicle is driven in dusty areas, used to tow a trailer, or driven frequently at slow speeds (idling in traffic) or on short journeys.*

Every 15 000 miles or 12 months, whichever occurs first
In addition to the item listed in the previous service, carry out the following:
☐ Check the battery and clean the terminals (Section 7)
☐ Check the auxiliary drivebelt (Section 8)
☐ Check the electrical system (Section 9)
☐ Check under the bonnet for fluid leaks and hose condition (Section 10)
☐ Check the condition of the fuel filter and drain the water (Section 11)
☐ Renew the fuel filter according to condition (Section 12)
☐ Check the condition of all engine compartment wiring (Section 13)
☐ Check the condition of all air conditioning system components (Section 14)
☐ Check the seat belts (Section 15)
☐ Check the antifreeze concentration (Section 16)
☐ Check the steering, suspension and roadwheels (Section 17)
☐ Check the driveshaft rubber gaiters and CV joints (Section 18)
☐ Check the exhaust system (Section 19)
☐ Check the underbody, and all fuel/brake lines (Section 20)
☐ Check the brake pad lining thickness (Section 21)
☐ Check the operation and adjustment of the handbrake (Section 22)
☐ Check the doors and bonnet, and lubricate their hinges and locks (Section 23)
☐ Check the security of all roadwheel nuts (Section 24)
☐ Road test (Section 25)
☐ Reset the service interval indicator (Section 26)

Every 30,000 miles or 2 years, whichever occurs first
In addition to the relevant items listed in the previous services, carry out the following:
☐ Renew the air filter element (Section 27)
☐ Check the transmission oil level (Section 28)
☐ Pollen filter renewal (Section 29)
☐ Renew the brake fluid (Section 30)
☐ Renew the remote control battery (Section 31)
☐ Renew the coolant (Section 32)*

Note: *Vehicles using Ford Super Plus coolant do not need the coolant renewed on a regular basis.*

Every 150,000 miles or 10 years, whichever occurs first
In addition to the relevant items listed in the previous services, carry out the following:
☐ Renew the auxiliary drivebelts (Section 33)

3 Maintenance –
component location

Underbonnet view of a 2.0 litre model

1 Engine oil level dipstick
2 Engine oil filler cap
3 Air cleaner assembly
4 Brake (and clutch) fluid reservoir
5 Fuse/relay box
6 Coolant expansion tank
7 Screen washer fluid reservoir
8 Positive (+) cable connection point
9 Power steering fluid reservoir

Underbonnet view of a 2.2 litre model

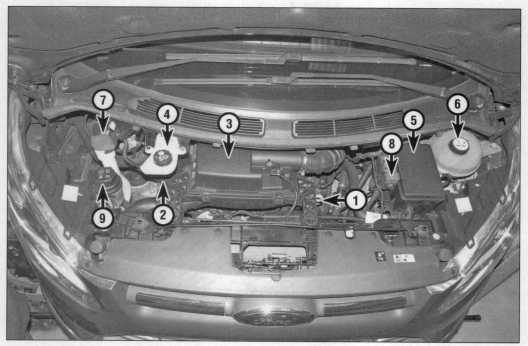

1 Engine oil level dipstick
2 Engine oil filler cap
3 Air cleaner assembly
4 Brake (and clutch) fluid reservoir
5 Fuse/relay box
6 Coolant expansion tank
7 Screen washer fluid reservoir
8 Positive (+) cable connection point
9 Power steering fluid reservoir

Front underbody view of a 2.0 litre model

1 Engine oil drain plug
2 Oil filter
3 Front brake calipers
4 Intercooler
5 Screen washer fluid
   reservoir
6 Transmission
7 Steering track rods
8 Front suspension lower
   arms
9 Front subframe
10 Engine/transmission rear
   mounting
11 Catalytic converter
12 Driveshaft intermediate
   shaft

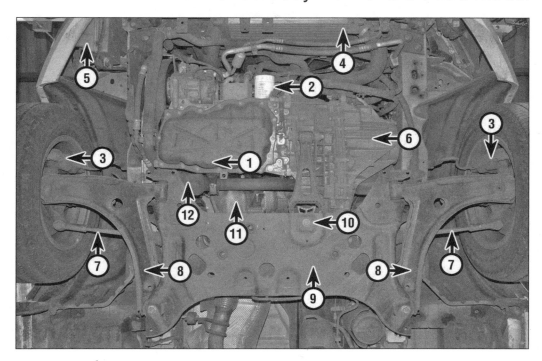

Front underbody of a 2.2 litre model

1 Engine oil drain plug
2 Oil filter
3 Front brake calipers
4 Intercooler
5 Screen washer fluid
   reservoir
6 Transmission
7 Steering track rods
8 Front suspension lower
   arms
9 Front subframe
10 Engine/transmission rear
   mounting
11 Catalytic converter
12 Driveshaft intermediate
   shaft

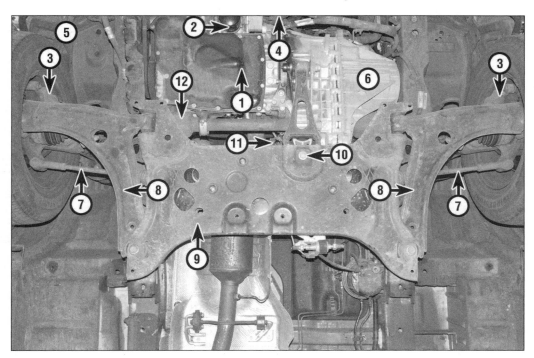

Rear underbody view

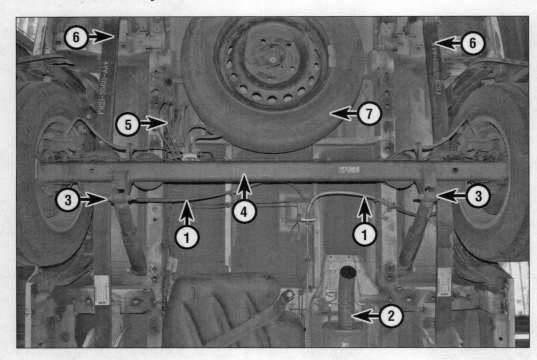

1 Handbrake cables
2 Exhaust tailpipe
3 Shock absorber lower mountings
4 Beam axle
5 Brake hydraulic hoses
6 Leaf springs
7 Spare wheel

4 General Information

1 This Chapter is designed to help the home mechanic maintain his/her vehicle for safety, economy, long life and peak performance.
2 The Chapter contains a master maintenance schedule, followed by Sections dealing specifically with each task in the schedule. Visual checks, adjustments, component renewal and other helpful items are included. Refer to the accompanying illustrations of the engine compartment and the underside of the vehicle for the locations of the various components.
3 Servicing your vehicle in accordance with the mileage/time maintenance schedule and the following Sections will provide a planned maintenance programme, which should result in a long and reliable service life. This is a comprehensive plan, so maintaining some items but not others at the specified service intervals, will not produce the same results.
4 As you service your vehicle, you will discover that many of the procedures can – and should – be grouped together, because of the particular procedure being performed, or because of the proximity of two otherwise unrelated components to one another. For example, if the vehicle is raised for any reason, the exhaust can be inspected at the same time as the suspension and steering components.
5 The first step in this maintenance programme

is to prepare yourself before the actual work begins. Read through all the Sections relevant to the work to be carried out, then make a list and gather all the parts and tools required. If a problem is encountered, seek advice from a parts specialist, or a dealer service department.

5 Regular maintenance

1 If, from the time the vehicle is new, the routine maintenance schedule is followed closely, and frequent checks are made of fluid levels and high-wear items, as suggested throughout this manual, the engine will be kept in relatively good running condition, and the need for additional work will be minimised.
2 It is possible that there will be times when the engine is running poorly due to the lack of regular maintenance. This is even more likely if a used vehicle, which has not received regular and frequent maintenance checks, is purchased. In such cases, additional work may need to be carried out, outside of the regular maintenance intervals.
3 If engine wear is suspected, a compression test or leak-down test will provide valuable information regarding the overall performance of the main internal components. Such a test can be used as a basis to decide on the extent of the work to be carried out. If, for example, a compression or leak-down test indicates serious internal engine wear, conventional

maintenance as described in this Chapter will not greatly improve the performance of the engine, and may prove a waste of time and money, unless extensive overhaul work is carried out first.
4 The following series of operations are those most often required to improve the performance of a generally poor running engine:

Primary operations

a) Clean, inspect and test the battery (see 'Weekly checks' and Section 7).
b) Check all the engine related fluids (refer to 'Weekly checks').
c) Check the condition and tension of the auxiliary drivebelt (Section 8).
d) Check the condition of all hoses, and check for fluid leaks (Section 10 and Section 20).
e) Renew the fuel filter (Section 12).
Check the condition of the air filter, and renew if necessary (Section 27).
5 If the above operations do not prove fully effective, carry out the following secondary operations:

Secondary operations

6 All items listed under Primary operations, plus the following:
a) Check the charging system (refer to Chapter 5 Section 5).
b) Check the pre/post-heating system (refer to Chapter 5 Section 12).
c) Check the fuel system and emissions control systems (refer to Chapter 4A and Chapter 4B).

6 Engine oil and filter renewal

1 Before starting this procedure, gather together all the necessary tools and materials. Also, make sure that you have plenty of clean rags and newspapers handy, to mop up any spills. Ideally, the engine oil should be warm, as it will drain more easily and more built-up sludge will be removed with it. Take care not to touch the exhaust or any other hot parts of the engine when working under the vehicle. To avoid any possibility of scalding and to protect yourself from possible skin irritants and other harmful contaminants in used engine oils, it is advisable to wear gloves when carrying out this work.

2 Access to the underside of the vehicle will be greatly improved if it can be raised on a lift, driven onto ramps, or jacked up and supported on axle stands (see *Jacking and vehicle support*). Whichever method is chosen, make sure that the vehicle remains level, or if it is at an angle, that the drain plug is at the lowest point.

3 Remove the oil filler cap, then unscrew the engine oil drain plug (located at the lowest point of the sump) about half a turn (see illustration). Position the draining container under the drain plug, then remove the plug completely – recover the sealing washer.

 HAYNES HiNT *As the drain plug threads release, move it sharply away so the stream of oil issuing from the sump runs into the container, not up your sleeve.*

4 Allow some time for the oil to drain, noting that it may be necessary to reposition the container as the oil flow slows to a trickle.

5 After all the oil has drained, wipe off the drain plug with a clean rag, and fit a new sealing washer. Clean the area around the drain plug opening, and refit the plug. Tighten the plug to the specified torque.

6 Move the container into position under the oil filter, which is located on the front of the cylinder block.

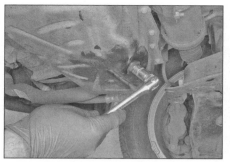
6.3 Engine oil drain plug location

7 Unscrew the oil filter from the front of the engine block (see illustration).

8 Use a cloth to clean the old oil from the filter-to-engine surface (see illustration).

9 Lubricate the new oil filter's seal with clean engine oil before screwing it into place. Tighten it by hand, or if a suitable tool is available, tighten it to the specified torque (see illustrations).

10 Remove the old oil and all tools from under the vehicle, then lower the vehicle to the ground.

11 Remove the dipstick, then unscrew the oil filler cap from the camshaft cover. Fill the engine, using the correct grade and type of oil (see *Lubricants, fluids and tyre pressures* on page 0•17). An oil can spout or funnel may help to reduce spillage. Pour in half the specified quantity of oil first, then wait a few minutes for the oil to fall to the sump. Continue adding oil, a small quantity at a time, until the level is up to the lower mark on the dipstick. Refit the filler cap.

12 Start the engine and run it for a few minutes, then check for leaks. Note that there may be a delay of a few seconds before the oil pressure warning light goes out when the engine is first started, as the oil circulates through the engine oil galleries and the new oil filter before the pressure builds up. Do not rev the engine.

13 Switch off the engine, and wait a few minutes for the oil to settle in the sump once more. With the new oil circulated and the filter completely full, recheck the level on the dipstick, and add more oil as necessary.

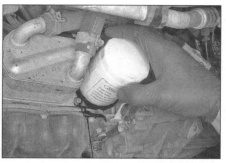
6.7 Unscrew the filter and discard it (2.0 litre engine shown)

14 Dispose of the used engine oil and filter safely, with reference to General repair procedures. Do not discard the old filter with domestic household waste. The facility for waste oil disposal provided by many local council refuse tips and/or recycling centers generally has a filter receptacle alongside.

7 Battery maintenance and charging

⚠ *Warning: Certain precautions must be followed when checking and servicing the battery. Hydrogen gas, which is highly flammable, is always present in the battery cells, so keep lighted tobacco and all other open flames and sparks away from the battery. The electrolyte inside the battery is actually dilute sulphuric acid, which will cause injury if splashed on your skin or in your eyes. It will also ruin clothes and painted surfaces.*

General

1 A routine preventive maintenance programme for the battery in your vehicle is the only way to ensure quick and reliable starts. For general maintenance, refer to *Weekly checks* at the start of this manual. Also, at the front of the manual, is information on jump starting. For details of removing and installing the battery, refer to Chapter 5 Section 4.

6.8 Clean the filter sealing surface

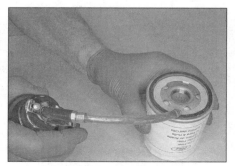
6.9a Lubricate the filter seal...

6.9b ...before tighten it by hand, or to the specified torque

Battery electrolyte level

2 On models not equipped with a sealed or 'maintenance-free' battery, check the electrolyte level of all six battery cells.

3 The level must be approximately 10 mm above the plates; this may be shown by maximum and minimum level lines marked on the battery's casing.

4 If the level is low, use a coin or screwdriver to release the filler/vent cap, and add distilled water. To improve access to the centre caps, it may be helpful to remove the battery hold-down clamp.

5 Install and securely retighten the cap, then wipe up any spillage.

Caution: Overfilling the cells may cause electrolyte to spill over during periods of heavy charging, causing corrosion or damage.

Charging

Note: *The following is intended as a guide only. Always refer to the manufacturer's recommendations (often printed on a label attached to the battery) before charging a battery.*

Warning: When batteries are being charged, hydrogen gas, which is very explosive and flammable, is produced. Do not smoke, or allow open flames, near a charging or a recently charged battery. Wear eye protection when near the battery during charging. Also, make sure the charger is unplugged before connecting or disconnecting the battery from the charger.

6 Slow-rate charging is the best way to restore a battery that's discharged to the point where it will not start the engine. It's also a good way to maintain the battery charge in a vehicle that's only driven a few miles between starts. Maintaining the battery charge is particularly important in winter, when the battery must work harder to start the engine, and electrical accessories that drain the battery are in greater use.

7 Check the battery case for any instructions regarding charging the battery. Some maintenance-free batteries may require a particularly low charge rate or other special conditions, if they are not to be damaged.

8 It's best to use a one- or two-amp battery charger (sometimes called a 'trickle' charger). They are the safest, and put the least strain on the battery. They are also the least expensive. For a faster charge, you can use a higher amperage charger, but don't use one rated more than 1/10th the amp/hour rating of the battery (ie, no more than 5 amps, typically). Rapid boost charges that claim to restore the power of the battery in one to two hours are hardest on the battery, and can damage batteries not in good condition. This type of charging should only be used in emergency situations.

9 The average time necessary to charge a battery should be listed in the instructions that come with the charger. As a general rule,

a trickle charger will charge a battery in 12 to 16 hours.

8 Auxiliary drivebelt check

General

1 Two auxiliary drivebelts are fitted at the right-hand end of the engine, driven from the crankshaft pulley. A multi-ribbed drivebelt is used to drive the alternator and air conditioning compressor (and power steering on 2.0 litre engines), tensioned by an automatic tensioner. A stretch-type, self-tensioning drivebelt is used to drive the power steering pump (which in turn drives the coolant pump via a coupling) on 2.2 litre engines, while on the 2.0 litre engine the stretch belt drives the coolant pump.

2 The good condition and proper tension of the auxiliary drivebelts are critical to the operation of the engine. They must, therefore, be regularly inspected.

Check

3 With the engine switched off, open and support the bonnet.

4 Firmly apply the handbrake, then jack up the front of the vehicle and support it securely on axle stands (see *Jacking and vehicle support*). Remove the right-hand roadwheel, then remove the auxiliary drivebelt cover (two or three fasteners) from under the wheel arch.

5 Using an inspection light or a small electric torch, and rotating the engine with a spanner applied to the crankshaft pulley bolt, check the whole length of the drivebelt for cracks, separation of the rubber, and torn or worn ribs. Also, check for fraying and glazing, which gives the drivebelt a shiny appearance.

6 Both sides of the drivebelt should be inspected, which means you will have to twist the drivebelt to check the underside. Use your fingers to feel the drivebelt where you can't see it. If you are in any doubt as to the condition of the drivebelt, renew it as described in Section 33.

A leak in the cooling system will usually show up as white- or rust-coloured deposits on the area adjoining the leak.

Drivebelt tension

7 The auxiliary drivebelts are tensioned by an automatic tensioner; regular tension checks are not required, and manual adjustment is not possible. The stretch-type of belt doesn't use tensioner.

8 If you suspect that a drivebelt is slipping and/or running slack, or that the tensioner is otherwise faulty, it must be renewed.

Drivebelt renewal

9 Refer to Section 33.

9 Electrical systems check

1 Check the operation of all external lights and indicators (front and rear).

2 Check for satisfactory operation of the instrument panel, its illumination and warning lights, the switches and their function lights.

3 Check the horn(s) for satisfactory operation.

4 Check all other electrical equipment for satisfactory operation.

10 Underbonnet check for fluid leaks and hose condition

1 Visually inspect the engine joint faces, gaskets and seals for any signs of water or oil leaks. Pay particular attention to the areas around the camshaft cover, cylinder head, oil filter and sump joint faces. Bear in mind that, over a period of time, some very slight seepage from these areas is to be expected – what you are really looking for is any indication of a serious leak. Should a leak be found, renew the offending gasket or oil seal by referring to the appropriate Chapters in this manual.

2 Also check the security and condition of all the engine related pipes and hoses, and all braking system pipes and hoses and fuel lines. Ensure that all cable ties or securing clips are in place, and in good condition. Clips which are broken or missing can lead to chafing of the hoses, pipes or wiring, which could cause more serious problems in the future.

3 Carefully check the radiator hoses and heater hoses along their entire length. Renew any hose which is cracked, swollen or deteriorated. Cracks will show up better if the hose is squeezed. Pay close attention to the hose clips that secure the hoses to the cooling system components. Hose clips can pinch and puncture hoses, resulting in cooling system leaks. If the crimped type hose clips are used, it may be a good idea to replace them with standard worm-drive clips.

4 Inspect all the cooling system components (hoses, joint faces, etc) for leaks **(see Haynes Hint)**.

5 Where any problems are found on system components, renew the component or gasket with reference to Chapter 3.

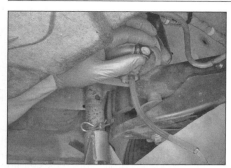

11.1 Loosen the drain screw and allow the filter to drain into a suitable container

11 Fuel filter water draining

Caution: Before starting any work on the fuel filter, wipe clean the filter assembly and the surrounding area as it is essential that no dirt or other foreign matter is allowed into the system. Obtain a suitable container into which the filter can be drained and place rags or similar material under the filter assembly to catch any spillages. Do not allow diesel fuel to contaminate components such as the alternator and starter motor, the coolant hoses and engine mountings, and any wiring.

1 If possible (depending on model), attach a length of hose to the base of the filter housing, to direct the liquid into a suitable container. Loosen the drain screw one to two complete turns and allow the filter to drain until clean fuel, free of dirt or water, emerges from the base or tube (approximately 100 cc is usually sufficient). If it was illuminated, the 'water in fuel' warning message on the dashboard should now disappear **(see illustration)**.

2 Remove the pipe and tighten the drain screw securely.

3 On completion, dispose of the drained fuel safely.

12 Fuel filter renewal

Caution: Before starting any work on the fuel filter, wipe clean the filter assembly and the surrounding area as it is essential that no dirt or other foreign matter is allowed into the system. Place rags or similar material under the filter assembly to catch any spillages. Do not allow diesel fuel to contaminate components such as the alternator and starter motor, the coolant hoses and engine mountings, and any wiring.

Note: *Before carrying out the following procedure, read carefully the precautions given in Chapter 4A Section 1.*

1 Raise the front of the vehicle and support it on axle stands (see *Jacking and vehicle support*).

2 The fuel filter is located at the rear of the engine compartment, on the left-hand side of the bulkhead.

3 If not already done, drain the water from the filter as described in Section 11.

2.0 litre engines

4 Place a cloth beneath the outermost pipe. Use a flat-bladed screwdriver to push up the top section of the clip before pushing up the lower section. Disconnect the pipe from the top of the filter housing **(see illustration)**.

5 Place a container beneath the filter and, unscrew the base of the housing and withdraw the filter from the vehicle **(see illustration)**.

6 Install the new filter by hand and then tighten it until the lug reaches the stop **(see illustrations)**.

7 Reattach the pipe at the top of the housing, securing the clip.

8 Wipe away any spilled fuel, then prime and bleed the fuel system as described in Chapter 4A Section 4.

9 On completion, dispose of the old filter safely.

2.2 litre engines

10 Disconnect the wiring plugs at the top and the bottom of the filter housing and release the wiring retaining clips **(see illustrations)**.

11 To change the filter, rotate the lower housing clockwise then remove the housing from the beneath the vehicle, keeping it

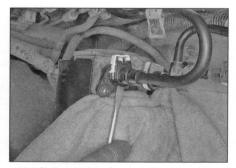

12.4 Release the clip and disconnect the hose from the fuel filter housing

12.5 Unscrew the base of the housing to extract the filter

12.6a Install the new filter into the housing and screw it on by hand…

12.6b …then tighten with the wrench until the lug reaches the stop

12.10a Disconnect the wiring plug at the top of the housing…

12.10b …and the one at the bottom, then free the wiring clip

12.11 Use a strap tool to undo the lower housing to access the filter element

12.12 Disconnect the fuel hoses

upright. Unscrew the top of the cannister, emptying the diesel into a suitable container, and remove the filter element. Discard it and the two O-rings – new items will be required **(see illustration)**.

12 To change the fuel filter housing, disconnect the four fuel hoses at the top of the fuel filter and plug the ends of the pipes to prevent dirt ingress **(see illustration)**.

13 Undo the two retaining nuts and manoeuvre the filter housing from beneath the vehicle.

14 Refitting is the reverse of removal.

15 Wipe away any spilled fuel, then prime and bleed the fuel system as described in Chapter 4A Section 4.

16 On completion, dispose of the old filter safely.

13 Engine compartment wiring check

1 With the vehicle parked on level ground, apply the handbrake firmly and open the bonnet. Using an inspection light or a small electric torch, check all visible wiring within and beneath the engine compartment.

2 What you are looking for is wiring that is obviously damaged by chafing against sharp edges, or against moving suspension/transmission components and/or the auxiliary drivebelt, by being trapped or crushed between carelessly refitted components, or melted by being forced into contact with the hot engine castings, coolant pipes, etc. In almost all cases, damage of this sort is caused in the first instance by incorrect routing on reassembly after previous work has been carried out.

3 Depending on the extent of the problem, damaged wiring may be repaired by rejoining the break or splicing-in a new length of wire, using solder to ensure a good connection, and remaking the insulation with adhesive insulating tape or heat-shrink tubing, as appropriate. If the damage is extensive, given the implications for the vehicle's future reliability, the best long-term answer may well be to renew that entire section of the loom, however expensive this may appear.

4 When the actual damage has been repaired, ensure that the wiring loom is re-routed correctly, so that it is clear of other components, and not stretched or kinked, and is secured out of harm's way using the plastic clips, guides and ties provided.

5 Check all electrical plugs, ensuring that they are clean, securely fastened, and that each is locked by its plastic tabs or wire clip, as appropriate. If any plug shows external signs of corrosion (accumulations of white or green deposits, or streaks of 'rust'), or if any is thought to be dirty, it must be unplugged and cleaned using electrical contact cleaner. If the pins are severely corroded, the plug must be renewed; note that this may mean the renewal of that entire section of the loom – see your local Ford dealer for details.

6 If the cleaner completely removes the corrosion to leave the plug in a satisfactory condition, it would be wise to pack it with a suitable material which will exclude dirt and moisture, preventing the corrosion from occurring again. A Ford dealer may be able to recommend a suitable product.

7 Use the same techniques to ensure that all earth points in the engine compartment provide good electrical contact through clean, metal-to-metal joints, and that all are securely fastened.

14 Air conditioning system check

1 The following maintenance checks will ensure that the air conditioner operates at peak efficiency:

a) *Check the auxiliary drivebelt (see Section 8).*

b) *Check the system hoses for damage or leaks.*

c) *Inspect the condenser fins for leaves, insects and other debris. Use a clean paint brush to clean the condenser.*

d) *Check that the drain tube from the front of the evaporator is clear – note that it is normal to have clear fluid (water) dripping from this while the system is in operation, to the extent that quite a large puddle can be left under the vehicle when it is parked.*

2 It's a good idea to operate the system for

about 30 minutes at least once a month, particularly during the winter (with the temperature turned up) when air conditioning is useful for the rapid demisting of fogged windows. Long term non-use can cause hardening of the seals, and subsequent failure.

3 Because of the complexity of the air conditioning system and the special equipment necessary to service it, in-depth fault diagnosis and repairs are not included in this manual.

4 The most common cause of poor cooling is simply a low system refrigerant charge. If a noticeable drop in cool air output occurs, the following quick check will help you determine if the refrigerant level is low.

5 Warm the engine up to normal operating temperature.

6 Place the air conditioning temperature selector at the coldest setting, and put the blower at the highest setting. Open the doors – to make sure the air conditioning system doesn't cycle off as soon as it cools the passenger compartment.

7 With the compressor engaged – the clutch will make an audible click, and the centre of the clutch will rotate – feel the inlet and outlet pipes at the compressor. One side should be cold, and one hot. If there's no perceptible difference between the two pipes, there's something wrong with the compressor or the system. It might be a low charge – it might be something else. Take the vehicle to a dealer service department or an automotive air conditioning specialist.

15 Seat belt check

1 Check the seat belts for satisfactory operation and condition. Inspect the webbing for fraying and cuts. Check that they retract smoothly and without binding into their reels.

2 Check that the seat belt mounting bolts are tight, and if necessary tighten them to the specified torque wrench setting (see Chapter 11).

16 Antifreeze concentration check

1 The cooling system should be filled with the recommended antifreeze and maintained at the correct concentration all year round. Over a period of time, the concentration of fluid may be reduced due to topping-up (this can be avoided by topping-up with the correct antifreeze mixture) or fluid loss. If loss of coolant has been evident, it is important to make the necessary repair before adding fresh fluid. The exact mixture of antifreeze-to-water which you should use depends on the relative weather conditions. The mixture should contain at least 40% antifreeze, but not more than 70%. Consult the mixture ratio chart on the antifreeze container before adding coolant. Use antifreeze which meets the vehicle manufacturer's specifications.

2 With the engine cold, carefully remove the cap from the expansion tank. If the engine is not completely cold, place a cloth rag over the cap before removing it, and remove it slowly to allow any pressure to escape.

3 Antifreeze checkers are available from car accessory shops. Draw some coolant from the expansion tank and observe how many plastic balls are floating in the checker. Usually, 2 or 3 balls must be floating for the correct concentration of antifreeze, but follow the manufacturer's instructions.

4 If the concentration is incorrect, it will be necessary to either withdraw some coolant and add antifreeze, or alternatively drain the old coolant and add fresh coolant of the correct concentration.

17 Steering, suspension and roadwheel check

Front suspension and steering

1 Firmly apply the handbrake, then jack up the front of the vehicle and support it securely on axle stands (see *Jacking and vehicle support*).

2 Visually inspect the balljoint dust covers and the steering rack-and-pinion gaiters for splits, chafing or deterioration. Any wear of these components will cause loss of lubricant, together with dirt and water entry, resulting in rapid deterioration of the balljoints or steering gear.

3 Check the power steering fluid hoses for chafing or deterioration, and the pipe and hose unions for fluid leaks. Also, check for signs of fluid leakage under pressure from the steering gear rubber gaiters, which would indicate failed fluid seals within the steering gear.

4 Grasp the roadwheel at the 12 o'clock and 6 o'clock positions, and try to rock it **(see illustration)**. Very slight free play may be felt, but if the movement is appreciable, further investigation is necessary to determine the source. Continue rocking the wheel while an assistant depresses the footbrake. If the movement is now eliminated or significantly reduced, it is likely that the hub bearings are at fault. If the free play is still evident with the footbrake depressed, then there is wear in the suspension joints or mountings.

5 Now grasp the wheel at the 9 o'clock and 3 o'clock positions, and try to rock it as before. Any movement felt now may again be caused by wear in the hub bearings or the steering track rod balljoints. If the outer track rod balljoint is worn, the visual movement will be obvious. If the inner joint is suspect, it can be felt by placing a hand over the rack-and-

17.4 Checking for wear in the front suspension and hub bearings

pinion rubber gaiter and gripping the track rod. If the wheel is now rocked, movement will be felt at the inner joint if wear has taken place.

6 Using a large screwdriver or flat bar, check for wear in the suspension mounting bushes by levering between the relevant suspension component and its attachment point. Some movement is to be expected, as the mountings are made of rubber, but excessive wear should be obvious. Also check the condition of any visible rubber bushes, looking for splits, cracks or contamination of the rubber.

7 With the vehicle standing on its wheels, have an assistant turn the steering wheel back-and-forth, about an eighth of a turn each way. There should be very little, if any, lost movement between the steering wheel and roadwheels. If this is not the case, closely observe the joints and mountings previously described. In addition, check the steering column universal joints for wear, and also check the rack-and-pinion steering gear itself.

Rear suspension

8 Chock the front wheels, then jack up the rear of the vehicle and support securely on axle stands (see *Jacking and vehicle support*).

9 Working as described previously for the front suspension, check the rear hub bearings, the leaf spring mounting bushes and the shock absorber mountings for wear. Also check that the rear spring U-bolt nuts are tightened to the specified torque as given in Chapter 10 **(see illustration)**.

Shock absorbers

10 Check for any signs of fluid leakage around the shock absorber body, or from the rubber gaiter around the piston rod. Should any fluid be noticed, the shock absorber is defective internally, and should be renewed (see Chapter 10 Section 6 or Chapter 10 Section 13).

Note: *Shock absorbers should always be renewed in pairs on the same axle.*

11 The efficiency of the shock absorber may be checked by bouncing the vehicle at each corner. Generally speaking, the body will return to its normal position and stop after

17.9 Rear spring U-bolt nuts (2 of 4 shown)

being depressed. If it rises and returns on a rebound, the shock absorber is probably suspect. Also examine the shock absorber upper and lower mountings for any signs of wear.

Roadwheels

12 Periodically remove the roadwheels, and clean any dirt or mud from the inside and outside surfaces. Examine the wheel rims for signs of rusting, corrosion or other damage. Light alloy wheels are easily damaged by kerbing while parking, and similarly, steel wheels may become dented or buckled. Renewal of the wheel is very often the only course of remedial action possible.

13 The balance of each wheel and tyre assembly should be maintained, not only to avoid excessive tyre wear, but also to avoid wear in the steering and suspension components. Wheel imbalance is normally signified by vibration through the vehicle's bodyshell, although in many cases it is particularly noticeable through the steering wheel. Conversely, it should be noted that wear or damage in suspension or steering components may cause excessive tyre wear. Out-of-round or out-of-true tyres, damaged wheels and wheel bearing wear/maladjustment also fall into this category. Balancing will not usually cure vibration caused by such wear.

18 Driveshaft rubber gaiter and CV joint check

1 The driveshaft rubber gaiters on front wheel drive vehicles are very important, because they prevent dirt, water and foreign material from entering and damaging the constant velocity (CV) joints. External contamination can cause the gaiter material to deteriorate prematurely, so it's a good idea to wash the gaiters with soap and water occasionally.

2 With the vehicle raised and securely supported on axle stands (see *Jacking and vehicle support*), turn the steering onto full-lock, then slowly rotate each front wheel in turn. Inspect the condition of the outer constant velocity (CV) joint rubber gaiters,

18.2 Check the driveshaft gaiters by hand for cracks and/or leaking grease

squeezing the gaiters to open out the folds **(see illustration)**. Check for signs of cracking, splits, or deterioration of the rubber, which may allow the escape of grease, and lead to the ingress of water and grit into the joint. Also check the security and condition of the retaining clips. Repeat these checks on the inner CV joints. If any damage or deterioration is found, the gaiters should be renewed as described in Chapter 8 Section 3 or Chapter 8 Section 4.

3 At the same time, check the general condition of the outer CV joints themselves, by first holding the driveshaft and attempting to rotate the wheels. Repeat this check on the inner joints, by holding the inner joint yoke and attempting to rotate the driveshaft.

4 Any appreciable movement in the CV joint indicates wear in the joint, wear in the driveshaft splines, or a loose driveshaft retaining nut.

19 Exhaust system check

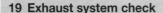

1 With the engine cold, check the complete exhaust system, from its starting point at the engine to the end of the tailpipe. If necessary, raise the front and rear of the vehicle and support it on axle stands (see *Jacking and vehicle support*).

2 Check the exhaust pipes and connections for evidence of leaks, severe corrosion, and damage. Make sure that all brackets

21.2 Check the thickness of the pad friction material through the caliper inspection window

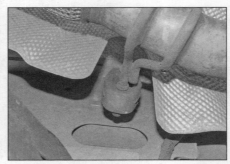

19.2 Check the condition of the rubber mountings

and mountings are in good condition **(see illustration)** and that all relevant nuts and bolts are tight. Leakage at any of the joints or in other parts of the system will usually show up as a black sooty stain in the vicinity of the leak.

3 Rattles and other noises can often be traced to the exhaust system, especially the brackets and rubber mountings. Try to move the pipes and silencers. If the components are able to come into contact with the body or suspension parts, secure the system with new mountings. Otherwise separate the joints (if possible) and twist the pipes as necessary to provide additional clearance.

20 Underbody and fuel/brake line check

1 With the vehicle raised and supported on axle stands (see *Jacking and vehicle support*), thoroughly inspect the underbody and wheel arches for signs of damage and corrosion. In particular, examine the bottom of the side sills, and any concealed areas where mud can collect.

2 Where corrosion and rust is evident, press and tap firmly on the panel with a screwdriver, and check for any serious corrosion which would necessitate repairs.

3 If the panel is not seriously corroded, clean away the rust, and apply a new coating of underseal. Refer to Chapter 11 Section 4 for more details of body repairs.

21.7 Checking the condition of a flexible brake hose

4 Inspect the fuel tank and filler neck for punctures, cracks and other damage. The connection between the filler neck and tank is especially critical. Sometimes a rubber filler neck or connecting hose will leak due to loose retaining clamps or deteriorated rubber.

5 Carefully check all rubber hoses and metal fuel lines leading away from the fuel tank. Check for loose connections, deteriorated hoses, crimped lines, and other damage. Pay particular attention to the vent pipes and hoses, which often loop up around the filler neck and can become blocked or crimped. Follow the lines to the front of the vehicle, carefully inspecting them all the way. Renew damaged sections as necessary. Similarly, while the vehicle is raised, take the opportunity to inspect all underbody brake fluid pipes and hoses.

6 From within the engine compartment, check the security of all fuel, vacuum, power steering and brake hose attachments and pipe unions, and inspect all hoses for kinks, chafing and deterioration.

21 Brake pad and brake shoe wear check

Front and rear disc brakes

1 Apply the handbrake, then jack up the front of the vehicle and support it on axle stands (see *Jacking and vehicle support*). For better access to the brake calipers, remove the front roadwheels.

2 Look through the inspection window in the caliper, and check that the thickness of the friction lining material on each of the pads is not less than the recommended minimum thickness given in the Specifications **(see illustration)**.

3 If it is difficult to determine the exact thickness of the pad linings, or if you are at all concerned about the condition of the pads, then remove them from the calipers for further inspection (refer to Chapter 9 Section 4).

4 Check the caliper on the other side in the same way.

5 If any one of the brake pads has worn down to, or below, the specified limit, all four pads must be renewed as a set.

6 Check both front brake discs with reference to Chapter 9 Section 5.

7 Before refitting the wheels, check the condition of all brake lines and flexible hoses. In particular, check the flexible hoses in the vicinity of the calipers, where they are subjected to most movement. Bend them between the fingers and check that this does not reveal previously hidden cracks, cuts or splits **(see illustration)**.

8 On completion, refit the roadwheels and lower the vehicle to the ground. Tighten the wheel nuts to the specified torque.

9 Chock the front wheels, then jack up the rear of the vehicle, and support it securely on axle stands (see *Jacking and vehicle support*).

For better access to the brake calipers, remove the rear roadwheels.
10 Repeat the checks described in paragraphs 2 to 8 on the rear brakes.

22 Handbrake operation and adjustment check

1 With the vehicle on a slight slope, apply the handbrake lever, and check that it holds the vehicle stationary, then release the lever and check that there is no resistance to movement of the vehicle.
2 If necessary, adjust the handbrake as follows. First, position the vehicle on level ground.
3 Chock the front wheels then jack up the rear of the vehicle and securely support it on axle stands (see Jacking and vehicle support).
4 Depress and release the brake pedal 10 times.
5 Firmly apply the handbrake lever, then release it, three or four times.
6 From under the vehicle, locate the handbrake cable adjuster nut at the cable compensator plate (see illustration).
7 With the handbrake fully released, unscrew the locknut, then slacken the handbrake cable adjuster nut until the handbrake operating lever on the brake caliper contacts its abutment stop, on both sides.
8 Insert a 1.0 mm feeler gauge between the handbrake operating lever on the brake caliper and its abutment stop, on both sides (see illustration).
9 Tighten the handbrake cable adjuster nut until movement is observed on one of the operating levers (ie until the feeler gauge drops out).
10 Remove the feeler gauges and tighten the handbrake cable adjuster nut two complete turns. Hold the adjuster nut and tighten the locknut.
11 Check that the rear wheels are free to rotate without binding.
12 On completion, lower the vehicle to the ground.

23 Door and bonnet check and lubrication

1 Check that the doors, bonnet and, where applicable, the liftgate or rear doors close securely. Check that the bonnet safety catch operates correctly. Check the operation of the door check straps.
2 Lubricate the hinges, door check straps, the striker plates and the bonnet catch sparingly with a little oil or grease.

24 Roadwheel nut tightness check

1 Apply the handbrake, chock the wheels, and engage first gear.
2 Remove the wheel nut covers (or wheel centre cover), using the flat end of the wheel brace supplied in the tool kit.
3 Check the tightness of all wheel nuts using a torque wrench (refer to the Specifications).

25 Road test

Instruments and electrical equipment
1 Check the operation of all instruments and electrical equipment.
2 Make sure that all instruments read correctly, and switch on all electrical equipment in turn, to check that it functions properly.

Steering and suspension
3 Check for any abnormalities in the steering, suspension, handling or road 'feel'.
4 Drive the vehicle, and check that there are no unusual vibrations or noises.
5 Check that the steering feels positive, with no excessive 'sloppiness', or roughness, and check for any suspension noises when cornering and driving over bumps.

Drivetrain
6 Check the performance of the engine, clutch, transmission and driveshafts.
7 Listen for any unusual noises or vibration from the engine, clutch and transmission.
8 Make sure that the engine runs smoothly when idling, and that there is no hesitation when accelerating.
9 Check that the clutch action is smooth and progressive, that the drive is taken up smoothly, and that the pedal travel is not excessive. Also listen for any noises when the clutch pedal is depressed.
10 Check that all gears can be engaged smoothly without noise, and that the gear lever action is smooth and not abnormally vague or 'notchy'.
11 Listen for a metallic clicking sound from the front of the vehicle as it is driven slowly in a circle with the steering on full-lock. Carry out this check in both directions. If a clicking noise is heard, this indicates wear in a driveshaft joint (see Chapter 8 Section 6).

Braking system
12 Make sure that the vehicle does not pull to one side when braking, and that the wheels do not lock when braking hard and the ABS activates.
13 Check that there is no vibration through the steering when braking.
14 Check that the handbrake operates correctly, without excessive movement of the lever, and that it holds the vehicle stationary on a slope.
15 Test the operation of the brake servo unit as follows. Depress the footbrake four or five times to exhaust the vacuum, then start the engine. As the engine starts, there should be a noticeable 'give' in the brake pedal as vacuum builds up. Allow the engine to run for at least two minutes, and then switch it off. If the brake pedal is now depressed again, it should be possible to detect a hiss from the servo as the pedal is depressed. After about four or five applications, no further hissing should be heard, and the pedal should feel considerably harder.

22.6 Handbrake cable adjuster nut

22.8 Insert a 1.0 mm feeler gauge between the lever and the stop

27.1a Undo the clamp...

27.1b ... and disconnect the outlet pipe

26 Service interval indicator reset

1 With the ignition off (position 0), simultaneously depress the brake pedal and accelerator pedal fully.
2 Switch the ignition on (position II) without starting the engine.
3 With the pedals still depressed, wait for at least 15 seconds until the service interval message indicates it has reset.

27 Air filter element renewal

27.2 Disconnect the sensor wiring plug

27.3 Pull the vacuum pipe from the left-hand side of the air filter cover

2.0 litre engine

1 Unscrew the air outlet pipe retaining clamp and remove the pipe **(see illustrations)**.
2 Disconnect the mass airflow sensor wiring plug from the top of the air cleaner cover **(see illustration)**.
3 Disconnect the vacuum pipe from the side of the air filter cover **(see illustration)**.
4 Release the 4 spring clips securing the air cleaner cover to the air cleaner housing **(see illustration)**.
5 Lift up the air cleaner cover at the front and remove the cover **(see illustration)**.
6 Lift out the element, and wipe out the housing with a cloth and brush, if necessary **(see illustration)**.
7 If carrying out a routine service, the element must be renewed regardless of its apparent condition.
8 If you are checking the element for any other reason, inspect its lower surface; if it is oily or very dirty, renew the element. If it is only moderately dusty, it can be re-used by blowing it clean with compressed air.
9 Fit the new element using a reversal of the removal procedure.

27.4 Release the spring clips securing the air cleaner cover to the air cleaner housing

27.5 Lift up the air cleaner cover at the front and remove it

2.2 litre engine

10 Unscrew the air outlet pipe retaining clamp and disconnect the pipe **(see illustration)**.
11 Disconnect the mass airflow sensor wiring plug from the top of the air cleaner cover **(see illustration)**.

27.6 Lift out the filter element

27.10 Undo the clamp and disconnect the pipe

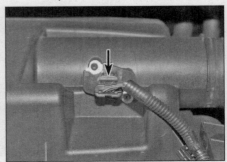

27.11 Release the clip and disconnect the mass airflow sensor plug

12 Release the 4 spring clips securing the air cleaner cover to the air cleaner housing **(see illustration)**.
13 Lift out the element, noting its direction of fitting, and wipe out the housing with a cloth and brush, if necessary **(see illustration)**.
14 If carrying out a routine service, the element must be renewed regardless of its apparent condition.
15 If you are checking the element for any other reason, inspect its lower surface; if it is oily or very dirty, renew the element. If it is only moderately dusty, it can be re-used by blowing it clean with compressed air.
16 Fit the new element using a reversal of the removal procedure.

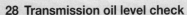

28 Transmission oil level check

Note: *The work in this Section is not a Ford service requirement. However, we consider it prudent to check the transmission oil level at least every 2 years.*
1 To check the oil level, raise the vehicle and support it securely on axle stands (see *Jacking and vehicle support*), making sure that the vehicle is level.
2 The filler/level plug is situated on the lower front side of the transmission housing.
3 Using a suitable Allen key or socket, unscrew and remove the filler/level plug – take care because it is likely to be very tight.
4 If the level is correct, it should be 21 mm below the lower edge of the filler/level plug hole. The best way to check the level is to use a 'dipstick' made up from a bent piece of wire. Put the wire in the hole (but don't drop it in) and check the level **(see illustration)**.
5 If the transmission needs topping-up, use a syringe or a plastic bottle and tube, to add more lubricant of the specified type (see *Lubricants, fluids and tyre pressures*) **(see illustration)**.
6 Stop filling the transmission when the lubricant reaches the correct level on the 'dipstick'.
7 Refit the filler/level plug, and tighten it to the specified torque setting. Drive the vehicle a short distance, then check for leaks.

27.12 Unclip the cover and remove it

28.4 Make your own 'dipstick' to check the transmission oil level

8 A need for regular topping-up can only be due to a leak, which should be found and rectified without delay.

29 Pollen filter renewal

1 To make access easier, open the glovebox fully by releasing the side stops **(see illustration)**.
2 Working under the passengers side of the facia, inside the footwell, release the clip on the right-hand side, open the cover and remove the filter **(see illustrations)**.
3 Fit the new filter using a reversal of the removal procedure, ensuring that the filter is fitted with the airflow arrows pointing in the correct direction, as noted on removal. Refit the cover and close the glovebox.

27.13 Lift out the filter element, noting its direction of fitting

28.5 Top-up the transmission oil

30 Brake fluid renewal

⚠ *Warning: Brake hydraulic fluid can harm your eyes and damage painted surfaces, so use extreme caution when handling and pouring it. Do not use fluid that has been standing open for some time, as it absorbs moisture from the air. Excess moisture can cause a dangerous loss of braking effectiveness.*
1 The procedure is similar to that for bleeding the hydraulic system as described in Chapter 9 Section 2 except that allowance should be made for the old fluid to be expelled when bleeding each section of the circuit.
2 Working as described in Chapter 9,

29.1 Use a screwdriver to release the glovebox side stops before opening it fully

29.2a Unclip and remove the cover...

29.2b ...then remove the pollen filter, noting any directional arrows as it is removed

30.2 Top up the fluid in the reservoir to the MAX level

Section 2, open the first bleed screw in the sequence, and pump the brake pedal gently until the level in the reservoir is approaching the MIN mark. Top-up to the MAX level with new fluid, and continue pumping until only new fluid remains in the reservoir, and new fluid can be seen emerging from the bleed screw. Tighten the screw and top the reservoir level up to the MAX level line **(see illustration)**.

3 Work through all the remaining bleed screws in the sequence until new fluid can be seen at all of them. Be careful to keep the master cylinder reservoir topped-up above the MIN level at all times, or air may enter the system. If this happens, further bleeding will be required, to remove the air.

4 When the operation is complete, check that all bleed screws are securely tightened, and that their dust caps are refitted. Wash off all traces of spilt fluid and recheck the master cylinder reservoir fluid level.

5 Check the operation of the brakes before taking the vehicle on the road.

31 Remote control battery

1 The remote control features a non-removable battery that is charged when the key is in the ignition and the engine is running. Ford recommend that all of the keys are used at least once a year – if they lose their charge they may need to be reprogrammed by a dealer.

32.3 Open the radiator tap and allow the coolant to drain into the tray

32 Coolant renewal

Note: *If the antifreeze used is Ford's Super Plus, or of similar quality, Ford state that coolant renewal is only necessary every 10 years. If the vehicle's history is unknown, if the antifreeze is of lesser quality, or if you prefer to follow conventional servicing intervals, the coolant should be changed as follows.*

⚠ **Warning: Do not allow antifreeze to come in contact with your skin or painted surfaces of the vehicle. Flush contaminated areas immediately with plenty of water. Don't store new coolant, or leave old coolant lying around, where it's accessible to children or pets – they're attracted by its sweet smell. Ingestion of even a small amount of coolant can be fatal. Wipe up garage-floor and drip-pan spills immediately. Keep antifreeze containers covered, and repair cooling system leaks as soon as they're noticed.**

⚠ **Warning: Never remove the expansion tank filler cap when the engine is running, or has just been switched off because the cooling system will be hot, and the consequent escaping steam and scalding coolant could cause serious injury.**

⚠ **Warning: Wait until the engine is cold before starting these procedures.**

Cooling system draining

1 To drain the system, first remove the expansion tank filler cap. Place a thick cloth over the expansion tank cap, then turn the cap anticlockwise as far as the first stop and wait for any pressure to be released, then depress it and turn it further anticlockwise to remove it.

2 Either remove the left-hand headlight as described in Chapter 12 Section 11, or jack up the front of the vehicle and support it on axle stands (see *Jacking and vehicle support*).

3 Place a large drain tray underneath the left-hand side of the radiator, and unscrew the radiator drain tap **(see illustration)**. Allow the coolant to drain into the tray. Attaching a hose to the outlet will help direct the coolant.

4 On completion, retighten the drain plug securely. Where necessary, lower the vehicle to the ground.

Cooling system flushing

5 If coolant renewal has been neglected, or if the antifreeze mixture has become diluted, then in time the cooling system may gradually lose efficiency as the coolant passages become restricted because of rust, scale deposits, and other sediment. The cooling system efficiency can be restored by flushing the system clean.

6 The radiator should be flushed independently of the engine, to avoid unnecessary contamination.

Radiator flushing

7 Disconnect the top and bottom hoses and any other relevant hoses from the radiator.

8 Insert a garden hose into the radiator top inlet. Direct a flow of clean water through the radiator, and continue flushing until clean water emerges from the radiator bottom outlet.

9 If after a reasonable period, the water still does not run clear, the radiator can be flushed with a good proprietary cleaning agent. It is important that the manufacturer's instructions are followed carefully. If the contamination is particularly bad, remove the radiator, insert the hose in the radiator bottom outlet, and reverse-flush the radiator.

Engine flushing

10 Remove the thermostat as described in Chapter 3, Section 3, then, if the radiator top hose has been disconnected from the engine, temporarily refit the thermostat housing cover and reconnect the hose.

11 With the top and bottom hoses disconnected from the radiator, insert a garden hose into the radiator top hose. Direct a clean flow of water through the engine, and continue flushing until clean water emerges from the radiator bottom hose.

12 On completion of flushing, refit the thermostat and reconnect the hoses with reference to Chapter 3, Section 3.

Antifreeze mixture

13 Ford state that, if the only antifreeze used is Ford's own purple Super Plus, it will last for ten years. This is subject to it being used in the recommended concentration, unmixed with any other type of antifreeze or additive, and topped-up when necessary using only that antifreeze type, mixed with clean water. If any other type of antifreeze is (or has been) added, the ten year life period no longer applies; in this case, the system must be drained and thoroughly flushed before fresh coolant mixture is poured in.

14 If any antifreeze other than Ford's is to be used, the coolant must be renewed at regular intervals to provide an equivalent degree of protection. The conventional recommendation is to renew the coolant every two years.

15 If the antifreeze used is to Ford's specification, the levels of protection it affords are indicated in the Specifications Section of this Chapter. To give the recommended standard mixture ratio for this antifreeze, 40% (by volume) of antifreeze must be mixed with 60% of clean, soft water. If you are using any other type of antifreeze, follow its manufacturer's instructions to achieve the correct ratio.

16 It is best to make up slightly more than the system's specified capacity, so that a supply is available for subsequent topping-up. However, note that you are unlikely to fully drain the system at any one time (unless the engine is being completely stripped), and the capacities quoted are therefore slightly academic for routine coolant renewal.

17 Before adding antifreeze, the cooling system should be completely drained, preferably flushed, and all hoses checked for condition and security. Fresh antifreeze will rapidly find any weaknesses in the system.

18 After filling with antifreeze, a label should be attached to the expansion tank, stating the type and concentration of antifreeze used, and the date installed. Any subsequent topping-up should be made with the same type and concentration of antifreeze. If topping-up using antifreeze to Ford's specification, note that a 50/50 mixture is permissible, purely for convenience.

19 Do not use engine antifreeze in the windscreen/tailgate washer system, as it will damage the vehicle's paintwork. A screen wash additive should be added to the washer system in its maker's recommended quantities.

Cooling system filling

20 Before attempting to fill the cooling system, make sure that all hoses and clips are in good condition, and that the clips are tight. Note that an antifreeze mixture must be used all year round, to prevent corrosion of the engine components.

21 Fill the system via the expansion tank, with the correct antifreeze mixture, until the coolant level is approximately 15 mm above the MAX mark on the side of the expansion tank **(see illustration)**. Refit the expansion tank filler cap. Gently squeeze the coolant hoses to help prevent the formation of air locks.

22 Start the engine and allow it to idle until it is at normal operating temperature.

Note: *Keep an eye on the coolant level as the engine is idling. If the level drops below minimum in the coolant reservoir, turn off the engine, allow it to cool and top up the level to the MAX mark.*

23 Switch off the engine and allow it to cool for at least 30 minutes.

24 Remove the filler cap and top-up the coolant level to the MAX mark on the expansion tank. Refit and tighten the cap.

Airlocks

25 If, after draining and refilling the system, symptoms of overheating are found which did not occur previously, then the fault is almost certainly due to trapped air at some point in the system, causing an airlock and restricting the flow of coolant; usually, the air is trapped because the system was refilled too quickly.

26 If an airlock is suspected, first try gently squeezing all visible coolant hoses. A coolant hose which is full of air feels quite different to one full of coolant when squeezed. After refilling the system, most airlocks will clear once the system has cooled, and been topped-up.

27 While the engine is running at operating temperature, switch on the heater and heater fan, and check for heat output. Provided there is sufficient coolant in the system, lack of heat output could be due to an airlock in the system.

28 Airlocks can have more serious effects than simply reducing heater output – a severe airlock could reduce coolant flow around the engine. Check that the radiator top hose is hot when the engine is at operating temperature – a top hose which stays cold could be the result of an airlock (or a non-opening thermostat).

29 If the problem persists, stop the engine and allow it to cool down **completely** before unscrewing the expansion tank filler cap or loosening the hose clips and squeezing the hoses to bleed out the trapped air. In the worst case, the system will have to be at least partially drained (this time, the coolant can be saved for re-use) and flushed to clear the problem. If all else fails, have the system evacuated and vacuum filled by a suitably-equipped garage.

33 Auxiliary drivebelt renewal

1 Disconnect the battery negative terminal as described in Chapter 5 Section 4. To improve access, remove the right-hand headlight as described in Chapter 12 Section 11.

2 Slacken the right-hand front roadwheel nuts, then jack up the front of the vehicle and support it securely on axle stands (see

32.21 Fill the coolant tank until the level is 15 mm above the MAX mark

Jacking and vehicle support). Remove the right-hand front roadwheel.

3 Remove the plastic shield **(see illustration)**.

4 Undo the pipe bracket retaining nut and move the pipe to one side **(see illustration)**.

5 Undo the bolts and nuts and remove the auxiliary drivebelt cover **(see illustration)**.

Stretch-type belt – vehicles with air conditioning

Note: *The stretch-type of belt drives the coolant pump on 2.0 litre engines or the power steering pump on 2.2 litre engines. A tensioner is not used. The belt is designed to be used once only and, after removal, a new belt must always be fitted.*

6 Remove the stretch-type drivebelt by cutting through it with a sharp knife or side-cutters.

7 Check the two pulleys, ensuring that their grooves are clean, and removing all traces of oil and grease.

8 The new drivebelt may not be supplied with a fitting tool (303-1596). It is possible to fit the new belt without the tool but it is not recommended because the belt can be damaged. Alternative equivalent tools are available from aftermarket suppliers.

9 Locate the new drivebelt in the grooves of the coolant pump/power steering pump pulley so that it is centred in the grooves, and not overlapping the raised sides. Position the belt under the crankshaft pulley and over the fitting tool. Rotate the crankshaft clockwise, by means of the crankshaft pulley, until the

33.3 Undo the three bolts and release the clip to remove the shield

33.4 Undo the nut and move the pipe away from the auxiliary belt cover

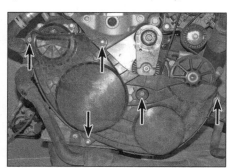

33.5 Remove the bolts and nuts and take off the cover (2.0 litre engine shown)

33.9a Locate the new stretch drivebelt in the grooves of the pulley...

33.9b ...then position the belt over the fitting tool and rotate the crankshaft clockwise

33.17a Locate the new alternator drivebelt in the grooves of the alternator pulley...

33.17b ...then position the belt under the crankshaft pulley and over the fitting tool

33.19 Rotate the crankshaft clockwise until the belt is seated in the grooves of the pulley

belt is seated in the grooves of the pulley. Remove the fitting tool **(see illustrations)**.

10 Rotate the crankshaft clockwise, through at least two full turns to settle the drivebelt on the pulleys, then check that the drivebelt is properly installed.

11 Refit the auxiliary drivebelt cover, plastic shield, power steering pipe bracket, then refit the roadwheel and tighten the wheel nuts to the specified torque.

12 Lower the vehicle to the ground and reconnect the battery.

Alternator drivebelt – vehicles without air conditioning

Note: *The drivebelt on non-air conditioning models is of the stretch type and a tensioner is not used. The belt is designed to be used once only and after removal, a new belt must always be fitted.*

13 Remove the power steering pump drivebelt as described previously in this Section.

14 Remove the alternator drivebelt by cutting through it with a sharp knife.

15 Check the two pulleys, ensuring that their grooves are clean, and removing all traces of oil and grease.

16 The new drivebelt will be supplied with a fitting tool which should be positioned over the crankshaft pulley grooves at approximately the 5 o'clock position.

17 Locate the new drivebelt in the grooves of the alternator pulley so that it is centred in the grooves, and not overlapping the raised sides. Position the belt under the crankshaft pulley and over the fitting tool **(see illustrations)**.

18 Push the tool around the crankshaft pulley, guiding the belt into pulley grooves, until the tool is at the 8 o'clock position.

19 Rotate the crankshaft clockwise, by means of the crankshaft pulley, until the belt is seated in the grooves of the pulley **(see illustration)**. Remove the fitting tool.

20 Rotate the crankshaft clockwise through at least two full turns to settle the drivebelt on

33.24 Insert a drill bit or rod to lock the tensioner in position

the pulleys, then check that the drivebelt is properly installed.

21 Fit a new power steering pump drivebelt as described previously in this Section.

Multi-ribbed drivebelt – vehicles with air conditioning

22 Remove the stretch-type belt as described previously in this Section.

23 If the existing multi-ribbed drivebelt is to be refitted, mark it, or note the maker's markings on its flat surface, so that it can be installed the same way round.

24 Rotate the tensioner pulley clockwise to release its pressure on the drivebelt then insert a 6 mm diameter drill bit or rod (2.0 litre engines) or a 4 mm drill bit (2.2 litre engines) or rod through the holes in the arm/body when they align to lock the tensioner in this position. Depending on model and equipment, the tensioner arm will either have a hex fitting for a spanner or socket, or a square hole into which a ratchet handle from a socket set can be fitted **(see illustration)**.

25 Remove the drivebelt from the pulleys.

26 Check all the pulleys, ensuring that their grooves are clean, and removing all traces of oil and grease. Check that the tensioner works properly, with strong spring pressure being felt when its pulley is rotated clockwise, and a smooth return to the limit of its travel when released.

**33.28a Auxiliary drivebelt arrangement –
2.0 models with air conditioning**

1 Alternator pulley
2 Idler pulley
3 Power steering pump pulley
4 Multi-ribbed drivebelt
5 Air conditioning compressor
   pulley
6 Crankshaft pulley
7 Coolant pump stretch belt
8 Coolant pump pulley
9 Tensioner pulley
10 Fuel pump sprocket
   cover

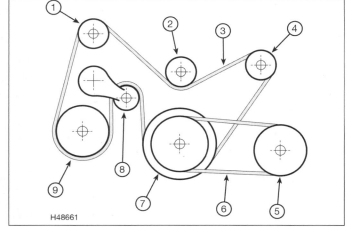

**33.28b Auxiliary drivebelt arrangement –
2.2 models with air conditioning**

1 Idler pulley
2 Idler pulley
3 Multi-ribbed drivebelt
4 Alternator pulley
5 Power steering pump pulley
6 Power steering pump drivebelt
7 Crankshaft pulley
8 Tensioner pulley
9 Air conditioning compressor
   pulley

27 If the original drivebelt is being refitted, use the marks or notes made on removal, to ensure that it is installed to run in the same direction as it was previously.
28 To fit the drivebelt, arrange it on the grooved pulleys so that it is centred in their grooves, and not overlapping their raised sides, (note that the flat surface of the drivebelt is engaged on one or more pulleys) and routed correctly **(see illustrations)**. Start at the top, and work down to finish at the bottom pulley.
29 Rotate the tensioner arm clockwise slightly, remove the locking drill bit/rod, and allow the tensioner to rotate anti-clockwise and gently tension the belt.

30 Rotate the crankshaft clockwise, by means of the crankshaft pulley, through at least two full turns to settle the drivebelt on the pulleys, then check that the drivebelt is properly installed.
31 Fit a new power steering pump or coolant pump drivebelt, as applicable, as described previously in this Section.

Chapter 2 Part A
2.0 litre engine in-vehicle repair procedures

Contents

Degrees of difficulty

Easy, suitable for novice with little experience	Fairly easy, suitable for beginner with some experience	Fairly difficult, suitable for competent DIY mechanic	Difficult, suitable for experienced DIY mechanic	Very difficult, suitable for expert DIY or professional

Specifications

General

Engine type.	Four-cylinder, in-line, double overhead camshaft
Designation	EcoBlue
Engine codes:	
77 kW engines	YLFS, YLF6
96 kW engines	YMFS, YMF6
125 kW engines	YNFS, YNF6
Capacity	1996 cc
Bore	84.01 mm
Stroke	90.03 mm
Compression ratio	16.5: 1
Firing order.	1-3-4-2 (No 1 cylinder at timing belt end)
Direction of crankshaft rotation	Clockwise (seen from right-hand side of vehicle)
Emissions level.	Euro Stage 6

Cylinder head

Piston protrusion: / **Thickness of cylinder head gasket**

0.671 to 0.720 mm	1.30 mm (1 tooth)
0.721 to 0.770 mm	1.35 mm (2 teeth)
0.771 to 0.820 mm	1.40 mm (3 teeth)
0.821 to 0.870 mm	1.45 mm (4 teeth)
0.871 to 0.920 mm	1.50 mm (5 teeth)
Maximum permissible gasket surface distortion	0.10 mm

Lubrication

Engine oil type/specification	See *Lubricants, fluids and tyre pressures* on page 0•17
Engine oil capacity	See Chapter 1 Specifications
Oil pressure – minimum (engine at operating temperature):	
At idle	1.0 bars
At 2000 rpm	1.5 bars

Torque wrench settings	Nm	lbf ft
Auxiliary drivebelt idler pulley	48	35
Auxiliary drivebelt tensioner bolt	48	35
Big-end bearing cap bolts: *		
Stage 1	5	4
Stage 2	25	18
Stage 3	40	30
Stage 4	Angle-tighten a further 90°	
Camshaft housing/cover bolts:		
Stage 1	5	4
Stage 2 – bolts 1 to 18 (see text)	10	7
Stage 3 – bolt 19 (see text)	23	17
Crankshaft rear oil seal carrier bolts		
Stage 1	5	4
Stage 2	10	7
Crankshaft position sensor bracket bolt(s)	10	7
Crankshaft idler pulley bolt*:		
Stage 1	60	44
Stage 2	Loosen 90°	
Stage 3	20	15
Stage 4	45	33
Stage 5	Angle-tighten 45°	
Crankshaft pulley bolt*:		
Stage 1	10	7
Stage 2	Loosen 60°	
Stage 3	20	15
Stage 4	70	52
Stage 5	150	111
Stage 6	Loosen 90°	
Stage 7	100	74
Stage 8	300	222
Stage 9	Angle-tighten 90°	
Cylinder head bolts: *		
Stage 1	15	11
Stage 2	25	18
Stage 3	40	30
Stage 4	Angle-tighten a further 90°	
Stage 5	Angle-tighten a further 90°	
Stage 6 (using service tools)	Angle tighten a further 90°	
Service tool 303-1611-03 retaining bolts	10	7
Engine/transmission mountings:		
Left-hand mounting:		
To inner wing panel – bolts	70	52
To transmission – lower bolts	70	52
To transmission – nuts	133	98
Right-hand mounting:		
To engine bracket – nuts	115	85
To inner wing panel – bolts	70	52
Rear mounting:		
Mounting-to-subframe*	133	98
Mounting through-bolt: *		
M14x1.5	150	111
M14x2.0	175	129
Flywheel bolts: *		
Stage 1	15	11
Stage 2	30	22
Stage 3	75	55
Stage 4	Angle-tighten a further 45°	
Lower crankcase/ladder to cylinder block:		
Bolts 1-7, 9-10, 12-13	23	17
Bolts 8, 11	13	10
Main bearing cap bolts: *		
Stage 1	6	4
Stage 2	15	11
Stage 3	20	15
Stage 4	35	26
Stage 5	80	59
#Stage 6	Angle-tighten a further 90°	

Torque wrench settings (continued)

	Nm	lbf ft
Oil filter/cooler housing bolts:		
Housing bolts	10	7
Oil filter mounting thread	55	41
Oil pressure sensor	20	15
Oil pump bolts:		
Stage 1	5	4
Stage 2	10	7
Oil pump drivebelt cover	10	7
Oil pump pick-up pipe	10	7
Piston cooling jets bolts	10	7
Roadwheel nuts	200	148
Sump bolts:		
Stage 1	5	4
Stage 2	10	7
Sump oil drain plug*	39	29
Timing belt cover:		
M6 bolts	10	7
M6 bolts	18	13
Central bolt*	40	30
Timing belt tensioner	25	18
Transmission-to-engine bolts	40	30

*Do not re-use

1 General Information

How to use this Chapter

1 This Part of Chapter 2 is devoted to repair procedures possible while the engine is still installed in the vehicle. Since these procedures are based on the assumption that the engine is installed in the vehicle, if the engine has been removed and mounted on a stand, some of the preliminary dismantling steps outlined will not apply.

2 Information concerning engine/transmission removal and refitting and engine overhaul can be found in Part C of this Chapter.

Engine description

3 The 2.0 litre diesel engines covered in this Part of Chapter 2 are all in-line four-cylinder, turbocharged units, with 16-valve, double overhead camshaft (DOHC) arrangement. The engine is mounted transversely at the front of the vehicle, with the transmission on the left-hand end.

4 The engine cylinder block casting is of cast-iron and has a lower aluminium crankcase which is bolted to the underside of the cylinder block, with a pressed steel sump bolted under that.

5 The crankshaft runs in five main bearings, the centre main bearing's upper half incorporating thrust washers to control crankshaft endfloat. The connecting rods rotate on horizontally-split bearing shells at their big-ends. The pistons are attached to the connecting rods by gudgeon pins which are a floating fit in the connecting rod small-end eyes, secured by circlips. The aluminium alloy pistons are fitted with three piston rings – two compression rings and an oil control ring.

6 The inlet and exhaust valves are each closed by coil springs, and they operate in guides which are a shrink-fit in the cylinder head, as also are the valve seat inserts.

7 The double overhead camshaft sprockets are driven by a belt from a sprocket on the crankshaft. The belt on these engines is unusual as it runs inside the timing cover, and is continuously immersed in engine oil. The camshafts operate the 16-valves via roller-rocker arms with hydraulic clearance adjusters. The rocker arms and clearance adjusters are located in an aluminium carrier bolted to the cylinder head. Each camshaft rotates in five bearings that are machined directly in the camshaft cover and the (bolted on) bearing caps. This means that the bearing caps are not available separately from the cylinder head, and must not be interchanged with caps from another engine.

8 The vacuum pump (used for the brake servo and other vacuum actuators) is located on the transmission end of the cylinder head, driven by a slot in the end of the exhaust camshaft. The high-pressure fuel injection pump is gear driven by an idler gear, itself driven by the crankshaft.

9 Lubrication is by means of a belt driven oil pump driven from a sprocket on the crankshaft. The oil pump is mounted below the lower crankcase, and draws oil through a strainer located in the sump. The pump forces oil through an externally-mounted full-flow cartridge-type filter. From the filter, the oil is pumped into a main gallery in the cylinder block/crankcase, from where it is distributed to the crankshaft (main bearings) and cylinder head. An oil cooler is fitted next to the oil filter, at the front of the block. The cooler is supplied with coolant from the engine cooling system.

10 While the crankshaft and camshaft bearings receive a pressurised supply, the camshaft lobes and valves are lubricated by splash, as are all other engine components. On higher powered engines, the undersides of the pistons are cooled by oil, sprayed from nozzles fitted above the upper main bearing shells. The turbocharger receives its own pressurised oil supply.

Repairs with the engine in the vehicle

11 The following major repair operations can be accomplished without removing the engine from the vehicle. However, owners should note that any operation involving the removal of the timing belt, camshafts or cylinder head requires careful forethought, depending on the level of skill and the tools and facilities available. Refer to the relevant text for details.

a) Compression pressure – testing.
b) Camshaft cover – removal and refitting.
c) Timing belt – renewal.
d) Timing belt tensioner and sprockets – removal and refitting.
e) Camshafts and hydraulic rockers – removal and refitting.
f) Cylinder head – removal, overhaul and refitting.
g) Crankshaft pulley – removal and refitting.
i) Sump – removal and refitting.
j) Pistons, connecting rods and big-end bearings – removal and refitting*.
k) Crankshaft oil seals – renewal.
l) Oil pump – removal and refitting.
m) Flywheel – removal and refitting.
n) Engine/transmission mountings – removal and refitting.

Note: *Although the operation marked with an asterisk can be carried out with the engine in the vehicle (after removal of the sump), it is preferable for the engine to be removed, in the interests of cleanliness and improved access. For this reason, the procedure is described in Chapter 2C.

3.7a Marks on the crankshaft sprocket and idler gear

3.7b Holes in the camshaft sprockets in the 12 o'clock position

2 Compression and leakdown tests – description and interpretation

Compression test

Note: *A compression tester suitable for use with diesel engines will be required for this test.*

Note: *The following procedure is likely to log a fault code in the powertrain control module memory. If the engine management warning light is illuminated after the test, it will be necessary to have the fault code cleared by a Ford dealer or suitably equipped garage using specialist diagnostic equipment.*

1 When engine performance is down, or if misfiring occurs which cannot be attributed to the fuel or emissions systems, a compression test can provide diagnostic clues as to the engine's condition. If the test is performed regularly, it can give warning of trouble before any other symptoms become apparent.

2 The engine must be fully warmed-up to normal operating temperature and the battery must be fully charged. The aid of an assistant will also be required.

3 Remove the glow plugs as described in Chapter 5 Section 13.

4 Fit a compression tester to the No 1 cylinder glow plug hole. A compression tester specifically intended for diesel engines must be used, because of the higher pressures involved. The tester is connected to an adapter (special tool 303-1051 or equivalent), which screws into the glow plug bore.

5 Crank the engine for several seconds on the starter motor. After one or two revolutions, the compression pressure should build up to a maximum figure and then stabilise. Record the highest reading obtained.

6 Repeat the test on the remaining cylinders, recording the pressure in each.

7 The cause of poor compression is less easy to establish on a diesel engine than on a petrol engine. The effect of introducing oil into the cylinders (wet testing) is not conclusive, because there is a risk that the oil will sit in the recess on the piston crown, instead of passing to the rings. However, the following can be used as a rough guide to diagnosis.

8 An actual compression pressure value is not stated by Ford, however all cylinders should produce very similar pressures. Any significant difference indicates the existence of a fault. Note that the compression should build-up quickly in a healthy engine. Low compression on the first stroke, followed by gradually increasing pressure on successive strokes, indicates worn piston rings. A low compression reading on the first stroke, which does not build-up during successive strokes, indicates leaking valves or a blown head gasket (a cracked head could also be the cause).

9 A low reading from two adjacent cylinders is almost certainly due to the head gasket having blown between them and the presence of coolant in the engine oil will confirm this.

10 On completion, remove the compression tester, and refit the glow plugs as described in Chapter 5 Section 13.

Leakdown test

11 A leakdown test measures the rate at which compressed air fed into the cylinder is lost. It is an alternative to a compression test, and in many ways it is better, since the escaping air provides easy identification of where pressure loss is occurring (piston rings, valves or head gasket).

12 The equipment required for leakdown testing is unlikely to be available to the home mechanic. If poor compression is suspected, have the test performed by a suitably equipped garage.

3 Engine timing – setting

Note: *Only turn the engine in the normal direction of rotation – clockwise viewed from the right-hand side of the vehicle.*

General information

1 Top Dead Centre (TDC) is the highest point in the cylinder that each piston reaches as it travels up and down when the crankshaft turns. Each piston reaches TDC at the end of the compression stroke and again at the end of the exhaust stroke, but TDC generally refers to piston position on the compression stroke. No 1 piston is at the timing chain end of the engine.

2 Setting No 1 piston at TDC (Top Dead Centre) is an essential part of many procedures, such as timing belt removal and cylinder head removal.

3 The design of the engines covered in this Chapter is such that piston-to-valve contact may occur if the camshaft or crankshaft is turned with the timing belt removed. For this reason, it is important to ensure that the camshaft and crankshaft do not move in relation to each other once the timing belt has been removed from the engine.

Setting

Note: *Ford service tool 303-1637 (or equivalent) – will be required to set the timing at TDC. Suitable alternatives to the Ford tool may be available from after-market suppliers, Eg: www.asttools.co.uk.*

4 Remove the timing belt cover as described in Section 5.

5 Remove the flywheel locking tool.

6 Temporarily refit the old crankshaft pulley retaining bolt, but only finger-tighten it.

7 Using a socket on the crankshaft pulley bolt, rotate the crankshaft clockwise until the mark on the crankshaft sprocket aligns with the corresponding mark on the idler gear, and the circular holes in the camshaft sprockets are in the 12 o'clock position **(see illustrations)**.

8 Carefully remove the old crankshaft pulley retaining bolt.

9 To lock the crankshaft in this position attach

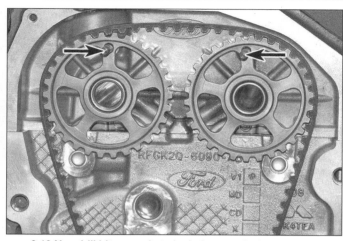

3.9 The special tool secures to the engine block to lock the crankshaft in position

3.10 Use drill bits or rods to lock the camshaft sprockets

Ford special tool No. 303-1637 (or equivalent) to the end of the crankshaft and cylinder block **(see illustration)**.

10 Lock the camshaft sprockets in position using two 6 mm drill bits/rods. Insert the rods through the circular holes in the sprockets into the corresponding holes in the cylinder head **(see illustration)**.

11 The crankshaft and camshafts are now set at TDC for No.1 cylinder.

12 Before rotating the crankshaft again, make sure that the special tool (and, where applicable, the camshaft sprocket timing pins) are removed. Refit all other components removed for access. **Do not** use the crankshaft timing setting tool to prevent the crankshaft from rotating.

4 Camshaft cover – removal and refitting

Caution: Do not carry out any work on the fuel system with the engine running. Wait for at least 2 minutes after the engine has been stopped before any work is carried out on the fuel system, to make sure the fuel pressure and temperature has dropped sufficiently. Make sure that all the fuel lines are kept clean. Fit blanking plugs

to the end of the fuel lines when they are disconnected, to prevent foreign matter entering the components.
Caution: Only turn the engine in the normal direction of rotation – clockwise viewed from the right-hand side of the vehicle.

Removal

1 Disconnect the battery negative terminal as described in Chapter 5 Section 4.

2 Refer to Section 7 and remove the timing belt.

3 Refer to Chapter 5 Section 7 and remove the alternator.

4 Refer to Chapter 4A Section 13 and remove the common fuel rail.

5 Refer to Chapter 4A Section 12 and remove the fuel injectors.

6 Disconnect the number one cylinder glow plug, unclip the wiring loom, undo the two retaining bolts and remove the bracket above the high pressure pump **(see illustration)**.

7 Disconnect the fuel return hoses from the fuel rail, high pressure pump and unclip the return union (from the left-hand end of the cylinder head) **(see illustrations)**. Remove the fuel return pipe assembly.

8 Depress the buttons, disconnect the fuel supply pipe from the high pressure pump and move it to one side **(see illustration)**.

9 Disconnect the wiring plug, undo the

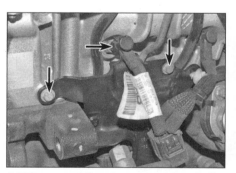

4.6 Disconnect the glow plug and undo the bracket retaining bolts

4.7a Unclip the union from the bracket on the left-hand end of the cylinder head

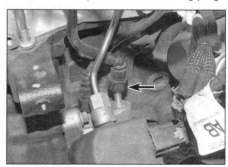

4.7b Disconnect the fuel return hose from the high pressure pump…

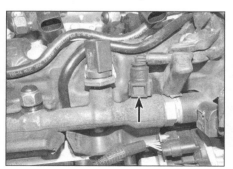

4.7c …and the fuel rail

4.8 Depress the release buttons, and disconnect the pipe

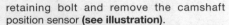

4.9 Disconnect the camshaft position sensor plug and undo the retaining bolt

4.10 Lift off the acoustic engine cover

4.12 Engine oil dipstick guide tube retaining nut

retaining bolt and remove the camshaft position sensor **(see illustration)**.

10 Remove the acoustic engine cover **(see illustration)**.

11 Refer to Chapter 9 Section 14 and remove the brake vacuum pump, pipes and gasket.

12 Undo the retaining nut and remove the engine oil dipstick guide tube from the camshaft cover. Renew the O-ring seal **(see illustration)**.

13 Working in the reverse of the sequence shown in illustration 4.16, undo the retaining bolts and lift the camshaft cover off the cylinder head. Recover the gasket and discard it – a new gasket and fuel injector seals will be required for refitting.

Refitting

14 Thoroughly clean the sealing surfaces of the camshaft cover and the cylinder head using brake cleaner.

15 Locate a new gasket on the camshaft cover ensuring that it fits correctly on the two locating dowels.

16 Lower the camshaft cover into place, ensuring it fits correctly over the locating dowels. Tighten the retaining bolts gradually and evenly to the specified torque in the sequence shown **(see illustration)**.

17 The remainder of refitting is a reversal of removal. Tighten all fasteners to the specified torque, where given.

5 Timing belt cover – removal and refitting

Note: *To carry out this task with the engine/transmission installed in the vehicle will require the equipment necessary to support the engine with the right-hand engine mounting removed, and to raise and support the front of the vehicle. Ford technicians use an engine support beam arrangement, which locates in the vehicle underbody and front crossmember. If such an arrangement is not available, use an engine crane; either way, use a suitable length of chain and hooks to attach the lifting gear to the engine lifting eye. If the engine must be supported from below, use a large piece of wood on a trolley jack to spread the load and reduce the chance of damage to the sump. Precise details of the procedure will depend on the equipment available and the following description is typical.*

Note: *Ford technicians use special tools for removing the oil seal and aligning the timing chain cover – see text. A new timing belt cover will be required for refitting because the cover will be irreparably distorted during removal.*

Removal

1 Disconnect the battery negative lead as described in Chapter 5 Section 4.

2 Drain the cooling system as described in Chapter 1 Section 32.

3 Remove the air cleaner assembly as described in Chapter 4A Section 5.

4 Remove the starter motor as described in Chapter 5 Section 10.

5 Remove the auxiliary drivebelt(s) as described in Chapter 1 Section 33.

6 Remove the right-hand headlight as described in Chapter 12 Section 11.

7 Drain the engine oil as described in Chapter 1 Section 6.

8 To prevent the crankshaft from rotating, install Ford special tool No.303-1643 (or equivalent) in the starter motor aperture. This tool engages with the flywheel ring gear, locking the crankshaft in place **(see illustration)**. In the absence of this tool it is possible to lock the flywheel by inserting a suitable lever into the flywheel teeth.

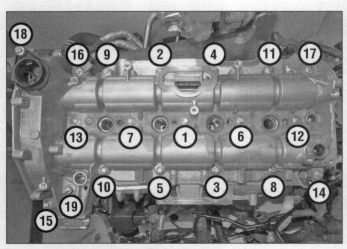

4.16 Camshaft cover bolt tightening sequence

5.8 Use a special tool or equivalent to lock the flywheel ring gear

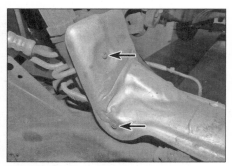

5.9 Remove the steering rack shield before supporting the engine

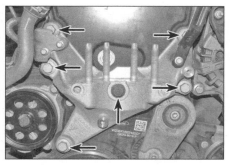

5.10 Right-hand engine mounting bracket retaining bolts

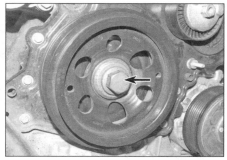

5.11 Slacken the crankshaft pulley bolt

5.12 Disconnect the coolant hose next to the timing belt cover

5.13 Release the clamps and remove the hose

5.14 Undo the nut and move the electric coolant pump to one side

9 Undo the 2 retaining bolts and remove the shield over the steering rack **(see illustration)**.
10 With the engine adequately supported (see earlier Note), remove the right-hand engine mounting, as described in Section 17, then undo the bolts and remove the engine mounting bracket from the cylinder head/block **(see illustration)**.
11 Slacken the crankshaft pulley bolt 2 complete revolutions **(see illustration)**.
12 Disconnect the coolant pipe/hose at the right-hand end of the engine, adjacent to the timing belt cover **(see illustration)**.
13 Remove the hose connecting the intercooler to the throttle body **(see illustration)**.
14 Undo the nut and move the electric coolant pump to one side **(see illustration)**. Unclip the coolant pump hose from the timing belt cover where necessary.
15 Slightly lift the sound insulation material from the top of the timing belt cover.
16 Undo the retaining Torx bolt and remove the auxiliary drivebelt tensioner **(see illustration)**.
17 Undo the 3 retaining bolts and move the power steering pump to one side **(see illustration)**. There's no need to disconnect the pipes.
18 Remove the crankshaft pulley as described in Section 6.
19 Slacken and remove the timing belt cover retaining bolts. Note that the larger diameter central nut/bolt must be renewed **(see illustrations)**.

5.16 Drivebelt tensioner retaining bolt

5.17 Undo the bolts and move the power steering pump to one side (pipes disconnected for clarity)

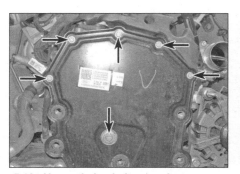

5.19a Upper timing belt cover fasteners...

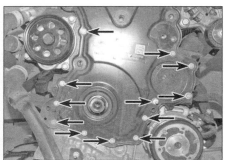

5.19b ...lower timing belt cover fasteners

5.20 Separate the cover from the engine

5.22a Apply a 4 mm bead of sealant to the timing belt cover…

20 The cover is secured to the engine and sump with sealant. Use a suitable tool to separate the cover from the engine (see illustration).
Caution: Take care not to damage the mating surfaces of the engine.
Note: *The timing belt cover must not be re-used – the removal procedure will distort it.*

Refitting

21 Plug the auxiliary drivebelt tensioner retaining bolt hole to prevent sealant ingress.
22 Make sure that the mating surfaces of the cover and the engine casing are clean. Apply a 4 mm bead of suitable sealant (Ford No. WSE-M4G323-A4 or equivalent) around the mating surface of the timing belt cover,

ensuring that the sealant bead passes around the inside of the retaining bolt holes. Also apply a 9 mm diameter bead of sealant to the areas where the camshaft carrier joins the cylinder head, the cylinder head joins the cylinder block, and the cylinder block joins the lower crankcase (see illustrations).
Caution: Install the timing chain cover within 5 minutes of applying the sealer to the engine casing. Make sure the cover does not come into contact with the engine casing until the correct position for fitting is obtained.
23 Fit the new timing belt cover, ensuring it locates correctly over the dowels. The help of an assistant may be required.
24 Insert 2 retaining bolts at the top of the cover, 2 at the centre and 2 at the lower corners. Only finger-tighten the bolts at this stage (see illustration).
25 Refit the engine mounting bracket and tighten the retaining bolts to the specified torque (see illustration).
26 Refit the remaining bolts around the circumference of the cover and tighten them

5.22b …and a 9 mm bead to these areas on the engine block/cylinder head

5.24 Finger-tighten the first 6 cover retaining bolts

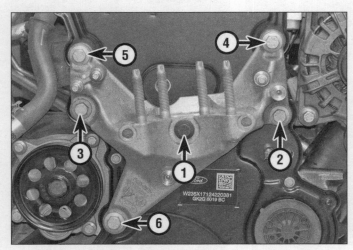

5.25 Engine mounting bracket bolts tightening sequence

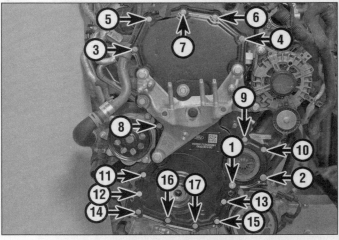

5.26a Timing belt cover bolts tightening sequence

to the specified torque, before installing the new larger diameter belt cover central bolt finger tight. You may need to remove one of the engine mounting bracket bolts to be able to tighten the central bolt to the specified torque **(see illustrations)**.

27 Remove the plug from the auxiliary drivebelt tensioner retaining bolt hole.

28 The remainder of refitting is a reversal of removal. Noting the following points:

a) *Refit the crankshaft pulley as described in Section 6.*

b) *Refit the auxiliary drivebelt(s) as described in Chapter 1 Section 33.*

c) *Refit the air cleaner assembly as described in Chapter 4A Section 5.*

d) *Refill the engine with oil as described in Chapter 1 Section 6.*

e) *Refill the cooling system as described in Chapter 1 Section 32.*

6 Crankshaft pulley – removal and refitting

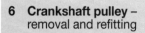

Removal

Note: *A new crankshaft pulley retaining bolt will be required for refitting.*

1 Disconnect the battery negative lead as described in Chapter 5 Section 4.

2 Slacken the right-hand front roadwheel nuts, then jack up the front of the vehicle and support it securely on axle stands (see *Jacking and vehicle support*). Remove the right-hand roadwheel.

3 Remove the auxiliary drivebelt(s), as described in Chapter 1 Section 33.

4 Remove the starter motor as described in Chapter 5 Section 10.

5 To prevent the crankshaft from rotating, install Ford special tool No.303-1643 (or equivalent) in the starter motor aperture. This tool engages with the flywheel ring gear, locking the crankshaft in place **(see illustration)**. In the absence of this tool it is possible to lock the flywheel by inserting a suitable lever into the flywheel teeth.

6 Loosen the crankshaft pulley bolt by five turns. Ensure that the vehicle is adequately supported, because considerable effort may be needed to slacken the bolt.

7 Use a two-leg puller to release the crankshaft pulley **(see illustration)**. Remove the bolt and remove the pulley. Discard the bolt – a new one must be fitted.

8 Remove the two-leg puller.

9 With the pulley removed, it is advisable to check the crankshaft oil seal for signs of oil leakage. If necessary, fit a new seal as described in Section 15.

Refitting

10 Refit the pulley to the end of the crankshaft, then fit the new pulley securing bolt and tighten the bolt to the specified torque settings and the specified angles.

11 Refitting is a reversal of removal.

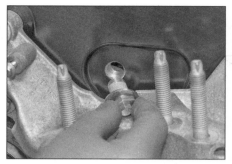

5.26b Temporarily remove the engine mounting bracket bolt to access the cover central bolt

7 Timing belt – removal, inspection and refitting

General

Note: *Only turn the engine in the normal direction of rotation – clockwise viewed from the right-hand side of the vehicle.*

1 The timing belt drives the camshafts from a toothed sprocket on the end of the crankshaft idler pulley. If the belt breaks or slips in service, the pistons are likely to hit the valve heads, resulting in expensive damage.

2 The timing belt should be renewed at the specific intervals, or earlier if it is contaminated with oil, or at all noisy in operation (a 'scraping' noise due to uneven wear).

Removal

Note: *Ford service tool 303-1650 (or equivalent) will be required to install the new timing belt. Suitable alternatives to the Ford tool may be available from after-market suppliers, EG: www.asttools.co.uk.*

Caution: The crankshaft or camshafts must not be rotated while the timing belt is removed.

3 Remove the timing belt cover, as described in Section 5.

4 Remove the Ford special service tool

6.7 Slacken the crankshaft pulley bolt before attaching the two-leg puller to remove the pulley

6.5 Use this special tool or a suitable lever to lock the flywheel ring gear

303-1643 or equivalent from the starter motor aperture.

5 Set the crankshaft and the camshafts in position as described in Section 3.

6 Slacken the timing belt tension by inserting a hexagon key into the access hole at the top of the tensioner and rotate it clockwise until you are able to insert a 6 mm drill bit/rod through the locking hole **(see illustration)**.

7 Noting its routing, remove the timing belt from the sprockets.

8 Undo the timing belt tensioner bolt and remove and discard the tensioner. A new one will be required.

Inspection

9 Renew the belt as a matter of course, regardless of its apparent condition. The cost of a new belt is nothing compared with the cost of repairs should the belt break in service. The tensioner bolt must always be replaced.

10 Examine the teeth of the camshaft and crankshaft sprockets for excessive wear and damage.

Refitting and tensioning

11 Ensure that the crankshaft and camshafts are still set to TDC on No 1 cylinder, as described in Section 3.

12 Fit the new timing belt tensioner, tightening the bolt to the specified torque **(see illustration)**.

7.6 Rotate the timing belt tensioner clockwise before inserting a bit or rod to lock it

7.12 Ensure the tensioner dowel is located into the hole on the engine block

7.13 Fit the special tool to the end of the crankshaft

7.14 The camshaft sprockets service tool makes it easier to fit a new timing belt

7.15a Locate the timing belt around the crankshaft idler sprocket first…

7.15b …around the tensioner and then over the camshaft sprockets

7.16 Release the tensioner so it comes into contact with the belt

13 Lock the crankshaft in position by attaching Ford special tool No. 303-1637 (or equivalent) to the end of the crankshaft and cylinder block **(see illustration)**.

14 Fit Ford service tool no.303-1650 (comprising two parts) over both camshaft sprockets, ensuring they locate over the drill bits/rods **(see illustration)**. Do not rotate the sprockets.

15 Locate the new timing belt on the crankshaft idler sprocket, making sure the teeth are engaged properly. Then position the belt around the tensioner and then locate it over the left-hand element of service tool no.303-1650 before sliding it onto the left-hand camshaft sprocket. Now do the same with the right-hand service tool/ camshaft sprocket, making sure the belt has engaged with all of the teeth on both sprockets **(see illustrations)**.

16 With the new belt fitted correctly over all of the sprockets, insert the hexagon key into the tensioner's access hole, remove the drill bit/rod and gently release the tensioner anti-clockwise until it rests against the timing belt **(see illustration)**.

17 Remove Ford service tool no.303-1650 from the camshaft sprockets and remove the 6 mm drill bits/rods that were used to lock the sprockets in position.

18 Remove Ford service tool no.303-1637 (used for TDC purposes) before fitting the original (old) crankshaft pulley bolt. Only finger-tighten the bolt at this stage.

19 Using a socket on the crankshaft pulley bolt, rotate the crankshaft clockwise four

revolutions. Do not turn it anticlockwise. Make sure the new timing belt is engaged properly on all of the sprockets.

20 Now remove and discard the crankshaft pulley bolt.

21 Refit Ford special service tool 303-1637 to the crankshaft pulley and cylinder block. Only finger-tighten the bolt at this stage **(see illustration 7.14)**.

22 Make sure the mark on the crankshaft sprocket aligns with the corresponding mark on the idler gear, and the circular holes in the camshaft sprockets are in the 12 O'clock position. Refit the 6 mm bits/rods to the camshaft sprockets to verify this before removing them. Remove Ford special service tool 303-1637.

23 Install Ford special service tool 303-1643 in the starter motor aperture.

8.4 Insert 4 mm rods or drill bits to lock the crankshaft and fuel pump pulley sprockets

24 The remainder of refitting is a reversal of removal.

8   Timing belt tensioner and sprockets – removal, inspection and refitting

Timing belt tensioner

1 The timing belt tensioner can be removed by referring to the timing belt renewal procedure, in Section 7.

Camshaft sprockets

2 The camshaft sprockets are integral with the camshafts, which are integral with the camshaft cover. Check with your Ford dealer or parts specialist. Refer to Section 4 for details of the procedure.

Crankshaft idler gear

Removal

3 Remove the timing belt as described in Section 7.

4 Insert 4 mm drill bits or rods through the holes in the crankshaft idler pulley sprocket and the fuel pump pulley sprocket **(see illustration)**.

5 Mark the position of the fuel pump pulley sprocket in relation to the engine block **(see illustration)**.

6 Undo the retaining bolt, then remove the crankshaft idler gear inner hub and sprocket **(see illustrations)**. Discard the bolt – a new one must be fitted.

Refitting

7 Use a new bolt and refit the crankshaft idler gear inner hub and sprocket, ensuring the alignment marks on the sprocket match up with the crankshaft sprocket, and that the drill bit/rod can pass through the hole in the sprocket. Also make sure that the drill bit in the fuel pump sprocket has not become dislodged and that the gears' teeth are still aligned. If not, realign them and reinsert the drill bit/rod **(see illustration)**.

8 Refit the oil pump sprocket and belt.

9 Refit the timing belt as described in Section 7.

9 Camshafts, rocker arms and hydraulic tappets – removal and refitting

Note: *Only turn the engine in the normal direction of rotation – clockwise viewed from the right-hand side of the vehicle.*

Camshafts

1 The camshafts are integral with the camshaft cover. Check with your Ford dealer or parts specialist. Removal of the camshaft cover is described in Section 4.

Rocker arms and hydraulic tappets

Removal

2 Remove the camshaft cover as described in Section 4.

3 Noting their fitted positions, carefully lift the rocker arms and hydraulic tappets from place.

4 Carefully lift the rocker arms and hydraulic tappets from their bores, and store them with the valve contact surface facing downwards, to prevent the oil from draining out **(see illustration)**. It is recommended that the tappets are kept immersed in oil while they are removed from the cylinder head. Keep the tappets in order because they must be refitted to their original valves – accelerated wear, leading to early failure, may result if they are interchanged.

Refitting

5 Fit the rocker arms and hydraulic tappets in their original positions, lubricating them with clean oil once they have been fitted **(see illustration)**.

6 The remainder of refitting is a reversal of removal.

10 Cylinder head – removal, inspection and refitting

Removal

1 Disconnect the battery negative lead as described in Chapter 5 Section 4.

2 Remove the rocker arms and hydraulic tappets as described in Section 9.

3 Remove the inlet manifold as described in Chapter 4A Section 16.

4 Unbolt the thermostat as described in Chapter 3 Section 3 and position it to one side.

5 Disconnect the glow plugs from cylinders 3 and 4.

6 Remove the bracket, wiring plugs and

clips on the left end of the cylinder head **(see illustration)**.

7 Depress the release button each side and disconnect the heater hose from the right-hand side heater matrix pipe stub **(see illustration)**.

8.5 Mark the position of the fuel pump pulley sprocket

8.6a Remove the crankshaft idler gear inner hub...

8.6b ...followed by the sprocket

8.7 Tighten the new idler gear bolt to the specified torque and angle

9.4 Store the tappets with the valve contact surface facing downwards

9.5 Fit the rocker arms and tappets and lubricate with clean oil

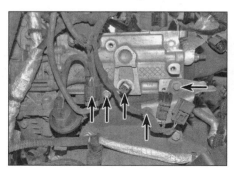

10.6 Remove the bracket, wiring plugs, and unclip the harnesses from the cylinder head

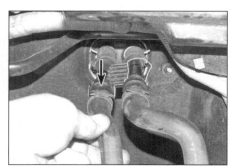

10.7 Disconnect the right-hand heater matrix pipe

10.8 Release the clamp and disconnect the hose

10.9 Disconnect the EGR valve wiring plug

10.10a Undo the bolt beneath the EGR cooler…

10.10b …and the EGR valve retaining bolts

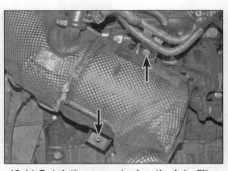

10.11 Catalytic converter/particulate filter retaining bolts

10.12 Undo the bolts and remove the lifting eye

8 Disconnect the hose from the EGR cooler **(see illustration)**.

9 Disconnect the wiring plug from the top of the EGR valve assembly **(see illustration)**.

10 Undo the 7 retaining bolts and remove the EGR cooler and valve assembly **(see illustrations)**.

11 Undo the catalytic converter/particulate filter retaining bolts, then release the clamp securing the assembly to the **(see illustration)**. Gently move the catalytic converter/particulate filter assembly to one side.

12 Undo the two bolts and remove the engine lifting eye **(see illustration)**.

13 Depress the release button each side and disconnect the coolant pipe from the cylinder head **(see illustration)**.

14 Disconnect the turbo oil supply and return pipes, as described in Chapter 4A Section 15.

15 Make a final check to ensure all relevant hoses, pipes and wiring have been disconnected from the cylinder head.

16 Working in the reverse order of the tightening sequence **(see illustration 10.38)**, and using a power tool, loosen the cylinder head bolts by half a turn at a time until they are all loose. Remove the head bolts and discard them – they must be renewed.

17 Using assistance, lift the cylinder head away – be carefully, it's heavy. Do not, under any circumstances, lever the head between the mating surfaces, because this may damage the sealing surfaces for the gasket, leading to leaks. *Caution: The glow plugs protrude through the bottom of the cylinder head, so support the head on wooden blocks to prevent the plugs becoming damaged.*

18 Once the head has been removed, recover the gasket from the two dowels and discard the gasket.

19 If required, dismantling and inspection of the cylinder head is covered in Chapter 2C Section 6 and Chapter 2C Section 7.

Cylinder head gasket selection

20 Examine the old cylinder head gasket for manufacturer's identification markings. These will be in the form of teeth (one, two or three) on the front edge of the gasket and/or holes in the gasket, which indicate the gasket's thickness **(see illustration)**.

21 Unless new components have been fitted, or the cylinder head has been machined (skimmed), the new cylinder head gasket must be of the same type as the old one. Purchase the required gasket, and proceed to paragraph 27.

22 If the head has been machined, or if new pistons have been fitted, it is likely that a head gasket of different thickness to the original will be needed. Gasket selection is made on the basis of the measured piston protrusion above the cylinder head gasket surface (the protrusion must fall within the range specified here).

Piston protrusion (mm)	Thickness of gasket (mm)
0.671-0.720	1.30 (one tooth) Grade 1
0.721-0.770	1.35 (two teeth) Grade 2
0.771-0.820	1.40 (three teeth) Grade 3
0.821-0.870	1.45 (four teeth) Grade 4
0.871-0.920	1.50 (five teeth) Grade 5

23 To measure the piston protrusion, anchor a dial test indicator (DTI) to the top face (cylinder head gasket mating face) of the

10.13 Disconnect the pipe from the cylinder head

10.20 Teeth and holes in the gasket, which indicate the gasket's thickness

cylinder block, and zero the gauge on the gasket mating face **(see illustration)**.

24 Rest the gauge probe above No 1 piston crown, and turn the crankshaft slowly by hand until the piston reaches TDC (its maximum height). Measure and record the maximum piston projection at TDC.

25 Repeat the measurement for the remaining pistons, and record the results.

26 If the measurements differ from piston to piston, take the highest figure, and use this to determine the thickness of the head gasket required.

Preparation for refitting

27 The mating faces of the cylinder head and cylinder block must be perfectly clean before refitting the head. Use a hard plastic or wooden scraper to remove all traces of gasket and carbon; also clean the piston crowns.
Note: *The new head gasket has rubber coated surfaces, which could be damaged from sharp edges or debris left by a metal scraper.*

28 Take particular care when cleaning the piston crowns, as the soft aluminium alloyis easily damaged.

29 Make sure that the carbon is not allowed to enter the oil and water passages – this is particularly important for the lubrication system, because carbon could block the oil supply to the engine's components. Using adhesive tape and paper, seal the water, oil and bolt holes in the cylinder block.

30 To prevent carbon entering the gap between the pistons and bores, smear a little grease in the gap. After cleaning each piston, use a small brush to remove all traces of grease and carbon from the gap, then wipe away the remainder with a clean rag. Clean all the pistons in the same way.

31 Check the mating surfaces of the cylinder block and the cylinder head for nicks, deep scratches and other damage. If slight, they may be removed carefully with a file, but if excessive, machining may be the only alternative to renewal.

32 If warpage of the cylinder head gasket surface is suspected, use a straight-edge to check it for distortion. Refer to Chapter 2C Section 7 if necessary.

33 Ensure that the cylinder head bolt holes in the crankcase are clean and free of oil. Syringe or soak up any oil left in the bolt holes. This is most important in order that the correct bolt tightening torque can be applied, and to prevent the possibility of the block being cracked by hydraulic pressure when the bolts are tightened.

Refitting

34 Wipe clean the mating surfaces of the cylinder head and block, and check that the two locating dowels are in position on the block.

35 Turn the crankshaft and position Nos 1 and 4 pistons at TDC, then turn the crankshaft a quarter turn (90°) anti-clockwise. This will eliminate any risk of piston-to-valve contact as the cylinder head is refitted.

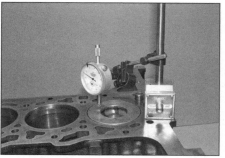

10.23 Using a dial test indicator to measure the piston protrusion

36 Position the new gasket over the dowels. The gasket can only be fitted one way round – check carefully that the holes in the gasket align with the holes in the block surface, and that none are blocked **(see illustration)**.

37 With the help of an assistant, lower the cylinder head into position on the gasket, ensuring that it engages correctly over the dowels.

38 Fit the new cylinder head bolts in the order shown **(see illustration)**, screwing them in as far as possible by hand before tightening them in the same order to the specified torque settings and angles.

39 The remainder of the refitting procedure is a reversal of the removal procedure, noting the following points:

a) *Refit the rocker arms and hydraulic tappets as shown in Section 9.*

b) *Check and if necessary top-up the engine oil level as described in 'Weekly checks'.*

c) *Before starting the engine, read through the section on engine restarting after overhaul, in Chapter 2C Section 17.*

10.36 Locate the new cylinder head gasket over the dowels

11 Sump –
removal and refitting

Removal

1 Firmly apply the handbrake, then jack up the front of the vehicle and support it securely on axle stands (see *Jacking and vehicle support*).

2 Drain the engine oil as described in Chapter 1 Section 6. Although not strictly necessary as part of the dismantling procedure, owners are advised to remove and discard the oil filter, so that it can be renewed with the oil. Refer to Chapter 1 Section 6 if necessary.

3 Progressively unscrew and remove the sump-retaining bolts and nuts.

4 Carefully remove the sump. Ford recommend that once removed, the sump should not be re-used due to deformation during the removal process. With care, it is possible to remove the sump without deforming it, making it suitable for reuse.

10.38 Tightening sequence for the cylinder head bolts

11.6 Apply a 7 mm bead of sealant to the sump flange

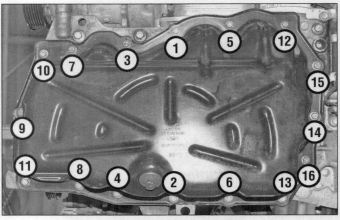

11.7 Sump retaining bolts/nuts tightening sequence

Caution: The use of sealant can make removal of the sump more difficult. If care is taken not to damage the surfaces, the sealant can be cut around using a putty knife or similar (special service tool 303-428). On no account lever between the mating faces, because this will almost certainly damage them, resulting in leaks when finished.

Refitting

5 Thoroughly clean and degrease the mating surfaces of the cylinder block lower crankcase and sump.

Note: *Take care not to allow sealant to enter the sump retaining bolt holes.*

6 Apply a 7 mm bead of suitable sealant (Ford No. LB 2U7J-M4G323-AB or equivalent to specification WSE-M4G323-A4) to the sump flange, making sure the bead is around the inside edge of the bolt holes (see illustration). The sump must be refitted within 5 minutes of applying the sealant.

7 Refit the sump, and tighten all the bolts and nuts to the specified torque settings in the sequence shown (see illustration).

8 Fit a new oil sump plug, tightening it to the specified torque setting.

9 Lower the vehicle to the ground and refill the engine with oil. If removed, fit a new oil filter with reference to Chapter 1 Section 6. Make a point of checking around the sump after filling to make sure there are no leaks.

12 Oil pump – removal and refitting

Note: *The following procedure is for removal and refitting of the oil pump. If the oil pump drive belt or tensioner requires renewal, the engine timing belt will need to be removed (see Section 7).*

Removal

1 Remove the sump as described in Section 11.

2 Unclip the pipe attached to the oil pick-up tube (see illustration).

3 Undo the retaining bolt and remove the drivebelt cover (see illustration).

4 Undo the four retaining bolts and remove the oil pump, complete with oil pick-up tube, from the lower crankcase. Withdraw the oil pump belt from the sprocket, taking care not to damage the belt. Note the oil pump's locating pegs (see illustrations).

Refitting

5 Offer up the oil pump to the lower crankcase, installing the drive belt to the sprocket on the oil pump before making sure the pump's locating pegs are correctly located.

6 Tighten the four oil pump retaining bolts to the specified torque settings.

7 The remainder of refitting is a reversal of removal.

13 Oil pressure sensor – removal and refitting

Removal

1 The sensor is located at the front of the engine block, above the engine oil cooler.

2 To improve access to the switch, it may be necessary to apply the handbrake, then jack up the front of the vehicle and support it on axle stands (see *Jacking and vehicle support*).

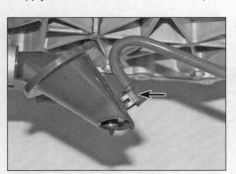

12.2 Unclip the pipe

12.3 Undo the bolt and remove the drivebelt cover

12.4a Oil pump retaining bolts

12.4b With the pump on the bench, the oil pick-up pipe and O-rings can be renewed

3 Disconnect the wiring plug and unscrew the sensor from the engine block **(see illustrations)**. Be prepared for oil spillage.

Refitting

4 Apply a thin smear of suitable sealant to the threads, then screw the sensor into place, and tighten it to the specified torque.

5 The remainder of refitting is a reversal of removal.

6 Check the engine oil level and top-up as necessary (see *Weekly checks*).

7 Check for correct warning light operation and for signs of oil leaks, once the engine has been restarted and warmed-up to normal operating temperature.

14 Oil filter housing and oil cooler – removal and refitting

Removal

1 Disconnect the battery negative lead as described in Chapter 5 Section 4.

2 Drain the cooling system as described in Chapter 1 Section 32.

3 Drain the engine oil as described in Chapter 1 Section 6.

4 The oil filter housing and cooler is located on the front of the cylinder block.

5 Firmly apply the handbrake, then jack up the front of the vehicle and support it securely on axle stands (see *Jacking and vehicle support*).

6 Position a container beneath the oil filter to catch escaping oil and coolant.

7 Release the clips and disconnect the two coolant hoses from the oil cooler **(see illustration)**. Be prepared for coolant spillage.

8 Using an oil filter removal tool, slacken the filter initially, then unscrew it by hand the rest of the way. Discard the filter – a new one must be fitted..

9 Undo the oil filter mounting threaded fitting with a socket and unscrew the four filter/cooler housing bolts.Withdraw the housing from the cylinder block. Remove and discard the gasket and O-ring seals from the housing's mating surface **(see illustrations)**.

Note: *The oil cooler is intergral with the filter housing and cannot be renewed separately.*

Refitting

10 Refitting is a reversal of removal, bearing in mind the following points:

a) *Use a new gasket and two new O-ring seals.*

b) *Fit the oil filter housing mounting bolts finger tight initially.*

c) *Tighten the oil filter housing retaining bolts to the specified torque.*

d) *Lubricate the oil filter's seal with clean oil before screwing on by hand only.*

e) *Replace the manufacturer's hose clips with worm-drive clips.*

13.3a Disconnect the wiring plug…

f) *On completion, refill the oil and coolant as described in Chapter 1, then start the engine and check for signs of oil or coolant leakage.*

15 Crankshaft oil seals – renewal

Timing belt end seal

1 The oil seal is integral with the timing belt cover. Refer to Section 5 for the timing belt cover replacement procedure.

Flywheel end seal

2 Remove the transmission as described in Chapter 7 Section 7 and the clutch assembly as described in Chapter 6 Section 6.

14.7 Disconnect the coolant pipes from the oil cooler

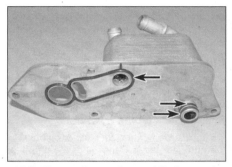
14.9b Renew the gasket and O-ring seals

13.3b …and unscrew the oil pressure sensor

3 Drain the engine oil as described in Chapter 1 Section 6.

4 Remove the flywheel as described in Section 16.

5 Undo the retaining bolts, and remove the oil seal carrier **(see illustration)**.

6 Clean the end of the crankshaft, polishing off any burrs or raised edges, which may have caused the seal to fail in the first place. Clean also the seal carrier mating face on the engine block, using a suitable solvent for degreasing if necessary **(see illustration)**.

7 Apply a 4 mm bead of suitable sealant (Ford No. WSE-M4G323-A4 or equivalent) around the mating surface of the engine block, ensuring that the sealant bead passes around the inside of the retaining bolt holes. Also apply a 9 mm bead of the sealant to the recesses as shown **(see illustration)**.

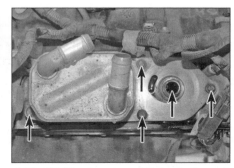
14.9a Oil filter housing retaining bolts and oil filter mounting thread

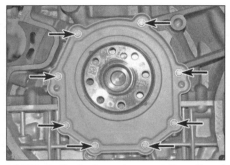
15.5 Undo the bolts and remove the oil seal carrier

15.6 Carefully remove all traces of the old sealant

15.7 Apply the sealant as shown

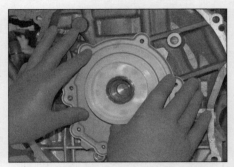

15.8 Fit the new seal over the end of the crankshaft using the locating sleeve

15.9a With the oil seal carrier centred around the crankshaft, tighten the retaining bolts

15.9b Remove the locating sleeve

Note: *The seal carrier must be fixed in position within 5 minutes of the silicone sealant having been applied to the engine block.*
Caution: Take care not to damage the mating surfaces when positioning the seal carrier.
8 Position the carrier into position, locating the fitting sleeve over the end of the crankshaft **(see illustration)**. Insert and finger-tighten the seal carrier retaining bolts.
9 Ensuring that the correct alignment of the carrier is maintained, work in a diagonal sequence, tightening the retaining bolts to the specified torque. Remove the locating sleeve **(see illustrations)**.
10 The remainder of the reassembly procedure is the reverse of dismantling, referring to the relevant text for details where required. Bear in mind the following points:

16.2 Fit the special service tool in the starter motor aperture

a) Make sure to fit a new engine oil sump plug.
b) Check for signs of oil leakage when the engine is restarted.

16 Flywheel –
removal, inspection and refitting

Removal

1 Remove the transmission as described in Chapter 7 Section 7, and the clutch assembly as described in Chapter 6 Section 6.
2 Install Ford special service tool 303-1643 or equivalent in the starter motor aperture. This tool engages with the flywheel ring gear, locking the crankshaft in place **(see illustration)**.
3 Unscrew the flywheel retaining bolts. Discard the bolts – new ones must be fitted.
4 Withdraw the flywheel, remembering that it is very heavy – do not drop it.

Inspection

5 A conventional solid flywheel or a dual-mass flywheel may be fitted, depending on engine power output and year of manufacture.

Single-mass (solid) flywheel

6 Examine the flywheel for wear or chipping of the ring gear teeth. Renewal of the ring gear is not possible and if the wear or chipping is significant, a new flywheel will be required.
7 Examine the flywheel for scoring of the clutch face. If the clutch face is scored significantly, a new flywheel will be required.
8 If there is any doubt about the condition of the flywheel, seek the advice of a Ford dealer or engine reconditioning specialist.

Dual-mass flywheel

9 A dual-mass flywheel has the effect of reducing engine and transmission vibrations and harshness. The flywheel consists of a primary mass and a secondary mass constructed in such a way that the secondary mass is allowed to rotate slightly in relation to the primary mass. Springs within the assembly restrict this movement to set limits.
10 Dual-mass flywheels have earned an unenviable reputation for unreliability and have been known to fail at quite low mileages (sometimes as low as 20,000 miles). As well as the checks described above in paragraphs 6 and 7, some additional checks should be performed as follows.
11 Look through the bolt hole and inspection openings in the secondary mass and check for any visible damage in the area of the centre bearing.
12 Place your thumbs on the clutch face of the secondary mass at the 3 o'clock and 9 o'clock positions and try to rock it. The maximum movement should not exceed 3 mm. Repeat this check with your thumbs at the 12 o'clock and 6 o'clock positions.
13 Rotate the secondary mass clockwise and anti-clockwise. It should move freely in both directions until spring resistance is felt, with no abnormal grating or rattling noises. The maximum rotational movement should not exceed a distance of five teeth of the ring gear.
14 If there is any doubt about the condition of the flywheel, seek the advice of a Ford dealer or engine reconditioning specialist. They will be able to advise if the flywheel is an acceptable condition, or whether renewal is necessary.

Refitting

15 Fit the flywheel to the crankshaft so that all bolt holes align, and make sure it is in full contact with the crankshaft flange before installing and finger-tightening the new retaining bolts.
16 If removed, reinstall Ford special service

Chapter 2 Part B
2.2 litre engine in-vehicle repair procedures

Contents

Degrees of difficulty

Easy, suitable for novice with little experience	Fairly easy, suitable for beginner with some experience	Fairly difficult, suitable for competent DIY mechanic	Difficult, suitable for experienced DIY mechanic	Very difficult, suitable for expert DIY or professional

Specifications

General

Engine type.	Four-cylinder, in-line, double overhead camshaft
Designation	DuraTorq-TDCi
Engine codes:	
74 kW engines	DRFF
92 kW engines	CYFF
114 kW engines	CVFF
Capacity	2198 cc
Bore	86.0 mm
Stroke	94.6 mm
Compression ratio	15.5 : 1
Firing order.	1-3-4-2 (No 1 cylinder at timing chain end)
Direction of crankshaft rotation	Clockwise (seen from right-hand side of vehicle)

Cylinder head

Piston protrusion:	**Thickness of cylinder head gasket**
0.430 to 0.520 mm	1.10 mm (1 hole/tooth)
0.521 to 0.570 mm	1.15 mm (2 holes/teeth)
0.571 to 0.620 mm	1.20 mm (3 holes/teeth)
Maximum permissible gasket surface distortion	0.10 mm

Lubrication

Engine oil type/specification	See *Lubricants, fluids and tyre pressures* on page 0•17
Engine oil capacity	See Chapter 1 Specifications
Oil pressure – minimum (engine at operating temperature):	
At idle	1.25 bars
At 2000 rpm	2.00 bars

Torque wrench settings

	Nm	lbf ft
Auxiliary drivebelt idler pulleys:		
Lower pulley nut	43	32
Upper pulley bolt	25	19
Auxiliary drivebelt tensioner bolts	25	19
Big-end bearing cap bolts: *		
Stage 1	8	6
Stage 2	25	19
Stage 3	37	27
Stage 4	Angle-tighten a further 90°	
Camshaft carrier bolts:		
Stage 1 – bolts 1 to 20	10	7
Stage 1 – bolts 21 to 24	5	4
Stage 2 – bolts 1 to 20	23	17
Stage 2 – bolts 21 to 24	10	7
Camshaft cover	10	7
Camshaft position sensor mounting bracket	10	7
Camshaft sprocket bolts	33	24
Crankshaft oil seal carrier bolts*	10	7
Crankshaft position sensor mounting bracket bolt	7	5
Crankshaft pulley bolts: *		
Stage 1	45	33
Stage 2	Angle-tighten a further 120°	
Cylinder head bolts: *		
Stage 1:		
Bolts 1 to 10	10	7
Bolts 11 to 18	5	4
Stage 2:		
Bolts 1 to 10	20	15
Bolts 11 to 18	10	7
Stage 3:		
Bolts 1 to 10	35	26
Bolts 11 to 18	20	15
Stage 4:		
Bolts 1 to 10	45	33
Bolts 11 to 18	25	18
Stage 5:		
Bolts 1 to 10	Angle-tighten a further 90°	
Bolts 11 to 18	Angle-tighten a further 90°	
Stage 6:		
Bolts 1 to 10	Angle-tighten a further 90°	
Bolts 11 to 18	Angle-tighten a further 90°	
Engine/transmission mountings: *		
Left-hand mounting:		
To inner wing panel	70	52
To transmission – bolts	115	85
To transmission – nut	133	98
Right-hand mounting:		
To engine bracket	125	92
To inner wing panel	70	52
Right-hand mounting engine bracket:		
Upper bolts:		
Stage 1	30	22
Stage 2	50	37
Stage 3	120	89
Stage 4	Angle-tighten a further 45°	
Lower stud bolt:		
Stage 1	20	15
Stage 2	25	18
Stage 3	50	37
Stage 4	Angle-tighten a further 45°	
Rear mounting:		
Mounting-to-subframe	133	98
Mounting through-bolt	150	111
Flywheel bolts: *		
Stage 1	15	11
Stage 2	30	22
Stage 3	75	55
Stage 4	Angle-tighten a further 45°	

Torque wrench settings (continued)

	Nm	lbf ft
Main bearing cap bolts: *		
Stage 1	15	11
Stage 2	20	15
Stage 3	35	26
Stage 4	80	59
Stage 5	Angle-tighten a further 90°	
Oil filter housing bolts	23	17
Oil pump bolts	10	7
Oil pump pick-up pipe	10	7
Roadwheel nuts	200	148
Rocker arm carrier bolts:		
Stage 1	10	7
Stage 2	Angle-tighten a further 30°	
Sump bolts/nuts:		
Stage 1	7	5
Stage 2	14	10
Sump oil drain plug	40	30
Timing chain cover:		
Nuts	10	7
Bolts	14	10
Timing chain guide retaining bolts:		
Lower fixed guide	15	11
Tensioner guide	40	30
Upper fixed guide	15	11
Timing chain tensioner	15	11
Transmission-to-engine bolts	40	30

Use new nuts/bolts

1 General Information

How to use this Chapter

1 This Part of Chapter 2 is devoted to repair procedures possible while the engine is still installed in the vehicle. Since these procedures are based on the assumption that the engine is installed in the vehicle, if the engine has been removed and mounted on a stand, some of the preliminary dismantling steps outlined will not apply.

2 Information concerning engine/transmission removal and refitting and engine overhaul can be found in Part C of this Chapter.

Engine description

3 The 2.2 litre diesel engines covered in this Part of Chapter 2 are all in-line four-cylinder, turbocharged units, with 16-valve, double overhead camshaft (DOHC) arrangement. The engine is mounted transversely at the front of the vehicle, with the transmission on its left-hand end.

4 The engine cylinder block casting is of cast-iron and has a lower aluminium crankcase which is bolted to the underside of the cylinder block, with a pressed steel sump bolted under that.

5 The crankshaft runs in five main bearings, the centre main bearing's upper half incorporating thrust washers to control crankshaft endfloat. The connecting rods rotate on horizontally-split bearing shells at their big-ends. The pistons are attached to the connecting rods by gudgeon pins which are a floating fit in the connecting rod small-end eyes, secured by circlips. The aluminium alloy pistons are fitted with three piston rings – two compression rings and an oil control ring.

6 The inlet and exhaust valves are each closed by coil springs, and they operate in guides which are a shrink-fit in the cylinder head, as also are the valve seat inserts.

7 The double overhead camshaft sprockets are driven by a chain from a sprocket on the crankshaft. The camshafts operate the 16 valves via roller-rocker arms with hydraulic clearance adjusters. The rocker arms and clearance adjusters are located in an aluminium carrier bolted to the cylinder head. Each camshaft rotates in five bearings that are machined directly in the cylinder head and the (bolted on) bearing caps. This means that the bearing caps are not available separately from the cylinder head, and must not be interchanged with caps from another engine.

8 The vacuum pump (used for the brake servo and other vacuum actuators) is located on the transmission end of the cylinder head, driven by a slot in the end of the exhaust camshaft. The high-pressure fuel injection pump is also located on the transmission end of the cylinder head, driven by a slot in the end of the inlet camshaft.

9 Lubrication is by means of a chain-driven oil pump driven from a sprocket on the crankshaft. The oil pump is mounted below the lower crankcase, and draws oil through a strainer located in the sump. The pump forces oil through an externally-mounted full-flow cartridge-type filter. From the filter, the oil is pumped into a main gallery in the cylinder block/crankcase, from where it is distributed to the crankshaft (main bearings) and cylinder head. An oil cooler is fitted next to the oil filter, at the front of the block. The cooler is supplied with coolant from the engine cooling system.

10 While the crankshaft and camshaft bearings receive a pressurised supply, the camshaft lobes and valves are lubricated by splash, as are all other engine components. On higher powered engines, the undersides of the pistons are cooled by oil, sprayed from nozzles fitted above the upper main bearing shells. The turbocharger receives its own pressurised oil supply.

Repairs with the engine in the vehicle

11 The following major repair operations can be accomplished without removing the engine from the vehicle. However, owners should note that any operation involving the removal of the timing chain, camshafts or cylinder head requires careful forethought, depending on the level of skill and the tools and facilities available. Refer to the relevant text for details.

a) Compression pressure – testing.
b) Camshaft cover – removal and refitting.
c) Timing chain cover – removal and refitting.
d) Timing chain – renewal.
e) Timing chain tensioner and sprockets – removal and refitting.
f) Camshaft oil seal – renewal.
g) Camshafts and hydraulic rockers – removal and refitting.
h) Cylinder head – removal, overhaul and refitting.
i) Crankshaft pulley – removal and refitting.
j) Sump – removal and refitting.

k) *Pistons, connecting rods and big-end bearings – removal and refitting*.
l) *Crankshaft oil seals – renewal.*
m) *Oil pump – removal and refitting.*
n) *Flywheel – removal and refitting.*
o) *Engine/transmission mountings – removal and refitting.*

Note: *Although the operation marked with an asterisk can be carried out with the engine in the vehicle (after removal of the sump), it is preferable for the engine to be removed, in the interests of cleanliness and improved access. For this reason, the procedure is described in Chapter.*

2 Compression and leakdown tests – description and interpretation

Compression test

Note: *A compression tester suitable for use with diesel engines will be required for this test.*

Note: *The following procedure is likely to log a fault code in the powertrain control module memory. If the engine management warning light is illuminated after the test, it will be necessary to have the fault code cleared by a Ford dealer or suitably equipped garage using specialist diagnostic equipment.*

1 When engine performance is down, or if misfiring occurs which cannot be attributed to the fuel or emissions systems, a compression test can provide diagnostic clues as to the engine's condition. If the test is performed regularly, it can give warning of trouble before any other symptoms become apparent.

2 The engine must be fully warmed-up to normal operating temperature and the battery must be fully charged. The aid of an assistant will also be required.

3 Remove the glow plugs as described in Chapter 5, Section 13.

4 Fit a compression tester to the No 1 cylinder glow plug hole. A compression tester specifically intended for diesel engines must be used, because of the higher pressures involved. The tester is connected to an adapter (special tool 303-1051 or equivalent), which screws into the glow plug bore.

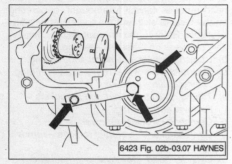

3.7 The special tool will only fit in one position on the crankshaft, and must align with the hole in the crankcase

5 Crank the engine for several seconds on the starter motor. After one or two revolutions, the compression pressure should build up to a maximum figure and then stabilise. Record the highest reading obtained.

6 Repeat the test on the remaining cylinders, recording the pressure in each.

7 The cause of poor compression is less easy to establish on a diesel engine than on a petrol engine. The effect of introducing oil into the cylinders (wet testing) is not conclusive, because there is a risk that the oil will sit in the recess on the piston crown, instead of passing to the rings. However, the following can be used as a rough guide to diagnosis.

8 An actual compression pressure value is not stated by Ford, however all cylinders should produce very similar pressures. Any significant difference indicates the existence of a fault. Note that the compression should build-up quickly in a healthy engine. Low compression on the first stroke, followed by gradually increasing pressure on successive strokes, indicates worn piston rings. A low compression reading on the first stroke, which does not build-up during successive strokes, indicates leaking valves or a blown head gasket (a cracked head could also be the cause).

9 A low reading from two adjacent cylinders is almost certainly due to the head gasket having blown between them and the presence of coolant in the engine oil will confirm this.

10 On completion, remove the compression tester, and refit the glow plugs as described in Chapter 5, Section 13.

Leakdown test

11 A leakdown test measures the rate at which compressed air fed into the cylinder is lost. It is an alternative to a compression test, and in many ways it is better, since the escaping air provides easy identification of where pressure loss is occurring (piston rings, valves or head gasket).

12 The equipment required for leakdown testing is unlikely to be available to the home mechanic. If poor compression is suspected, have the test performed by a suitably equipped garage.

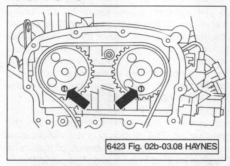

3.8 Insert a 6 mm drill bit/rod through the holes in the camshaft sprockets, and into the holes in the cylinder head

3 Engine timing – setting

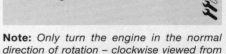

Note: *Only turn the engine in the normal direction of rotation – clockwise viewed from the right-hand side of the vehicle.*

General information

1 Top Dead Centre (TDC) is the highest point in the cylinder that each piston reaches as it travels up and down when the crankshaft turns. Each piston reaches TDC at the end of the compression stroke and again at the end of the exhaust stroke, but TDC generally refers to piston position on the compression stroke. No 1 piston is at the timing chain end of the engine.

2 Setting No 1 piston at TDC is an essential part of many procedures, such as timing chain removal, cylinder head removal and camshaft removal.

3 The design of the engines covered in this Chapter is such that piston-to-valve contact may occur if the camshaft or crankshaft is turned with the timing chain removed. For this reason, it is important to ensure that the camshaft and crankshaft do not move in relation to each other once the timing chain has been removed from the engine.

Setting

Note: *Ford service tool 303-1587 – obtainable from Ford dealers or a tool supplier – will be required to set the crankshaft in the correct position.*

4 Disconnect the battery negative terminal, as described in Chapter 5 Section 4.

5 Firmly apply the handbrake, then jack up the front of the vehicle and support it securely on axle stands (see Chapter 13 Section 5). Remove the right-hand roadwheel, then remove the auxiliary drivebelt cover (two or three fasteners) from under the wheel arch.

6 Remove the timing chain cover as described in Section 5.

7 Re-insert the old crankshaft pulley bolts, and rotate the crankshaft clockwise until Ford Special tool No. 303-1587 (or equivalent) can be fitted to the crankshaft, with the hole in the end of the tool aligned with the threaded hole in the crankcase **(see illustration)**.

8 Examine the camshaft sprocket positions. If the 6 mm holes in the sprocket at in the 6 o'clock position and align with the corresponding holes in the cylinder head, the engine is set at TDC for No.1 cylinder. If the holes are at the 12 o'clock position, remove the crankshaft tool, and rotate the crankshaft a further complete turn (360°) clockwise to bring the holes in the camshaft sprockets to the 6 o'clock position. With the holes correctly aligned, insert a 6 mm drill bit/rod into the holes in the sprockets and into the holes in the cylinder head, then bolt the end of the crankshaft special tool to the crankcase **(see illustration)**.

Caution: *Do not use the crankshaft timing*

4.4a Loosen the fuel supply pipe union at the fuel pump...

4.4b ...and at the fuel rail

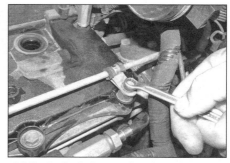

4.6 Undo the bolt securing the fuel supply pipe clamp to the camshaft cover bolt

4.7 Remove the fuel supply pipe and discard it

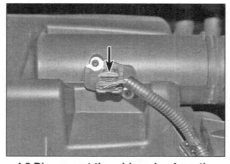

4.8 Disconnect the wiring plug from the mass airflow sensor

4.9 Disconnect the crankcase ventilation hose from the rear of the camshaft cover

setting tool to prevent the crankshaft from rotating.

9 The engine is now set at TDC for No.1 cylinder.

4 Camshaft cover – removal and refitting

Caution: Do not carry out any work on the fuel system with the engine running. Wait for at least 2 minutes after the engine has been stopped before any work is carried out on the fuel system, to make sure the fuel pressure and temperature has dropped sufficiently. Make sure that all the fuel lines are kept clean. Fit blanking plugs to the end of the fuel lines when they are disconnected, to prevent foreign matter entering the components.

Removal

1 Disconnect the battery negative terminal, as described in Chapter 5 Section 4.
2 Remove the fuel injectors, as described in Chapter 4A Section 12.
3 Use a brush and suitable solvent to clean the area around the fuel pipe unions on the injection pump and fuel rail. Allow time for any solvent used to dry.
4 Carefully loosen the fuel supply pipe union at the fuel pump and the one to the fuel rail **(see illustrations)**.
5 Once the unions are loose, wrap clean absorbent tissue or rag around them briefly, to soak away any dirt which may otherwise enter. If available, Ford recommend using a vacuum line to suck any dirt away from the opening union – do not use an airline, as this may blast dirt inwards, rather than cleaning it away.
6 Undo the bolt securing the fuel supply

pipe clamp to the camshaft cover bolt **(see illustration)**.
7 Remove the fuel supply pipe, and discard it – a new one must be used **(see illustration)**. Plug or suitably cover the open connections.
8 Disconnect the wiring plug from the mass airflow sensor on the air cleaner air outlet duct **(see illustration)**.
9 Disconnect the crankcase ventilation hose from the rear of the camshaft cover **(see illustration)**.
10 Slacken the clip securing the air outlet duct to the turbocharger and remove the duct from the engine **(see illustrations)**.
11 Where fitted, undo the retaining screw and remove the engine oil filler pipe from the camshaft cover.
12 Note the locations of the different bolt types, then unscrew the twelve retaining bolts and lift the camshaft cover off the cylinder head **(see illustration)**. Note that the bolts

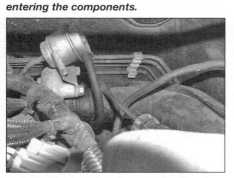

4.10a Slacken the clip securing the air outlet duct to the turbocharger...

4.10b ...and remove the duct from the engine

4.12 Unscrew the twelve bolts and lift the camshaft cover off the cylinder head

4.14a Remove the fuel injector seals from the camshaft cover...

4.14b ...and press new seals into position

4.15 Ensure the camshaft cover gasket fits correctly in the cover groove

are captive in the camshaft cover and cannot be completely removed. Recover the gasket and discard it – a new gasket and fuel injector seals will be required for refitting.

Refitting

13 Thoroughly clean the sealing surfaces of the camshaft cover and the cylinder head.

14 If fitted, using a screwdriver, remove the fuel injector seals from the camshaft cover and press new seals into position **(see illustrations)**.

15 Locate a new gasket on the camshaft cover ensuring that it fits correctly in the cover groove **(see illustration)**.

16 The remainder of refitting is a reversal of removal, noting the following points:

a) Renew the fuel supply pipe and tighten the pipe unions to the specified torque.

b) Refit the fuel injectors as described in Chapter 4A Section 12.

5 Timing chain cover – removal and refitting

Note: *To carry out this task with the engine/transmission installed in the vehicle will require the equipment necessary to support the engine with the right-hand engine mounting removed, and to raise and support the front of the vehicle. Ford technicians use an engine support beam arrangement, which locates in the vehicle underbody and front crossmember. If such an arrangement is not available, use an engine crane; either way, use a suitable length of chain and hooks to attach the lifting gear to the engine lifting eye. If the engine must be supported from below, use a large piece of wood on a trolley jack to spread the load and reduce the chance of damage to*

the sump. Precise details of the procedure will depend on the equipment available and the following description is typical.

Note: *Ford technicians use special tools for removing the oil seal and aligning the timing chain cover – see text. A new timing chain cover will be required for refitting because the cover will be irreparably distorted during removal.*

Removal

1 Disconnect the battery negative terminal, as described in Chapter 5 Section 4.

2 Firmly apply the handbrake, then jack up the front of the vehicle and support it securely on axle stands (see *Jacking and vehicle support*). Remove the right-hand roadwheel.

3 Remove the air cleaner assembly as described in Chapter 4A Section 5.

4 Remove the auxiliary drivebelt(s) as described in Chapter 1 Section 33.

5 On models with air conditioning, undo the two bolts and remove the auxiliary drivebelt tensioner, then unbolt the drivebelt idler pulley located above the tensioner.

6 Remove the crankshaft pulley as described in Section 6.

7 Remove the crankshaft timing chain end oil seal as described in Section 15.

8 Remove the retaining bolts and nuts from the lower part of the timing chain cover.

9 Depending on the equipment available, support the engine either from the top using an engine crane or from underneath the sump using a suitable jack.

10 Undo the retaining bolts and nuts, then remove the engine mounting from the right-hand inner front wing panel and from the mounting bracket on the engine **(see illustrations)**.

11 On models with air conditioning, undo the retaining nut and slide the idler pulley from the engine mounting bracket stud **(see illustration)**.

Note: *The pulley will not come all the way off the stud at this point.*

12 Undo the two upper bolts and one lower stud bolt, and remove the engine mounting bracket, complete with idler pulley (where fitted) from the timing chain cover **(see illustrations)**.

13 Remove the retaining bolts/nuts from the upper part of the timing chain cover.

5.10a Undo the three retaining nuts on the engine-side bracket...

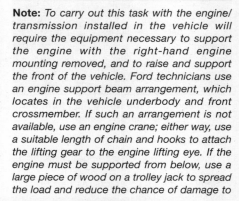

5.10b ...and the four bolts holding the bracket to the body (two shown)

5.11 Undo the retaining nut and slide the idler pulley away from the engine

5.12a Undo the two upper bolts and one lower stud bolt...

5.12b ...and remove the engine mounting bracket from the timing chain cover

5.14a Using a scraper or similar tool prise free the timing chain cover...

5.14b ...then remove the cover from the engine...

5.14c ...and collect the inner gasket

5.17 Insert the special tool over the end of the crankshaft to align the cover, before tightening the retaining bolts

14 Using a couple of scrapers or similar, carefully work your way around the timing chain cover and prise it away from the engine. The cover will become distorted on removal, discard it, as a new cover must be used on refitting. With the cover removed, collect the inner gasket from the engine mounting bracket area, if fitted **(see illustrations)**.

Refitting

15 Make sure that the mating surfaces of the cover and the engine casing are clean. Apply a 3 mm bead of sealant around the mating surface of the timing chain cover, ensuring that the sealant bead passes around the inside of the retaining bolt holes.
Caution: Install the timing chain cover within 5 minutes of applying the sealer to the engine casing. Make sure the cover does not come into contact with the engine casing, until the correct position for fitting is obtained.
16 With the help of an assistant, fit the new timing chain cover and install the retaining nuts and bolts hand-tight.
17 Using a cover aligning tool (Ford special tool 303-682), insert the tool over the end of the crankshaft to align the cover **(see illustration)**, then tighten all the timing chain cover retaining nuts and bolts to the specified torque. Remove the tool once the cover is in position.
18 Further refitting is a reversal of removal, noting the following points:
a) *Fit a new crankshaft oil seal as described in Section 15.*
b) *Refit the crankshaft pulley as described in Section 6.*
c) *Refit the auxiliary drivebelt(s) as described in Chapter 1 Section 33.*
d) *Refit the air cleaner assembly as described in Chapter 4A Section 5.*

6 Crankshaft pulley – removal and refitting

Removal

Note: *New crankshaft pulley retaining bolts will be required for refitting.*
1 Move the driver's seat fully forward, open the battery box cover and disconnect the battery negative terminal as described in Chapter 5 Section 4.
2 Firmly apply the handbrake, then jack up the front of the vehicle and support it securely on axle stands (see *Jacking and vehicle support*). Remove the right-hand roadwheel.
3 Remove the auxiliary drivebelt(s), as described in Chapter 1 Section 33.
4 The three bolts which secure the crankshaft pulley must now be slackened. Ensure that the vehicle is adequately supported, as considerable effort may be needed to slacken the bolts.
5 Ford technicians use a special holding tool (303-1310) which locates over two of the three pulley retaining bolts and prevents it from turning. If this is not available, select a gear, and have an assistant firmly apply the footbrake as the bolts are loosened. If this

method is unsuccessful, remove the starter motor as described in Chapter 5 Section 10, and jam the flywheel ring gear, using a suitable tool, to prevent the crankshaft from rotating **(see illustration)**.
6 Unscrew the bolts securing the pulley to the crankshaft, and remove the pulley **(see illustration)**. Discard the bolts and obtain new bolts for refitting.
7 With the pulley removed, it is advisable to check the crankshaft oil seal for signs of oil leakage. If necessary, fit a new seal as described in Section 15.

Refitting

8 Refit the pulley to the end of the crankshaft, then fit the new pulley securing bolts and tighten them as far as possible before the crankshaft starts to rotate.

6.5 Jam the flywheel ring gear, using a suitable tool, to prevent the crankshaft from rotating

6.6 Crankshaft pulley retaining bolts (arrowed)

6.10a Mark the pulley bolts with quick-drying paint then similarly mark the pulley two flats further on

6.10b Tighten the bolts until the marks align

9 Holding the pulley against rotation as for removal, first tighten the bolts to the specified Stage 1 torque.

10 Stage 2 involves tightening the bolts though an angle, rather than to a torque. The bolts must be rotated through the specified angle – special angle gauges are available from tool outlets. As a guide, a 120° angle is equivalent to two flats on the retaining bolt, and this is easily judged by marking each bolt with quick-drying paint then similarly marking the pulley two flats further on. Tighten the bolts until the marks align **(see illustrations)**.

11 Refit the auxiliary drivebelts as described in Chapter 1 Section 33.

12 Refit the roadwheel, lower the vehicle to the ground, and reconnect the battery negative lead. Tighten the wheel nuts to the specified torque.

7 Timing chain – removal, inspection and refitting

Caution: Only turn the engine in the normal direction of rotation – clockwise viewed from the right-hand side of the vehicle.

Removal

1 Remove the timing chain cover, as described in Section 5.

2 Set the engine timing as described in Section 3 **(see illustration)**.

3 If the timing chain is not being fitted straight away (or if the chain is being removed as part of another procedure, such as cylinder head removal), temporarily refit the engine

right-hand mounting and tighten the nuts/bolts securely.

4 Slacken the timing chain tensioner by inserting a small screwdriver into the access hole in the tensioner and releasing the pawl mechanism. Press against the timing chain guide to depress the piston into the tensioner housing. When fully depressed, insert a locking pin (approximately 2 mm diameter) to lock the piston in its compressed position **(see illustration)**.

5 To remove the timing chain tensioner, undo the two retaining bolts and remove the tensioner from the cylinder block **(see illustration)**. Note that a new tensioner will be required for refitting.

6 Undo the retaining bolts and remove the fixed timing chain guides and tensioner timing chain guide from the cylinder block **(see illustrations)**.

7 With the camshafts held in position, undo the camshaft sprocket retaining bolts and remove the camshaft sprockets and timing chain. Do not rotate the crankshaft until the timing chain is refitted.

Note: *Do not rely on the timing pins (6 mm drill bit) to hold the sprockets in position.*

8 To remove the timing chain sprocket from the crankshaft, the oil pump drive chain will need to be removed first. Lift the tensioner arm and insert a suitable drill bit through the hole in the arm and behind the spring blade. With the tensioner now locked in the released position, slide the tensioner off the pivot stud. The chain can now be removed from the sprocket. Undo

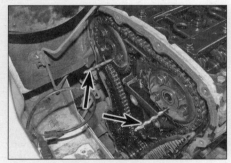

7.2 Insert 6 mm drill bits to align the camshaft sprockets

7.4 Insert a locking pin to lock the piston in its compressed position

7.5 Remove the timing chain tensioner from the cylinder block, taking care not to remove the locking pin

7.6a Undo the retaining bolts and remove the upper fixed timing chain guide...

7.6b ...the lower fixed timing chain guide...

7.6c ...and the tensioner timing chain guide

7.8a Lift the tensioner arm and insert a drill bit through the hole in the arm and behind the spring blade...

7.8b ...then slide the tensioner off the pivot stud

7.8c Collect the spacer plate from inside the crankshaft sprocket

7.15a Place the timing chain around the camshaft sprockets...

7.15b ...with the arrows on the sprockets aligned with the coloured links in the chain

7.16 Locate the chain and the two sprockets in position on the camshafts

the retaining bolt and withdraw the sprocket from the crankshaft. Collect the spacer plate from inside the sprocket (**see illustrations**).

Inspection

Note: *Keep all components identified for position to ensure correct refitting.*

9 Clean all components thoroughly and wipe dry.

10 Examine the chain tensioner guides for deep grooves made by the timing chain, and for any other damage.

11 Examine the timing chain for excessive wear. Hold it horizontally and check how much movement exists in the chain links. If there is any doubt, compare it to a new chain. Renew as necessary.

12 Examine the teeth of the camshaft and crankshaft sprockets for excessive wear and damage.

Refitting

13 Ensure that the crankshaft and camshafts are still as described in Section 3.

14 If not already fitted, refit the crankshaft drive sprocket onto the crankshaft and securely tighten the retaining bolt. Refit the oil pump drive chain and tensioner, then hold pressure against the tensioner arm and withdraw the tensioner locking pin. (see Section 12 for further information on refitting the oil pump).

15 Place the timing chain around the inlet and exhaust camshaft sprockets, with the arrows on the sprockets aligned with the coloured links in the chain (**see illustrations**).

16 Hold the timing chain in position on

the camshaft sprockets and feed the chain around the crankshaft sprocket. Locate the two sprockets in position on the camshafts (**see illustration**).

17 Refit the camshaft sprocket retaining bolts but DO NOT tighten the bolts at this stage.

18 Fit the new timing chain tensioner to the cylinder block and tighten the retaining bolts to the specified torque. Take care not to remove the locking pin.

19 Refit the timing chain tensioner guide and the fixed timing chain guides to the cylinder block and tighten the retaining bolts to the specified torque.

20 With all the timing chain guides fitted, hold pressure against the bottom of the tensioner guide and withdraw the tensioner locking pin. This will then tension the timing chain (**see illustration**).

Note: *Do not rely on the timing pins (6 mm drill bits) to hold the sprockets in position.*

21 Tighten the camshaft sprocket retaining bolts to the specified torque (**see illustration**).

22 Check that the engine is still set as described in Section 3, then remove the timing pins (6 mm drill bits) from the sprockets and the special tool from the crankshaft.

23 Turn the engine (in the direction of engine rotation) two full turns. Refit the timing pins and crankshaft timing tool to make sure the engine timing is still set as describe in Section 3.

24 Check the tension of the chain then remove the timing pins (6 mm drill bits) from the sprockets and the timing tool from the crankshaft.

25 Refit the timing chain cover as described in Section 5.

7.20 Hold pressure against the bottom of the tensioner guide and withdraw the tensioner locking pin

7.21 Tighten the camshaft sprocket retaining bolts to the specified torque

9.7a Progressively slacken and remove the 10 retaining bolts...

9.7b ...and lift off the rocker arm carrier

8 Timing chain tensioner and sprockets – removal, inspection and refitting

Timing chain tensioner

1 The timing chain tensioner is removed as part of the timing chain renewal procedure, in Section 7.

Camshaft sprockets

2 The camshaft sprockets are removed as part of the timing chain renewal procedure, in Section 7.

9.12a Lubricate the camshafts and cylinder head bearing journals...

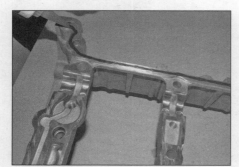

9.13a Apply a 2.5 mm bead of sealant around the outer mating surface of the camshaft carrier

Crankshaft sprocket

3 The crankshaft sprocket is removed as part of the timing chain renewal procedure, in Section 7.

9 Camshafts and hydraulic rockers – removal and refitting

Note: New rocker arm carrier retaining bolts will be required for refitting.

Caution: Only turn the engine in the normal direction of rotation – clockwise

9.12b ...then carefully lower the camshafts into position

9.13b ...then place the carrier in position on the cylinder head

viewed from the right-hand side of the vehicle.

Removal

1 Remove the timing chain cover, as described in Section 5.

2 Set the engine timing as described in Section 3.

3 Remove the camshaft cover, as described in Section 4.

4 Remove the fuel rail as described in Chapter 4A Section 13.

5 Remove the brake servo vacuum pump as described in Chapter 9 Section 14.

6 Remove the high-pressure fuel pump as described in Chapter 4A Section 11.

7 Progressively slacken and remove the 10 retaining bolts and lift off the rocker arm carrier **(see illustrations)**. Note that new retaining bolts will be required for refitting. Note also that further dismantling of the rocker arm carrier is not possible because the rocker arms and hydraulic clearance adjusters are not available separately.

8 Working as described in Section 7, remove the timing chain tensioner, timing chain guides and camshaft sprockets.

9 Slacken the camshaft carrier retaining bolts in the **reverse** of the sequence shown **(see illustration 9.14)**, then lift the camshaft carrier from the cylinder head.

10 Carefully lift out the camshafts, and place them somewhere clean and safe – the lobes must not be scratched.

Refitting

11 Make sure that the top surfaces of the cylinder head, and in particular the camshaft bearing surfaces and the mating surfaces for the camshaft carrier, are completely clean; use a plastic scraper and primer H-BW or equivalent.

12 Lubricate the camshafts and cylinder head bearing journals with clean engine oil, then carefully lower the camshafts into position in the cylinder head **(see illustrations)**.

Note: Install the camshaft carrier within 5

minutes of applying the sealer to the mating surface. Make sure the carrier does not come into contact with the cylinder head, until the correct position for fitting is obtained.

13 Apply a 2.5 mm bead of sealant around the outer mating surface of the camshaft carrier, then place the carrier in position on the cylinder head **(see illustrations)**.

14 Install the camshaft carrier retaining bolts and tighten them to the specified torque in the sequence shown **(see illustration)**.

15 Refit the timing chain, sprockets, guides and tensioner as described in Section 7.

16 Install the rocker arm carrier using new retaining bolts, then tighten the bolts to the specified torque.

17 Refit the timing chain cover, as described in Section 5.

18 Refit the camshaft cover, as described in Section 4.

19 Refit the fuel rail as described in Chapter 4A Section 13.

20 Refit the brake servo vacuum pump as described in Chapter 9 Section 14.

21 Refit the high-pressure fuel pump as described in Chapter 4A Section 11.

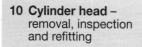

10 Cylinder head –
removal, inspection and refitting

Removal

1 Disconnect the battery negative lead, as described in Chapter 5 Section 4.

2 Drain the cooling system as described in Chapter 1 Section 32.

3 Remove the camshafts and hydraulic rockers as described in Section 9.

4 Remove the exhaust manifold as described in Chapter 4A Section 17.

5 Remove the inlet manifold as described in Chapter 4A Section 16.

6 Remove the brake vacuum pump as described in Chapter 9 Section 14.

7 Undo the retaining nuts and disconnect the glow plug wiring harness from the glow plugs and cylinder head.

8 Check around the head and the engine bay that there is nothing still attached to the cylinder head, nor anything which would prevent it from being lifted away.

9 Working in the reverse order of the tightening sequence **(see illustration 10.33)**, loosen the cylinder head bolts by half a turn at a time, until they are all loose. Remove the head bolts, and discard them – Ford state that they must not be re-used, even if they appear to be serviceable.

10 With the help of an assistant, lift the cylinder head away – be careful, it's heavy. Do not, under any circumstances, lever the head between the mating surfaces, because this will damage the sealing surfaces for the gasket, leading to leaks.

11 Once the head has been removed, recover the gasket from the two dowels and

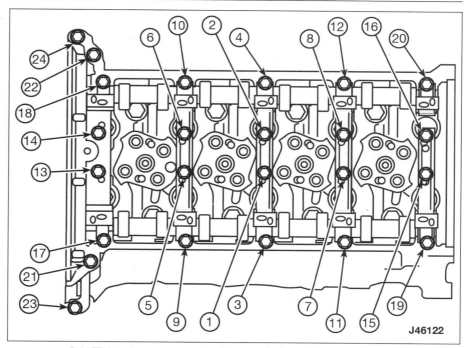

9.14 Tightening sequence for the camshaft carrier retaining bolts

discard the gasket, because a new one will be required on refitting – see paragraph 13.

Inspection

12 If required, dismantling and inspection of the cylinder head is covered in Chapter 2C Section 6 and Chapter 2C Section 7.

Cylinder head gasket selection

13 Examine the old cylinder head gasket for manufacturer's identification markings. These will be in the form of teeth (one, two or three) on the front edge of the gasket and/or holes in the gasket, which indicate the gasket's thickness **(see illustration)**.

14 Unless new components have been fitted, or the cylinder head has been machined (skimmed), the new cylinder head gasket must be of the same type as the old one. Purchase the required gasket, and proceed to paragraph 20.

15 If the head has been machined, or if new pistons have been fitted, it is likely that a head

gasket of different thickness to the original will be needed. Gasket selection is made on the basis of the measured piston protrusion above the cylinder head gasket surface (the protrusion must fall within the range specified at the start of this Chapter).

16 To measure the piston protrusion, anchor a dial test indicator (DTI) to the top face (cylinder head gasket mating face) of the cylinder block, and zero the gauge on the gasket mating face **(see illustration)**.

17 Rest the gauge probe above No 1 piston crown, and turn the crankshaft slowly by hand until the piston reaches TDC (its maximum height). Measure and record the maximum piston projection at TDC.

18 Repeat the measurement for the remaining pistons, and record the results.

19 If the measurements differ from piston to piston, take the highest figure, and use this to determine the thickness of the head gasket required (see the Specifications at the start of this Chapter).

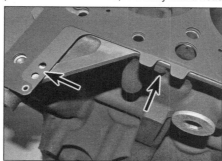

10.13 Teeth and holes in the gasket (arrowed), which indicate the gasket's thickness

10.16 Using a dial test indicator to measure the piston protrusion

10.29 Locate the new cylinder head gasket over the dowels correctly

Preparation for refitting

20 The mating faces of the cylinder head and cylinder block must be perfectly clean before refitting the head. Use a hard plastic or wooden scraper to remove all traces of gasket and carbon; also clean the piston crowns. **Note:** *The new head gasket has rubber coated surfaces, which could be damaged from sharp edges or debris left by a metal scraper.*

21 Take particular care when cleaning the piston crowns, as the soft aluminium alloy is easily damaged.

22 Make sure that the carbon is not allowed to enter the oil and water passages – this is particularly important for the lubrication system, as carbon could block the oil supply to the engine's components. Using adhesive tape and paper, seal the water, oil and bolt holes in the cylinder block.

23 To prevent carbon entering the gap between the pistons and bores, smear a little grease in the gap. After cleaning each piston,

use a small brush to remove all traces of grease and carbon from the gap, then wipe away the remainder with a clean rag. Clean all the pistons in the same way.

24 Check the mating surfaces of the cylinder block and the cylinder head for nicks, deep scratches and other damage (refer to the Note in paragraph 20). If slight, they may be removed carefully with a file, but if excessive, machining may be the only alternative to renewal.

25 If warpage of the cylinder head gasket surface is suspected, use a straight-edge to check it for distortion. Refer to Chapter 2C Section 7 if necessary.

26 Ensure that the cylinder head bolt holes in the crankcase are clean and free of oil. Syringe or soak up any oil left in the bolt holes. This is most important in order that the correct bolt tightening torque can be applied, and to prevent the possibility of the block being cracked by hydraulic pressure when the bolts are tightened.

Refitting

27 Make sure the timing is still set at 50° BTDC (see Section 3). This will eliminate any risk of piston-to-valve contact as the cylinder head is refitted.

28 To guide the cylinder head into position, screw two long studs into the end cylinder head bolt locations on the manifold side of the cylinder block. As an alternative to the studs, use old cylinder head bolts with their heads cut off, and slots cut in the ends to enable the bolts to be unscrewed.

29 Ensure that the cylinder head locating dowels are in place in the cylinder block, then fit the new cylinder head gasket over

the dowels **(see illustration)**. The gasket can only be fitted one way, with the teeth to determine the gasket thickness at the front **(see illustration 10.13)**. Take care to avoid damaging the gasket's rubber coating.

30 Lower the cylinder head into position on the gasket, ensuring that it engages correctly over the guide studs (if fitted) and dowels.

31 Fit the new cylinder head bolts to the remaining bolt locations and screw them in as far as possible by hand.

32 If fitted, unscrew the two guide studs from the cylinder block, then screw in the two remaining new cylinder head bolts as far as possible by hand.

33 Working in the sequence shown, tighten all the cylinder head bolts through the specified Stages as given in the Specifications at the beginning of this Chapter **(see illustration)**.

34 The last Stage involves tightening the bolts through an angle, rather than to a torque. Each bolt in sequence must be rotated through the specified angle – special angle gauges are available from tool outlets. As a guide, a 90° angle is equivalent to a quarter turn, and this is easily judged by assessing the start and end positions of the socket handle.

35 The remainder of the refitting procedure is a reversal of the removal procedure, bearing in mind the following points:

a) *Reconnect the wiring harness to the glow plugs and cylinder head.*

b) *Refit the brake vacuum pump as described in Chapter 9 Section 14.*

c) *Refit the inlet manifold as described in Chapter 4A Section 16.*

d) *Refit the exhaust manifold as described in Chapter 4A Section 17.*

e) *Refit the camshafts and hydraulic rockers as described in Section 9.*

f) *Refit the timing chain as described in Section 7.*

g) *Refit the camshaft cover as described in Section 4.*

h) *Refill the cooling system as described in Chapter 1 Section 32.*

i) *Check and if necessary top-up the engine oil level as described in 'Weekly checks'.*

j) *Before starting the engine, read through the section on engine restarting after overhaul, in Chapter 2C Section 17.*

11 Sump –
removal and refitting

Removal

1 Firmly apply the handbrake, then jack up the front of the vehicle and support it securely on axle stands (see *Jacking and vehicle support*).

2 Referring to Chapter 1 Section 6 if necessary, drain the engine oil, then clean and fit a new engine oil drain plug, tightening it to the specified torque. Although not strictly necessary as part of the dismantling

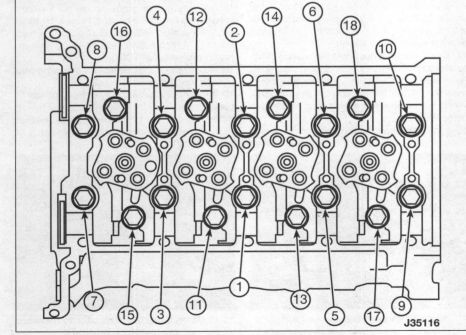

10.33 Tightening sequence for the cylinder head bolts

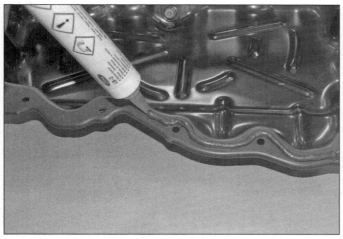

11.9 Apply a 3 mm bead of sealant to the lower casing

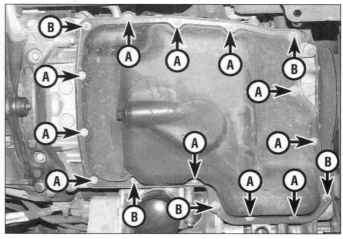

11.11 Tighten the sump retaining bolts (A) and nuts (B)

procedure, owners are advised to remove and discard the oil filter, so that it can be renewed with the oil.

3 If fitted, undo the retainers and relocate the pipes running from front to back, along the left-hand side of the sump.

4 A conventional sump gasket is not used – sealant is used instead.

5 Progressively unscrew and remove the 11 sump retaining bolts and then the 5 nuts.

6 The use of sealant can make removal of the sump more difficult. If care is taken not to damage the surfaces, the sealant can be cut around using a scraper or a sharp knife. On no account lever between the mating faces, because this will almost certainly damage them, resulting in leaks when finished.

Refitting

7 Thoroughly clean and degrease the mating surfaces of the cylinder block lower crankcase and sump, removing all traces of sealant, then use a clean rag to wipe out the sump and the engine's interior.

8 If the studs have been removed, they must be refitted before the sump is offered up, to ensure that it is aligned correctly. If this is not done, some of the sealant may enter the blind holes for the sump bolts, preventing the bolts from being fully fitted.

Note: *The sump must be refitted within 5 minutes of applying the sealant.*

9 Apply a 3 mm bead of sealant LB, or equivalent, to the sump flange, making sure the bead is around the inside edge of the bolt holes **(see illustration)**.

10 With the help of an assistant, fit the sump over the studs, and insert the sump bolts and nuts, tightening them by hand only at this stage.

11 Now tighten all the bolts to the specified torques before tightening the nuts to the same values **(see illustration)**.

12 Lower the vehicle to the ground and refill the engine with oil. Take the vehicle for a test drive and check for leaks.

12 Oil pump – removal and refitting

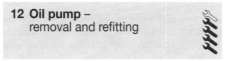

Note: *The following procedure is for removal and refitting of the oil pump. If the oil pump drive chain or tensioner requires renewal, the engine timing chain will need to be removed (see Section 7).*

Removal

1 Remove the sump as described in Section 11.

2 Ford special tool (303-705) or a DTI gauge are used to align the oil pump sprocket – bolt the tool/plate to the sump flange so that it sits flush with oil pump drive sprocket **(see illustration)**.

3 Undo the retaining bolts and remove the pick-up pipe from the oil pump **(see illustration)**.

4 Undo the retaining bolts and remove the oil pump from the lower crankcase **(see illustration)**. Pull down on the oil pump chain, then withdraw the chain from the sprocket on removal.

Caution: The oil pump sprocket and crankshaft sprocket must be kept in line with each other, so that the chain runs straight. Use Ford's special tool or a DTI gauge to make sure they are aligned correctly.

Refitting

5 Refit the oil pump to the lower crankcase, installing the drive chain to the sprocket on the oil pump. Only finger-tighten the oil pump retaining bolts at this stage.

6 Slide the oil pump until the drive sprocket sits flush with the special tool, as aligned on removal **(see illustration 12.2)**. With the oil pump in position, tighten the retaining bolts to the specified torque.

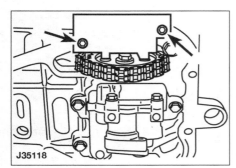

12.2 Aligning the oil pump sprocket using a plate bolted to the lower crankcase

12.3 Removing the oil pick-up pipe from the oil pump

12.4 Oil pump retaining bolts

12.9 Mount the DTI gauge on the cylinder block with the probe against the inner teeth of the crankshaft sprocket

12.10 Move the probe to the oil pump sprocket and move the pump as necessary until the two gauge readings are the same

13.3 Unplug the wiring from the oil pressure switch and unscrew it from the filter housing

7 Ensuring that the alignment of the pump is correct, undo the special tool's retaining bolts and remove it from the sump flange.

8 If the oil pump has been removed as part of an engine overhaul procedure, and the timing chain cover has been removed, the oil pump sprocket alignment can be checked with a DTI gauge.

9 Mount the gauge on the cylinder block with the probe against the inner teeth of the crankshaft sprocket **(see illustration)**. Zero the gauge in this position.

10 Without moving the gauge body, move the probe to the oil pump sprocket **(see illustration)**. Move the oil pump as necessary until the two gauge readings are the same, then tighten the pump retaining bolts to the specified torque.

11 Refit the pick-up pipe to the oil pump.

12 Refit the sump with reference to Section 11.

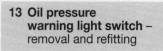

13 Oil pressure warning light switch – removal and refitting

Removal

1 The switch is screwed into the upper part of the oil filter housing.

2 To improve access to the switch, it may be necessary to apply the handbrake, then jack up the front of the vehicle and support it on axle stands (see *Jacking and vehicle support*).

3 Unplug the wiring from the switch and unscrew it from the filter housing **(see illustration)**. Be prepared for some oil loss.

Refitting

4 Refitting is the reverse of the removal procedure. Apply a thin smear of suitable sealant to the switch threads, and tighten it securely.

5 Check the engine oil level and top-up as necessary (see *Weekly checks*).

6 Check for correct warning light operation and for signs of oil leaks, once the engine has been restarted and warmed-up to normal operating temperature.

14 Oil filter housing and oil cooler – removal and refitting

Removal

1 The oil filter housing is mounted on the front facing side of the cylinder block, with the oil cooler bolted to its side.

2 Firmly apply the handbrake, then jack up the front of the vehicle and support it securely on axle stands (see *Jacking and vehicle support*).

3 Position a container beneath the oil filter to catch escaping oil and coolant.

4 Clamp the oil cooler coolant hoses to minimise spillage, then remove the clips and disconnect the hoses from the oil cooler. Be prepared for coolant spillage.

5 Disconnect the oil pressure warning light switch wiring plug (see Section 13).

6 Unscrew the three bolts and withdraw

the oil filter housing from the cylinder block **(see illustration)**. Collect the gasket – a new gasket must be used on refitting.

7 With the filter housing removed, if required, undo the four bolts and separate the oil cooler from the filter housing. Collect the gasket noting a new gasket must be used on refitting.

Refitting

8 Refitting is a reversal of removal, bearing in mind the following points:

a) *Use new gaskets.*

b) *Fit the oil cooler mounting bolts and tighten them securely.*

c) *Tighten the oil filter housing retaining bolts to the specified torque.*

d) *On completion, lower the vehicle to the ground. Check and if necessary top-up the oil and coolant levels, then start the engine and check for signs of oil or coolant leakage.*

15 Crankshaft oil seals – renewal

Timing chain end seal

1 Remove the crankshaft pulley as described in Section 6.

2 Ford technicians use a special seal-removing and refitting tool (303-679), but an adequate substitute can be achieved using a three-legged puller and three bolts **(see illustrations)**. Turn the seal anticlockwise,

14.6 Oil filter housing retaining bolts

15.2a Tool for removing the oil seal, using a three-legged puller and three bolts...

15.2b ...insert the bolts into the recesses (arrowed) in the seal...

15.2c ...and rotate the seal anticlockwise to remove

15.5a Locate the new seal over the end of the crankshaft using the locating sleeve...

15.5b ...then remove the locating sleeve

using the tool, to remove the crankshaft oil seal from the timing chain cover.

3 Wipe clean the oil seal contact surfaces and seating, and clean up any sharp edges or burrs which might damage the new seal as it is fitted, or which might cause the seal to leak once in place.

4 The new oil seal may be supplied fitted with a locating sleeve, which must **not** be removed prior to fitting.

5 Locate the new seal (lips facing inwards) over the end of the crankshaft, and press the seal squarely and fully into position in the cover. Remove the locating sleeve **(see illustrations)**.

6 Using the special tool used on removal, turn the seal clockwise until it is located securely into the timing chain cover.

7 Refit the crankshaft pulley with reference to Section 6.

Flywheel end seal

8 Remove the transmission as described in Chapter 7 Section 7 and the clutch assembly as described in Chapter 6 Section 6.

9 Remove the flywheel as described in Section 16.

10 Unbolt and remove the oil seal carrier. The seal is renewed complete with the carrier, and is not available separately. A complete set of new carrier retaining bolts should also be obtained for reassembly.

11 Clean the end of the crankshaft, polishing off any burrs or raised edges, which may have caused the seal to fail in the first place. Also clean the seal carrier mating face on the engine block, using a suitable solvent for degreasing if necessary.

12 The new oil seal is supplied fitted with a locating sleeve, which must not be removed prior to fitting **(see illustration)**. A centring sleeve is also supplied with the seal.

13 Apply sealant (LB, or equivalent) to the recesses on each side of the seal carrier **(see illustration)**.

14 Offer up the carrier into position, feeding the locating sleeve over the end of the crankshaft **(see illustrations)**. Insert the new seal carrier retaining bolts and tighten them all by hand. Remove the locating sleeve.

15 If a special centring sleeve is supplied with the seal, use it to centre the oil seal

15.12 A locating/centring sleeve is supplied with the new oil seal

carrier around the end of the crankshaft **(see illustration)**.

16 Ensuring that the correct alignment of the carrier is maintained, work in a diagonal

15.14a Locate the new seal over the end of the crankshaft using the locating sleeve...

15.15 Use the centring sleeve to centre the oil seal carrier

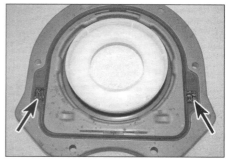

15.13 Apply sealant to the recesses on each side of the oil seal carrier

sequence, tightening the retaining bolts to the specified torque **(see illustration)**. Remove the seal centring sleeve.

17 The remainder of the reassembly procedure

15.14b ...then remove the locating sleeve

15.16 With the oil seal carrier centred around the crankshaft, tighten the retaining bolts

16.2 Locating dowel to align the flywheel when refitting

16.3 Special tool used to lock the flywheel, while the retaining bolts are slackened

is the reverse of dismantling, referring to the relevant text for details where required. Check for signs of oil leakage when the engine is restarted.

16 Flywheel – removal, inspection and refitting

Removal

1 Remove the transmission as described in Chapter 7 Section 7, and the clutch assembly as described in Chapter 6 Section 6.

2 There is a locating dowel in the end of the crankshaft, to ensure correct alignment during refitting **(see illustration)**.

3 Prevent the flywheel from turning by locking the ring gear teeth, or by bolting a strap between the flywheel and the cylinder block/crankcase **(see illustration)**.

4 Slacken the bolts evenly until all are free and ensure that new replacements are obtained for reassembly. These bolts are subjected to severe stresses and so must be renewed regardless of their apparent condition, whenever they are disturbed.

5 With the help of an assistant, withdraw the flywheel; it is very heavy – do not drop it.

Inspection

6 A conventional solid flywheel or a dual-mass flywheel may be fitted, depending on engine power output and year of manufacture.

Single-mass (solid) flywheel

7 Examine the flywheel for wear or chipping of the ring gear teeth. Renewal of the ring gear is not possible and if the wear or chipping is significant, a new flywheel will be required.

8 Examine the flywheel for scoring of the clutch face. If the clutch face is scored significantly, a new flywheel will be required.

9 If there is any doubt about the condition of the flywheel, seek the advice of a Ford dealer or engine reconditioning specialist.

Dual-mass flywheel

10 A dual-mass flywheel has the effect of reducing engine and transmission vibrations and harshness. The flywheel consists of a primary mass and a secondary mass

constructed in such a way that the secondary mass is allowed to rotate slightly in relation to the primary mass. Springs within the assembly restrict this movement to set limits.

11 Dual-mass flywheels have earned an unenviable reputation for unreliability and have been known to fail at quite low mileages (sometimes as low as 20,000 miles). As well as the checks described above in paragraphs 7 and 8, some additional checks should be performed as follows.

12 Look through the bolt hole and inspection openings in the secondary mass and check for any visible damage in the area of the centre bearing.

13 Place your thumbs on the clutch face of the secondary mass at the 3 o'clock and 9 o'clock positions and try to rock it. The maximum movement should not exceed 3 mm. Repeat this check with your thumbs at the 12 o'clock and 6 o'clock positions.

14 Rotate the secondary mass clockwise and anti-clockwise. It should move freely in both directions until spring resistance is felt, with no abnormal grating or rattling noises. The maximum rotational movement should not exceed a distance of five teeth of the ring gear.

15 If there is any doubt about the condition of the flywheel, seek the advice of a Ford dealer or engine reconditioning specialist. They will be able to advise if the flywheel is an acceptable condition, or whether renewal is necessary.

Refitting

16 Fit the flywheel to the crankshaft so that all bolt holes align (it will fit only one way), and also check that the dowel is located correctly. Apply a drop of locking compound to the threads of each of the new flywheel retaining bolts (unless they are already pre-coated) then install the new bolts.

17 Lock the flywheel by the method used on dismantling. Working in a diagonal sequence, tighten the bolts to the specified Stage 1 torque wrench setting.

18 Working in the same diagonal sequence, tighten them to the specified Stage 2 torque wrench setting followed by the Stage 3 setting.

19 Stage 4 involves tightening the bolts

though an angle, rather than to a torque. Each bolt must be rotated through the specified angle – special angle gauges are available from tool outlets.

20 The remainder of reassembly is the reverse of the removal procedure, referring to the relevant text for details where required.

17 Engine/transmission mountings – inspection and renewal

General

1 The engine/transmission mountings seldom require attention, but broken or deteriorated mountings should be renewed immediately, or the added strain placed on the driveline components may cause damage or wear.

2 While separate mountings may be removed and refitted individually, if more than one is disturbed at a time (such as if the engine/transmission unit is removed from its mountings) they must be reassembled and their fasteners tightened in the position marked on removal.

3 On reassembly, the complete weight of the engine/transmission unit must not be taken by the mountings until all are correctly aligned with the marks made on removal. Tighten the engine/transmission mounting nuts/bolts to their specified torque settings.

Inspection

4 During the check, the engine/transmission unit must be raised slightly, to remove its weight from the mountings.

5 Firmly apply the handbrake, then jack up the front of the vehicle and support it securely on axle stands (see *Jacking and vehicle support*). Position a jack under the sump, or under the transmission, with a large block of wood between the jack head and the sump/transmission, then carefully raise the engine/transmission just enough to take the weight off the mountings.

⚠️ *Warning: Do not place any part of your body under the engine when it is supported only by the jack.*

6 Check the mountings to see if the rubber is cracked, hardened or separated from the metal components. Sometimes the rubber will split right down the centre.

7 Check for relative movement between each mounting's brackets and the engine/transmission or body (use a large screwdriver or lever to attempt to move the mountings). If movement is noted, lower the engine and check the tightness of the mounting fasteners.

Renewal

Note: *The following paragraphs assume the engine is supported beneath the sump or transmission as described earlier.*

Right-hand mounting

8 Mark the position of the mounting on the right-hand inner wing panel.

17.9 Right-hand engine/transmission mounting-to-engine bracket retaining nuts

17.10 Right-hand engine/transmission mounting-to-inner wing panel rear mounting bolts (two of four shown)

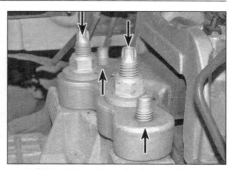

17.13 Left-hand engine/transmission mounting retaining nuts

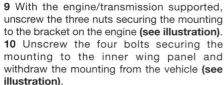

9 With the engine/transmission supported, unscrew the three nuts securing the mounting to the bracket on the engine **(see illustration)**.
10 Unscrew the four bolts securing the mounting to the inner wing panel and withdraw the mounting from the vehicle **(see illustration)**.
11 On refitting, tighten the nuts and bolts to the specified torque. Tighten the nuts securing the mounting to the engine bracket first, then release the jack to allow the mounting bracket to rest on the inner wing panel. Re-align the marks made on removal then tighten the mounting bracket bolts to the specified torque.

Left-hand mounting

12 With the engine/transmission supported, mark the position of the mounting on the left-hand inner wing panel.
13 Undo the nuts securing the mounting to the transmission mounting bracket **(see illustration)**.
14 Undo the two bolts from below, securing the mounting to the transmission mounting bracket.
15 Unscrew the four bolts securing the mounting to the inner wing panel and withdraw the mounting from the vehicle **(see illustration)**.

17.15 Right-hand inner wing panel mounting bolts

16 On refitting, tighten the nut and bolts to the specified torque. Tighten the nuts and bolts securing the mounting to the transmission bracket first, then release the jack to allow the mounting bracket to rest on the inner wing panel. Re-align the marks made on removal then tighten the mounting bracket bolts to the specified torque.

Rear mounting

Caution: The through-bolt securing the mounting to the transmission will be a M14 x 1.5 or a M14 x 2.0, depending

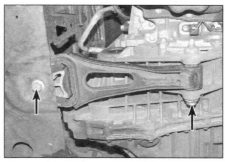

17.17 Undo the bolts securing the engine/transmission rear mounting

on model. Make sure you obtain the correct new bolt for refitting. They also have different torque settings (refer to Specifications at the beginning of this chapter).
17 Undo and discard the bolt securing the engine/transmission rear mounting to the front subframe. Undo the through-bolt securing the mounting to the transmission and remove the mounting from under the vehicle **(see illustration)**.
18 On refitting, tighten the bolts to the specified torque.

Chapter 2 Part C
Engine removal and overhaul procedures

Contents

Degrees of difficulty

Easy, suitable for novice with little experience	Fairly easy, suitable for beginner with some experience	Fairly difficult, suitable for competent DIY mechanic	Difficult, suitable for experienced DIY mechanic	Very difficult, suitable for expert DIY or professional

Specifications

Engine identification

Engine type	Manufacturer's engine code
2.0 litre engines:	
77 kW engines	YLFS and YLF6
96 kW engines	YMFS and YMF6
125 kW engines	YNFS and YNF6
2.2 litre engines:	
74 kW engines	DRFF
92 kW engines	CYFF
114 kW engines	CVFF

2.0 litre engines

Cylinder head
Valve stem-to-guide clearance:
Inlet	0.026-0.061 mm
Exhaust.	0.036-0.705 mm

Cylinder block
Cylinder bore diameter.	84.000-84.020 mm

Pistons and piston rings
Piston diameter	83.915-83.931 mm
Piston-to-cylinder bore clearance	0.07 to 0.11 mm
Piston ring end gaps*:	
Top compression ring.	0.25 to 0.40 mm
Second compression ring.	0.85 to 1.10 mm
Oil scraper ring	0.20 to 0.40 mm

Piston ring end gaps should be offset at 120° to each other when fitted

Crankshaft and bearings
Crankshaft endfloat	0.090 to 0.305 mm
Big-end bearing journal standard diameter	53.000 to 53.013 mm
Big-end bearing shell running clearance	0.017 mm to 0.029 mm
Main bearing journals standard diameter (1 to 5).	59.970 to 59.990 mm
Main bearing shell running clearance:	
1, 2, 4, 5	0.019 to 0.035 mm
3	0.023 to 0.039 mm

Torque wrench settings
Refer to Chapter 2A Specifications

2.2 litre engines

Cylinder head
Valve stem-to-guide clearance:
Inlet .... 0.045 mm
Exhaust .... 0.055 mm

Cylinder block
Cylinder bore diameter:
    Class 1 .... 86.000 to 86.010 mm
    Class 2 .... 86.010 to 86.020 mm
    Class 3 .... 86.020 to 86.030 mm

Pistons and piston rings
Piston diameter:
    Class A .... 85.94 to 85.95 mm
    Class B .... 85.95 to 85.96 mm
    Class C .... 85.96 to 85.97 mm
Piston-to-cylinder bore clearance .... 0.05 to 0.07 mm
Piston ring end gaps*:
    Top compression ring............................... 0.25 to 0.40 mm
    Second compression ring........................... 0.85 to 1.10 mm
    Oil scraper ring .... 0.20 to 0.40 mm
*Piston ring end gaps should be offset at 120° to one another when fitted

Crankshaft and bearings
Crankshaft endfloat .... 0.090 to 0.305 mm
Big-end bearing journal standard diameter .... 52.980 to 53.000 mm
Big-end bearing shell running clearance .... 0.034 mm to 0.100 mm
Main bearing journals standard diameter:
    1 to 4 .... 64.950 to 64.970 mm
    5 .... 69.950 to 69.970 mm
Main bearing shell running clearance:
    1 to 4 .... 0.033 to 0.080 mm
    5 .... 0.034 to 0.083 mm

Torque wrench settings
Refer to Chapter 2B Specifications

---

1 General Information

1 Included in this Part of Chapter 2 are details of removing the engine/transmission from the vehicle and general overhaul procedures for the cylinder head, cylinder block/crankcase and all other engine internal components.

2 The information given ranges from advice concerning preparation for an overhaul and the purchase of new parts, to detailed step-by-step procedures covering removal, inspection, renovation and refitting of engine internal components (where possible).

3 After Section 6, all instructions are based on the assumption that the engine has been removed from the vehicle. For information concerning in-vehicle engine repair, as well as the removal and refitting of those external components necessary for full overhaul, refer to Parts A and B of this Chapter (as applicable) and to Section 6. Ignore any preliminary dismantling operations described in Parts A to D that are no longer relevant once the engine has been removed from the vehicle.

4 Apart from torque wrench settings, which are given at the beginning of Parts A and B (as applicable), all specifications relating to engine overhaul are at the beginning of this Part of Chapter 2.

Note: *Before carrying out any major engine dismantling, consult a Ford dealer or engine reconditioning specialist on the availability of replacement parts. Major components such as the crankshaft, pistons, connecting rods, camshafts etc are not available as separate items from Ford although they may be available from alternative sources.*

2 Engine overhaul – general information

1 It's not always easy to determine when, or if, an engine should be completely overhauled, because a number of factors must be considered.

2 High mileage is not necessarily an indication that an overhaul is needed, while low mileage doesn't preclude the need for an overhaul. Frequency of servicing is probably the most important consideration. An engine that has had regular and frequent oil and filter changes, as well as other required maintenance, will most likely give many thousands of miles of reliable service. Conversely, a neglected engine may require an overhaul very early in its life.

3 Excessive oil consumption is an indication that piston rings, valve seals and/or valve guides are in need of attention. Make sure that oil leaks are not responsible before deciding that the rings and/or guides are worn. Perform a cylinder compression test (refer to Part A or B of this Chapter) to determine the likely cause of the problem.

4 Check the oil pressure with a gauge fitted in place of the oil pressure switch, and compare it with the value given in the Specifications. If it is extremely low, the main and big-end bearings and/or the oil pump are probably worn out.

5 Loss of power, rough running, knocking or metallic engine noises, excessive valve gear noise, and high fuel consumption may also point to the need for an overhaul, especially if they are all present at the same time. If a complete service does not cure the situation, major mechanical work is the only solution.

6 A full engine overhaul involves restoring all internal parts to the specification of a new engine. During a complete overhaul, the pistons and the piston rings are renewed, and the cylinder bores are reconditioned. New main and big-end bearings are generally fitted.

If necessary, the crankshaft may be reground, to compensate for wear in the journals. The valves are also serviced as well, since they are usually in less-than-perfect condition at this point. Always pay careful attention to the condition of the oil pump when overhauling the engine, and renew it if there is any doubt as to its serviceability. The end result should be an as-new engine that will give many trouble-free miles.

Note: *Critical cooling system components such as the hoses, thermostat and coolant pump should be renewed when an engine is overhauled. The radiator should also be checked carefully, to ensure that it is not clogged or leaking.*

7 Before beginning the engine overhaul, read through the entire procedure to familiarise yourself with the scope and requirements of the job. Overhauling an engine is not difficult if you follow all of the instructions carefully, have the necessary tools and equipment, and pay close attention to all specifications; however, it can be time-consuming. Plan on the vehicle being tied up for a minimum of two weeks, especially if parts must be taken to an engineering works for repair or reconditioning. Check on the availability of parts, and make sure that any necessary special tools and equipment are obtained in advance. Most work can be done with typical hand tools, although a number of precision measuring tools are required for inspecting parts to determine if they must be renewed. Often the engineering works will handle the inspection of parts, and offer advice concerning reconditioning and renewal.

8 The services provided by an engineering machine shop or engine reconditioning specialist will almost certainly be required, particularly if major repairs such as crankshaft regrinding or cylinder reboring are necessary. Apart from carrying out machining operations, these establishments will normally handle the inspection of parts, offer advice concerning reconditioning or renewal and supply new components such as pistons, piston rings and bearing shells. It is recommended that the establishment used is a member of the Federation of Engine Re-Manufacturers, or a similar society.

9 Always wait until the engine has been completely dismantled, and all components, especially the engine block, have been inspected before deciding what service and repair operations must be performed by an engineering works. Since the condition of the block will be the major factor to consider when determining whether to overhaul the original engine or buy a reconditioned unit, do not purchase parts or have overhaul work done on other components until the block has been thoroughly inspected. As a general rule, time is the primary cost of an overhaul, so it does not pay to fit worn or substandard parts.

10 As a final note, to ensure maximum life and minimum trouble from a reconditioned engine, everything must be assembled with care, in a spotlessly clean environment.

3 Engine/transmission removal – methods and precautions

1 If you have decided that the engine must be removed for overhaul or major repair work, several preliminary steps should be taken.

2 Locating a suitable place to work is extremely important. Adequate work space, along with storage space for the vehicle, will be needed. If a garage isn't available, at the very least, a flat, level, clean work surface made of concrete or asphalt is required.

3 Cleaning the engine compartment and engine before beginning the removal procedure will help keep tools clean and organised.

4 The help of an assistant is essential. Apart from the safety aspects involved, there are many instances when one person cannot simultaneously perform all of the operations required during engine/transmission removal.

5 Plan the operation ahead of time. Arrange for (or obtain) all of the tools and equipment you'll need prior to beginning the job. Some of the equipment necessary to perform engine/transmission removal and installation safely and with relative ease, and which may have to be hired or borrowed, includes:
a) An engine dolly (a low, wheeled platform capable of taking the weight of the engine/transmission, so that it can be removed and then moved easily when on the ground).
b) Heavy duty trolley jacks.
c) A strong pair of axle stands.
d) An assortment of wooden blocks and assorted wooden strips.
e) A complete set of spanners and sockets.
f) Rags and cleaning solvent for mopping-up spilled oil, coolant and fuel.

6 Plan for the vehicle to be out of use for quite a while. An engineering machine shop or engine reconditioning specialist will be required to perform some of the work which cannot be accomplished without special equipment. These places often have a busy schedule, so it would be a good idea to consult them before removing the engine, in order to accurately estimate the amount of time required to rebuild or repair components that may need work.

7 During the engine/transmission removal procedure, it is advisable to note the locations of all brackets, cable ties, earthing points, etc, as well as how the wiring harnesses, hoses and electrical connections are attached and routed around the engine and engine compartment. The best way of doing this is to take a series of photographs of the various components with your phone before they are disconnected or removed. The resulting photos will prove invaluable when the engine/transmission is refitted.

Caution: Always be extremely careful when removing and refitting the engine/transmission. Serious injury can result from careless actions. Plan ahead and take your time, and a job of this nature, although major, can be accomplished successfully.

8 On all models, the engine/transmission is removed as an assembly from the front of the vehicle, after removal of the front bumper, radiator and body upper crossmember. The engine is then separated from the transmission after removal.

4 Engine/transmission – removal, separation and refitting

Note: *Read through the entire Section, as well as reading the advice in Section 3, before beginning this procedure. The engine and transmission are removed as a unit, from the front of the vehicle, then separated after removal.*

Removal

1 On models with air conditioning, have the refrigerant discharged at a dealer service department or an automotive air conditioning repair facility.

2 Disconnect the battery negative terminal as described in Chapter 5 Section 4.

3 Remove the air cleaner assembly as described in Chapter 4A Section 5.

4 Slacken the clamp and remove the air duct from the right-hand end of the engine **(see illustration)**.

5 Where fitted, undo the retaining screw at the top of the engine oil filler pipe and unscrew the base and lift the pipe away from the camshaft cover **(see illustrations)**.

4.4 Remove the air intake duct

4.5a Undo the retaining screw...

4.5b …and rotate the fitting anticlockwise to remove the engine oil filler pipe from the camshaft cover

4.8 Disconnect the starter motor positive cable from the positive cable terminal box stud

4.9 Disconnect the earth lead from left-hand chassis member

4.10 Disconnect the wiring harness plugs at the left-hand side of the engine compartment

4.17 Slide the power steering reservoir upwards from the bracket

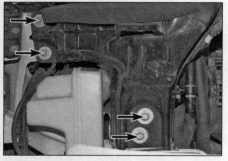

4.19 Undo the mounting bolts on each side of the slam panel assembly

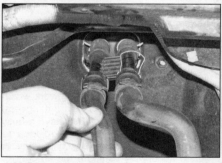

4.22 Disconnect the heater hoses from the matrix pipe stubs

4.23 Disconnect the fuel supply and return hose at the quick-release connections

4.24 Carefully release the pipe from the brake servo

6 Remove the engine management powertrain control module as described in Chapter 4A Section 10.

7 Unclip the cooling system expansion tank hose from the battery positive (+) cable connection point, then lift off the connection point cover. Unclip and remove the fuse/relay box cover and the positive cable terminal box cover.

8 Undo the retaining nut and disconnect the starter motor positive cable from the positive cable terminal box stud **(see illustration)**.

9 Undo the retaining bolt and disconnect the earth lead from left-hand chassis member **(see illustration)**.

10 Disconnect the wiring harness plugs at the left-hand side of the engine compartment so that the harness is free to be removed with the engine/transmission **(see illustration)**. Release the wiring from any retaining clips as necessary.

11 Undo the brake/clutch fluid reservoir retaining screws, release the reservoir and suspend it with wire. Do not remove any of its hoses.

12 Remove the front bumper cover as described in Chapter 11 Section 22.

13 Remove the radiator electric cooling fan assembly as described in Chapter 3 Section 4.

14 Remove the intercooler as described in Chapter 3 Section 5.

15 Remove the radiator as described in Chapter 3 Section 5.

16 Remove the condensor as described in Chapter 3 Section 10.

17 Slide the power steering reservoir upwards from the mounting bracket and move it to one side **(see illustration)**.

18 Detach the gear shift cables from the connections on the transmission housing as described in Chapter 7 Section 4.

19 Undo the mounting bolts each side, and remove the bonnet slam panel assembly **(see illustration)**. Disconnect any wiring plugs etc. as necessary.

20 Disconnect the power steering pipes as described in Chapter 10 Section 21.

21 Disconnect the air conditioning compressor pipes as described in Chapter 3 Section 10.

22 Release the quick-release fittings and disconnect both heater hoses at the heater matrix pipe stubs. Depress the release button each side to disconnect the right-hand hose, and prise up the left-hand hose retaining clip **(see illustration)**.

23 Disconnect the fuel supply and return hoses at the quick-release connections, then release the hoses from their support brackets **(see illustration)**. Plug or cap all open fittings.

24 Disconnect the vacuum pipe from the brake servo or vacuum pump **(see illustration)**.

25 Prise out the retaining clip, disconnect the fluid pressure pipe from the clutch slave cylinder and free the pipe from any retaining clips. Cover both the union and the pipe ends to minimise fluid loss and prevent the entry of dirt into the hydraulic system **(see illustration)**.
Caution: While the hydraulic hose/pipe is disconnected, DO NOT depress the clutch pedal.
26 Remove the driveshafts as described in Chapter 8 Section 2.
27 Remove protective heat cap and disconnect the diesel additive pipe (2.0 litre engines only) **(see illustration)**.
28 Remove the engine/transmission rear mounting as described in Chapter 2A Section 17 or Chapter 2B Section 17.
29 Remove the catalytic converter and particulate filter as described in Chapter 4B Section 3.
30 Position an engine dolly (a low, wheeled platform capable of taking the weight of the engine/transmission) under the engine transmission/assembly. Lower the engine until the sump is resting on the dolly, then use suitable wooden blocks to securely support the engine/transmission assembly on the dolly.
31 Remove the engine/transmission left-hand and right-hand mountings as described in Chapter 2A Section 17 or Chapter 2B Section 17.
32 Make a final check to ensure that nothing else remains connected to the engine/transmission. Ensure that the engine/transmission is securely supported on the dolly, then wheel the dolly out through the front of the vehicle. It may be necessary to tilt the assembly slightly to clear the underbody, in which case the use an assistant will be essential. Great care must be taken to ensure that no components are trapped or damaged during the removal procedure.

Separation

33 With the engine/transmission assembly removed, support the assembly on suitable blocks of wood, on a work bench (or failing that, on a clean area of the workshop floor).
34 Remove the starter motor as described in Chapter 5 Section 10.
35 Ensure that engine and transmission are adequately supported, then slacken and remove the remaining bolts securing the transmission housing to the engine. Note the correct fitted positions of each bolt (and relevant brackets) as they are removed, to use as a reference on refitting.
36 Carefully withdraw the transmission from the engine, ensuring that the weight of the transmission is not allowed to hang on the input shaft while it is engaged with the clutch friction disc.
37 While the engine/transmission is removed, check the mountings and renew them if they are worn or damaged. Similarly, check the condition of all coolant and vacuum hoses and pipes. Components that are normally hidden

can now be checked properly, and should be renewed if there is any doubt at all about their condition. Also take the opportunity to overhaul the clutch components (see Chapter 6). It is regarded by many as good working practice to renew the clutch assembly as a matter of course, whenever major engine overhaul work is carried out. Check also the condition of all components (such as the transmission oil seals) disturbed on removal, and renew any that are damaged or worn.

Refitting

38 Refitting is the reverse of the removal procedure, noting the following points.
a) *Tighten all nuts/bolts to the torque settings given in the Specifications Sections of Chapter 2A and Chapter 2B, and in the other applicable Chapters of this manual.*
b) *Always renew any circlips and self-locking nuts disturbed on removal.*
c) *Where wiring was secured by cable ties which had to be cut on removal, ensure that it is secured with new ties on refitting.*
d) *With all overhaul operations completed, refit the transmission to the engine as described in Chapter 7 Section 7.*
e) *Manoeuvre the engine/transmission unit into the engine compartment, then raise or lower the vehicle as necessary, and refit the engine mountings as described in Chapter 2A Section 17 or Chapter 2B Section 17.*
f) *Refit (and where applicable adjust) all engine related components and systems with reference to the Chapters concerned.*
g) *Prior to refitting the radiator/condenser assembly, refit the radiator/intercooler lower crossmember.*
h) *Add coolant, engine oil, and brake and transmission fluids as needed (see Chapter 1).*
i) *When installation is complete, prime and bleed the fuel system as described in Chapter 4A Section 4 and the power steering system as described in Chapter 10 Section 23.*
j) *Run the engine, and check for proper operation and the absence of leaks. Shut off the engine and recheck the fluid levels.*
k) *On models with air conditioning, have the system evacuated, charged and leak-tested by the specialist who discharged it.*

5 Engine overhaul – dismantling sequence

Note: *Before carrying out any major engine dismantling, consult a Ford dealer or engine reconditioning specialist on the availability of replacement parts. Major components such as the crankshaft, pistons, connecting rods, camshafts etc are not available as separate items from Ford although they may be available from alternative sources.*

4.25 Prise out the retaining clip and disconnect the clutch hydraulic pipe from the transmission

1 It is much easier to dismantle and work on the engine if it is mounted on a portable engine stand. These stands can often be hired from a tool hire shop. Before the engine is mounted on a stand, the flywheel should be removed so that the engine stand bolts can be tightened into the end of the cylinder block/crankcase.
2 If a stand is not available it is possible to dismantle the engine with it mounted on blocks, on a sturdy workbench or on the floor. Be extra careful not to tip or drop the engine when working without a stand.
3 If you are going to obtain a reconditioned ('recon') engine, all external components must be removed first to be transferred to the new engine (just as they will if you are doing a complete engine overhaul yourself).
Note: *When removing the external components from the engine, pay close attention to details that may be helpful or important during refitting. Note the fitted position of gaskets, seals, spacers, pins, washers, bolts and other small items. These external components include the following:*
a) *Alternator, starter and mounting brackets.*
b) *Glow plug/preheating system components.*
c) *Cooling system/thermostat housings.*
d) *Oil level dipstick and dipstick tube.*
e) *All fuel injection system components.*
f) *Brake vacuum pump.*
g) *All electrical switches and sensors and engine wiring harness.*
h) *Inlet and exhaust manifolds.*
i) *Engine/transmission mounting brackets.*
j) *Flywheel.*

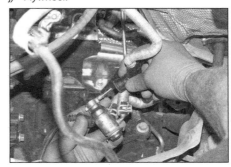

4.27 Disconnect the diesel additive pipe from the rear of the engine

6.3 The EGR hose pipe stub bracket retaining bolt

6.6a Compress the valve springs using a spring compressor tool...

6.6b ...and remove the split collets

6.6c Release the tool and remove the upper spring seat...

6.6d ...and the valve spring

4 If you are obtaining a 'short' engine (which consists of the engine cylinder block/crankcase, crankshaft, pistons and connecting rods all assembled), then the cylinder head, sump, oil pump, oil filter cooler/housing and timing chains will also have to be removed.

5 If you are planning a complete overhaul, the engine can be dismantled and the internal components removed in the following order.
Inlet manifold (Chapter 4A Section 16).
a) *Exhaust manifold (Chapter 4A Section 17).*
b) *Timing belt/chain, tensioners and sprockets (Chapter 2A Section 7, Chapter 2A Section 8, and Chapter 2B Section 7, Chapter 2B Section 8.*
c) *Cylinder head (Chapter 2A Section 10, Chapter 2B Section 10 and Section 6).*
d) *Flywheel (Chapter 2A Section 16 and Chapter 2B Section 16.*
e) *Sump (Chapter 2A Section 11, and Chapter 2B Section 11).*

f) *Oil pump (Chapter 2A Section 12 and Chapter 2B Section 12).*
g) *Piston/connecting rod assemblies (Section 16).*
h) *Crankshaft (Section 10).*

6 Before beginning the dismantling and overhaul procedures, make sure that you have all of the correct tools necessary. Refer to *Tools and working facilities* for further information.

6 Cylinder head – dismantling

Note: *New and reconditioned cylinder heads are available from the manufacturers and from engine overhaul specialists. Due to the fact that some specialist tools are required for the dismantling and inspection procedures and new components may not be readily available,*

it may be more practical and economical for the home mechanic to purchase a reconditioned head, rather than to dismantle, inspect and recondition the original head.

1 With the cylinder head removed as described in the relevant Part of Chapters 2A or 2B, clean away all external dirt, and remove any remaining components as applicable.

2.0 litre engines

Caution: The glow plugs protrude from the bottom of the cylinder head. Support the cylinder head with a block at each end to avoid the plugs being damaged.

2 Undo the two retaining bolts and remove the engine lifting eye.

3 Undo the bolt and remove the exhaust gas recirculation pipe stub mounting bracket **(see illustration)**.

4 Remove the exhaust manifold complete with the turbocharger, as described in Chapter 4A Section 17.

All engines

5 Remove the glow plugs as described in Chapter 5 Section 13.

6 With the cylinder head resting on one side, using a valve spring compressor compress each valve spring in turn until the split collets can be removed. A special valve spring compressor will be required to reach into the deep wells in the cylinder head without risk of damaging the tappet bores. Such compressors are widely available from most good motor accessory shops. Release the compressor and lift off the spring upper seat and spring **(see illustrations)**.

7 If, when the valve spring compressor is screwed down, the spring upper seat refuses to free and expose the split collets, gently tap the top of the tool, directly over the upper seat, with a light hammer. This will free the seat to remove the collets.

8 Withdraw the valve through the combustion chamber. If it binds in the guide (will not pull through), push it back in and deburr the area around the collet groove with a fine file or whetstone.

9 Use a pair of pliers or a special tool to extract the valve spring lower seat/stem oil seal from the valve guides **(see illustration)**.

10 It is essential that the valves are kept

6.9 Use a removal tool to extract the valve stem oil seal

6.10 Use clearly marked containers to identify components and to keep matched assemblies together

together with their collets, spring seats and springs, and in their correct sequence (unless they are so badly worn that they are to be renewed). If they are going to be kept and used again, place them in a labelled polythene bag or similar small container (see illustration).

7 Cylinder head and valves – cleaning and inspection

Note: *If the engine has been severely overheated, it is best to assume that the cylinder head is warped, and to check carefully for signs of this.*

1 Thorough cleaning of the cylinder head and valve components followed by a detailed inspection, will enable you to decide how much valve service work must be carried out during the engine overhaul.

Cleaning

2 Using a degreasing agent, remove all traces of oil deposits from the cylinder head, paying particular attention to the journal bearings, camshaft bores, valve guides and oilways.

3 Scrape away all traces of old gasket material and sealing compound from the cylinder head, taking great care not to score or gouge the surfaces.

4 Scrape away the carbon from the combustion chambers and ports, then wash the cylinder head thoroughly with paraffin or a suitable solvent to remove the remaining debris.

5 Scrape off any heavy carbon deposits that may have formed on the valves, then use a power-operated wire brush to remove deposits from the valve heads and stems.

Inspection

Note: *Be sure to perform all the following inspection procedures before concluding that the services of a machine shop or engine overhaul specialist are required. Make a list of all items that require attention.*

Cylinder head

6 Inspect the head very carefully for cracks, evidence of coolant leakage, and other damage. If cracks are found, a new cylinder head should be obtained.

7 Use a straight-edge and feeler blade to check that the cylinder head gasket surface is not distorted, check the head across a number of different ways to find any distortion (see illustration). If it is, it may be possible to resurface it.

8 Examine the valve seats in each of the combustion chambers. If they are severely pitted, cracked or burned, then they will need to be renewed or recut by an engine overhaul specialist. If they are only slightly pitted, this can be removed by grinding-in the valve heads and seats with fine valve-grinding compound as described below.

9 If the valve guides are worn, indicated by a side-to-side motion of the valve, new guides must be fitted. Measure the diameter of the

existing valve stems (see below) and the bore of the guides, then calculate the clearance, and compare the result with the specified value. If the clearance is excessive, renew the valves or guides as necessary.

10 Valve guides may be renewed using a press and a suitable mandrel, however, the work is best carried out by an engine overhaul specialist, since if it is not done skilfully, there is a risk of damaging the cylinder head.

11 If the valve seats are to be recut, this must be done only after the guides have been renewed.

Valves

12 Examine the head of each valve for pitting, burning, cracks and general wear, and check the valve stem for scoring and wear ridges. Rotate the valve and check for any obvious indication that it is bent. Look for pits and excessive wear on the tip of each valve stem. Renew any valve that shows any such signs of wear or damage.

13 If the valve appears satisfactory at this stage, measure the valve stem diameter at several points using a micrometer (see illustration). Any significant difference in the readings obtained indicates wear of the valve stem. Should any of these conditions be apparent, the valve(s) must be renewed.

14 If the valves are in satisfactory condition, they should be ground (lapped) into their respective seats to ensure a smooth gas-tight seal. If the seat is only lightly pitted, or if it has been recut, fine grinding compound only should be used to produce the required finish. Coarse valve-grinding compound should not be used unless a seat is badly burned or deeply pitted. If this is the case, the cylinder head and valves should be inspected by an expert to decide whether seat recutting, or even the renewal of the valve or seat insert, is required.

15 Valve grinding is carried out as follows. Place the cylinder head upside-down on a bench, with a block of wood at each end to give clearance for the valve stems.

16 Smear a trace of the appropriate grade of coarse carborundum paste on the seat face, and press a suction grinding tool onto the valve head. With a semi-rotary action, grind the valve head to its seat, lifting the valve occasionally to redistribute the grinding compound (see illustration). A light spring

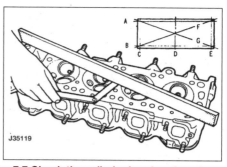

7.7 **Check the cylinder head surface for warping in the planes indicated. Using feeler blades under the straight-edge**

placed under the valve head will greatly ease this operation.

17 If coarse grinding compound is being used, work only until a dull, matt even surface is produced on both the valve seat and the valve, then wipe off the used compound and repeat the process with fine compound. When a smooth unbroken ring of light grey matt finish is produced on both the valve and seat, the grinding operation is complete. Do not grind in the valves any farther than absolutely necessary, or the seat will be prematurely sunk into the cylinder head.

18 When all the valves have been ground-in, carefully wash off all traces of grinding compound using paraffin or a suitable solvent, before reassembly of the cylinder head.

Valve components

19 Examine the valve springs for signs of damage and discolouration, and also measure their free length by comparing each of the existing springs with a new component.

20 Stand each spring on a flat surface and check it for squareness. If any of the springs are damaged, distorted, or have lost their tension, obtain a complete set of new springs.

21 Check the spring upper seats and collets for obvious wear and cracks. Any questionable parts should be renewed, as extensive damage will occur if they fail during engine operation. Any damaged or excessively-worn parts must be renewed. The valve spring lower seat/stem oil seals must be renewed as a matter of course whenever they are disturbed.

7.13 **Measure the diameter of the valve stems with a micrometer**

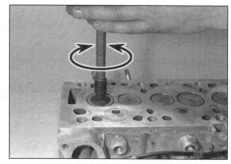

7.16 **Grind-in the valves with a reciprocating rotary motion**

8.2a Fit the new valve spring lower seat/ stem oil seal...

8.2b ...then use a suitable socket or metal tube to press the seal firmly onto the guide

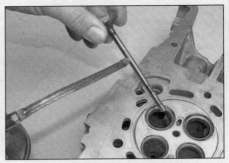

8.3 Apply clean engine oil to the valve stem, and refit the valve

8.4a Refit the valve spring...

8.4b ...and the upper spring seat

8.5 Compress the spring and install the collets. Use grease to hold the two halves of the split collet in the groove

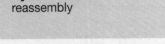

8 Cylinder head – reassembly

 Warning: Wear eye protection when using compressed air.

1 Regardless of whether or not the head was sent away for repair work of any sort, make sure that it is clean before beginning reassembly. Be sure to remove any metal particles and abrasive grit that may still be present from operations such as valve grinding or head resurfacing. Use compressed air, if available, to blow out all the oil holes and passages.
2 Beginning at one end of the head, fit the new valve spring lower seat/stem oil seal. Use a suitable socket or metal tube to press the seal firmly onto the guide (**see illustrations**).
3 Apply clean engine oil to the valve stem, and refit the valve (**see illustration**). Where the original valves are being re-used, ensure that each is refitted in its original guide. If new valves are being fitted, insert them into the locations to which they have been ground.
4 Refit the valve spring and upper seat (**see illustrations**).
5 Compress the spring with the valve spring compressor, and carefully install the collets in the stem groove. Apply a small dab of grease to each collet to hold it in place if necessary (**see illustration**). Slowly release the compressor and make sure the collets seat properly.

6 When the valves are installed, use a hammer and interposed block of wood (to prevent the end of the valve stem being damaged) to tap the end of the valve stem gently in order to settle the components.
7 Repeat the procedure for the remaining valves. Be sure to return the valve assembly components to their original locations – don't mix them up.

9 Piston/connecting rod assemblies – removal and inspection

Note: *While this task is theoretically possible when the engine is in place in the vehicle, in practice it requires so much preliminary dismantling and is so difficult to carry out*

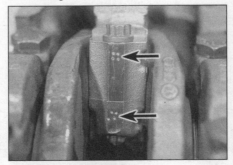

9.4 If necessary, make your own marks to correspond with the connecting rod location

due to the restricted access, that owners are advised to remove the engine from the vehicle first. The following paragraphs assume that the engine has been removed.

Removal

1 Remove the cylinder head and sump with reference to Part A or B of this Chapter.
2 Remove the oil pump and pick-up pipe as described in Chapter 2A Section 12 or Chapter 2B Section 12.
3 Unscrew the bolts securing the lower crankcase to the cylinder block. Loosen the bolts gradually and evenly, then separate the lower crankcase from the cylinder block. Remove the gasket.
4 Temporarily refit the crankshaft pulley so that the crankshaft can be rotated. Note that each piston/connecting rod assembly can be identified by its cylinder number (counting from the timing chain end of the engine) etched into the flat-machined surface of both the connecting rod and its cap. Furthermore, each piston has an arrow stamped into its crown, pointing towards the timing chain end of the engine. If no marks can be seen, make your own before disturbing any of the components so that you can be certain of refitting each piston/connecting rod assembly the right way round, and to its correct (original) bore, with the cap also the right way round (**see illustration**).
5 Use your fingernail to feel if a ridge has formed at the upper limit of ring travel (about 6 mm down from the top of each

cylinder). If carbon deposits or cylinder wear have produced ridges, they must be completely removed with a special tool called a ridge reamer **(see illustration)**. Follow the manufacturer's instructions provided with the tool.

Caution: Failure to remove the ridges before attempting to remove the piston/ connecting rod assemblies may result in piston ring breakage.

6 Slacken each of the big-end bearing cap bolts half a turn at a time, until they can be removed by hand. Remove the No 1 cap and bearing shell. Don't drop the shell out of the cap.

7 Caution: The connecting rod/bearing cap mating surfaces are not machined flat, since the big-end bearing caps are 'cracked' off from the rod during production and left untouched to ensure the cap and rod mate perfectly. Great care must be taken to ensure the mating surfaces of the cap and rod are not marked or damaged in anyway. Any damage to the mating surfaces will adversely affect the strength of the connecting rod and could lead to premature failure.

8 Remove the upper bearing shell and push the connecting rod/piston assembly out through the top of the cylinder block. Use a wooden hammer handle to push on the connecting rod's bearing recess. If resistance is felt, double-check that all of the ridge was removed from the cylinder. Repeat the procedure for the remaining cylinders.

9 After removal, reassemble the big-end bearing caps and shells on their respective connecting rods, and refit the bolts finger-tight. Leaving the old shells in place until reassembly will help prevent the bearing recesses from being accidentally nicked or gouged. New shells should be used on reassembly.

10 Remove the retaining screws and withdraw the piston cooling jets from the bottom of the cylinder bores **(see illustrations)**.

Inspection

11 Before the inspection process can be carried out, the piston/connecting rod assemblies must be cleaned and the original piston rings removed from the pistons. The rings should have smooth, polished working surfaces, with no dull or carbon-coated sections and no traces of wear on their top and bottom surfaces. Any discoloured sections will show that the ring is not sealing correctly against the bore wall, so allowing combustion gases to blow by. The end gaps should be clear of carbon but not polished (indicating a too-small end gap), and all the rings (including the elements of the oil control ring) should be free to rotate in their grooves, but without excessive up-and-down movement. If the rings appear to be in good condition, they are probably fit for further use; if so, check the end gaps (in an unworn part of the bore) as described in Section 14. If any of

the rings appears to be worn or damaged, or has an end gap significantly different from the specified value, the usual course of action is to renew all of them as a set.

Note: *While it is usual to renew piston rings when an engine is overhauled, they may be re-used if in acceptable condition. If re-using the rings, make sure that each ring is marked during removal to ensure that it is refitted correctly.*

12 Using a piston ring removal tool, carefully remove the rings from the pistons. Be careful not to nick or gouge the pistons in the process, and mark or label each ring as it is removed, so that its original top surface can be identified on reassembly, and so that it can be returned to its original groove. Take care also with your hands – piston rings are sharp **(see Tool Tip)**.

> **TOOL TIP** *If a piston ring removal tool is not available, the rings can be removed by hand, expanding them over the top of the pistons. The use of two or three old feeler blades will be helpful in preventing the rings dropping into empty grooves.*

13 Scrape all traces of carbon from the top of the piston. A hand-held wire brush or a piece of fine emery cloth can be used once the majority of the deposits have been scraped away. Do not under any circumstances use a wire brush mounted in a drill motor to remove deposits from the pistons because the piston

9.5 A ridge reamer may be required, to remove the ridge from the top of each cylinder

material is soft, and may be eroded away by the wire brush.

14 Use a piston ring groove-cleaning tool to remove carbon deposits from the ring grooves. If a tool isn't available, but replacement rings have been found, a piece broken off the old ring will do the job. Be very careful to remove only the carbon deposits (don't remove any metal) and do not nick or scratch the sides of the ring grooves **(see illustrations)**. Wear suitable gloves if possible, because the piston rings are sharp.

⚠ *Warning: Wear eye protection when using compressed air.*

15 Once the deposits have been removed, clean the piston/rod assemblies with solvent and dry them with compressed air if available. Make sure the oil return holes in the back sides of the ring grooves and the oil hole in the lower end of each rod are clear.

9.10a Remove the piston cooling jet-retaining screws...

9.10b ...and remove the jets from their mounting holes

9.14a The piston ring grooves can be cleaned with a special tool as shown here...

9.14b ...or alternatively a section of a broken piston ring may be used, if available

10.1 Measure the crankshaft endfloat using a DTI gauge

10.3 If a DTI gauge is not available, measure the endfloat using feeler gauges

16 If the pistons and cylinder walls are not damaged or worn excessively and if the cylinder block/crankcase is not rebored, new pistons will not be necessary. Normal piston wear appears as even vertical wear on the piston thrust surfaces, and slight looseness of the top ring in its groove.

17 Carefully inspect each piston for cracks around the skirt, at the pin bosses, and at the ring lands (between the ring grooves).

18 Look for scoring and scuffing on the thrust faces of the piston skirt, holes in the piston crown, and burned areas at the edge of the crown. If the skirt is scored or scuffed, the engine may have been suffering from overheating and/or abnormal combustion which caused excessively high operating temperatures. The cooling and lubrication systems should be checked thoroughly. A hole in the piston crown, or burned areas at the edge of the piston crown indicates that abnormal combustion (knocking or detonation) has been occurring. If any of the above problems exist, the causes must be investigated and corrected or the damage will occur again. The causes may include intake air leaks, incorrect fuel/air mixture or EGR system malfunctions.

19 Corrosion of the piston in the form of small pits indicates that coolant is leaking into the combustion chamber and/or the crankcase. Again, the cause must be corrected or the problem may persist in the rebuilt engine.

20 Check the piston-to-rod clearance by twisting the piston and rod in opposite directions. Any noticeable play indicates excessive wear which

must be corrected. The piston/connecting rod assemblies should be taken to an engine reconditioning specialist to have the pistons, gudgeon pins and rods checked, and new components fitted as required.

21 Check the connecting rods for cracks and other damage. Temporarily remove the big-end bearing caps and the old bearing shells, wipe clean the rod and cap bearing recesses, and inspect them for nicks, gouges and scratches. After checking the rods, refit the old shells, slip the caps into place, and tighten the bolts finger-tight.

10 Crankshaft – removal and inspection

Note: *This procedures applies only to the 2.2 litre engine. Ford recommends that the crankshaft isn't removed from the 2.0 litre engine.*

Removal

Note: *The crankshaft can be removed only after the engine/transmission has been removed from the vehicle. It is assumed that the transmission, flywheel, timing chain, lower crankcase, cylinder head, sump, oil pump, and piston/connecting rod assemblies have already been removed. The crankshaft oil seal carrier must be unbolted from the cylinder block/crankcase before proceeding with crankshaft removal.*

1 Before the crankshaft is removed, check the endfloat. Mount a DTI (Dial Test Indicator, or dial gauge) with the probe in line with the

crankshaft and just touching the crankshaft **(see illustration)**.

2 Push the crankshaft fully away from the gauge and zero the gauge. Next, lever the crankshaft towards the gauge as far as possible, and check the reading obtained. The distance that the crankshaft moved is its endfloat. If it is greater than specified, check the crankshaft thrust surfaces for wear. If no wear is evident, new thrustwashers (integral with No 3 main bearing upper shell) should correct the end-float.

3 If a dial gauge is not available, feeler gauges can be used. Gently lever or push the crankshaft all the way towards the right-hand end of the engine. Slip feeler gauges between the crankshaft and the right-hand face of No 3 (centre) main bearing to determine the clearance **(see illustration)**.

4 The main bearing caps may already be numbered consecutively from the timing chain end of the engine. If not, mark them with a pencil. The caps also have an embossed arrow pointing to the timing belt/chain end of the engine **(see illustrations)**. Slacken the cap bolts a quarter-turn at a time each, starting with the end caps and working toward the centre, until they can be removed by hand.

5 Gently tap the caps with a soft-faced hammer, then separate them from the cylinder block/crankcase. If necessary, use the bolts as levers to remove the caps. Take care not to drop the bearing shells as the bearing caps are removed.

6 Carefully lift the crankshaft out of the engine **(see illustration)**. Use an assistant since the crankshaft is heavy. With the bearing shells in place in the cylinder block/crankcase and main bearing caps, return the caps to their respective locations on the block and tighten the bolts finger-tight. Leaving the old shells in place until reassembly will help prevent the bearing recesses from being accidentally nicked or gouged. New shells should be used on reassembly.

Inspection

⚠ **Warning: Wear eye protection when using compressed air.**

7 Clean the crankshaft, and dry it with compressed air if available. Be sure to clean the oil holes with a pipe cleaner or similar probe.

10.4a Note the main bearing caps may be numbered to indicate their locations...

10.4b ...and the caps have an embossed arrow pointing to the timing chain end of the engine

10.6 Carefully remove the crankshaft from the cylinder block

8 Check the main and crankpin (big-end) bearing journals carefully. If uneven wear, scoring, pitting and cracking are evident then the crankshaft should be reground (where possible) by an engineering workshop, and refitted to the engine with new undersize bearings.

9 Rather than attempt to determine the crankshaft journal sizes and the bearing clearances, take the crankshaft to an automotive engineering workshop. Have them perform the necessary measurements, grind the journals if necessary and supply the appropriate new shell bearings.

10 Check the oil seal journals at each end of the crankshaft for wear and damage. If either seal has worn an excessive groove in its journal, it may cause the new seals to leak when the engine is reassembled. Consult an engine overhaul specialist, who will be able to advise whether a repair is possible or whether a new crankshaft is necessary.

11 Cylinder block/crankcase – cleaning and inspection

Cleaning

Note: *If the crankshaft position sensor mounting bracket is removed, its new fitted position will have to be established on reassembly (see Section 16).*

1 For complete cleaning, make sure that all the external components have been removed, including mounting brackets, oil cooler and filter housing, piston cooling jets, fuel injection pump mounting bracket (where applicable) and all electrical switches/sensors.

2 Remove the main bearing caps and separate the bearing shells from the caps and the cylinder block. Mark or label the shells, indicating which bearing they were removed from, and whether they were in the cap or the block, then set them aside **(see illustration)**. Wipe clean the block and cap bearing recesses and inspect them for nicks, gouges and scratches.

3 Scrape all traces of gasket from the cylinder block, taking care not to damage the sealing surfaces.

4 Remove all oil gallery plugs (where fitted). The plugs are usually very tight and they may have to be drilled out and the holes retapped. Use new plugs when the engine is reassembled.

5 If any of the castings are extremely dirty, they should be steam-cleaned.

6 After the castings are returned from steam-cleaning, clean all oil holes and oil galleries one more time. Flush all internal passages with warm water until the water runs clear, then dry thoroughly and apply a light film of oil to all machined surfaces, to prevent rusting. If you have access to compressed air, use it to speed the drying process, and to blow out all the oil holes and galleries.

11.2 Felt marker pens can be used as shown to identify bearing shells without damaging them

⚠ *Warning: Wear eye protection when using compressed air.*

7 If the castings are not very dirty, you can do an adequate cleaning job with hot soapy water and a stiff brush. Take plenty of time and do a thorough job. Regardless of the cleaning method used, be sure to clean all oil holes and galleries very thoroughly and to dry all components completely. Protect the machined surfaces as described above to prevent rusting.

8 The threaded holes in the cylinder block must be clean to ensure accurate torque readings when tightening nuts/bolts during reassembly. Run the correct-size tap (which can be determined from the size of the relevant bolt) into each of the holes to remove rust, corrosion, thread sealant or other contamination, and to restore damaged threads **(see illustration)**. If possible, use compressed air to clear the holes of debris produced by this operation. Do not forget to clean the threads of all bolts and nuts which are to be re-used, as well.

9 Where applicable, apply suitable sealant to the new oil gallery plugs and insert them into the relevant holes in the cylinder block. Tighten the plugs securely. Refit the piston cooling jets into the block and secure with the new retaining bolts tightened securely.

10 Refit the main bearing caps and tighten the bolts finger-tight. If the engine is not going to be reassembled right away, cover it with a large plastic bag to keep it clean. Apply a thin coat of engine oil to all machined surfaces to prevent rusting.

Inspection

11 Visually check the castings for cracks and corrosion. Look for stripped threads in the threaded holes. If there has been any history of internal coolant leakage, it may be worthwhile having an engine overhaul specialist check the cylinder block/crankcase for cracks with special equipment. If defects are found, have them repaired, if possible, or renew the assembly.

12 Check each cylinder bore for scuffing and scoring. Any evidence of this kind of damage should be double-checked with an inspection of the pistons (see Section 9). If the damage is in its early stages, it may be possible to repair

11.8 All bolt holes in the block, particularly the main bearing cap and head bolt holes, should be cleaned and restored with a tap

the block by reboring it. Seek the advice of an engineering workshop.

13 Place the cylinder block on a level surface, crankcase downwards. Use a straight-edge and set of feeler blades to measure the distortion of the cylinder head mating surface in both planes. Ford quotes a maximum distortion figure – measured longitudinally and diagonally – of 0.10mm. If the measurement exceeds this figure, repair may be possible by machining (consult an engineering workshop for advice).

14 To allow an accurate assessment of the wear in the cylinder bores to be made, take the cylinder block to an automotive engineering workshop and have them carry out the measurement procedures. If necessary, they will be able to rebore the cylinders and supply the appropriate piston kits.

15 Even if the cylinder bores are not excessively worn, they must be honed. This process involves using an abrasive tool to produce a fine, cross-hatch pattern on the inner surface of the bore. This has the effect of seating the piston rings, resulting in a good seal between the piston and cylinder. Again, an engineering workshop will be able to carry out the job for you at a reasonable cost.

16 Refit all the components removed in paragraph 1.

12 Main and big-end bearings – inspection

1 Even though the main and big-end bearing shells should be renewed during the engine overhaul, the old shells should be retained for close examination because they may reveal valuable information about the condition of the engine **(see illustration)**.

2 Bearing failure occurs because of lack of lubrication, the presence of dirt or other foreign particles, overloading the engine or corrosion – or a combination of these. Regardless of the cause of bearing failure, it must be corrected before the engine is reassembled, to prevent it from happening again.

3 When examining the bearing shells, remove them from the cylinder block/crankcase and main bearing caps, and from the connecting

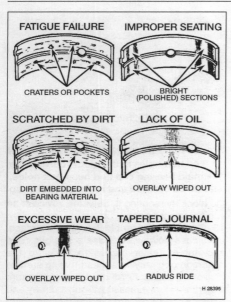

12.1 Look for any of these problems when inspecting the main and big end bearings

FATIGUE FAILURE — CRATERS OR POCKETS

IMPROPER SEATING — BRIGHT (POLISHED) SECTIONS

SCRATCHED BY DIRT — DIRT EMBEDDED INTO BEARING MATERIAL

LACK OF OIL — OVERLAY WIPED OUT

EXCESSIVE WEAR — OVERLAY WIPED OUT

TAPERED JOURNAL — RADIUS RIDE

H 28395

rods and the big-end bearing caps, then lay them out on a clean surface in the same general position as their location in the engine. This will enable you to match any bearing problems with the corresponding crankshaft journal.

4 Dirt or other foreign matter gets into the engine in a variety of ways. It may be left in the engine during assembly or it may pass through filters or the crankcase ventilation system. It may get into the oil and from there into the bearings. Metal chips from machining operations and normal engine wear are often present. Abrasives are sometimes left in engine components after reconditioning, especially when parts are not thoroughly cleaned using the proper methods.

5 Whatever the source, these foreign objects often end up embedded in the soft bearing material and are easily recognised. Large particles will not embed in the material, and will score or gouge the shell and journal. The best prevention for this cause of bearing failure is to clean all parts thoroughly and to keep everything spotlessly clean during

engine assembly. Frequent and regular engine oil and filter changes are also recommended.

6 Lack of lubrication (or lubrication breakdown) has a number of inter-related causes. Excessive heat which thins the oil, overloading which squeezes the oil from the bearing face and oil leakage (from excessive bearing clearances, worn oil pump or high engine speeds) all contribute to lubrication breakdown. Blocked oil passages, which usually are the result of misaligned oil holes in a bearing shell, will also starve a bearing of oil and destroy it. When lack of lubrication is the cause of bearing failure, the bearing material is wiped or extruded from the steel backing of the shell. Temperatures may increase to the point where the steel backing turns blue from overheating.

7 Driving habits can have a definite effect on bearing life. Full-throttle, low-speed operation (labouring the engine) puts very high loads on bearings, which tends to squeeze out the oil film. These loads cause the shells to flex, which produces fine cracks in the bearing face (fatigue failure). Eventually, the bearing material will loosen in pieces and tear away from the steel backing.

8 Driving the vehicle for short distances leads to corrosion of bearings, because insufficient engine heat is produced to drive off condensed water and corrosive gases. These products collect in the engine oil, forming acid and sludge. As the oil is carried to the engine bearings, the acid attacks and corrodes the bearing material.

9 Incorrect shell refitting during engine assembly will also lead to bearing failure. Tight-fitting shells leave insufficient bearing running clearance and will result in oil starvation. Dirt or foreign particles trapped behind a bearing shell result in high spots on the bearing which lead to failure.

10 *Do not* touch the internal bearing surface of any shell with your fingers during reassembly because there is a risk of scratching the delicate surface or of depositing particles of dirt on it.

11 As mentioned at the beginning of this Section, the bearing shells should be renewed as a matter of course during an engine overhaul. To do otherwise is false economy.

13 Engine overhaul – reassembly sequence

1 Before reassembly begins, ensure that all new parts have been obtained and that all necessary tools are available. Read through the entire procedure to familiarise yourself with the work involved, and to ensure that all items necessary for reassembly of the engine are at hand. In addition to all normal tools and materials, jointing and thread-locking compound will be needed during engine reassembly. A suitable tube of sealant will also be required for certain type of joint faces that are without gaskets. It is recommended that the manufacturer's own products are used because these are specially formulated for the purpose.

2 In order to save time and avoid problems, engine reassembly can be carried out in the following order:

a) *Crankshaft and main bearings (Section 10).*
b) *Pistons/connecting rods and main bearing ladder. (Section 9).*
c) *Oil pump (Chapter 2A Section 12 and Chapter 2B Section 12).*
d) *Sump (Chapter 2A Section 11 and Chapter 2B Section 11).*
e) *Flywheel (Chapter 2A Section 16 and Chapter 2B Section 16).*
f) *Cylinder head (Chapter 2A Section 10 and Chapter 2B Section 10).*
g) *Timing belt/chain, tensioners and sprockets (Chapter 2A Section 8 and Chapter 2B Section 8).*
h) *Inlet manifold (Chapter 4A Section 16).*
i) *Exhaust manifold (Chapter 4A Section 17).*
j) *Engine external components and ancillaries.*

3 Ensure that everything is clean prior to reassembly. As mentioned previously, dirt and metal particles can quickly destroy bearings and result in major engine damage. Use clean engine oil to lubricate during reassembly.

14 Piston rings – refitting

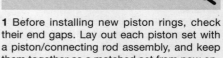

1 Before installing new piston rings, check their end gaps. Lay out each piston set with a piston/connecting rod assembly, and keep them together as a matched set from now on.

2 Insert the top compression ring into the first cylinder, and square it up with the cylinder walls by pushing it in with the top of the piston **(see illustration)**. The ring should be near the bottom of the cylinder, at the lower limit of ring travel.

3 To measure the end gap, slip feeler gauges between the ends of the ring until a gauge equal to the gap width is found **(see illustration)**. The feeler gauge should slide between the ring ends with a slight amount of drag. Compare the measurement to the value

14.2 When checking the piston ring end gap, the ring must be square in the cylinder bore

14.3 With the ring square in the bore, measure the end gap with a feeler gauge

given in the Specifications. If the gap is larger or smaller than specified, double-check to make sure you have the correct rings before proceeding. If you are assessing the condition of used rings, have the cylinder bores checked and measured by a Ford dealer or similar engine reconditioning specialist, so that you can be sure of exactly which component is worn, and seek advice as to the best course of action to take.

4 If the end gap is still too small, it must be opened up by careful filing of the ring ends using a fine file. If it is too large, this is not as serious, unless the specified limit is exceeded, in which case very careful checking is required of the dimensions of all components, as well as of the new parts.

5 Repeat the procedure for each ring that will be installed in the first cylinder, and for each ring in the remaining cylinders. Remember to keep rings, pistons and cylinders matched up.

6 Refit the piston rings as follows. Where the original rings are being refitted, use the marks or notes made on removal, to ensure that each ring is refitted to its original groove and the same way up. New rings generally have their top surfaces identified by markings, often an indication of size (such as STD or the word TOP). The rings must be fitted with such markings uppermost **(see illustration)**.

Note: *Always follow the instructions printed on the ring package or box as different manufacturers may require different approaches. Do not mix up the top and second compression rings as they usually have different cross-sections.*

7 The oil control ring (lowest one on the piston) is usually installed first. It is usually composed of three separate elements. Slip the spacer/expander into the groove. Next, install the lower side rail. Do not use a piston ring installation tool on the oil ring side rails because they may be damaged. Instead, place one end of the side rail into the groove between the spacer/expander and the ring land, hold it firmly in place, then slide a finger around the piston while pushing the rail into the groove. Next, install the upper side rail in the same manner.

8 After all the oil ring components have been installed, check that both the upper and lower

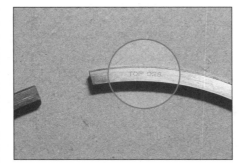

14.6 Piston ring 'TOP' markings

side rails can be turned smoothly in the ring groove.

9 The second compression (middle) ring is installed next, followed by the top compression ring. Make sure their marks are uppermost. Do not expand either ring any more than necessary to slide it over the top of the piston.

10 With all the rings in position, space the ring gaps (including the elements of the oil control ring) uniformly around the piston at 120° intervals. Repeat the procedure for the remaining pistons and rings.

15 Crankshaft – refitting

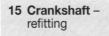

Note: *This procedures applies only to the 2.2 litre engine. Ford recommends that the crankshaft isn't removed from the 2.0 litre engine. However, for details of how to renew the 2.0 litre engine's lower crankcase-to-cylinder block seal see the next Section.*

Note: *New main bearing cap retaining bolts must be used when refitting the crankshaft.*

1 Crankshaft refitting is the first major step in engine reassembly. It is assumed at this point that the cylinder block/crankcase and crankshaft have been cleaned, inspected and repaired or reconditioned as necessary. Where removed, the oil jets must be refitted at this stage and their mounting bolts tightened securely.

2 Place the cylinder block on a clean, level

work surface, with the crankcase facing upwards. Wipe out the inner surfaces of the main bearing caps and crankcase with a clean cloth because they must be kept spotlessly clean.

3 Clean the rear surface of the new main bearing shells with a lint-free cloth. Fit the shells with an oil groove in each main bearing location in the block. Note the thrustwashers integral with the No 3 (centre) upper main bearing shell **(see illustrations)**. Fit the other shell from each bearing set in the corresponding main bearing cap. The oil holes in the block must line up with one of the oil holes in the bearing shell. Don't hammer the shells into place and don't nick or gouge the bearing faces. It is critically important that the surfaces of the bearings are kept free from damage and contamination.

4 Clean the bearing surfaces of the shells in the block and the crankshaft main bearing journals with a clean, lint-free cloth. Check or clean the oil holes in the crankshaft because any dirt will become embedded in the new bearings when the engine is first started.

5 Apply a thin, uniform layer of clean engine oil to each surface **(see illustration)**. Coat the thrustwasher surfaces as well.

6 Making sure the crankshaft journals are clean, lay the crankshaft back in place in the block.

7 Lubricate the crankshaft oil seal journals with clean engine oil.

8 Clean the bearing surfaces of the shells in the caps then lubricate them. Refit the caps in their respective positions, with the arrows pointing to the timing chain end of the engine.

9 Apply a smear of clean engine oil to the threads and underneath the heads of the new main bearing cap bolts. Fit the bolts, tightening them all by hand.

10 Working on one cap at a time, from the centre main bearing outwards (and ensuring that each cap is tightened down squarely and evenly onto the block), tighten the main bearing cap bolts to the specified Stage 1 torque setting given in Chapter 2B **(see illustration)**.

11 When all the bolts have been tightened to the Stage 1 setting, go around again and tighten them to the Stage 2 setting, then Stage 3 and Stage 4.

15.3a Fitting the shells in each main bearing location

15.3b Note the thrustwashers integral with the No 3 (centre) upper main bearing shell

15.5 Ensure the bearing shells are absolutely clean and lubricate liberally

15.10 Tighten the main bearing cap bolts in the initial Stages using a torque wrench

15.12 Using an angle-tightening gauge to tighten the main bearing cap bolts to the final Stage

12 The final stage involves tightening the bolts though an angle, rather than to a torque. The bolts must be rotated through the specified angle – special angle gauges are available from tool outlets **(see illustration)**. As a guide, a 90° angle is equivalent to a quarter-turn, and this is easily judged by assessing the start and end positions of the socket handle.

13 Rotate the crankshaft a number of times by hand, to check for any obvious binding.

14 Check the crankshaft endfloat (see Section 10). It should be correct if the crankshaft thrust faces are not worn or damaged, and if the thrust control bearings have been renewed.

15 Referring to Part A or B of this Chapter,

fit a new crankshaft oil seal, then refit the flywheel.

16 Refit the piston connecting rod assemblies as described in Section 9.

16 Piston/connecting rod assemblies – refitting

Note: *At this point, it is assumed that the crankshaft has been measured, renewed/reground as necessary, and has been fitted to the engine as described in Section 15.*

Note: *New retaining bolts must be used when refitting the big-end bearing caps.*

1 Before refitting the piston/connecting rod

16.3 Press the bearing shells into the connecting rods and caps ensuring they sit centrally

16.6 Insert the piston/connecting rod assembly into the top of the cylinder

16.8 Using a hammer handle to tap the piston into its bore

16.9 Note the markings on the bearing cap with respect to the connecting rod on refitting

assemblies, the cylinder bores must be perfectly clean, the top edge of each cylinder must be chamfered, and the crankshaft must be in place.

2 Remove the big-end bearing cap from No 1 cylinder connecting rod (refer to the marks noted or made on removal). Remove the original bearing shells, and wipe the bearing recesses of the connecting rod and cap with a clean, lint-free cloth. They must be kept spotlessly clean.

3 Ensure that all traces of the protective grease on the new bearing shells are cleaned off using paraffin, then wipe the shells dry with a lint-free cloth. Press the bearing shells into the connecting rods and caps ensuring they sit centrally within the rods and caps **(see illustration)**.

4 Lubricate the cylinder bores, the pistons, piston rings and upper bearing shells with clean engine oil. Lay out each piston/connecting rod assembly in order on a clean work surface. Take care not to scratch the crankpins and cylinder bores when the pistons are refitted.

5 Start with piston/connecting rod assembly No 1. Make sure that the piston rings are still spaced as described in Section 14, then clamp them in position with a piston ring compressor.

6 Insert the piston/connecting rod assembly into the top of cylinder No 1 **(see illustration)**. Lower the big-end in first, guiding it to protect the cylinder bores. Take particular care not to damage or break off the oil spray jets when guiding the connecting rods onto the crankpins.

7 Ensure that the orientation of the piston in its cylinder is correct. The piston crown, connecting rod and big-end bearing caps should have markings which must be aligned in the position noted on removal (see Section 9).

8 Using a block of wood or hammer handle against the piston crown, tap the assembly into the cylinder until the piston crown is flush with the top of the cylinder **(see illustration)**.

9 Ensure that the bearing shell is still correctly installed. Liberally lubricate the crankpin and both bearing shells with clean engine oil. Taking care not to mark the cylinder bores, tap the piston/connecting rod assembly down the bore and onto the crankpin. Oil the threads and underside of the new retaining bolt heads, then fit the big-end bearing cap, tightening its retaining bolts finger tight at first. Note that the orientation of the bearing cap with respect to the connecting rod must be correct when the two components are reassembled **(see illustration)**.

10 Tighten the retaining bolts to the specified Stage 1 torque setting, then to the Stage 2 and Stage 3 settings. The final involves tightening the bolts though an angle rather than to a torque. The bolts must be rotated through the specified angle (special angle gauges are available from tool outlets). As a guide, a 90° angle is equivalent to a quarter-turn, and this is easily judged by assessing the start

16.10a Tighten the big-end bearing cap bolts to the Stage 1, 2 and 3 torque settings using a torque wrench...

16.10b ...then tighten the bolts to the Stage 4 setting using an angle-tightening gauge

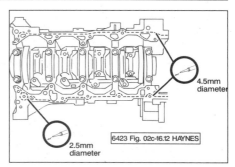

16.13 Apply the sealant to the 2.0 litre engine's cylinder block

16.14a Fit the new lower crankcase-to-cylinder block gasket on the 2.2 litre engine...

16.14b ...then refit the lower crankcase to the cylinder block

16.15a Place a straight-edge across the transmission mating surface of the cylinder block...

and end positions of the socket handle (see illustrations).

11 Repeat the entire procedure for the remaining piston/connecting rod assemblies.

12 After all the piston/connecting rod assemblies have been properly installed, rotate the crankshaft a number of times by hand to check for any obvious binding or tight spots.

13 The 2.0 litre engine's lower crankcase-to-cylinder block seal takes the form of silicone sealant LB (to Ford specification WSE-M4G323-A4), while the 2.2 litre engine uses a gasket. The sealant should be applied as

shown as a 4.5mm wide bead. In addition, a 2.5mm bead should be added in the recess (see illustration). This must be completed within 5 minutes.

14 With the new gasket or sealant in place, refit the lower crankcase to the cylinder block, then insert the bolts and hand-tighten (see illustrations).

15 Place a straight-edge across the transmission mating surface of the cylinder block and the lower crankcase to check the lower crankcase-to-cylinder block alignment. The lower crankcase should be flush with

the cylinder block. If not flush, the alignment should be within –0.01 mm overlap to a +0.2 mm gap at the rear of the cylinder block. Repeat this check by placing the straight-edge against the two projecting bosses on the side of the cylinder block (see illustrations). In this instance the alignment should be –0.05 mm overlap to a +0.05 mm gap

16 Once the alignment is within tolerance, tighten the lower crankcase bolts to the specified torque. All of the 2.2 litre engine's bolts have the same torque rating but the 2.0 litre engine's bolts have different ratings (see illustration).

16.15b ...and against the two projecting bosses on the fuel injection pump side of the cylinder block

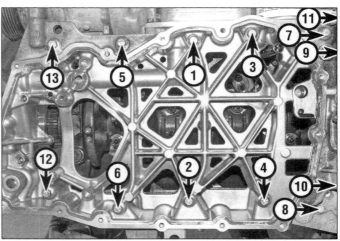

16.16 Tighten the 2.0 litre engine's lower crankcase bolts in the order shown

16.21 Make up an arrow pointer out of stiff tin plate and bolt it to the cylinder block using suitable washers as necessary

16.23b Mark the position of the flywheel using a white marker pen (or similar) in relation to the arrow pointer

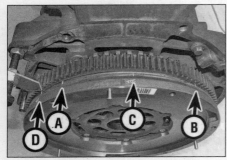

16.28 Arrangement of the flywheel markings

A First mark
B Second mark
C Established TDC position
D Established 50° BTDC position

16.29 Align the newly established 50° BTDC position with the arrow pointer

16.23a Rotate the crankshaft until No 1 piston is approximately 10 mm before top dead centre, then zero the dial gauge

16.26 Measure the distance between the two marks made on the flywheel

17 Clean off any excess sealant on the outside of the 2.0 litre engine's crankcase.

18 Where applicable, set the position of the crankshaft position sensor mounting bracket, then refer to Part A or B of this Chapter (as applicable) and refit the relevant assemblies.

Setting the crankshaft position sensor mounting bracket

Note: *Ford service tool 303-698 – obtainable from Ford dealers or a tool supplier – will be required for this procedure.*

19 If the crankshaft position sensor mounting bracket was removed from the cylinder block during the cleaning and reconditioning procedures described previously, its position in relation to the flywheel will need to be reset as follows.

20 Refit the crankshaft position sensor mounting bracket and install the bolts, tightened finger tight.

21 Make up an arrow pointer out of stiff tin plate or similar. Drill a hole in the plate and bolt it to the cylinder block using the upper left-hand transmission mounting bolt hole. Use suitable washers as necessary so that the pointer lies just flush with the flywheel periphery **(see illustration)**. Once the pointer is in place, do not move it during the setting procedure.

22 Mount a DTI (Dial Test Indicator, or dial gauge) on the cylinder head mating face of the cylinder block, with the probe in line with No 1 cylinder piston.

23 Rotate the crankshaft until No 1 piston is approximately 10 mm before top dead centre (TDC). Zero the dial gauge and mark the position of the flywheel using a white marker pen or similar, in relation to the arrow pointer **(see illustrations)**.

24 Turn the flywheel anti-clockwise until the dial gauge indicates 'O'. Again, mark the position of the flywheel, using a white marker pen or similar, in relation to the arrow pointer.

25 Repeat paragraphs 21 and 22 to make sure that the markings on the flywheel are correct.

26 Using a dressmaker's tape measure (or a suitable length of string) measure the distance between the two marks on the flywheel **(see illustration)**. Divide this measurement by 2 and mark that measurement on the flywheel. This will be the TDC position.

27 Again, using a tape measure or a suitable length of string, wrap it around the flywheel outer periphery to measure the flywheel circumference. Record this measurement.

28 Multiply the circumference measurement by 0.1388 and mark this new figure on the flywheel by measuring anti-clockwise from the previously marked TDC position. This new figure will be the 50° BTDC position **(see illustration)**.

29 Turn the flywheel to align the newly established 50° BTDC position with the arrow pointer **(see illustration)**.

30 Insert the Ford special tool into the crankshaft position sensor mounting bracket, and move the bracket within the limit of the elongated bolt holes until the tool drops into position in the flywheel **(see illustrations)**.

16.30a Insert the Ford tool into the crankshaft position sensor mounting bracket...

16.30b ...and move the bracket until the tool drops into position in the flywheel

Now tighten the crankshaft position sensor mounting bracket retaining bolts to the specified torque. Remove the special tool on completion.

17 Engine – initial start-up after overhaul

1 With the engine refitted in the vehicle, double-check the engine oil and coolant levels. Make a final check that everything has been reconnected, and that there are no tools or rags left in the engine compartment.

2 Turn the engine on the starter until the oil pressure warning light goes out. If the lamp fails to extinguish after several seconds of cranking, check the engine oil level and oil filter security. Assuming these are correct, check the security of the oil pressure switch wiring. **Do not** progress any further until you are satisfied that oil is being pumped around the engine at sufficient pressure.

3 Prime and bleed the fuel system as described in Chapter 4A Section 4, then start the engine, noting that this may take a little longer than usual.

4 While the engine is idling, check for fuel, water and oil leaks. Don't be alarmed if there are some odd smells and smoke from parts getting hot and burning off oil deposits.

5 Assuming all is well, run the engine until it reaches normal operating temperature, then switch off the engine.

6 After a few minutes, recheck the oil and coolant levels as described in *Weekly checks*, and top-up as necessary.

7 Note that there is no need to retighten the cylinder head bolts once the engine has first run after reassembly.

8 If new pistons, rings or crankshaft bearings have been fitted, the engine must be treated as new and run-in for the first 600 miles. Do not operate the engine at full-throttle or allow it to labour at low engine speeds in any gear. It is recommended that the oil and filter be changed at the end of this period.

Notes

Chapter 3
Cooling, heating and air conditioning systems

Contents

Degrees of difficulty

Easy, suitable for novice with little experience	Fairly easy, suitable for beginner with some experience	Fairly difficult, suitable for competent DIY mechanic	Difficult, suitable for experienced DIY mechanic	Very difficult, suitable for expert DIY or professional

Specifications

Coolant
Mixture type	See *Lubricants, fluids and tyre pressures* on page 0•17
Cooling system capacity	See Chapter 1 Specifications

Expansion tank filler cap
Pressure rating..	1.45 bar (21 psi)

Air conditioning system
Refrigerant	R134a
Refrigerant quantity	740 g

Torque wrench settings

	Nm	lbf ft
Air conditioning compressor bolts	25	19
Crossmember bolts:		
Thru A-pillar bolts.....................................	30	22
In-cabin bolts	25	19
Compressor mounting bolts..................................	25	19
Compressor refrigerant shield bolts:		
Shield-to-compressor bolt	25	19
Shield-to-engine-block bolts	15	11
Coolant pump bolts	24	18
Electric coolant pump bolts:		
Mounting bracket to engine	10	7
Pump to mounting bracket..............................	8	6
Refrigerant union to compressor	20	15
Refrigerant union to condenser	8	6
Thermostat housing cover bolts...............................	10	7

1 General information and precautions

Engine cooling system

1 The cooling system is of pressurised type, comprising a coolant pump, a crossflow radiator, electric cooling fan, and thermostat. The coolant pump is bolted to the right-hand of the engine cylinder block, and is driven by a drivebelt off the crankshaft pulley on 2.0 litre engines, or is coupled to the power steering pump on 2.2 litre engines.

2 The thermostat is located in a housing on the left-hand end of the cylinder block, beneath the brake vacuum pump.

3 The system functions as follows. Cold coolant from the radiator passes to the coolant pump, where it is pumped around the cylinder block, head passages and heater matrix. After cooling the cylinder bores, combustion surfaces and valve seats, the coolant reaches the underside of the thermostat which is initially closed. The coolant passes through the heater and is returned to the coolant pump.

4 When the engine is cold, the coolant circulates only through the cylinder block, cylinder head and heater. When the coolant reaches a predetermined temperature, the thermostat opens and the coolant also passes through to the radiator. As the coolant circulates through the radiator, it is cooled by the inrush of air when the vehicle is in forward motion. Airflow is supplemented by the action of the electric cooling fan when necessary. Once the coolant has passed through the radiator and has cooled, the cycle is repeated.

5 The electric cooling fan, mounted on the rear of the radiator, is controlled by the engine management system powertrain control module. At a predetermined coolant temperature, the fan is actuated.

6 An expansion tank is fitted to the left-hand side of the engine compartment to accommodate expansion of the coolant when hot.

Heating/ventilation system

7 The heating system consists of a blower fan and heater matrix (radiator) located in the air distribution housing, with hoses connecting the heater matrix to the engine cooling system. Hot engine coolant is circulated through the heater matrix. Incoming fresh air for the ventilation system enters the vehicle through the scuttle intake air duct. The ventilation system air distribution is controlled by a number of flap doors in the air distribution housing. When the heater controls are operated, the flap doors open to direct the air to the chosen areas of the passenger compartment. When the blower control is operated, the blower fan forces air through the unit according to the setting selected.

Air conditioning system

8 See Section 10.

Precautions

⚠️ *Warning: DO NOT attempt to remove the expansion tank filler cap, or to disturb any part of the cooling system, while it or the engine is hot, as there is a very great risk of scalding. If the expansion tank filler cap must be removed before the engine and radiator have fully cooled down (even though this is not recommended) the pressure in the cooling system must first be released. Cover the cap with a thick layer of cloth, to avoid scalding, and slowly unscrew the filler cap until a hissing sound can be heard. When the hissing has stopped, showing that pressure is released, slowly unscrew the filler cap further until it can be removed, however, if more hissing sounds are heard, wait until they have stopped before unscrewing the cap completely. At all times, keep well away from the filler opening.*

⚠️ *Warning: Do not allow antifreeze to come in contact with your skin, or with the painted surfaces of the vehicle. Rinse off spills immediately with plenty of water. Never leave antifreeze lying around in an open container, or in a puddle in the driveway or on the garage floor. Children and pets are attracted by its sweet smell, but antifreeze is fatal if ingested.*

⚠️ *Warning: If the engine is hot, the electric cooling fan may start rotating even if the engine is not running, so be careful to keep hands, hair and loose clothing well clear when working in the engine compartment.*

⚠️ *Warning: Refer to Section 9 for precautions to be observed when working on models equipped with air conditioning.*

2 Cooling system hoses – disconnection and renewal

Note: *Refer to the warnings given in Section 1 of this Chapter before starting work.*

3.3 Disconnect the thermostat wiring plugs

1 If the checks described in Chapter 1 Section 10 reveal a faulty hose, it must be renewed as follows.

2 First drain the cooling system as described in Chapter 1 Section 32. If the antifreeze is not due for renewal, the drained coolant may be re-used if it is collected in a clean container.

3 To disconnect any hose, use a pair of pliers to release the spring clamps (or a screwdriver to slacken screw-type clamps), then move them along the hose clear of the union. Carefully work the hose off its stubs. The hoses can be removed with relative ease when new, however, on an older vehicle they may have stuck.

4 If a hose proves stubborn, try to release it by rotating it on its unions before attempting to work it off. Gently prise the end of the hose with a blunt instrument (such as a flat-bladed screwdriver), but do not apply too much force, and take care not to damage the pipe stubs or hoses. Note in particular that the radiator hose unions are fragile, therefore do not use excessive force when attempting to remove the hoses. If all else fails, cut the hose with a sharp knife, then slit it so that it can be peeled off in two pieces. While expensive, this is preferable to buying a new radiator. Check first, however, that a new hose is readily available.

5 When refitting a hose, first slide the clamps onto the hose, then work the hose onto its stubs. If the hose is stiff, use soap or washing-up liquid as a lubricant, or soften it by soaking it in boiling water (take care to prevent scalding).

6 Work each hose end fully onto its stub, then check that the hose is settled correctly and is properly routed. Slide each clip along the hose until it is behind the stub flared end, before tightening it securely.

7 Refill the system with coolant as described in Chapter 1 Section 32.

8 Check carefully for leaks as soon as possible after disturbing any part of the cooling system.

3 Thermostat – removal, testing and refitting

Note: *Refer to the warnings given in Section 1 of this Chapter before starting work.*

Removal

1 Drain the cooling system as described in Chapter 1 Section 32. If the coolant is relatively new or in good condition, drain it into a clean container and re-use it.

2 To improve access, remove the radiator electric cooling fan and shroud as described in Section 4.

3 On the 2.0 litre engine, disconnect the two wiring plugs from the top and bottom of the thermostat **(see illustration)**.

4 Release the clamps and disconnect the coolant hoses from the thermostat housing **(see illustration)**.

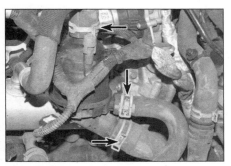

3.4 Disconnect the three hoses from the thermostat housing (2.0 litre engine shown)

3.6a Unscrew the bolts (2.0 litre engine)

3.6b Separate the cover from the thermostat housing (2.2 litre engine)

3.6c Remove the thermostat housing (2.0 litre engine)

3.7 Remove the thermostat (2.2 litre engines)

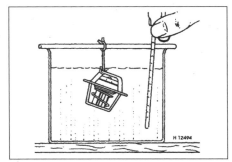

3.10 Method of checking thermostat opening temperature

5 Where applicable, unclip the wiring loom in front of the thermostat and move it out of the way.

6 Unscrew the three bolts and separate the thermostat body (2.0 litre engine) or cover from the thermostat housing (2.2 litre engine) **(see illustrations)**.

7 On the 2.2 litre engine, withdraw the thermostat from the housing **(see illustration)**.

8 Recover the O-ring seal(s).

Testing

9 The contruction of the 2.0 litre engine's thermostat makes testing impossible, so diagnosis will have to be made via the vehicle's onboard diagnostics socket (see Chapter 4A Section 9).

10 A rough test of the 2.2 litre engine's thermostat may be made by suspending it with a piece of string in a container full of water, so that it is immersed in the water but not touching the sides or bottom of the container **(see illustration)**. Heat the water to bring it to the boil, and check that the thermostat opens by the time the water boils. If not, renew it.

11 If a thermometer is available, the precise opening temperature of the thermostat may be determined. Compare the figures with the opening temperature marked on the thermostat.

12 A thermostat which fails to close as the water cools must also be renewed.

Refitting

13 Refitting is a reversal of removal, but clean all sealing surfaces, fit a new O-ring seal and tighten the bolts to the specified torque. Refill

the cooling system as described in Chapter 1 Section 32.

<table>
<tr><td>4</td><td>Radiator electric cooling fan assembly – testing, removal and refitting</td></tr>
</table>

Note: *Refer to the warnings given in Section 1 of this Chapter before starting work.*

Testing

1 The radiator cooling fan is controlled by the engine management system's powertrain control module, acting on the information received from the cylinder head temperature sensor.

2 First, check the relevant fuses and relays (see Chapter 12 Section 3).

3 To test the fan motor, unplug the wiring plug and use fused jumper wires to connect the fan

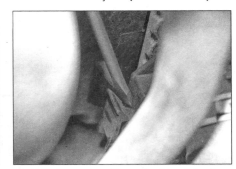

4.8 Disconnect both cooling fan wiring plugs

directly to the battery. If the fan still does not work, renew the motor.

4 If the motor is satisfactory, the fault lies in the cylinder head temperature sensor (see Chapter 4A Section 10) or in the wiring loom or in the engine management system.

Removal

5 Disconnect the battery negative terminal as described in Chapter 5 Section 4.

6 Remove the air cleaner assembly and air ducts as described in Chapter 4A Section 5.

7 Suitably support the bonnet in the open position, then disengage the stay from the bonnet.

8 Disconnect the cooling fan wiring plugs and release the retaining clips **(see illustration)**.

9 Detach the expansion tank pipe fasteners that run across the top of the fan assembly.

10 Release the retaining clip each side and lift the fan assembly out **(see illustration)**.

4.10 Release the clip each side of the fan shroud assembly

4.11 Motor retaining screws and wiring plug

11 If required, undo the three retaining Torx screws and lift the motor off the shroud. Disconnect the wiring plug and remove the motor **(see illustration)**.

Refitting

12 Refitting is a reversal of removal.

5 Radiator –
removal, inspection and refitting

Note: *Refer to the warnings given in Section 1 of this Chapter before starting work.*
Note: *If leakage is the reason for removing the radiator, bear in mind that minor leaks can often be cured using a radiator sealant added to the coolant without removing the radiator.*

5.4 Disconnect the expansion tank coolant hose at the quick release connector

5.5b ...and bottom hoses from the radiator

Removal

1 Drain the cooling system as described in Chapter 1 Section 32. If the coolant is relatively new or in good condition, drain it into a clean container and re-use it.
2 Remove the radiator electric cooling fan assembly as described in Section 4.
3 Remove the intercooler as described in Chapter 4A Section 18.
4 Depress the release buttons and disconnect the expansion tank coolant hose at the right-hand side of the radiator **(see illustration)**.
5 Release the retaining clamps and disconnect the top and bottom hoses from the radiator **(see illustrations)**.
6 On models with air conditioning, depress the retaining clip each side and lift the air conditioning condenser slightly **(see illustration)**. Disengage the two mounting lugs each side from the guides on the radiator. Suitably secure the condenser.

 Warning: Do not disconnect the refrigerant hoses.

7 Remove the cable ties, where applicable, and ease the radiator downwards and manoeuvre it from under the vehicle.
8 Remove the rubber radiator mounting bushes from the top and bottom retaining brackets, and inspect them for wear and damage. If necessary, obtain and fit new ones before refitting the radiator **(see illustration)**.

Inspection

9 With the radiator removed, it can be

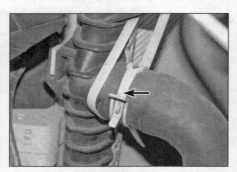

5.5a Release the retaining clamps and disconnect the top...

5.6 Depress the retaining clip and lift the condenser slightly to free the radiator

inspected for leaks and damage. If it needs repair, have a radiator specialist or dealer service department perform the work, as special techniques are required.
10 Insects and dirt can be removed from the radiator with a garden hose or a soft brush. Take care not to bend the cooling fins.

Refitting

11 Refitting is the reverse of the removal procedure, but refill the cooling system as described in Chapter 1 Section 32.

6 Coolant pumps –
removal and refitting

Note: *Refer to the warnings given in Section 1 of this Chapter before starting work.*
Note: *The 2.0 litre engine has two coolant pumps. The first is driven by the crankshaft pulley using a drive belt. The second is electrically powered and supplies coolant to the diesel exhaust fluid injector. It is located above the alternator.*

Coolant pump

Removal

Note: *To carry out this task on the 2.0 litre engine with the engine/transmission installed in the vehicle will require the equipment necessary to support and raise the engine with the right-hand engine mounting removed, and to raise and support the front of the vehicle. Ford technicians use an engine support beam arrangement, which locates in the front crossmember. If the engine must be supported from below, use a large piece of wood on a trolley jack to spread the load and reduce the chance of damage to the sump. Precise details of the procedure will depend on the equipment available. There is no need to support the 2.2 litre engine to remove the coolant pump, but follow the instructions below.*

1 Drain the cooling system as described in Chapter 1 Section 32. If the coolant is relatively new or in good condition, drain it into a clean container and re-use it. If you are working on the 2.2 litre engine, proceed to paragraph 4.

5.8 Inspect the bushes for damage and replace if necessary

6.3 Home-made tool to support and raise the engine, without damaging the sump

6.5a Undo the three bolts securing the coolant pump to the power steering pump (2.2 litre engine)

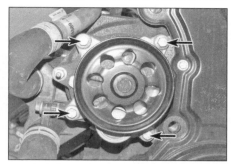

6.5b Coolant pump retaining bolts (2.0 litre engine)

2 Remove the coolant pump drive belt as described in Chapter 1 Section 33.

3 With the engine adequately supported, remove the right-hand engine mounting bracket as described in Chapter 2A Section 17, then raise the engine as necessary to create clearance for the coolant pump removal **(see illustration)**.

4 On 2.2 litre engines, release the retaining clamps and disconnect the two coolant hoses from the rear of the coolant pump.

5 Suitably support the 2.2 litre engine's coolant pump, then working through the holes in the power steering pump pulley, undo the three bolts securing the coolant pump to the power steering pump **(see illustration)**. The 2.0 litre engine's coolant pump is retained by four bolts **(see illustration)**.

6 On the 2.0 litre engine, pull the coolant pump from place. On the 2.2 litre engine, using a large screwdriver, ease the coolant pump drive coupling away from the drive dog on the shaft; disengage the drive coupling then move the coolant pump clear of the power steering pump **(see illustrations)**.

7 On 2.2 litre engines, recover the coolant pipe O-ring from the top of the pump and obtain a new O-ring for refitting.

8 On 2.0 litre engines, if required, undo the retaining bolts, disconnect the 2 coolant hoses and remove the coolant pump outlet housing. Renew the two seals **(see illustration)**.

Refitting

9 Refitting is a reversal of removal, but tighten

6.6a Ease the coolant pump drive coupling away from the power steering pump drive dog...

the mounting bolts/nuts to the specified torque. Refill the cooling system as described in Chapter 1 Section 32.

Electric coolant pump (2.0 litre engine)

Removal

10 Apply suitable clamp to seal the hoses, then release the clamps and disconnect the two hoses to the top and sides of the pump **(see illustration)**. Be prepared for fluid to be released. Also disconnect the wiring plug and unclip it from the pump's mounting bracket.

11 Undo the 3 Torx screws and detach the pump from its' mounting bracket.

Refitting

12 Refitting is a reversal of removal.

6.6b ...then disengage the drive coupling and move the coolant pump clear of the power steering pump (2.2 litre engines)

7 Heater/ventilation components – removal and refitting

Heater blower motor

Removal

1 Working in the passenger footwell, undo the three retaining screws and release the tabs to remove the cover beneath the glovebox **(see illustration)**.

2 Undo the two screws and manoeuvre the air ducting to one side **(see illustration)**.

3 Disconnect the heater blower motor wiring plug and release the wiring, if attached **(see illustration)**.

4 Undo the three retaining screws and lower

6.8 Renew the seals on the coolant pump outlet housing (2.0 litre engine)

6.10 Disconnect the hoses and wiring plug

7.1 Undo the screws and remove the heater blower motor cover

7.2 Air ducting retaining screws

7.3 Disconnect the heater blower motor wiring plug

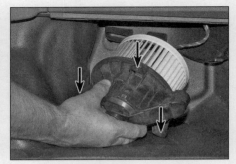

7.4 Undo the screws and remove the blower motor

7.7 Remove the heater support bracket screws and nuts

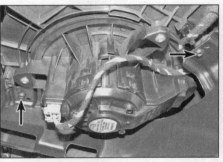

7.8a Lower ducting retaining screws

7.8b Upper ducting retaining screw

the heater blower motor out of the vehicle **(see illustration)**.

Refitting

5 Refitting is a reversal of removal.

Blower motor resistor

Note: *Vehicles with climate control (instead of manual air-conditioning) have a blower control module fitted instead of a blower motor resistor.*

Removal

6 Remove the glovebox as described in Chapter 11 Section 27.

7 Undo the two retaining screws and two nuts, and remove the heater support bracket, releasing the blower motor case fastener from it as it is removed **(see illustration)**.

8 Undo the retaining screws and remove the air ducting **(see illustrations)**.

9 Disconnect the resistor wiring plug **(see illustration)**.

10 Undo the resistor retaining Torx screw **(see illustration)**.

11 Manoeuvre the blower motor resistor out from place.

Refitting

12 Refitting is a reversal of removal.

Air inlet blend door actuator

Removal

13 Remove the glovebox as described in Chapter 11 Section 27.

14 Working through the glovebox aperture, disconnect the wiring plug, undo the three screws and remove the actuator **(see illustration)**.

Refitting

15 Refitting is a reversal of removal.

Air distribution housing

Removal

16 On models with air conditioning, have the refrigerant discharged at a dealer service department or an automotive air conditioning repair facility.

17 Drain the cooling system as described in Chapter 1 Section 32. If the coolant is relatively new or in good condition, drain it into a clean container and re-use it.

18 Remove the windscreen cowl panel as described in Chapter 12 Section 15.

19 Undo the nut and disconnect the refrigerant pipes from the expansion valve at the rear of the engine compartment **(see illustration)**. Plug the openings to prevent contamination. New O-ring seals will be required.

20 Disconnect the heater hoses at the heater matrix pipe stubs at the engine compartment

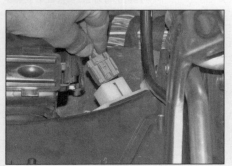

7.9 Disconnect the resistor wiring plug

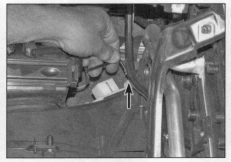

7.10 Use a Torx key to access the resistor retaining screw

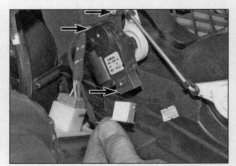

7.14 Disconnect the plug and undo the screws and remove the actuator

7.19 Undo the nut and pull the pipes from the expansion valve

7.20 Disconnect the heater hoses from the matrix stubs

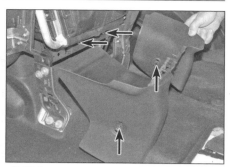

7.25 Centre bottom facia panel retaining screws

bulkhead **(see illustration)**. Depress the release buttons to disconnect the right-hand hose, and prise up the wire clip to disconnect the left-hand hose.

21 Remove both front doors as decribed in Chapter 11 Section 10.
22 Remove both A-pillar trim panels as described in Chapter 11 Section 24.
23 Remove the complete facia as described in Chapter 11 Section 27.
24 Remove the steering column as described in Chapter 10 Section 17.
25 Remove the screw covers and then undo four screws securing the centre bottom facia panel. Remove the panel **(see illustration)**.
26 Disconnect the gearchange outer and inner cables from the gear lever assembly as described in Chapter 7 Section 4.
27 Undo the retaining nuts and remove the gear change lever assembly **(see illustration)**.
28 Undo the bolt ahead of the steering column mounting bracket **(see illustration)**.
29 Disconnect the wiring plugs from the base of the A-pillars, the fuse boxes, base of the A-pillar, then undo the bolt securing the wiring loom plug on the left-hand side of the crossmember **(see illustrations)**.
30 Undo the four bolts on each side and remove the crossmember floor mounting plates. Each plate comprises two parts **(see illustration)**.
31 Remove the rubber grommets, then undo the crossmember retaining bolts each side **(see illustration)**. Have an assistant support the crossmember as the bolts are removed.

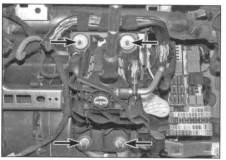

7.27 Gear change lever assembly retaining nuts

⚠️ *Warning: The crossmember is heavy, and has sharp edges.*

32 Mark the fitted positions, then undo the

7.29a Starting on the right-hand side, disconnect this wiring plug...

7.28 Undo the bolt in front of the steering column mounting bracket

two crossmember retaining bolts each side. Check that all wiring has been disconnected, then manoeuvre the crossmember and climate control assembly from the vehicle.

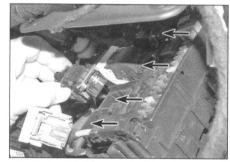

7.29b ...wiring plugs from the fuse box...

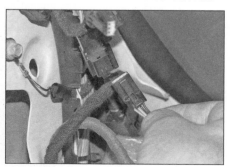

7.29c ...the wiring plugs and aerial connection at the base of the left-hand A-pillar...

7.29d ...then undo the retaining bolt and disconnect the wiring loom plug

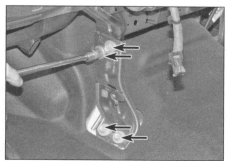

7.30 Undo the bolts and remove the floor mounting plates

7.31 Undo the crossmember retaining bolt each side

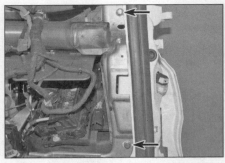

7.32 Mark the position of the crossmember retaining bolts

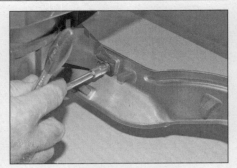

7.33a Undo the blower motor case nut from the bracket...

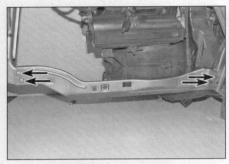

7.33b ...and undo the bracket's retaining screws

7.34 Release the clamps and disconnect the hoses

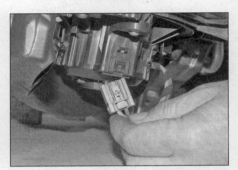

7.35 Disconnect the blower motor wiring plug

Guide the heater matrix (and, where fitted, the evaporator) pipes through the bulkhead as the housing is withdrawn. Be prepared for coolant spillage. **(see illustration).**

33 With the assembly on the bench, undo the retaining screws and remove the heater support bracket, releasing the blower motor case fastener from it as it is removed **(see illustrations).**

34 Release the clamps and remove the heater hose extension pipes attached to the matrix stubs **(see illustration).**

35 Disconnect the heater blower wiring plug and unclip the wiring harness **(see illustration).**

36 Disconnect the wiring plug for the air inlet blend door actuator motor **(see illustration).**

37 Disconnect the wiring plug for the blower motor resistor **(see illustration).**

38 Disconnect all of the wiring plugs on the right-hand side of the air distribution housing **(see illustration).**

39 Undo the screw and disconnect the right-hand side footwell airflow duct **(see illustration).**

40 Remove the wiring loom from the top of the assembly.

41 Undo the four nuts and one bolt retaining the air distribution housing. An assistant may be required to hold the crossmember whilst the housing is removed. **(see illustrations).**

7.36 Unplug the air inlet blend door actuator motor

7.37 Blower motor resistor wiring plug

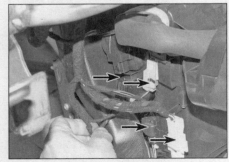

7.38 Disconnect the plugs on the right-hand side of the housing

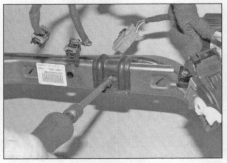

7.39 Remove the right-hand side footwell duct

7.41a Undo the upper...

7.41b ...and lower nuts...

7.41c ...and the bolt securing the housing to the crossmember

7.45 Pull off the moulding from the matrix pipe stubs

7.46 Undo the three screws and remove the heater matrix guide bracket

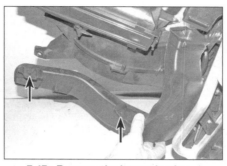

7.47a Remove the lower ducting...

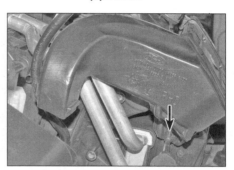

7.47b ...and the upper ducting

Refitting

42 Refitting is a reversal of removal, bearing in mind the following points:
a) *Refit the facia as described in Chapter 11 Section 27.*
b) *On models with air conditioning, renew all disturbed refrigerant pipe seals.*
c) *Refill the cooling system as described in Chapter 1 Section 32.*
d) *Have the air conditioning system evacuated, charged and leak-tested by the specialist who discharged it.*

Heater matrix

Removal

43 Remove the air distribution housing as described previously in this Section.
44 Release the clips and remove the heater hose extension pipes attached to the matrix stubs **(see illustration 7.34)**.
45 Remove the sponge moulding from the pipe stubs **(see illustration)**.
46 Undo the three screws and remove the heater matrix guide bracket from the front of the air distribution housing **(see illustration)**.
47 Undo the two retaining screws and remove the lower ducting, then undo the single screw and remove the upper ducting **(see illustrations)**.
48 Undo the two screws and disconnect the small ventilation pipe off the lower stub **(see illustration)**.
49 Undo the three screws, release the clip beneath and separate the air inlet assembly from the air distribution assembly **(see illustrations)**.

50 Undo the screw and remove the matrix-retaining clip **(see illustration)**.

51 Carefully withdraw the matrix from the air distribution housing **(see illustration)**.

7.48 Undo the screws and disconnect the small ventilation pipe

7.49a Undo the three screws...

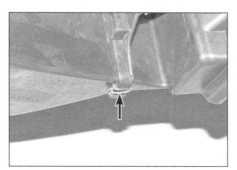

7.49b ...and release the clip

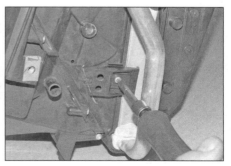

7.50 Undo the screw and remove the clip

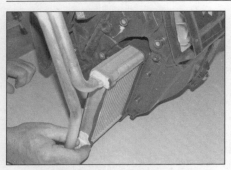

7.51 Withdraw the matrix from the air distribution housing

7.54 Remove the ducting to access the electric booster heater

7.55 Undo the electric booster heater retaining screws

Refitting

52 Refitting is a reversal of removal.

Electric booster heater

53 Remove the air distribution housing as described in Section 7.
54 Undo the screw and remove the ducting above the heater **(see illustration)**.
55 Release the heater wiring clips and undo the two Torx screws retaining the heater **(see illustration)**.
56 Withdraw the heater control unit and element from the housing **(see illustration)**.

Dashboard air vents

Outer air vents

57 Remove the single Torx screw on the outside edge of the facia and use a trim removal tool to carefully ease the vent assembly free of the dashboard **(see illustration)**.
58 Refitting is a reversal of removal.

Centre air vents

59 Remove the infotainment console as described in Chapter 12 Section 5.
60 Undo the two Torx screws at the rear of each vent and release the various clips to free the air vent **(see illustrations)**.
61 Refitting is a reversal of removal.

8 Heater/air conditioning controls – removal and refitting

Note: *This procedure also applies to vehicles equipped with climate control.*

Removal

1 Disconnect the battery negative terminal as described in Chapter 5 Section 4.
2 Remove the facia upper centre trim panel as described in Chapter 11, Section 27.
Note: *Take care not to damage surrounding trim when using the wedge tool.*
3 Using a wedge tool, gently ease the surround away from the ventilation controls. Disconnect any wiring plugs as the surround is removed **(see illustration)**.
4 Undo the retaining screws and remove the ventilation control panel **(see illustration)**.
5 Disconnect the wiring plugs from the rear of the panel **(see illustration)**.

Refitting

6 Refitting is a reversal of removal.

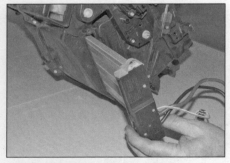

7.56 Slide the heater element from the housing

7.57 Undo the screw (1) before levering the assembly from the dashboard (2)

7.60a Undo the screws…

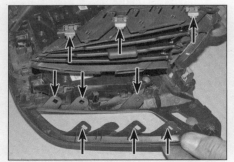

7.60b …and release the clips to remove the air vent

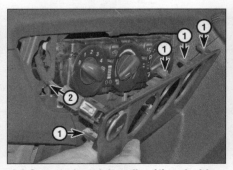

8.3 Surround retaining clips (1) and wiring plug (2)

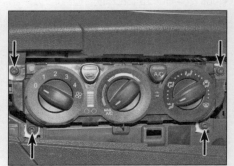

8.4 Ventilation control panel retaining screws

9 Air conditioning system – general information and precautions

General information

1 The air conditioning system consists of a condenser mounted in front of the radiator, an evaporator mounted adjacent to the heater matrix, a compressor driven by the auxiliary drivebelt, an accumulator/dehydrator and the pipes connecting all of the above components.

2 The cooling side of the system works in the same way as a domestic refrigerator. Refrigerant gas at low pressure is drawn into a belt-driven compressor and passes into a condenser mounted on the front of the radiator, where it loses heat and becomes liquid. The liquid passes through an expansion valve to an evaporator, where it changes from liquid under high pressure to gas under low pressure. This change is accompanied by a drop in temperature, which cools the evaporator. The refrigerant returns to the compressor, and the cycle begins again.

3 Air blown through the evaporator passes through the air distribution housing, where it is mixed with hot air blown through the heater matrix to achieve the desired temperature in the passenger compartment.

4 The heating side of the system works in the same way as on models without air conditioning.

Air conditioning service ports

5 Both service ports are located in front of the fuse box, on the left-hand side of the engine compartment **(see illustration)**.

Precautions

⚠️ **Warning: The air conditioning system is under high pressure. Do not loosen any fittings or remove any components until after the system has been discharged. Air conditioning refrigerant should be properly discharged into an approved type of container, at a dealer service department or an automotive air conditioning repair facility capable of handling R134a refrigerant. Always wear eye protection when disconnecting air conditioning system fittings.**

6 When an air conditioning system is fitted, it is necessary to observe the following special precautions whenever dealing with any part of the system, its associated components, and any items which necessitate disconnection of the system:

a) *While the refrigerant used (R134a) is less damaging to the environment than the previously used R12, it is still a very dangerous substance. It must not be allowed into contact with the skin or eyes, or there is a risk of frostbite. It must also not be discharged in an enclosed space since, while it is not toxic, there is a risk of*

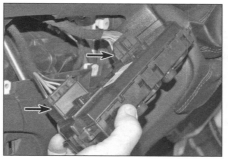

8.5 Disconnect the wiring plugs

suffocation. The refrigerant is heavier than air, and so must never be discharged over a pit.

b) *The refrigerant must not be allowed to come in contact with a naked flame, otherwise a poisonous gas will be created and under certain circumstances, this can form an explosive mixture with air. For similar reasons, smoking in the presence of refrigerant is highly dangerous, particularly if the vapour is inhaled through a lighted cigarette.*

c) *Never discharge the system to the atmosphere. R134a is not an ozone-depleting ChloroFluoroCarbon (CFC) like R12, but is instead a hydrofluorocarbon, which causes environmental damage by contributing to the 'greenhouse effect' if released into the atmosphere.*

d) *R134a refrigerant must not be mixed with R12. The system uses different seals (now green-coloured, previously black) and has different fittings requiring different tools, so that there is no chance of the two types of refrigerant becoming mixed accidentally.*

e) *If for any reason the system must be disconnected, entrust this task to your Ford dealer or a refrigeration engineer.*

f) *It is essential that the system be professionally discharged prior to using any form of heat (welding, soldering, brazing, etc) in the vicinity of the system, before having the vehicle oven-dried at a temperature exceeding 70°C after repainting, and before disconnecting any part of the system.*

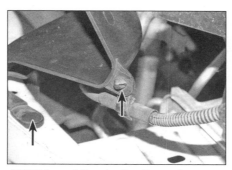

10.3 Take out the plastic clips and remove both air deflectors

9.5 Air conditioning system high-pressure service port (A) and low-pressure service port (B)

10 Air conditioning system components – removal and refitting 🔧

⚠️ **Warning: The air conditioning system is under high pressure. Do not loosen any fittings or remove any components until after the system has been discharged. Air conditioning refrigerant should be properly discharged into an approved type of container, at a dealer service department or an automotive air conditioning repair facility capable of handling R134a refrigerant. Cap or plug the pipe lines as soon as they are disconnected, to prevent the entry of moisture. Always wear eye protection when disconnecting air conditioning system fittings.**

Condenser

Removal

1 Have the refrigerant evacuated at a dealer service department or an automotive air conditioning repair facility.

2 Remove the front bumper cover as described in Chapter 11 Section 22.

3 Release the retaining clips and any attached wiring, and remove the right- and left-hand air deflectors from the side of the condenser **(see illustration)**.

4 Remove the intercooler as described in Chapter 4A Section 18.

5 Disconnect the refrigerant pipes from the condenser and immediately cap the openings

10.5 Undo the nuts and disconnect the refrigerant pipes

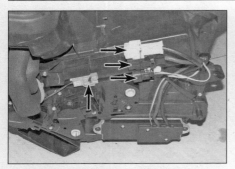

10.9 Disconnect the wiring plugs on the right side of the housing

10.10a Remove the thermostatic expansion valve…

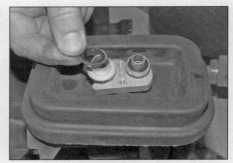

10.10b …before extracting the seals…

10.10c …and the pipe bracket

10.11 Pull off the foam pad on the stubs

10.12 Undo the two screws and separate the evaporator pipe guide bracket

to prevent the entry of dirt and moisture **(see illustration)**. Discard the O-ring seals and obtain new ones for refitting.

6 Depress the clip each side and lift the condenser slightly, disengage the mounting lug each side from the guides on the radiator, then manoeuvre it down and out from under the vehicle.

Refitting

7 Refitting is a reversal of removal, but fit new O-ring seals. The O-ring seals must be coated with clean refrigerant oil before refitting them. Have the system evacuated, charged and leak-tested by the specialist who discharged it.

Evaporator

Removal

8 Remove the heater matrix as described in Section 7.

9 If not already done, detach the wiring from the right-hand side of the evaporator housing **(see illustration)**.

10 Undo the thermostatic expansion valve retaining screws, remove the valve and extract the pipe seals and pipe bracket **(see illustrations)**.

11 Remove the foam pad from the end of the evaporator pipe stubs **(see illustration)**.

12 Remove the evaporator pipe guide bracket **(see illustration)**.

13 Undo the retaining screws and remove the evaporator lower cover **(see illustration)**.

14 Undo the retaining screws and remove the upper cover **(see illustration)**.

15 Withdraw the evaporator from the air distribution housing.

Refitting

16 Refitting is a reversal of removal.

Compressor

Removal

17 Have the refrigerant evacuated at a dealer service department or an automotive air conditioning repair facility.

18 Disconnect the battery negative terminal as described in Chapter 5 Section 4.

19 Firmly apply the handbrake, then jack up the front of the vehicle and support it securely on axle stands (see *Jacking and vehicle support*).

20 Remove the auxiliary drivebelt as described in Chapter 1 Section 33.

21 If fitted, undo the three retaining bolts securing the shield that covers the refrigerant pipes leading to the compressor. Remove the shield.

22 Undo the two mounting bolts that secure the refrigerant pipes to the engine and then undo the two nuts and disconnect the refrigerant pipes from the compressor. Plug the openings to prevent contamination.

23 Disconnect the wiring plugs from the air conditioning compressor **(see illustration)**.

24 Support the compressor, then unscrew the three mounting bolts (one may have been removed already if the shield was taken off earlier). Withdraw the compressor from the engine. Discard the O-ring seals. Tape over or plug the compressor apertures and line ends to prevent entry of dust and dirt.

Refitting

25 Refitting is a reversal of removal, but fit new O-ring seals after coating them with clean refrigerant oil, and tighten the mounting bolts to the specified torque. Have the system

10.13 Evaporator lower cover screws

10.14 Remove the evaporator upper cover

evacuated, charged and leak-tested by the specialist that discharged it.

Accumulator/dehydrator

Note: *The accumulator/dehydrator housing is attached to the right-hand side of the condensor and is accessed from beneath the vehicle.*

26 Have the refrigerant discharged at a dealer service department or an automotive air conditioning repair facility.

27 Remove the intercooler as described in Chapter 4A Section 18.

28 Undo the four retainers and remove the shield from beneath the radiator.

29 Unscrew the cover and remove the accumulator/dehydrator **(see illustration)**.

30 Refitting is a reversal of removal.

10.23 Disconnect the wiring plugs from the compressor

10.29 Remove the cover to extract the accumulator/dehydrator

Chapter 4 Part A
Fuel and exhaust systems

Contents

Degrees of difficulty

Easy, suitable for novice with little experience	Fairly easy, suitable for beginner with some experience	Fairly difficult, suitable for competent DIY mechanic	Difficult, suitable for experienced DIY mechanic	Very difficult, suitable for expert DIY or professional

Specifications

General

System type	Turbocharged Direct Common-rail injection (TDCi), intercooled, controlled by engine management powertrain control module (PCM)
Firing order.	1-3-4-2 (No 1 at timing chain/belt end)
Idle speed.	850 rpm (regulated by engine management system – no adjustment possible)

Torque wrench settings

	Nm	lbf ft
Accelerator pedal retaining nuts.	8	6
Air conditioning compressor bolts	25	19
Alternator mounting bolts.	48	35
Camshaft position sensor bolt:		
2.0 litre engine	8	6
2.2 litre engine	10	7
Catalytic converter support bracket bolts	25	19
Catalytic converter-to-turbocharger nut(s): *		
2.0 litre engine	9	7
2.2 litre engine	48	35
Crankshaft position sensor bolts:		
2.0 litre engine	10	7
2.2 litre engine	7	5
Cylinder head temperature sensor.	10	7
EGR outlet pipe retaining bolts	10	7
Exhaust manifold heat shield bolts	10	7
Exhaust manifold-to-cylinder head: *		
2.0 litre engines:		
Stage 1	12	9
Stage 2	23	17
2.2 litre engine:		
Front-side fixings (2)	10	7
Manifold-to-cylinder head (8 nuts and bolts)	40	30
Exhaust manifold gasket retaining studs*	10	7
Exhaust manifold-to-EGR cooler*	23	17
Exhaust system clamp nuts	45	33
Exhaust system flange nuts*	48	35

Torque wrench settings (continued)

	Nm	lbf ft
Fuel injection pump retaining bolts	23	17
Fuel injection pump sprocket retaining bolt:		
2.0 litre engine:		
Stage 1	25	19
Stage 2	75	55
2.2 litre engine	55	41
Fuel injection pump support bracket bolts	10	7
Fuel injector clamp bracket bolts: *		
2.0 litre engine:		
Stage 1	9	7
Stage 2	Loosen 45°	
Stage 3	6	4
Stage 4	Angle-tighten a further 180°	
2.2 litre engine:		
Stage 1	6	4
Stage 2	Angle-tighten a further 360°	
Fuel rail mounting bolts:		
2.0 litre engine	13	10
2.2 litre engine	25	19
Fuel rail pressure sensor:		
2.0 litre engine	10	7
2.2 litre engine	30	22
Fuel supply pipe clamp to camshaft cover bolt (2.2 litre engine)	10	7
Fuel supply pipe union nuts:		
2.0 litre engine:		
Stage 1	12	9
Stage 2	16	12
Stage 3	Angle-tighten a further 55°	
2.2 litre engine:		
Stage 1	15	11
Stage 2	30	22
Fuel tank strap bolts	35	26
Inlet housing/manifold-to-cylinder head:		
2.0 litre engine:		
Stage 1	10	7
Stage 2	23	17
2.2 litre engine	25	19
Inlet housing to throttle body bolts	10	7
Mass air flow sensor retaining bolts	5	4
Power control module plug mounting bracket retaining nut and bolts	10	7
Radiator support bracket bolts	10	7
Temperature and manifold absolute pressure sensor:		
2.0 litre engine	8	6
2.2 litre engine	5	4
Turbocharger oil return pipe nut(s)	10	7
Turbocharger oil supply pipe bolt (2.0 litre engine)	10	7
Turbocharger oil supply pipe banjo union bolt (2.2 litre engine)	20	15
Turbocharger retaining nuts*	23	17
Turbocharger shield retaining bolts	10	7
Turbocharger support bracket bolts	23	17

* Do not re-use

1 General information and precautions

General information

1 The fuel system consists of a fuel tank, fuel gauge sender unit mounted in the fuel tank, fuel filter, high-pressure fuel injection pump, fuel rail, fuel pipes, injectors, and powertrain control module (PCM).

2 Fuel is drawn from the tank via a transfer pump, then it passes through the fuel filter located in the engine compartment, where foreign matter and water are removed, then onto the high-pressure fuel pump.

3 The pump supplies fuel at very high pressure to a common rail (fuel rail) supplying all four injectors, which are then opened as signalled by the PCM. On reaching the high-pressure pump, the fuel is pressurised according to demand, and accumulates in the fuel rail, which acts as a fuel reservoir. The pressure in the rail is accurately maintained using a pressure sensor in the end of the rail and the pump's metering valve, with fuel return being controlled according to fuel temperature. The PCM determines the exact timing and duration of the injection period according to engine operating conditions. The four fuel injectors operate sequentially according to the firing order of the cylinders.

4 There are four pipes from the fuel rail (one for each of the injectors), and one from the fuel pump to the fuel rail. Each injector disperses the fuel evenly, and sprays fuel directly into the combustion chamber as its piston approaches TDC on the compression stroke.

5 The DuraTorq TDCi and EcoBlue engines feature a full electronic engine management system. An extensive array of sensors are fitted, which supply information on many different parameters to the PCM.

6 Cold-starting performance is automatically controlled by the PCM. Under cold start conditions, the cylinder head temperature (CHT) sensor informs the PCM on the engine temperature, this determines the preheat time. The glow plugs are located in the side of the cylinder head, one for each cylinder, and are electrically heated. A warning light illuminates when the ignition is switched on, showing that the glow plugs are in operation. When the light goes out, preheating is complete and the engine can be started.

7 The fuel system on common rail diesel engines is normally very reliable. Provided that clean fuel is used, that the specified maintenance is conscientiously carried out, and absolute cleanliness is observed during any maintenance or repair operation, no problems should be experienced. The injection pump and injectors may require overhaul after a high mileage has been covered, but this cannot be done on a DIY basis.

Precautions

⚠ **Warning: It is necessary to take certain precautions when working on the fuel system components, particularly the high-pressure side of the system. Before carrying out any operations on the fuel system, refer to the precautions given in 'Safety first!' at the beginning of this manual, and to any additional warning notes at the start of the relevant Sections. Also refer to the additional information contained in Section 2.**

⚠ **Warning: Do not operate the engine if any of air intake ducts are disconnected or the filter element is removed. Any debris entering the engine will cause severe damage to the turbocharger.**

Caution: To prevent damage to the turbocharger, do not race the engine immediately after start-up, especially if it is cold. Allow it to idle smoothly to give the oil a few seconds to circulate around the turbocharger bearings. Always allow the engine to return to idle speed before switching it off – do not blip the throttle and switch off, as this will leave the turbo spinning without lubrication.

Caution: Observe the recommended intervals for oil and filter changing, and use a reputable oil of the specified quality. Neglect of oil changing, or use of inferior oil, can cause carbon formation on the turbo shaft, leading to subsequent failure.

2 Common rail diesel injection system – special information

Warnings and precautions

1 It is essential to observe strict precautions when working on the fuel system components, particularly the high-pressure side of the

system. Before carrying out any operations on the fuel system, refer to the precautions given at the beginning of this manual, and to the following additional information.

Do not carry out any repair work on the high-pressure fuel system unless you are competent to do so, have all the necessary tools and equipment required, and are aware of the safety implications involved.

Before starting any repair work on the fuel system, wait at least 30 seconds after switching off the engine to allow the fuel circuit to return to atmospheric pressure. Never work on the high-pressure fuel system with the engine running.

Keep well clear of any possible source of fuel leakage, particularly when starting the engine after carrying out repair work. A leak in the system could cause an extremely high-pressure jet of fuel to escape, which could result in severe personal injury.

Never place your hands or any part of your body near to a leak in the high-pressure fuel system.

Do not use steam cleaning equipment or compressed air to clean the engine or any of the fuel system components.

Repair procedures and general information

2 Strict cleanliness must be observed at all times when working on any part of the fuel system. This applies to the working area in general, the person doing the work, and the components being worked on.

3 Before working on the fuel system components, they must be thoroughly cleaned with a suitable degreasing fluid. Cleanliness is particularly important when working on the fuel system connections at the following components:

a) *Fuel filter.*
b) *Fuel injection pump.*
c) *Fuel rail.*
d) *Fuel injectors.*
e) *High-pressure fuel pipes.*

4 After disconnecting any fuel pipes or components, the open union or orifice must be immediately sealed to prevent the entry of dirt or foreign material. Plastic plugs and caps in various sizes are available in packs from motor factors and accessory outlets, and are particularly suitable for this application **(see illustration)**. Fingers cut from disposable rubber gloves should be used to protect components such as fuel pipes, fuel injectors and wiring plugs, and can be secured in place using elastic bands. Suitable gloves of this type are available at no cost from most petrol station forecourts.

5 Whenever any of the high-pressure fuel pipes are disconnected or removed, a new pipe(s) must be obtained for refitting.

6 The torque wrench settings given in the Specifications must be strictly observed when tightening component mountings and connections. This is particularly important when tightening the high-pressure fuel pipe unions.

2.4 Typical plastic plug and cap set for sealing disconnected fuel pipes and components

3 Fuel pipes and fittings – general information and disconnection

1 Disconnect the cable from the negative battery terminal as described in Chapter 5 Section 4.

2 The fuel supply pipe connects the fuel pump in the fuel tank to the fuel rail on the engine.

3 Whenever you're working under the vehicle, be sure to inspect all fuel and evaporative emission pipes for leaks, kinks, dents and other damage. Always replace a damaged fuel pipe immediately.

4 If you find signs of dirt in the pipes during disassembly, disconnect all pipes and blow them out with compressed air. Inspect the fuel strainer on the fuel pump pick-up unit for damage and deterioration.

Steel tubing

5 It is critical that the fuel pipes be replaced with pipes of equivalent type and specification.

6 Some steel fuel pipes have threaded fittings. When loosening these fittings, hold the stationary fitting with a spanner while turning the union nut.

Plastic tubing

⚠ **Warning: When removing or installing plastic fuel tubing, be careful not to bend or twist it too much, which can damage it. Also, plastic fuel tubing is NOT heat resistant, so keep it away from excessive heat.**

7 When replacing fuel system plastic tubing, use only original equipment replacement plastic tubing.

Flexible hoses

8 When replacing fuel system flexible hoses, use original equipment replacements, or hose to the same specification.

9 Don't route fuel hoses (or metal pipes) within 100 mm of the exhaust system or within 280 mm of the catalytic converter. Make sure that no rubber hoses are installed directly against the vehicle, particularly in places where there is any vibration. If allowed to touch some vibrating part of the vehicle, a hose can easily become chafed and it might start leaking. A good rule of thumb is to maintain a minimum of 8.0 mm clearance around a hose (or metal pipe) to prevent contact with the vehicle underbody.

Disconnecting Fuel pipe Fittings

10 Typical fuel pipe fittings:

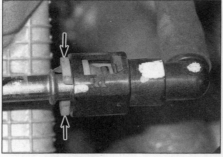

3.10a Two-tab type fitting; depress both tabs with your fingers, then pull the fuel pipe and the fitting apart

3.10b On this type of fitting, depress the two buttons on opposite sides of the fitting, then pull it off the fuel pipe

3.10c Threaded fuel pipe fitting; hold the stationary portion of the pipe or component (A) while loosening the union nut (B) with a flare-nut spanner

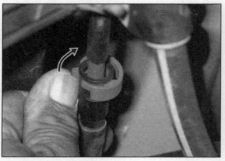

3.10d Plastic collar-type fitting; rotate the outer part of the fitting

3.10e Metal collar quick-connect fitting; pull the end of the retainer off the fuel pipe and disengage the other end from the female side of the fitting…

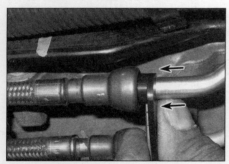

3.10f …insert a fuel pipe separator tool into the female side of the fitting, push it into the fitting and pull the fuel pipe off the pipe

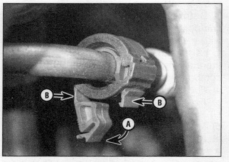

3.10g Some fittings are secured by lock tabs. Release the lock tab (A) and rotate it to the fully-opened position, squeeze the two smaller lock tabs (B)…

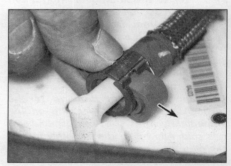

3.10h …then push the retainer out and pull the fuel pipe off the pipe

3.10i Spring-lock coupling; remove the safety cover, install a coupling release tool and close the tool around the coupling…

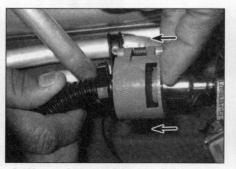

3.10j …push the tool into the fitting, then pull the two pipes apart

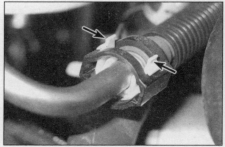

3.10k Hairpin clip type fitting: push the legs of the retainer clip together, then push the clip down all the way until it stops and pull the fuel pipe off the pipe

4 Fuel system – priming and bleeding

Note: *Refer to the warnings and precautions contained in Section 1 and Section 2 before proceeding.*

1 After disconnecting any part of the fuel system or running out of fuel, it is necessary to prime the fuel system and bleed off any air which may have entered the system components.

2 Turn the ignition key to the ON (II) position and wait 30 seconds before turning it to the OFF position (0). Repeat this twice more before starting the engine. If the 2.2 litre engine will not start, proceed as follows.

Note: *The following procedure should be carried out on the 2.2 litre engine only.*

3 It will be necessary to obtain the special Ford priming hose (kit No. 310-110A) or a suitable alternative hand-priming pump, together with various adaptors to enable the pump to be connected to the fuel lines. Hand-priming pump and adaptor kits are readily available from motor factors and tool supply outlets at moderate cost **(see illustration)**.

4 A valve is incorporated in the fuel return pipe to allow attachment of the hand-priming pump **(see illustration)**.

5 Using the adaptors supplied with the hand priming pump, connect the pump into the fuel return pipe. Ensure that the arrow on the pump is pointing towards the fuel tank.

6 Squeeze and release the pump to draw fuel from the tank, through the filter, through the high-pressure fuel pump and back to the tank via the fuel return line. Continue to squeeze and release the pump until fuel without air bubbles can be seen flowing through the clear plastic adaptor on the pump. Note that it may take some time before the fuel flow is completely free of air bubbles.

7 When no more air bubbles can be seen, operate the starter for a maximum of 10 seconds, waiting 30 seconds between each attempt. If the engine does not start after two attempts, continue operating the priming pump as there may still be air in the system.

4.3 Typical hand-priming pump

8 Once the engine starts and runs satisfactorily, switch it off, disconnect the priming pump and reconnect the fuel return pipe.

5 Air cleaner assembly and air ducts – removal and refitting

2.0 litre models

Removal

1 Unclip the wiring loom, undo the bolt and detach the pressure sensor from the left-hand side of the air cleaner assembly **(see illustration)**.

2 Depress the quick release button and disconnect the airflow pipe **(see illustration)**.

3 Slacken the clamp and disconnect the air outlet duct from the right-hand side of the air

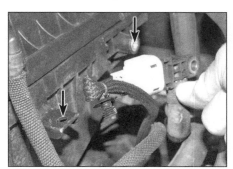

5.1 Undo the bolt and unclip the wiring loom

4.4 Hand-priming pump connection point

cleaner lid. Disconnect the wiring plug from the mass airflow sensor on the air cleaner lid and release the wiring retaining clip on the assembly. **(see illustration)**.

4 Remove the air intake duct **(see illustration)**.

5 Lift the front of the air cleaner assembly to release the front mountings, then slide the assembly forwards, detaching it from the rear support **(see illustrations)**.

Refitting

6 Refitting is the reverse of the removal procedure.

2.2 litre models

Removal

7 Slacken the clamp and disconnect the air outlet duct on the left side of the air cleaner assembly **(see illustration)**.

5.2 Disconnect the airflow pipe

5.3 Slacken the clamp, disconnect the air outlet duct, and disconnect the mass airflow sensor wiring plug

5.4 Detach the air intake duct

5.5a Lift the air cleaner off the mountings...

5.5b ...and fromt the rear support

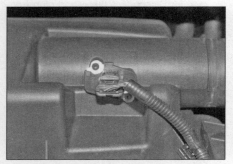

5.8 Disconnect the mass airflow sensor wiring plug

8 Disconnect the wiring plug from the mass airflow sensor at the front of the air cleaner cover **(see illustration)**. Unclip the wiring loom from the air cleaner housing.

5.10 Disengage the air cleaner from the mountings at the front and the support bar at the rear

7.4a Disconnect the wiring plug on top of the fuel tank...

5.7 Pull off the air outlet duct once the clamp has been slackened

5.9 Detach the air intake duct from the front panel

9 Remove the air intake duct from the right-hand side of the air cleaner assembly and front panel **(see illustration)**.
10 Pull the air cleaner assembly upwards

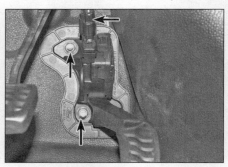

6.1 Disconnect the wiring plug, undo the nuts and remove the accelerator pedal assembly

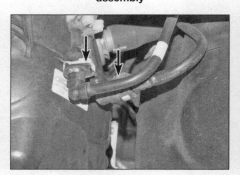

7.4b ...undo the supply and return hoses on the diesel additive tank...

to disengage the front mountings, then pull it forward to release it at the rear **(see illustration)**.

Refitting

11 Refitting is the reverse of the removal procedure.

6 Accelerator pedal – removal and refitting

Removal

1 Disconnect the wiring plug from the accelerator pedal position sensor, then unscrew the two nuts and remove the accelerator pedal assembly **(see illustration)**.

Refitting

2 Refitting is the reverse of the removal procedure, tightening the nuts to the specified torque. On completion, check the action of the pedal with the engine running.

7 Fuel tank – removal and refitting

Note: *Refer to the warnings and precautions contained in Section 1 and Section 2 before proceeding.*

Removal

1 Before removing the fuel tank, all fuel must be drained from the tank. Since a fuel tank drain plug is not provided, this procedure should be undertaken when the tank is nearly empty. The remaining fuel can then be syphoned or hand-pumped from the tank.
2 Disconnect the battery negative lead as described in Chapter 5 Section 4.
3 Firmly apply the handbrake, then jack up the front of the vehicle and support it securely on axle stands (see *Jacking and vehicle support*).
4 Disconnect the fuel tank sender/pump wiring plug, slacken the retaining clips and disconnect the fuel tank filler hose, the fuel supply and return hoses and unclip the ventilation hose **(see illustrations)**.

7.4c ...and disconnect the fuel tank filler hose. You will need to clamp the pipe if the tank is more than a third full

5 Support the weight of the fuel tank on a jack with interposed block of wood, making sure you can access all of the fuel tank support straps' retaining bolts.

6 Undo the fuel tank front support strap inner and outer retaining bolts and remove the three straps **(see illustration)**.

7 Carefully lower the tank and manoeuvre it out from under the vehicle.

8 Lower the tank to the ground and remove it from under the vehicle.

9 If the tank contains sediment or water, it may cleaned out with two or three rinses of clean diesel. Remove the fuel gauge sender unit as described in Section 8. Shake the tank vigorously and change the fuel as necessary to remove all contamination from the tank.

10 Any repairs to the fuel tank should be carried out by a professional. Do not under any circumstances attempt any form of DIY repair to a fuel tank.

Refitting

11 Refitting is the reverse of the removal procedure, noting the following points:

a) *When raising the tank back into position, take care to ensure that none of the fuel lines become trapped between the tank and vehicle body. Refit the retaining straps and tighten the bolts to the specified torque.*

b) *Ensure all pipes and hoses are correctly routed and all hose unions are securely joined.*

c) *On completion, refill the tank with a small*

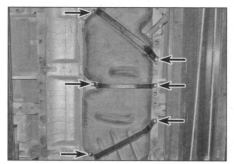

7.6 Undo the six bolts and remove the three support straps

amount of fuel and check for signs of leakage prior to taking the vehicle out on the road.

8 Fuel gauge sender, pump and control unit – removal and refitting

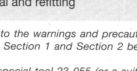

Note: *Refer to the warnings and precautions contained in Section 1 and Section 2 before proceeding.*

Note: *Ford special tool 23-055 (or a suitable alternative) will be required to unscrew the sender unit retaining ring.*

Removal

1 Remove the fuel tank as described in Section 7.

Sender and pump unit

2 Push the fuel pipes and collar in to release them, and disconnect the wiring plug from the top of the sender unit **(see illustration)**.

3 Using a suitable tool, unscrew and remove the sender unit retaining ring **(see illustration)**.

4 Lift the sender/pump unit out of the fuel tank, taking care not to damage the float or bend the float arm. Remove and discard the O-ring seal – a new seal will be required **(see illustration)**.

5 If required, release the wiring, depress the clips and slide the sender unit from the mounting **(see illustration)**.

6 If required, the sender unit can be checked by connecting a multimeter to the sender terminals, and measuring the resistance at full and zero deflection.

Sender unit resistance	Ohms
Full deflection (full tank)	10
Zero deflection (empty tank)	180

7 If the resistance measured differs greatly from these figures the sender unit may be defective.

Pump control unit

8 Disconnect the wiring plug from the top of the fuel tank and depress the clip to remove the pump control unit **(see illustrations)**.

Refitting

9 Refitting is the reverse of the removal procedure. Use a new O-ring seal (the old

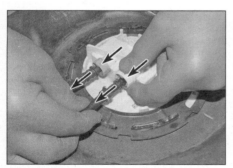

8.2 Push the collar towards to the pipe before pulling each out

8.3 Rotate the fuel gauge sender unit retaining ring anti-clockwise

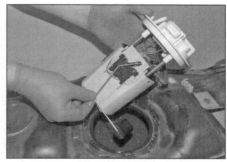

8.4 Lift the pump assembly out of the tank, taking care not to damage it

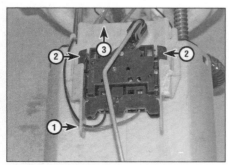

8.5 Release the wiring (1), depress the tabs (2) and slide the sender from the mounting (3)

8.8a Disconnect the wiring plug...

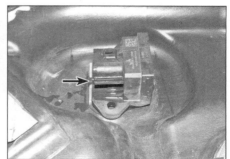

8.8b ...and depress the clip to remove the pump control unit

8.9 Use a new O-ring seal when refitting the sender unit

9.2 Diagnostic connector location

10 Injection system electronic components – removal and refitting

Crankshaft position sensor

Note: *Ford stipulate that a new crankshaft position sensor must be fitted if the fitted position of the original sensor is disturbed.*

1 Disconnect the battery negative terminal as described in Chapter 5 Section 4.

2 On the 2.0 litre engine, the sensor is located beside the sump and is accessed from below the vehicle. On the 2.2 litre engine it is in the top of the bellhousing at the rear.

3 Firmly apply the handbrake, then jack up the front of the vehicle and support it securely on axle stands (see *Jacking and vehicle support*).

2.0 litre engine

4 Place a drain container beneath the sensor before disconnecting the wiring plug and unscrewing the mounting bolt towards the front edge of the sump. Undo the second mounting bolt and withdraw the sensor. Be ready to collect escaping fluid **(see illustration)**.

5 Refitting is a reversal of removal, making sure the mounting bolts are tightened to the specified torque.

2.2 litre engine

6 Undo the nut and remove the shield above the sensor (where fitted), then disconnect the wiring plug, unscrew the mounting bolt and withdraw the sensor from the mounting bracket **(see illustrations)**.

7 Look down through the centre of the crankshaft position sensor mounting bracket and make sure that one of the trigger teeth on the flywheel is directly below the centre of the mounting bracket. If necessary turn the engine crankshaft, by means of the crankshaft pulley, to align the trigger tooth.

8 Insert the new sensor into the mounting bracket and push it down until the pip on the underside of the sensor rests on the flywheel trigger tooth. Refit the retaining bolt and tighten it securely.

9 Reconnect the sensor wiring plug, and where applicable, refit the shield.

one may have swollen, making refitting very difficult) and tighten the sender unit retaining ring until it is secure **(see illustration)**.

9 Diesel injection system – checking

Note: *Refer to the warnings and precautions contained in Section 1 and Section 2 before proceeding.*

1 If a fault appears in the diesel injection system, first ensure that all the system wiring plugs are securely connected and free of corrosion. Then ensure that the fault is not due to poor maintenance; ie, check that the air cleaner filter element is clean, the cylinder compression pressures are correct, the fuel filter has been drained (or changed) and the engine breather hoses are clear and undamaged.

2 If these checks fail to reveal the cause of the problem, the vehicle should be taken to a Ford dealer or suitably equipped repairer for testing. A diagnostic connector (located under the facia on the driver's side) is incorporated in the engine management system wiring harness, into which dedicated electronic test equipment can be plugged **(see illustration)**. To gain access, remove the right-hand lower trim panel by pulling it away from the facia to release the retaining clips.

3 The test equipment is capable of 'interrogating' the powertrain control module (PCM) electronically and accessing its internal fault log (reading fault codes).

4 Fault codes can only be extracted from the PCM using a dedicated fault code reader. Ford dealers have such readers, but they are inexpensive and available from other suppliers.

5 Using this equipment, faults can be pinpointed quickly and simply, even if their occurrence is intermittent. Testing all the system components individually in an attempt to locate the fault by elimination is a time-consuming operation that is unlikely to be fruitful (particularly if the fault occurs dynamically), and carries a high risk of damage to the PCM's internal components.

6 Experienced home mechanics equipped with a diesel tachometer or other diagnostic equipment may be able to check the engine idle speed; if found to be out of specification, the vehicle must be taken to a suitably equipped Ford dealer for assessment. The engine idle speed is not manually adjustable; incorrect test results indicate the need for maintenance (possibly, injector cleaning or recalibration) or a fault within the injection system.

7 If excessive smoking or knocking is evident, there may be a problem with the fuel injectors. Proprietary treatments are available which can be added to the fuel, in order to clean the injectors. Injectors deteriorate with prolonged use, however, and it is reasonable to expect them to need reconditioning or renewal after 60,000 miles or so. Accurate testing, overhaul and calibration of the injectors must be left to a specialist.

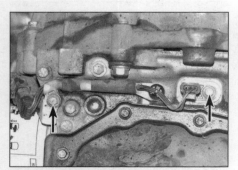

10.4 Undo the two mounting bolts and remove the crankshaft position sensor

10.6a Unscrew the mounting bolt...

10.6b ...and withdraw the crankshaft position sensor from the mounting bracket

10 Lower the vehicle to the ground and reconnect the battery.

Cylinder head temperature sensor

Note: *Ford stipulate that a new cylinder head temperature sensor must be fitted if the original sensor is disturbed.*

11 Disconnect the battery negative terminal as described in Chapter 5 Section 4.

12 The sensor is screwed into the left-hand (flywheel) end of the cylinder head, below and to the left of the vacuum pump **(see illustration)**.

13 Trace the wiring from the sensor and disconnect it at the plug on top of the engine.

14 The sensor can now be unscrewed and removed. Due to the length of the wiring it may prove difficult to gain access with a ring spanner. If necessary, cut the sensor wiring.

15 Refitting is a reversal of removal.

Temperature and manifold absolute pressure sensor

16 Disconnect the battery negative terminal as described in Chapter 5 Section 4.

17 On the 2.0 litre engine, to improve access, remove the air cleaner assembly as described in Section 5.

18 Disconnect the wiring plug from the sensor which is located on the inlet manifold **(see illustration)**.

19 Unscrew and remove the retaining screw, and withdraw the sensor from the manifold.

20 Refitting is a reversal of removal.

EGR valve

21 Refer to Chapter 4B Section 2.

Clutch pedal position switch

22 On models without engine stop-start the clutch pedal position switch is part of the clutch master cylinder assembly. Its wiring plug can be disconnected but it has to be replaced as part of that assembly. See Chapter 6 Section 3.

23 On models with engine stop-start, remove the lower facia trim panels beneath the steering wheel by pulling them away from the facia to release the retaining clips **(see illustration)**.

24 Disconnect the wiring plug from the clutch pedal position switch **(see illustration)**.

25 Rotate the clutch pedal position switch anti-clockwise by a quarter-turn and remove the switch from the pedal mounting bracket. Do not depress the clutch pedal during the removal or refitting procedure – the pedal must be 'at rest'.

26 To refit the switch, hold the clutch pedal in the raised ('rest') position and insert the clutch pedal position switch into the hole in the pedal mounting bracket. Rotate the switch clockwise to lock it in position. Reconnect the switch wiring plug.

27 Refit the facia trim panel, then reconnect the battery.

10.12 The cylinder head temperature sensor is located below the vacuum pump

10.23 Remove the facia lower trim panel by pulling it away to release the retaining clips

Brake stop-light switch/ pedal position switch

28 Disconnect the battery negative terminal as described in Chapter 5 Section 4.

29 Remove the facia right-hand lower trim panel by pulling it away from the facia to release the retaining clips **(see illustration 10.23)**.

30 Disconnect the wiring plug from the brake stop-light/position switch, located at the top of the brake pedal **(see illustration)**.

31 Rotate the switch clockwise by a quarter-turn and remove it from the pedal mounting bracket **(see illustration)**. Do not depress the brake pedal during the removal or refitting procedure – the pedal must be 'at rest'.

32 Hold the brake pedal in the raised position

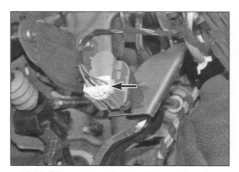

10.30 Disconnect the switch wiring plug

10.18 Disconnect the wiring plug from the temperature and manifold absolute pressure sensor

10.24 Disconnect the clutch pedal position switch wiring plug

and insert the stop-light switch and brake pedal position switch into the holes in the pedal mounting bracket. Push the switches down to depress the plungers, then turn the switches to lock them in position. Reconnect the wiring plugs to the switches.

33 Refit the facia trim panel, then reconnect the battery.

Accelerator pedal position sensor

34 The accelerator pedal sensor is integral with the pedal assembly, which is removed as described in Section 6.

Powertrain control module

Caution: The PCM is fragile. Take care not to drop it or subject it to any other kind of impact, and do not subject it to extremes of

10.31 Rotate the switch clockwise to remove it

10.39 Release the clip and lift the plastic shield

10.42 Pivot over the locking catches and disconnect the wiring plugs

10.40 Drill out the shear bolts and remove the shield

10.43 Undo the bolts/nut and remove the bracket

Mass airflow sensor

46 Disconnect the battery negative terminal as described in Chapter 5 Section 4.
47 Disconnect the wiring plug from the sensor which is located in the centre of the air cleaner cover **(see illustration)**.
48 Undo the retaining screws and remove the sensor.
49 Refitting is a reversal of removal.

Camshaft position sensor

50 Disconnect the battery negative terminal as described in Chapter 5 Section 4.
51 Remove the air cleaner assembly as described in Section 5.
52 Remove the engine oil filler shroud (where fitted) and pipe as one unit. Refit the oil filler cap.
53 Lift the plastic cover from the top of the engine.
54 Disconnect the wiring plug from the camshaft sensor **(see illustration)**.
55 Undo the sensor retaining bolt and remove the sensor.
56 Fit a new O-ring to the sensor, and lubricate it lightly with a general-purpose spray lubricant.
57 Refit the sensor, and tighten the retaining bolt securely. Reconnect the wiring plug, then refit the air cleaner assembly.
58 Reconnect the battery on completion.

Fuel pressure sensor

59 On the 2.2 litre engine, it is not possible to replace the sensor separately from the fuel rail. Ford advise that no attempt should be made to remove it. If the sensor is faulty, renew the fuel rail as described in Section 13.
60 On the 2.0 litre engine, remove the air cleaner assembly, as described in Section 5.
61 Release the clamps, undo the retaining bolts and remove the charge air pipe across the top of the engine.
62 Remove the sound insulation from the top of the engine.
63 Remove any dirt and debris around the sensor, then disconnect the wiring plug, and unscrew the sensor from the common fuel rail **(see illustration)**.
64 Refitting is a reversal of removal.

ABS wheel speed sensors

65 Refer to Chapter 9 Section 20 for removal and refitting details.

temperature, or allow it to get wet. Do not touch the PCM terminals because there is a chance that static electricity may damage the internal electronic components.
Note: *If renewing the powertrain control module, note that it must be reprogrammed for the specific model by a Ford dealer using Ford diagnostic equipment. Failure to do so will result in the PCM assuming its 'limited operating strategy' (LOS) settings, giving poor performance and economy.*
35 Disconnect the battery negative terminal as described in Chapter 5 Section 4.
36 Remove the left-hand headlight as described in Chapter 12 Section 11.
37 The powertrain control module is located on the left-hand side of the engine compartment, underneath the cooling system expansion tank.
38 Undo the mounting bolts and move the

coolant expansion tank upwards to improve access.
39 Release the clip at the rear and lift the plastic shield from above the PCM **(see illustration)**.
40 Drill out the shear bolts, and remove the PCM security shield, if fitted **(see illustration)**.
41 Remove the glow plug control module as described in Chapter 5 Section 14.
42 Disconnect the wiring plugs from the base of the PCM **(see illustration)**.
43 Undo the bolts/nut, remove the bracket, then remove the PCM **(see illustration)**.
44 Refitting is a reversal of removal, using new shear bolts to secure the security shield.

Glow plug control module

45 Removal and refitting of the glow plug control module is described in Chapter 5 Section 14.

10.47 Disconnect the mass airflow sensor wiring plug (2.0 litre engine shown)

10.54 Disconnect the camshaft position sensor wiring plug

10.63 Unscrew the sensor from the fuel rail

11.6 Remove the fuel pump cover

11.7a Disconnect the wiring plug from the fuel injection pump…

11.7b …disconnect the glow plug 1 and 2 wiring plugs and release the wiring loom from the clips on the metal bracket

11.8 Bracket retaining bolts

11.9 Tensioner retaining bolt

11.10 Undo the bolts and move the power steering pump (pipes removed for clarity)

---

11 Fuel injection pump – removal and refitting

Caution: Be careful not to allow dirt into the injection pump or injector pipes during this procedure.

Removal

Note: *Refer to the warnings and precautions contained in Sections 1 and 2 before proceeding.*
Note: *If a new injection pump is fitted, there is a possibility that the engine may not run properly (or even at all) until the powertrain control module (PCM) has been electronically reconfigured using Ford diagnostic equipment, or a compatible alternative.*

1 Disconnect the battery negative terminal as described in Chapter 5 Section 4.

2 Remove the air cleaner assembly and air intake duct as described in Section 5.

2.0 litre engines

3 Remove the auxiliary drivebelt as described in Chapter 1 Section 33.
4 Remove the starter motor as described in Chapter 5 Section 10.
5 Remove the alternator as described in Chapter 5 Section 7.
6 Remove the fuel injection pump cover **(see illustration)**.
7 Disconnect the wiring plug from the fuel injection pump and the wiring plugs from glow plugs nos 1 and 2. Release the two wiring loom clips **(see illustrations)**.
8 Undo the two bolts and remove the metal bracket above the fuel pump **(see illustration)**.
9 Undo the retaining Torx bolt and remove the auxiliary drivebelt tensioner **(see illustration)**.

10 Undo the 3 retaining bolts and move the power steering pump to one side **(see illustration)**. There's no need to disconnect the pipes.
11 Rotate the fuel pump sprocket access cover anticlockwise and remove it **(see illustration)**.
Note: *Seal all fuel pipes with blanking caps to prevent contaminants entering the system, and be prepared for fuel spillage.*
12 Undo the union and remove high pressure pipe, then depress the release buttons and disconnect the two low pressure pipes **(see illustration)**. Discard the high pressure pipe – a new one must be fitted.
13 Using a socket on the crankshaft pulley bolt, rotate the crankshaft clockwise until the mark on the fuel injection pump sprocket aligns with the corresponding mark on the crankshaft idler pulley sprocket **(see illustration)**.

11.11 Turn the sprocket cover anticlockwise and remove it

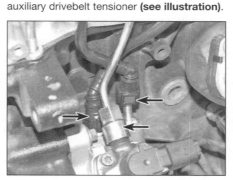

11.12 Disconnect the low pressure pipes and the high-pressure pipe

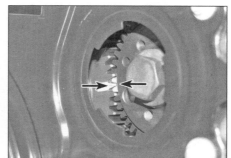

11.13 Rotate the crankshaft pulley bolt until the marks align

11.14 Insert the special tool to lock the crankshaft in place

11.15 Undo the four bolts from the timing cover

11.16a Screw in the special service tool bolts...

11.16b ...then remove the fuel injection pump sprocket retaining bolt

11.18 Tighten the special service tool bolts and nuts

11.19 Install the service tool

Caution: Do not rotate the crankshaft pulley anti-clockwise.

14 To prevent the crankshaft from rotating, install Ford special tool No.303-1643 (or equivalent) in the starter motor aperture. This tool engages with the flywheel ring gear, locking the crankshaft in place **(see illustration)**.

15 Remove the four retaining bolts from the timing cover **(see illustration)**.

16 Screw the three bolts from the special service tool 303-1635/3 through the holes in the fuel injection pump sprocket, then unscrew the sprocket bolt **(see illustrations)**. Discard the bolt – a new one must be fitted.

17 Remove special service tool 303-1643 from the starter motor aperture.

18 Install special service tool 303-1635 over the fuel injection pump sprocket. Tighten the

three retaining bolts, then tighten the inner nuts **(see illustration)**.

19 Install service tool 303-1635/2 in the aperture left by the sprocket bolt. Rotate it three times to secure it **(see illustration)**.

20 Undo the two retaining bolts from the rear of the fuel injection pump. Discard the bolts – new ones must be fitted.

21 Slowly rotate service tool 303-1635/2 clockwise and press the fuel injection pump from place **(see illustration)**.

Refitting

22 Installation is a reverse of removal, noting the following points:

a) *If refitting the same pump, fit a new seal and make sure the seal area is completely clean.*

b) *Ensure the key on the pump shaft aligns with the key way in the drive sprocket.*

c) *Fit and rotate service tool 303-1635/6 clockwise as the pump is installed.*

d) *Use new bolts to secure the pump.*

2.2 litre engines

23 Unscrew and remove the engine oil filler cap from the camshaft cover. Lift the hose(s) from their locations in the acoustic engine cover, then lift the cover off the camshaft cover. Refit the oil filler cap.

24 Before proceeding further, use a brush and suitable solvent to clean the area around the pump's fuel supply and return hose quick-release fittings. Also clean around the fuel supply pipe unions at the pump and fuel rail. It is essential that no dirt enters the pump. Allow time for any solvent used to dry.

25 Release the quick-release fittings and disconnect the fuel supply and return hoses at the fuel injection pump. Plug or suitably cover the open connections.

26 Disconnect the wiring plugs from the fuel temperature sensor and from the metering valve on the rear of the fuel injection pump. Suitably cover the plugs on the pump to prevent the entry of dirt and cleaning solvent.

27 Carefully loosen the fuel supply pipe union at the fuel pump and the one to the fuel rail, and undo the nut securing the retaining bracket **(see illustration)**.

28 Remove the fuel supply pipe and discard it – a new one must be used when refitting. Plug or suitably cover the open connections.

29 Undo the one injection pump retaining bolt and remove the pump from the cylinder

11.21 Turn the special tool clockwise and remove the pump

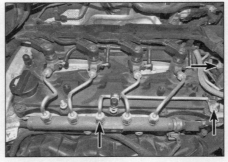

11.27 Carefully loosen the fuel supply pipe unions at the fuel injection pump and fuel rail

head and camshaft carrier. Recover the O-ring from the rear of the pump and discard it – a new one must be used when refitting.

30 If required, and if fitted, undo the bolt(s) and remove the injection pump adaptor plate from the cylinder head and camshaft carrier. Recover the O-ring from the adaptor plate and discard it – a new one must be used when refitting.

31 Remove the injection pump drive coupling from the end of the inlet camshaft.

Refitting

32 Refit the injection pump drive coupling to the inlet camshaft.

33 If removed, locate a new O-ring seal on the injection pump adaptor plate and place the adaptor plate in position on the cylinder head and camshaft carrier. Fit the retaining bolt and tighten to the specified torque.

34 With a new O-ring in place on the injection pump, engage the pump shaft with the drive coupling and position the pump on the cylinder head and camshaft carrier. Fit the retaining bolts and tighten them to the specified torque.

35 Place the new fuel supply pipe in position and screw on the union nuts at the fuel injection pump and fuel rail. When refitting, do not bend or strain the pipe, and make sure it is kept clean.

36 Tighten the fuel supply pipe unions at the fuel injection pump and fuel rail to their specified torque setting **(see illustration)**.

37 Refit the bolt securing the fuel supply pipe clamp to the camshaft cover bolt.

11.36 Tighten the fuel supply pipe unions at the fuel injection pump and fuel rail to the specified torque

38 Reconnect the wiring plugs to the fuel temperature sensor and metering valve on the rear of the pump.

39 Reconnect the fuel supply and return hoses to the fuel injection pump.

40 Refit the acoustic cover to the top of the engine.

41 Refit the air cleaner assembly and air outlet duct as described in Section 5.

42 Fit a new fuel filter as described in Chapter 1 Section 12.

43 Reconnect the battery negative terminal, then prime and bleed the fuel system as described in Section 4.

44 Once the engine starts, allow it to idle until it reaches normal operating temperature. As the engine warms-up, check for signs of leakage from the fuel unions.

12 Fuel injectors – removal and refitting

Note: *Refer to the warnings and precautions contained in Sections 1 and 2 before proceeding.* ***Caution: Be careful not to allow dirt into the injection system during this procedure.***

Removal

1 Disconnect the battery negative terminal as described in Chapter 5 Section 4.

2 Remove the air cleaner assembly as described in Section 5.

3 On the 2.0 litre engine, drain the cooling system as described in Section 1 Section 32.

4 Unscrew and remove the engine oil filler cap. On the 2.0 litre engine, undo the bolt and remove the oil filler shroud and attached pipe from the camshaft cover **(see illustration)**.

5 Unclip and move aside any pipes and hoses running across the top of the engine. Refit the oil filler cap to prevent any contamination **(see illustration)**.

6 On the 2.0 litre engine, slacken the retaining clamps, undo the two bolts and remove the turbocharger outlet hose assembly **(see illustrations)**.

7 Slacken the clamp, disconnect the wiring plug and remove the turbocharger inlet hose **(see illustration)**.

8 Remove the acoustic shield from the top of the engine **(see illustration)**.

9 Remove the alternator as described in Chapter 5 Section 7.

12.4 Engine oil filler shroud retaining bolt

12.5 Unclip and move any pipes running across the top of the engine

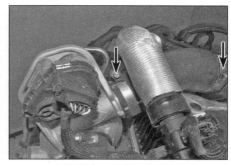
12.6a Release the clamps...

12.6b ...undo the bolts and remove the turbocharger outlet hose assembly

12.7 Slacken the clamp and disconnect the wiring plug

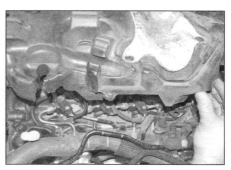
12.8 Lift the acoustic shield from the top of the engine

12.11a Slide out the grey locking tab (2.0 litre engines) and disconnect the wiring plugs

12.11b Lift the locking tab (2.2 litre engines)

12.11c Wiring loom clips on 2.0 litre engines

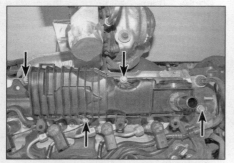

12.12 Oil separator retaining bolts

12.13 Push back the retaining clip and disconnect the fuel return hose from the top of each injector

12.14 Carefully loosen the fuel pipe unions at the fuel rail and pump

10 Before proceeding further, use a brush and suitable solvent to clean the area around the fuel supply pipe unions on the fuel rail and injectors.

11 Disconnect the wiring plugs from the fuel injectors **(see illustrations)**. Unclip the wiring loom as necessary.

12 On the 2.0 litre engine undo the four retaining bolts and lift off the oil separator assembly **(see illustration)**.

13 Disconnect the fuel return hose from each injector **(see illustration)**. Check the condition of the O-ring seal at each injector connection, if fitted – renew if necessary.

14 Carefully loosen the fuel pipe unions at the fuel rail and fuel pump **(see illustration)**. On 2.2 litre engines, use a second spanner to counter-hold the unions at the injectors. Once the unions are loose, wrap clean absorbent tissue or rag around them briefly, to soak away any dirt which may otherwise enter. If available, Ford recommend using a vacuum line to suck any dirt away from the opening union – do not use an airline, as this may blast dirt inwards, rather than cleaning it away.

15 Once the fuel pipe unions are loose, fully unscrew them and remove the fuel pipes. Discard the pipes – new ones should be used when refitting. Plug or suitably cover the open connections.

16 Undo the retaining bolt and lift the injector clamp bracket off each injector (2.0 litre engine) or each pair of injectors (2.2 litre engine) **(see illustrations)**. Discard the clamp brackets and their retaining bolts – new ones must be fitted.

17 Using an open-ended spanner, twist each injector from side-to-side to release them, then lift it from its location in the cylinder head **(see illustrations)**. On the 2.2 litre engine, fuel injectors that share a retaining clamp must be removed and installed in pairs. Discard the injectors sealing washers – new ones must be fitted.

12.16a Removing the bolts from each of the four brackets (2.0 litre engine)

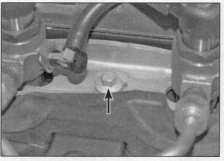

12.16b Injector bracket retaining bolt (2.2 litre engine)

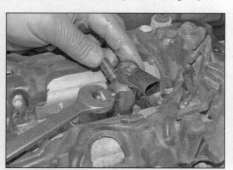

12.17a Using an open-ended spanner, twist each injector from side-to-side until it becomes free...

12.17b ...then lift it from its location in the cylinder head

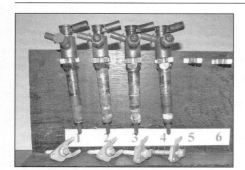

12.19 It is advisable to mount the injectors the right way up in a suitable stand after removal

12.20 Injector identification numbers are stamped on the top of the wiring plug location

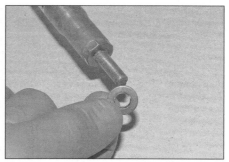

12.21 Fit a new sealing washer onto each injector

18 If fitted, using a flat-bladed screwdriver, remove the fuel injector seals from the camshaft cover and discard them – new ones must be fitted.

19 If the original injectors are to be refitted, it is absolutely essential that they are refitted in to their original positions. It is advisable to mount the injectors in a suitable stand, the right way up. This will help to prevent difficulties when priming and bleeding after refitting **(see illustration)**.

Refitting

20 If new injectors are being fitted, take a note of the identification numbers stamped on the top of the wiring plug location **(see illustration)**. These need to be uploaded into the PCM on completion of the work.

21 Fit a new sealing washer onto each injector **(see illustration)**. If necessary, use a suitable deep socket to push the sealing washers fully into place.

22 If fitting new injectors to the 2.0 engine, apply Ford grease FL-LL/HUJ-M1C227-AA to the sides (but not the end) of the injector tip.

23 Fit the injectors and clamp brackets into the cylinder head, then tighten the new clamp bracket bolts finger-tight only at this stage.

24 Working on one fuel injector at a time, remove the blanking plugs from the fuel pipe unions on the fuel rail and the relevant injector. Locate a new fuel pipe over the unions and screw on the union nuts. Take care not to cross-thread the nuts or strain the fuel pipes as they are fitted. Once the union nut threads have started, finger-tighten the nuts only at this stage, to the ends of the threads.

25 When all the fuel pipes are in place, tighten the injector clamp bracket retaining bolts to the specified torque and through the specified angle.

26 Tighten the fuel pipe union nuts to the specified torque using a torque wrench and crow's-foot adapter. On 2.2 litre engines, use a second spanner to counter-hold the unions at the injectors. Tighten all the disturbed union nuts in the same way.

27 Apply a thin coating of grease FL-LL to the O-ring seal, then refit the oil separator (2.0 litre engines).

28 If new injectors have been fitted, their

classification numbers must be programmed into the engine management PCM using dedicated diagnostic equipment. If this equipment is not available, entrust this task to a Ford dealer or suitably equipped repairer. Note that it should be possible to drive the vehicle, albeit with reduced performance/increased emissions, to a repairer for the numbers to be programmed.

29 The remainder of refitting is a reversal of removal.

30 On completion, fit a new fuel filter as described in Chapter 1 Section 12.

31 Reconnect the battery negative terminal, then prime and bleed the fuel system as described in Section 4.

32 Once the engine starts, allow it to idle until it reaches normal operating temperature. As the engine warms-up, check for signs of leakage from the fuel pipe unions.

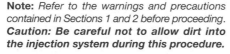

13 Fuel rail – removal and refitting

Note: *Refer to the warnings and precautions contained in Sections 1 and 2 before proceeding.*
Caution: Be careful not to allow dirt into the injection system during this procedure.

Removal

1 Disconnect the battery negative terminal as described in Chapter 5 Section 4.

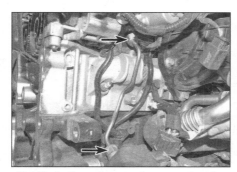

13.4 Undo the unions and remove the pipe from the fuel rail to the pump (2.0 litre engine shown)

2 Follow the fuel injector removal procedure as described in Section 12 until the fuel pipes connecting the fuel rail to the injectors have been removed.

3 Disconnect the wiring plug from the fuel rail.

4 Remove and discard the high pressure fuel pipe from the fuel rail to the fuel injector pump. On the 2.2 litre engine undo and remove any bolts securing the pipe to the camshaft cover **(see illustration 11.28)**. A new pipe must be used when refitting to both engines. Plug or suitably cover the open connections **(see illustration)**.

5 Where applicable, disconnect the fuel return hose union at the quick-release connector on the fuel rail.

6 Undo the retaining bolts and lift away the fuel rail **(see illustration)**. If necessary, move the wiring harness support bracket away to provide clearance for removal of the fuel rail.

Refitting

7 Offer the fuel rail into position, then refit and hand-tighten the retaining bolts.

8 Fit new fuel pipes to the fuel rail, injectors and fuel pump, leaving the union nuts hand-tight only at this stage. Do not bend or strain the pipes, and make sure they are kept clean.

9 Tighten the fuel rail mounting bolts to the specified torque.

10 With all the fuel injection pipes in place,

13.6 Fuel rail retaining bolts

fully tighten the union nuts to the specified torque using a torque wrench and crow's-foot adapter **(see illustration)**.

11 The remainder of refitting is a reversal of removal.

12 On completion, fit a new fuel filter as described in Chapter 1 Section 12.

13 Reconnect the battery negative terminal, then prime and bleed the fuel system as described in Section 4.

14 Once the engine starts, allow it to idle until it reaches normal operating temperature. As the engine warms-up, check for signs of leakage from the fuel pipe unions.

14 Turbocharger – general information

1 The turbocharger increases engine efficiency by raising the pressure in the inlet manifold above atmospheric pressure. Instead of the air simply being sucked into the cylinders, it is forced in. Additional fuel is supplied by the injection pump, in proportion to the increased amount of air.

2 Energy for the operation of the turbocharger comes from the exhaust gas. The gas flows through a specially-shaped housing (the turbine housing) and in so doing, spins the turbine wheel. The turbine wheel is attached to a shaft, at the end of which is another vaned wheel, known as the compressor wheel. The compressor wheel spins in its own

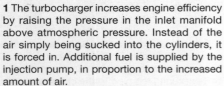

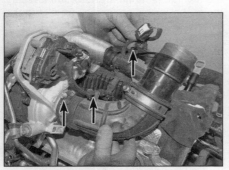

15.3 Release the clamps, disconnect the wiring plug and unclip the wiring loom

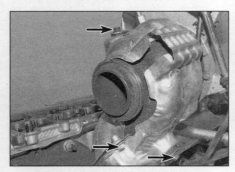

15.6 Turbocharger heat shield retaining bolts

13.10 Tighten the fuel pipe union nuts to the specified torque using a torque wrench and crow's-foot adapter

housing, and compresses the inducted air on the way to the intake manifold.

3 Between the turbocharger and the inlet manifold, the compressed air passes through an intercooler. The purpose of the intercooler is to remove from the inducted air some of the heat gained in being compressed. Because cooler air is denser, removal of this heat further increases engine efficiency.

4 The turbo shaft is pressure-lubricated by its own dedicated oil feed pipe. The shaft 'floats' on a cushion of oil. Oil is returned to the sump via a return pipe that connects to the sump.

5 The turbocharger is either of fixed vane type, or variable vane type according to engine type. On the fixed vane type there is a wastegate control valve, which opens a flap

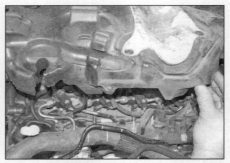

15.4 Remove the acoustic shield from the top of the engine

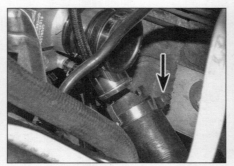

15.7 Slacken the retaining clip and disconnect the intercooler air duct from the turbocharger (2.2 engine shown)

at high engine speeds. On the variable vane type, as the engine speed increases the guide vanes in the turbine housing are progressively opened.

6 Refer to Chapter 1 for precautions to be observed with turbocharger operation.

15 Turbocharger – removal and refitting

Note: *The turbocharger should only be removed with the engine completely cool.*

Removal

1 Disconnect the battery negative terminal as described in Chapter 5 Section 4.

2 Remove the air cleaner assembly and air outlet duct as described in Section 5.

3 Remove the turbocharger-to-air-cleaner inlet pipe and disconnect the associated wiring plugs, clips and connections from the top of the engine **(see illustration)**.

4 Unscrew and remove the engine oil filler cap, shroud and filler pipe from the camshaft cover on the 2.0 litre engine. On the 2.2 engine remove the cap from the camshaft cover. Lift the front and rear coolant hoses from their locations in the engine cover, then lift the acoustic shield off the camshaft cover. Refit the oil filler cap **(see illustration)**.

5 Firmly apply the handbrake, then jack up the front of the vehicle and support it securely on axle stands (see *Jacking and vehicle support*).

6 Undo the three retaining bolts and remove the turbocharger heat shield on 2.0 litre engines **(see illustration)**.

7 Slacken the retaining clip and disconnect the intercooler air duct from the turbocharger **(see illustration)**.

8 Undo the bolt (two bolts on the 2.2 litre engine) and disconnect the oil return pipe flange from the cylinder block. Collect the flange gasket **(see illustration)**.

9 Undo the bolt(s) securing the turbocharger oil supply pipe to the cylinder block, and on 2.2 litre models release the pipe from the two retainers **(see illustration)**. Undo the oil supply pipe banjo union bolt and collect the two copper washers.

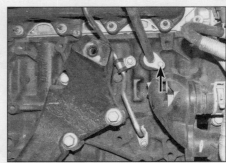

15.8 Undo the bolt and separate the oil return pipe

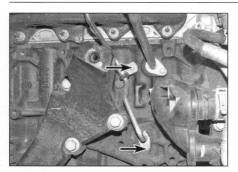

15.9 Disconnect the oil supply pipe from the block

10 On 2.2 models with air conditioning, remove the auxiliary drivebelt as described in Chapter 1 Section 33.

11 On 2.2 litre models models with air conditioning, disconnect the air conditioning compressor wiring plug. Undo the three mounting bolts and secure the compressor to one side using cable ties. Do not disconnect the refrigerant pipes.

12 On models with a variable vane turbocharger, disconnect the wiring plug from the vane actuator.

13 Remove the catalytic converter/particulate filter as described in Chapter 4B Section 3.

14 Undo the nuts securing the turbocharger to the exhaust manifold. Manoeuvre the turbocharger from place and recover the gasket. A new gasket will be required for refitting **(see illustration)**.

15 No further dismantling of the turbocharger is recommended. Interfering with the wastegate setting may lead to a reduction in performance, or could result in engine damage. No parts appear to be available separately for the turbocharger.

16 If on inspection there are any signs of internal oil contamination on the turbine or compressor wheels, this indicates failure of the turbocharger oil seals. Renewing these seals is a job best left to a turbocharger specialist. In the event of any problem with the turbocharger, one of these specialists will usually be able to rebuild a defective unit, or offer a rebuilt unit on an exchange basis, either of which will prove cheaper than a new unit.

Refitting

17 Refitting is a reversal of removal, noting the following points:

a) *Tighten all nuts/bolts to the specified torque, where given.*

b) *Renew the turbocharger mounting studs in the exhaust manifold and the turbocharger mounting nuts.*

c) *Use new gaskets on all disturbed joints.*

d) *Renew the oil supply pipe banjo union copper washers*

16 Throttle body/inlet manifold – removal and refitting

Removal

1 Disconnect the battery negative terminal as described in Chapter 5 Section 4.

2 Remove the air cleaner assembly and air outlet duct as described in Section 5.

3 Unscrew and remove the engine oil filler cap/the filler cap shroud and filler pipe, depending on model. Move the coolant hoses from their locations in the plastic engine cover (or above it), then lift the engine cover off the camshaft cover. Refit the oil filler cap.

4 On the 2.0 litre engine remove the exhaust gas recirculation outlet tube as described in Chapter 4B Section 2.

5 Release the clamp and disconnect the pipe

16.5a Release the clamp and disconnect the intercooler-to-throttle body pipe (2.0 litre engine)

15.14 Undo the nuts and remove the turbocharger

from the intercooler to the throttle body **(see illustrations)**.

6 Disconnect the wiring plugs from the manifold absolute pressure/temperature sensor and the throttle body motor, and release the wiring loom clips **(see illustration)**. Manoeuvre it clear of the housing.

7 On the 2.2 litre engine undo the bolt securing the oil dipstick guide tube to the cylinder block and remove the guide tube from the engine **(see illustration)**.

8 On the 2.2 litre engine remove the EGR valve as described in Chapter 4B Section 2.

2.0 litre engines

9 Undo the 3 retaining bolts and manoeuvre the inlet manifold from place **(see illustration)**.

10 If required, undo the retaining bolts and

16.5b Undo the clip and pull off the intercooler-to-throttle body pipe (2.2 litre engine)

16.6 Disconnect the wiring plugs and manoeuvre the wiring loom out of the way (2.0 litre engine shown)

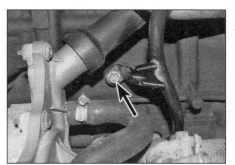

16.7 Undo the bolt securing the guide tube to the cylinder block and remove the tube from the engine

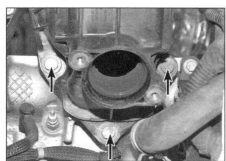

16.9 Undo the three bolts and remove the inlet manifold

16.10a Undo the bolts and remove the throttle body

16.10b Renew the throttle body seal

16.11 Undo the nine bolts securing the inlet manifold to the cylinder head and remove it, recovering the seals

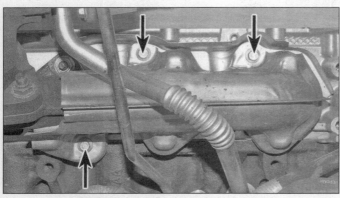

17.2 Exhaust manifold heat shield bolts

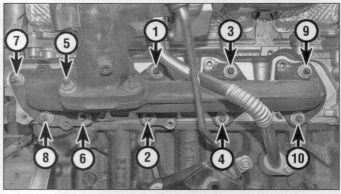

17.4 Manifold nuts tightening sequence

remove the throttle body. A new seal will be required for refitting **(see illustrations)**.

2.2 litre engines

11 Undo the nine bolts securing the inlet manifold to the cylinder head. Also undo the clip securing the intake pipe to the manifold and remove it. Remove the manifold and recover the rubber seals **(see illustration)**.

Refitting

12 Refitting is a reversal of removal, noting the following points:
a) *Tighten all nuts/bolts to the specified torque, where given.*
b) *Use new gaskets and/or sealing rings on all disturbed joints.*
c) *Where applicable, refit the EGR valve as described in Chapter 4B Section 2.*

---

17 Exhaust manifold –
     removal and refitting

2.0 litre engine

Removal

1 Remove the turbocharger as described in Section 15.

2 Remove the exhaust manifold heat shield, which may be fitted as two parts, either side of the turbocharger **(see illustration)**.

3 Working in reverse of the sequence shown **(see illustration 17.4)**, undo the nuts and

manoeuvre the manifold from place. Discard the nuts and gasket.

Refitting

4 Refit the manifold with a new gasket, then tighten the new retaining nuts to the specified torque, in the sequence shown **(see illustration)**.
5 Refitting is otherwise a reversal of removal, noting the following points:
a) *Renew all of the discarded items.*
b) *Tighten all nuts/bolts to the specified torque.*
c) *Refit the turbocharger as described in Section 15.*

2.2 litre engine

Removal

6 Remove the turbocharger as described in Section 15.
7 Remove the exhaust manifold heat shield, if fitted.
8 First, undo the 2 fixings securing the top side of the manifold to the heatshield, undo the 8 nuts and bolts securing the manifold to the cylinder head, then undo the 3 bolts securing the manifold to the EGR valve cooler **(see illustration)**.

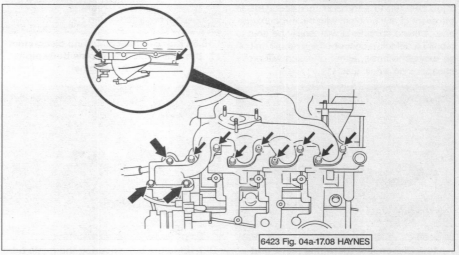

6423 Fig. 04a-17.08 HAYNES

17.8 Undo the 2 fixings on the top side of the manifold (inset), followed by the manifold-to-cylinder block nuts and bolts, and the manifold-to-EGR valve cooler bolts

9 Remove the manifold from the cylinder head and recover the EGR valve cooler gasket and the exhaust manifold heat shield, removing the gasket to manifold studs to do so **(see illustrations)**.

Refitting

10 Refitting is a reversal of removal, noting the following points:
a) *Renew the gaskets.*
b) *Tighten all nuts/bolts to the specified torque, where given.*
c) *Refit the turbocharger as described in Section 15.*

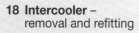
18 Intercooler –
removal and refitting

Removal

1 Disconnect the battery negative terminal as described in Chapter 5 Section 4.
2 Using suitable pieces of wire or cable ties, secure the radiator to the bonnet slam panel to prevent it dropping down when the lower support bracket is removed.
3 Firmly apply the handbrake, then jack up the front of the vehicle and support it securely on axle stands (see *Jacking and vehicle support*).
4 Undo the retaining screws along the front, remove the plastic rivet at the rear of the air deflector and remove it from under the intercooler **(see illustrations)**.
5 Slacken the retaining clips and disconnect the intake and outlet air ducts from the intercooler **(see illustration)**.
6 Unclip the radiator lower hose from the support bracket
7 Undo the two radiator support bracket bolts each side **(see illustration)**. Prise out the clips securing the top of the support to the plastic panel beneath the radiator. Note that new clips are likely to be required. Lower the radiator support bracket complete with intercooler and remove it from under the vehicle.
8 With the assembly on the bench, undo the two bolts each side and remove the intercooler from the radiator support bracket **(see illustration)**.

18.5 Slacken the clips and disconnect the intake and outlet air ducts at each end of the intercooler

17.9a Remove the manifold from the cylinder head...

Refitting

9 Refitting is a reversal of removal. Check the intake and outlet air ducts for signs of damage, and make sure that the clips are securely tightened. Check for leaks after taking the vehicle out for a short drive.

19 Exhaust system – general information and component renewal

⚠️ *Warning: Inspection and repair of exhaust system components should be done only after the system has cooled completely. This applies particularly to the catalytic converter, which runs at very high temperatures.*

18.4a Undo the retaining bolts at each end of the air deflector...

18.7 Undo the two bolts on each side securing the radiator support bracket to the underbody

17.9b ...and recover the exhaust manifold heat shield

General information

1 The exhaust system consists of three main sections; a front pipe incorporating a catalytic converter and a diesel particulate filter, an intermediate pipe incorporating the silencers, and a tailpipe.
2 The front pipe is fitted with a flexible section to allow for exhaust system movement and the system is suspended throughout its entire length by rubber mountings.
3 To remove a part of the system, first jack up the front or rear of the vehicle, and support it on axle stands (see *Jacking and vehicle support*). Alternatively, position the vehicle over an inspection pit, or on vehicle ramps.
4 Ford recommend that all nuts (such as flange joint nuts, clamp joint nuts, or converter-to-manifold nuts) are renewed on reassembly – given that they may be in less-

18.4b ...and the rear plastic rivet

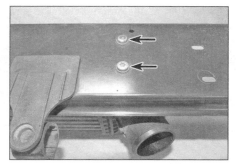
18.8 Undo the two bolts each side and remove the intercooler from the radiator support bracket

than-perfect condition as a result of corrosion, this seems a good idea, especially as it will make subsequent removal easier.

Component renewal

Note: *Refer to Chapter 4B Section 3 for details of catalytic converter/diesel particulate filter renewal.*

5 If any section of the exhaust is damaged or deteriorated, excessive noise and vibration will occur.

6 Carry out regular inspections of the exhaust system, to check security and condition. Look for any damaged or bent parts, open seams, holes, loose connections, excessive corrosion, or other defects which could allow exhaust fumes to enter the vehicle. Deteriorated sections of the exhaust system should be renewed.

7 If the exhaust system components are extremely corroded or rusted together, it may not be possible to separate them. In this case, simply cut off the old components with a hacksaw, and remove any remaining corroded pipe with a cold chisel. Be sure to wear safety glasses to protect your eyes, and wear gloves to protect your hands.

8 Here are some simple guidelines to follow when repairing the exhaust system:

a) *Work from the back to the front when removing exhaust system components.*
b) *Apply penetrating fluid to the flange nuts before unscrewing them.*
c) *Use new gaskets and rubber mountings when installing exhaust system components.*
d) *Apply anti-seize compound to the threads of all exhaust system studs during reassembly.*
e) *Be sure to allow sufficient clearance between newly installed parts and all points on the underbody, to avoid overheating the floorpan.*

Chapter 4 Part B
Emission control systems

Contents

Degrees of difficulty

Easy, suitable for novice with little experience	Fairly easy, suitable for beginner with some experience	Fairly difficult, suitable for competent DIY mechanic	Difficult, suitable for experienced DIY mechanic	Very difficult, suitable for expert DIY or professional

Specifications

Torque wrench settings

	Nm	lbf ft
Catalytic converter support bracket bolts	25	18
Catalytic converter-to-turbocharger clamp nut (2.0 litre engine)	9	7
Catalytic converter-to-turbocharger nuts (2.2 litre engine)*	48	35
Diesel additive reservoir retaining bolts	35	26
EGR cooler/valve retaining bolts (2.0 engine)*	10	7
EGR pipe retaining nuts/bolts	10	7
EGR valve-to-EGR cooler fixings:		
2.0 litre engine	10	7
2.2 litre engine	23	17
Exhaust manifold-to-EGR cooler (2.2 litre engine)*	23	17

* Use new nuts/bolts

1 General Information

1 All models are designed to meet strict emission requirements. The engines are fitted with a crankcase emission control system and a catalytic converter incorporating a diesel particulate filter to keep exhaust emissions to a minimum. An exhaust gas recirculation (EGR) system is also fitted to further decrease exhaust emissions.

2 The emission control systems function as follows.

Crankcase emission control

3 To reduce the release of unburned hydrocarbons from the crankcase into the atmosphere, the engine is sealed and the blow-by gases and oil vapour are drawn from inside the crankcase, through an oil separator, into the inlet tract to be burned by the engine during normal combustion.

4 Under all conditions the gases are forced out of the crankcase by the (relatively) higher crankcase pressure; if the engine is worn, the raised crankcase pressure (due to increased blow-by) will cause some of the flow to return under all manifold conditions.

5 The components of this system require no attention other than to check at regular intervals that the hose(s) are clear and undamaged.

Exhaust emission control

6 To minimise the level of exhaust pollutants released into the atmosphere, a catalytic converter/particulate filter is fitted in the exhaust system.

7 The catalytic converter consists of a canister containing a fine mesh impregnated with a catalyst material, over which the hot exhaust gases pass. The catalyst speeds up the oxidation of harmful carbon monoxide, unburned hydrocarbons and soot, effectively reducing the quantity of harmful products released into the atmosphere via the exhaust gases.

8 The diesel particulate filter contains a silicon carbide honeycomb block containing microscopic channels in which the exhaust gasses flow. As the gasses flow through the honeycomb channels, soot particles are deposited on the channel walls. To prevent clogging of the honeycomb channels, the soot particles are burned off at regular intervals during what is known as a 'regeneration phase'. Under the control of the engine management

system PCM, the injection characteristics are altered to raise the temperature of the exhaust gasses to approximately 600°C. At this temperature, the soot particles are effectively burned off the honeycomb walls as the exhaust gasses pass through. A differential pressure sensor and temperature sensors are used to inform the PCM of the condition of the particulate filter, and the temperature of the exhaust gasses during the regeneration phase. When the PCM detects that soot build-up is reducing the efficiency of the particulate filter, it will instigate the regeneration process. This occurs at regular intervals under certain driving conditions and will normally not be detected by the driver.

Exhaust gas recirculation (EGR) system

9 This system is designed to recirculate small quantities of exhaust gas into the inlet tract, and therefore into the combustion process. This process reduces the level of unburnt hydrocarbons present in the exhaust gas before it reaches the catalytic converter. The system is controlled by the powertrain control module (PCM), using the information from its various sensors, via the EGR valve.

4B•2 Emission control systems

2.3 Undo the bolts and discard the gasket

2.9 Disconnect the wiring plug from the top of the EGR valve

2.11 Undo the bolts securing the EGR outlet tube to the intake manifold

2.12a Undo the screws securing the EGR valve to the EGR cooler

2.12b Withdraw the EGR valve from the cooler and collect the gasket…

2.12c …and the EGR pipe-to-valve gasket

2 Exhaust Gas Recirculation (EGR) system – checking and component renewal

Checking

1 Checking of the system as a whole entails a close visual inspection of all hoses, pipes and connections for condition and security. Apart from this, any known or suspected faults should be attended to by a Ford dealer or suitably equipped specialist.

EGR valve renewal

2.0 litre models

2 Remove the EGR cooler and valve assembly as described in the following Section.
3 With the assembly on the bench, undo the seven bolts securing the cooler to the valve assembly and recover the gasket (see illustration).
4 Refitting is a reversal of removal, bearing in mind you will need a new gasket and that the retaining bolts should be tightened in a diagonal sequence to the specified torque settings.

2.2 litre models

5 Disconnect the battery negative terminal as described in Chapter 5 Section 4.
6 Remove the air cleaner assembly and air outlet duct as described in Chapter 4A Section 5.
7 Unscrew and remove the engine oil filler cap from the camshaft cover. Lift the front

and rear coolant hoses from their locations in the plastic engine cover, then lift the engine cover off the camshaft cover. Refit the oil filler cap.
8 Drain the cooling system as described in Chapter 1 Section 32. Alternatively, clamp the two coolant hoses leading to the EGR valve with suitable hose clamps, and be prepared for coolant spillage.
9 Disconnect the wiring plug from the EGR valve (see illustration).
10 Release the retaining clips and disconnect the two coolant hoses from the EGR valve.
11 Undo the two bolts securing the metal EGR outlet tube to the intake manifold (see illustration).
12 Undo the screws securing the EGR valve to the EGR cooler. Withdraw the EGR valve from the cooler and discard the gasket (see illustrations).

2.18 Undo the bolts and remove the cooler to intake manifold tube

13 Refitting is a reversal of removal, bearing in mind the following points:
a) Thoroughly clean the mating faces of the EGR valve, pipe and cooler and use a new gasket.
b) Tighten the retaining bolts to the specified torque.
c) Top-up the cooling system as described in 'Weekly checks'. If the coolant was drained, refill the cooling system as described in Chapter 1 Section 32.

EGR cooler renewal

14 Disconnect the battery negative terminal as described in Chapter 5 Section 4.
15 Remove the air cleaner assembly and air outlet duct as described in Chapter 4A Section 5.
16 On 2.0 litre engines remove the engine oil filler cap, the shroud and filler pipe from the camshaft cover. On 2.2 litre engines unscrew and remove the engine oil filler cap from the camshaft cover. Lift the front and rear coolant hoses from their locations in the plastic engine cover, then lift the engine cover off the camshaft cover. Refit the oil filler cap.
17 On 2.0 litre engines remove the thermostat as described in Chapter 3 Section 3.
18 On 2.0 litre engines remove the EGR outlet tube by undoing the two bolts at each end securing it to the intake manifold and the EGR cooler. Recover the bolts, gaskets and O-ring seal at the intake manifold end of the tube and discard them – new ones will be needed on refitting (see illustration).
19 If not already done, drain the cooling system as described in Chapter 1 Section 32.

2.20a Disconnect the coolant hose...

2.20b ...the wiring plug...

2.20c ...and the vacuum hose

Alternatively, clamp the coolant hoses leading to the EGR cooler with suitable hose clamps, and be prepared for coolant spillage.

20 On 2.0 litre engines release the retaining clip and disconnect the coolant hose from the top of the EGR cooler and disconnect the wiring plug at the top of the EGR valve. Also release the clip and disconnect the vacuum hose **(see illustrations)**.

21 On 2.2 litre engines release the retaining clips and disconnect the two coolant hoses from the EGR cooler.

22 Firmly apply the handbrake, then jack up the front of the vehicle and support it securely on axle stands (see *Jacking and vehicle support*).

23 On 2.0 litre engines, undo the one retaining bolt securing the cooler to the engine, then undo the six bolts securing the EGR valve and remove the gasket **(see illustrations)**. Remove the EGR cooler/valve assembly.

24 On 2.2 litre engines undo the three nuts securing the EGR cooler to the exhaust manifold.

25 On 2.2 litre engines, if not already done, undo the two bolts securing the EGR cooler to the EGR valve **(see illustration 2.12a)**.

26 On 2.2 litre engines undo the bolt securing the EGR cooler to the cylinder head. Withdraw the EGR cooler and collect the two gaskets.

27 Refitting is a reversal of removal, bearing in mind the following points:
Thoroughly clean the mating faces of the EGR valve, cooler and exhaust manifold and use new gaskets.

Tighten the retaining bolts to the specified torque.
Top-up the cooling system as described in Weekly checks. If the coolant was drained, refill the cooling system as described in Chapter 1 Section 32.

3 Catalytic converter/particulate filter – general information, precautions, removal and refitting

General information

Note: *The catalytic converter also incorporates the diesel particulate filter.*

1 The catalytic converter reduces harmful exhaust emissions by chemically converting the more poisonous gases to ones which (in theory at least) are less harmful. The chemical reaction is known as an 'oxidising' reaction, or one where oxygen is 'added'.

2 Inside the converter is a honeycomb structure, made of ceramic material and coated with the precious metals palladium, platinum and rhodium (the 'catalyst' which promotes the chemical reaction). The chemical reaction generates heat, which itself promotes the reaction – therefore, once the vehicle has been driven several miles, the body of the converter will be very hot.

3 The ceramic structure contained within the converter is understandably fragile, and will not withstand rough treatment. Since the converter runs at a high temperature, driving through deep standing water (in flood conditions, for example) is to be avoided,

since the thermal stresses imposed when plunging the hot converter into cold water may well cause the ceramic internals to fracture, resulting in a 'blocked' converter – a common cause of failure. A converter which has been damaged in this way can be checked by shaking it (do not strike it) – if a rattling noise is heard, this indicates probable failure.

Note: *Checking the operation of a catalytic converter requires expensive and sophisticated diagnostic equipment, starting with a high-quality exhaust gas analyser. If the level of CO in the exhaust gases is too high, a full check of the engine management system must be carried out to eliminate all other possibilities before the converter is suspected of being faulty. The vehicle should be taken to a Ford dealer for this work to be carried out using the correct diagnostic equipment. Do not waste time trying to test the system without such facilities.*

Precautions

4 The catalytic converter is a reliable and simple device which needs no maintenance in itself, but there are some facts of which an owner should be aware if the converter is to function properly for its full service life.

● DO NOT use fuel or engine oil additives – these may contain substances harmful to the catalytic converter.

● DO NOT continue to use the vehicle if the engine burns oil to the extent of leaving a visible trail of blue smoke.

● Remember that the catalytic converter operates at very high temperatures. DO NOT, therefore, park the vehicle in dry undergrowth or over long grass or piles of dead leaves after a long run.

● Remember that the catalytic converter is FRAGILE – do not strike it with tools during servicing work.

● The catalytic converter, used on a well-maintained and well-driven vehicle, should last for between 50,000 and 100,000 miles – if the converter is no longer effective it must be renewed.

Note: *Do not over bend the front exhaust flexible pipe as it is removed or damage will occur. Support the flexible pipe with a support wrap or a splint.*

2.23a Undo the bolt beneath the EGR cooler...

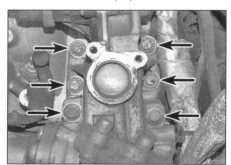

2.23b ...and the valve retaining bolts

5 Jack up the front of the vehicle (see *Jacking and vehicle support*).

6 Disconnect the battery negative terminal as described in Chapter 5 Section 4.

7 Remove the air cleaner assembly and air ducts as described in Chapter 4A Section 5.

2.0 litre engine

8 Disconnect the gearshift cables at the transmission end as described in Chapter 7 Section 4.

9 Noting their fitted locations, disconnect all relevant wiring plugs from catalytic converter/particulate filter.

10 Release the clamp securing the exhaust additive metal pipe to the top of the catalytic converter/particulate filter **(see illustration)**.

11 Undo the bolts securing the catalytic converter/particulate filter assembly mounting brackets to the left-hand and rear of the engine **(see illustrations)**.

Note: *The rear upper mounting fastener also secures the exhaust additive pipe bracket.*

12 Slacken the clamp securing the catalytic converter to the turbocharger **(see illustration)**.

13 Undo the two nuts and disconnect the flexible section of the exhaust pipe from the intermediate pipe **(see illustration)**.

14 With the help of an assistant, free the exhaust system from the rubber mountings and lower it from the vehicle. Recover and discard the flange gasket from the union between the exhaust and the particulate filter pipe **(see illustration)**.

Caution: Particular care must be taken not to damage wiring and sensors as the assembly is removed.

15 Refitting is a reversal of removal. Use new nuts, bolts and gaskets as necessary, and tighten all fasteners to the specified torque.

Note: *Exhaust sealant paste should not be used on any part of the exhaust system upstream of the catalytic converter (between the engine and the converter) – even if the sealant does not contain additives harmful to the converter, pieces of it may break off and foul the element, causing local overheating.*

2.2 litre engine

16 Undo the three nuts securing the top of the catalytic converter/particulate filter to the turbocharger.

17 Disconnect the oxygen sensor wiring plug.

18 Note their fitted positions, and disconnect the pressure pipes from the particulate filter. Trace the temperature sensor wiring back to its plug and disconnect it.

19 Undo the retaining nuts securing the catalytic converter to the intermediate pipe.

20 Suitably support the exhaust system and detach the front rubber mountings.

21 Where fitted, undo the retaining bolts and remove the catalytic converter support bracket, then remove the catalytic converter from under the vehicle. Collect the flange gaskets.

22 Refitting is a reversal of removal. Use new nuts, bolts and gaskets as necessary, and tighten all fasteners to the specified torque.

Note: *Exhaust sealant paste should not be used on any part of the exhaust system upstream of the catalytic converter (between the engine and the converter) – even if the sealant does not contain additives harmful to the converter, pieces of it may break off and foul the element, causing local overheating.*

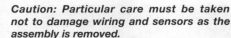

4 Diesel exhaust additive system components – removal and refitting

Caution: Always wear suitable gloves and eye protection when handling the additive fluid and immediately mop up/wash off spills with clean water.

1 The 2.0 litre engine uses a selective catalytic reduction system to reduce the amount of nitrogen oxides emitted from the exhaust system.

2 Firmly apply the handbrake, then jack up the front of the vehicle and support it securely on axle stands (see *Jacking and vehicle support*).

3 Remove the filler cap, and remove as much fluid as possible from the tank using a vacuum pump or similar. The angle of the filler pipe makes this difficult.

Pump

Removal

4 The pump is located beneath the additive

3.10 Undo the screw and release the clamp

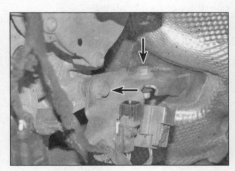

3.11a Undo the bolts at the rear of the engine...

3.11b ...and the bolt above the catalytic converter/particulate filter

3.12 Slacken the turbocharger-to-catalytic-converter securing clamp

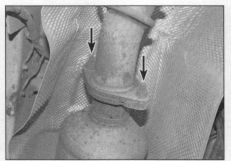

3.13 Remove the nuts securing the flexible exhaust section

3.14 Renew the gasket between the exhaust pipe flange and the particulate filter

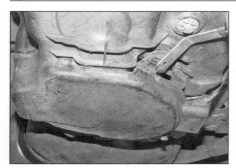

4.4 Prise out the clips and remove the pump shield

4.5a Slide out the locking catch and disconnect the wiring plug

4.5b Squeeze together the tabs and disconnect the pipe connector

4.6 Use a forked tool to remove the clips that retain the tank shield

4.8 Ensure the markings align when refitting the pump to the tank

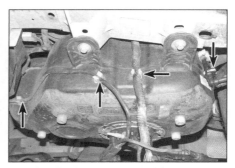

4.10 Unclip the hoses and wiring from the retainers on the tank

tank. Release the two clips and two fasteners, lever the hinges out and remove the pump shield (see illustration).

5 Slide out the grey locking catch and disconnect the wiring plug from the pump. The right-angled connector is released by squeezing the plastic tabs together and then pulling the pipe off – it may be difficult to remove. Be prepared for some fluid loss (see illustrations).

6 Prise out the plastic clips and remove the protective shield (see illustration).

7 Rotate the assembly anti-clockwise and lower the pump from the tank. Be prepared for fluid to leak out.

Refitting

8 Refitting is a reversal of removal, noting the alignment markings on the tank (see illustration). Use a new O-ring seal and refill the additive reservoir as described in the owner's handbook.

Reservoir

Note: *Access to the filler pipes will be improved if the fuel tank is removed as described in Chapter 4A Section 7.*

Removal

9 Disconnect the wiring plug and the hose from the pump, and remove the shield as described previously in this Section.

10 Unclip the hoses and wiring from the side of the reservoir and disconnect the two hoses at the rear of the reservoir that link it to the fuel tank. Be prepared for fluid loss (see illustration).

11 Disconnect the wiring plug at the upper front side of the reservoir (see illustration).

12 Disconnect the vent pipe that connects to the filler pipe (see illustration).

13 Support the reservoir with a suitable jack, undo the four retaining bolts – two of which hold the retaining bracket to the underside of the vehicle on the right-hand side – and lower the reservoir slightly (see illustration).

14 Disconnect the filler hose. Lowering the tank slightly will boost access but releasing the hose may still be difficult.

15 Unclip any wiring looms as necessary and lower the reservoir from place.

16 If necessary, the control module is located on top of the tank and can be removed by removing the wiring plug, undoing the retaining bolt and unclipping the module.

Refitting

17 Refitting is a reversal of removal. Refill the additive reservoir as described in the owner's handbook.

4.11 Disconnect the plug on the upper front side

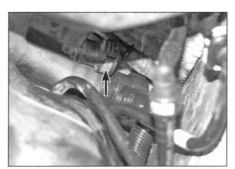

4.12 Depress the release button and disconnect the reservoir vent pipe

4.13 Undo the four bolts (two on bracket shown)

5 Diesel exhaust additive injector – removal and refitting

1 The injector is fitted to the catalytic converter. Refer to Section 3 for information on how to remove it.

Chapter 5
Starting and charging systems

Contents

Degrees of difficulty

Easy, suitable for novice with little experience	Fairly easy, suitable for beginner with some experience	Fairly difficult, suitable for competent DIY mechanic	Difficult, suitable for experienced DIY mechanic	Very difficult, suitable for expert DIY or professional

Specifications

General
Electrical system type . . . .   12 volt, negative-earth

Battery
Type   . . . .   Silver-calcium

Torque wrench settings

	Nm	lbf ft
Alternator idler pulley bolt	48	35
Alternator mounting bolts.	48	35
Glow plugs:		
Stage 1 (2.2 litre engines only)	8	6
Stage 2	13	10
Roadwheel nuts	200	148
Starter motor mounting bolts.	35	26
Starter motor wiring retaining nuts.	10	7
Thermostat mounting bracket bolt.	10	7

*Do not re-use

---

1 General information and precautions

General information

1 The engine electrical system consists mainly of the charging and starting systems, and the engine pre/post-heating system. Because of their engine-related functions, these components are covered separately from the body electrical devices such as the lights, instruments, etc (which are covered in Chapter 12).

2 The electrical system is of 12-volt negative earth type.

3 The battery is of the low-maintenance type, and is charged by the alternator, which is belt-driven from the crankshaft pulley.

4 The starter motor is of a pre-engaged type incorporating an integral solenoid. On starting, the solenoid moves the drive pinion into engagement with the flywheel ring gear before the starter motor is energised. Once the engine has started, a one-way clutch prevents the motor armature being driven by the engine until the pinion disengages.

5 Further details of the various systems are given in the relevant Sections of this Chapter. While some repair procedures are given, the usual course of action is to renew the component concerned.

Precautions

6 It is necessary to take extra care when working on the electrical system to avoid damage to semi-conductor devices (diodes and transistors), and to avoid the risk of personal injury. In addition to the precautions given in *Safety first!* at the beginning of this manual, observe the following when working on the system:

• *Always remove rings, watches, etc before working on the electrical system. Even with the battery disconnected, capacitive discharge could occur if a component's live terminal is earthed through a metal object. This could cause a shock or nasty burn.*

• *Do not reverse the battery connections. Components such as the alternator, electronic control units, or any other components having semi-conductor circuitry could be irreparably damaged.*

• *If the engine is being started using jump leads and a slave battery, connect the batteries positive-to-positive and negative-to-negative (see 'Jump starting'). This also applies when connecting a battery charger but in this case both of the battery terminals should first be disconnected.*

• *Never disconnect the battery terminals, the alternator, any electrical wiring or any test instruments when the engine is running.*

• *Do not allow the engine to turn the alternator when the alternator is not connected.*

• *Never test for alternator output by flashing the output lead to earth.*

• *Never use an ohmmeter of the type incorporating a hand-cranked generator for circuit or continuity testing.*
• *Always ensure that the battery negative lead is disconnected when working on the electrical system.*
• *Before using electric arc welding equipment on the vehicle, disconnect the battery, alternator and components such as the engine powertrain control module to protect them from the risk of damage.*

2 Electrical fault finding – general information

1 Refer to Chapter 13 Section 9.

3 Battery – testing and charging

Testing

1 The simplest way to test a battery is with a voltmeter (or multimeter set to voltage testing) – connect the voltmeter across the battery terminals, observing the correct polarity. The test is only accurate if the battery has not been subjected to any kind of charge for the previous six hours. If this is not the case, switch on the headlights for 30 seconds, then wait four to five minutes before testing the battery after switching off the headlights. All other electrical circuits must be switched off, so check that the doors and, where applicable, the tailgate are fully shut when making the test.
2 If the voltage reading is less than 12.0 volts, then the battery is less than healthy. Under 11.5 volts and the battery needs charging. However, as little as 11.0 volts will still usually be enough to start the engine, although a battery in this condition could not be relied on. A reading of around 10.0 volts suggests that one of the six battery cells has died – a common way for modern batteries to fail.
3 If the battery is to be charged, remove it from the vehicle (see Section 4) and charge it as described later in this Section.

Low maintenance battery

4 If the vehicle covers a small annual mileage, it is worthwhile checking the specific gravity of the electrolyte every three months to determine the state of charge of the battery. Use a hydrometer to make the check and compare the results with the tool maker's instructions (typically, there will be a colour-coded scale on hydrometers sold for battery testing).
5 If the battery condition is suspect, first check the specific gravity of electrolyte in each cell. A significant variation between any cells indicates loss of electrolyte or deterioration of the internal plates.
6 If the cell variation is satisfactory but the

battery is discharged, it should be charged as described later in this Section.

Maintenance-free battery

7 In cases where a 'sealed for life' maintenance-free battery is fitted, topping-up and testing of the electrolyte in each cell is not possible. The condition of the battery can therefore only be tested using a battery condition indicator or a voltmeter.

Charging

Note: *The following is intended as a guide only. Always refer to the manufacturer's recommendations (often printed on a label attached to the battery), and always disconnect both terminal leads (or preferably remove the battery) before charging.*

Low maintenance battery

8 It is advisable to remove the cell caps or covers if possible during charging, but note that the battery will be giving off potentially explosive hydrogen gas while it is being charged. Small amounts of acidic electrolyte may also escape as the battery nears full charge, so always wear eye protection and suitable gloves. Removing the cell caps will allow you to check whether all six cells are receiving charge – after a while, the electrolyte should start to bubble. If any cell does not bubble, this may indicate that it has failed, and the battery is no longer fit for use.
9 Charge the battery at a rate of 3.5 to 4 amps and continue to charge the battery at this rate until no further rise in specific gravity is noted over a four hour period.
10 Alternatively, a trickle charger charging at the rate of 1.5 amps can safely be used overnight.
11 Specially rapid 'boost' charges which are claimed to restore the power of the battery in 1 to 2 hours are not recommended, because they can cause serious damage to the battery plates through overheating.
12 While charging the battery, note that the temperature of the electrolyte should never exceed 38ºC.

Maintenance-free battery

13 This battery type takes considerably longer to fully recharge than the standard type, the time taken being dependent on the extent of discharge, but it will take anything up to three days.
14 A constant voltage type charger is required, to be set, when connected, to 13.9 to 14.9 volts with a charger current below 25 amps. Using this method, the battery should be usable within three hours, giving a voltage reading of 12.5 volts, but this is for a partially discharged battery and, as mentioned, full charging can take considerably longer.
15 If the battery is to be charged from a fully discharged state, have it recharged by your dealer or local automotive electrician, because the charge rate is higher and constant supervision during charging is necessary.

4 Battery – disconnection, removal and refitting

Disconnection

1 Numerous systems fitted to the vehicle require battery power to be available at all times, either to ensure their continued operation (such as the clock) or to maintain control unit memories which would be erased if the battery were to be disconnected. Whenever the battery is to be disconnected therefore, first note the following, to ensure that there are no unforeseen consequences of this action:
a) *First, on any vehicle with central locking, it is a wise precaution to remove the key from the ignition, and to keep it with you, so that it does not get locked in if the central locking should engage accidentally when the battery is reconnected.*
b) *Depending on vehicle and specification, the Ford anti-theft alarm system may be of the type which is automatically activated when the vehicle battery is disconnected and/or reconnected. To prevent the alarm sounding on models so equipped, switch the ignition on, then off, and disconnect the battery within15 seconds. If the alarm is activated when the battery is reconnected, deactivate the alarm by locking and unlocking one of the front doors.*
c) *The engine management powertrain control module (PCM) is of the 'self-learning' type, meaning that as it operates, it also monitors and stores the settings which give optimum engine performance under all operating conditions. When the battery is disconnected, these settings are lost and the PCM reverts to the base settings programmed into its memory at the factory. On restarting, this may lead to the engine running/idling roughly for a short while, until the PCM has re-learned the optimum settings. This process is best accomplished by taking the vehicle on a road test (for approximately 15 minutes), covering all engine speeds and loads, concentrating mainly in the 2500 to 3500 rpm region.*
d) *On all models, when reconnecting the battery after disconnection, switch on the ignition and wait 10 seconds to allow the electronic vehicle systems to stabilise and re-initialise.*

Removal

2 The battery is located inside the vehicle beneath the driver's seat. Two batteries may be fitted on certain models.
3 Raise the seat to its highest position, move the seat cushion as far forward as it will go

and tilt the seat backrest as far forward as possible **(see illustration)**.

4 Undo the two bolts, detach the cable clip and remove the retaining bracket from the top of the battery box, then remove the negative terminal cover, followed by the main battery cover **(see illustrations)**.

5 Disconnect the leads at the negative (–) terminal by slackening the retaining nut and pulling the clamp from the terminal with a twisting motion **(see illustration)**. Where two batteries are fitted, disconnect the lead at the negative (–) terminal on the second battery in the same way. Note that the battery negative (–) and positive (+) terminal connections are stamped on the battery case.

6 Lift the positive (+) terminal cover (where fitted), slacken the nut and pull the positive lead clamp from the battery terminal **(see illustration)**. Where two batteries are fitted, disconnect the lead at the positive (+) terminal on the second battery in the same way.

Caution: Take care – the battery is heavy.

7 Carefully lift the battery from its location and remove it from the vehicle. Make sure the battery is kept upright at all times.

Refitting

Note: *As a precaution, before refitting the battery check that all doors are unlocked.*

8 Refitting is a reversal of removal, but smear petroleum jelly on the terminals after reconnecting the leads to reduce corrosion, and always reconnect the positive lead(s) first, followed by the negative lead(s).

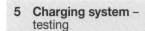

5 Charging system – testing

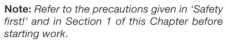

Note: *Refer to the precautions given in 'Safety first!' and in Section 1 of this Chapter before starting work.*

1 If a malfunction occurs in the charging circuit, don't automatically assume that the alternator is causing the problem. First check the following items:

a) *Check the tension and condition of the auxiliary drivebelt (see Chapter 1 Section 8) – renew it if it is worn or deteriorated (Chapter 1 Section 33).*

b) *Ensure the alternator mounting bolts are tight.*

c) *Inspect the alternator wiring harness and the electrical connections at the alternator; they must be in good condition and tight.*

d) *Check the large main fuses in the engine compartment fuse/relay box (see Chapter 12 Section 3). If any have blown, determine the cause, repair the circuit and renew the fuse (the engine won't start and/ or the accessories won't work if the fuse is blown).*

e) *Start the engine and check the alternator for abnormal noises – for example, a shrieking or squealing sound may indicate a badly worn bearing or bush.*

f) *Make sure the battery is fully charged – one bad cell in a battery can cause overcharging by the alternator.*

g) *Disconnect the battery leads (negative first, then positive). Inspect the battery posts and the lead clamps for corrosion. Clean them thoroughly if necessary (see 'Weekly checks'). Reconnect the lead to the positive terminal.*

h) *With the ignition and all accessories switched off, insert a test light between the battery negative post and the disconnected negative lead clamp:*

i) *If the test light does not come on, re-attach the clamp and proceed to the next step.*

j) *If the test light comes on, there is a short in the electrical system of the vehicle. The short must be repaired before the charging system can be checked.*

k) *To find the short, disconnect the alternator wiring harness. If the light goes out, the alternator is at fault. If the light stays on, remove each fuse until it goes out – this will tell you which component is short-circuited.*

2 Using a voltmeter, check the battery voltage with the engine off. It should be approximately 12.0 volts.

3 Start the engine and check the battery voltage again. Increase the engine speed until the voltmeter remains steady; it should now be approximately 13.5 to 14.8 volts.

4 Switch on as many electrical accessories (eg, the headlights and heater blower) as possible, and check that the alternator maintains the regulated voltage at around 13.05 to 14.8 volts. The voltage may drop and

4.3 Move the driver's seat up and fully forward

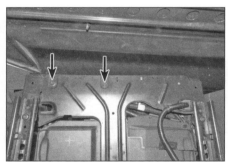

4.4a Undo the bolts, remove the retaining bracket...

4.4b ...the negative terminal cover...

4.4c ...and the battery main cover

4.5 Slacken the nut and pull the negative (–) lead clamp from the battery terminal

4.6 Slacken the nut and pull the positive lead clamp from the battery terminal

then come back up; it may also be necessary to increase engine speed slightly, even if the charging system is working properly.

5 If the regulated voltage is not as stated, the fault may be due to worn brushes, weak brush springs, a faulty voltage regulator, a faulty diode, a severed phase winding, or worn or damaged slip rings. The alternator should be renewed or taken to a dealer or auto electrician for testing and repair.

6 Auxiliary drivebelt – removal and refitting

1 Refer to Chapter 1 Section 33.

7 Alternator – removal and refitting

Removal

1 Disconnect the battery negative terminal as described in
Section 4.

2 Firmly apply the handbrake, then jack up the front of the vehicle and support it securely on axle stands (see *Jacking and vehicle support*).

3 To improve access on 2.0 litre engines, remove the right-hand headlight assembly as described in Chapter 12 Section 11, then

unclip and remove the air intake pipe from the front panel to the air cleaner housing.

4 On the 2.0 litre engine, release the clamps, undo the mounting bracket bolt and remove the air pipe from the intercooler to the throttle body **(see illustration)**.

5 Remove the auxiliary drivebelt(s) as described in Chapter 1 Section 33.

2.0 litre engines

6 Slide the power steering fluid reservoir upwards from its' mountings, and move it to one side.

7 Undo the retaining bolt and move the electric coolant pump and bracket to one side **(see illustration)**.

All engines

8 Disconnect the wiring plug from the alternator **(see illustrations)**.

9 Remove the plastic cover from the terminal stud, then undo the retaining nut and disconnect the wiring **(see illustration)**.

10 Slacken the mounting bolts, then tap the heads of the bolts lightly with a soft-faced hammer to release the adjusting sleeves. Completely, unscrew the mounting bolts and withdraw the alternator **(see illustration)**.

11 On 2.0 litre engines, if required, undo the retaining bolt and remove the alternator idler pulley.

Refitting

12 Refitting is a reversal of removal.

8 Alternator – testing and overhaul

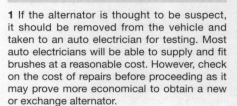

1 If the alternator is thought to be suspect, it should be removed from the vehicle and taken to an auto electrician for testing. Most auto electricians will be able to supply and fit brushes at a reasonable cost. However, check on the cost of repairs before proceeding as it may prove more economical to obtain a new or exchange alternator.

9 Starting system – testing

Note: *Refer to the precautions given in 'Safety first!' and in Section 1 of this Chapter before starting work.*

1 If the starter motor fails to operate during the normal starting procedure, the possible causes are as follows:

a) *The engine immobiliser is faulty.*
b) *The battery is faulty.*
c) *The electrical connections between the switch, solenoid, battery and starter motor are somewhere failing to pass the necessary current from the battery through the starter to earth.*
d) *The solenoid is faulty.*
e) *The starter motor is mechanically or electrically defective.*

7.4 Slacken the clamps, undo the bolt and remove the air pipe

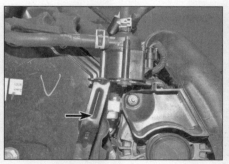

7.7 Move the pump and bracket to one side

7.8a Disconnect the wiring plug from the front of the alternator (2.0 litre engines)

7.8b Disconnect the wiring plug from the rear of the alternator (2.2 litre engines)

7.9 Undo the nut and disconnect the battery positive cable from the alternator

7.10 Alternator mounting bolts

2 To check the battery, switch on the headlights. If they dim after a few seconds, this indicates that the battery is discharged – recharge (see Section 3) or renew the battery. If the headlights glow brightly, operate the starter switch while watching the headlights. If they dim, then this indicates that current is reaching the starter motor, therefore the fault must lie in the starter motor. If the lights continue to glow brightly (and no clicking sound can be heard from the starter motor solenoid), this indicates that there is a fault in the circuit or solenoid – see the following paragraphs. If the starter motor turns slowly when operated, but the battery is in good condition, then this indicates either that the starter motor is faulty, or there is considerable resistance somewhere in the circuit.

3 If a fault in the circuit is suspected, disconnect the battery leads (including the earth connection to the body), the starter/solenoid wiring and the engine/transmission earth strap. Thoroughly clean the connections, and reconnect the leads and wiring. Use a voltmeter or test light to check that full battery voltage is available at the battery positive lead connection to the solenoid. Smear petroleum jelly around the battery terminals to prevent corrosion – corroded connections are among the most frequent causes of electrical system faults.

4 If the battery and all connections are in good condition, check the circuit by disconnecting the ignition switch supply wire from the solenoid terminal. Connect a voltmeter or test lamp between the wire end and a good earth (such as the battery negative terminal), and check that the wire is live when the ignition switch is turned to the 'start' position. If it is, then the circuit is sound – if not the circuit wiring can be checked as described in Chapter 12 Section 2.

5 The solenoid contacts can be checked by connecting a voltmeter or test light between the battery positive feed connection on the starter side of the solenoid and earth. When the ignition switch is turned to the 'start' position, there should be a reading or lighted bulb, as applicable. If there is no reading or lighted bulb, the solenoid is faulty.

6 If the circuit and solenoid are proved sound, the fault must lie in the starter motor. In this event, it may be possible to have the starter

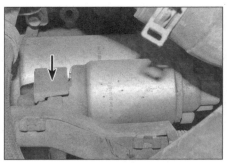
10.3a Remove the shield...

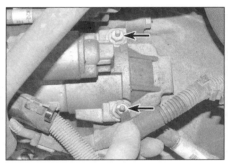
10.4 Undo the two nuts, and detach the wiring loom clip and earth lead

10.3b ...and undo the two nuts securing the wiring

10.6 The lower stud bolt secures the earth lead

motor overhauled by a specialist, but check on the cost of spares before proceeding, as it may prove more economical to obtain a new or exchange motor.

10 Starter motor – removal and refitting

Removal

1 Disconnect the battery negative terminal as described in Section 4.
2 Firmly apply the handbrake, then jack up the front of the vehicle and support it securely on axle stands (see Jacking and vehicle support).

2.0 litre engines

3 Remove the plastic shield on the right side of the starter motor solenoid and undo the nuts securing the wiring (see illustrations).
4 Undo the two retaining nuts, remove the wiring loom clip and earth lead from the lower nut, then withdraw the starter motor (see illustration).

2.2 litre engines

5 Remove the air cleaner assembly as described in Chapter 4A Section 5.
6 Lift the wiring harness retainer off the starter motor lower stud bolt, then undo the stud bolt and disconnect the earth lead (see illustration).
7 Slacken and remove the two retaining nuts and disconnect the wiring from the starter motor solenoid (see illustrations). Recover the washers under the nuts.
8 Unscrew the starter motor upper stud bolt, then manoeuvre the starter motor downwards and out from under the vehicle (see illustration).

10.7a Slacken and remove the two retaining nuts...

10.7b ...and disconnect the wiring from the starter motor solenoid

10.8 Manoeuvre the starter motor downwards and out from under the vehicle

13.14 Pull the connector off all four glow plugs (1 and 2 shown)

13.16 Unscrew the retaining nut (two of four arrowed) from each glow plug

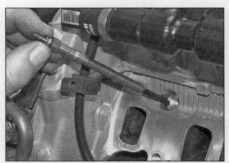

13.17 Remove the glow plug from the cylinder head

Refitting

9 Refitting is a reversal of removal, tightening the mounting bolts to the specified torque. Ensure all wiring is correctly routed and the retaining nuts are securely tightened.

11 Starter motor – testing and overhaul

1 If the starter motor is thought to be suspect, it should be removed from the vehicle and taken to an auto electrician for testing. Most auto electricians will be able to supply and fit brushes at a reasonable cost. However, check on the cost of repairs before proceeding as it may prove more economical to obtain a new or exchange motor.

12 Pre/post-heating system – general information

System description

1 Cold-starting performance is automatically controlled by the powertrain control module (PCM). Under cold start conditions, the cylinder head temperature (CHT) sensor informs the PCM of the engine temperature and this determines the pre/post-heat time.
2 Each cylinder of the engine is fitted with a glow plug screwed into it. The plugs are electrically operated before and during start-up when the engine is cold. Electrical feed to the glow plugs is controlled by the PCM via the glow plug relay.
3 A warning light in the instrument panel tells the driver that pre/post-heating is taking place. When the light goes out, the engine is ready to be started. The voltage supply to the glow plugs continues for several seconds after the light goes out. If no attempt is made to start, the PCM then cuts off the supply, in order to avoid draining the battery and overheating the glow plugs.
4 The glow plugs also provide a post-heating function, whereby the glow plugs remain switched on after the engine has started. The post-heating function only operates at below

2500 rpm, and below temperatures of 50°C. This helps the engine to run more smoothly during idling and reduces exhaust emissions through more efficient combustion just after starting.

Component locations

5 The pre/post-heating is controlled by the powertrain control module which is located in the engine compartment on the left-hand side. Refer to Chapter 4A Section 10 for removal and refitting details.
6 The cylinder head temperature sensor is screwed into the transmission end of the cylinder head. Refer to Chapter 4A Section 10 for removal and refitting details.

13 Glow plugs – testing, removal and refitting

Testing

1 If the system malfunctions, testing is ultimately by substitution of known good units, but some preliminary checks may be made as follows.
2 Connect a voltmeter or 12 volt test lamp between the glow plug supply cable and earth (engine or vehicle metal). Make sure that the live connection is kept clear of the engine and bodywork.
3 Have an assistant switch on the ignition, and check that voltage is applied to the glow plugs. Note the time for which the warning light is lit, and the total time for which voltage is applied before the system cuts out. Switch off the ignition.
4 If an ammeter of suitable range (0 to 50 amp) is available, connect it between the glow plug feed wire and the busbar (the wire that connects the four plugs together). During the pre-heating period, the ammeter should show a current draw of approximately 8 amps per working plug, ie, 32 amps if all four plugs are working. If one or more plugs appear not to be drawing current, remove the busbar and check each plug separately with a continuity tester or self-powered test light.
5 If there is no supply at all to the glow plugs, the relay or associated wiring may be at fault.

Otherwise this points to a defective cylinder head temperature sensor (see Chapter 4A Section 10), or to a problem with the powertrain control module.
6 To locate a defective glow plug, disconnect the main feed wire and the interconnecting busbar from the top of the glow plugs. Be careful not to drop the nuts and washers.
7 Use a continuity tester, or a 12 volt test lamp connected to the battery positive terminal, to check for continuity between each glow plug terminal and earth. The resistance of a glow plug in good condition is very low (less than 1 ohm), so if the test lamp does not light or the continuity tester shows a high resistance, the glow plug is certainly defective.
8 If an ammeter is available, the current draw of each glow plug can be checked. After an initial surge of 15 to 20 amps, each plug should draw 10 amps. Any plug which draws much more or less than this is probably defective.
9 As a final check, the glow plugs can be removed and inspected as described below.

Removal

10 Caution: If the pre/post-heating system has just been energised, or if the engine has been running, the glow plugs will be very hot.
11 Disconnect the battery negative terminal as described in Section.
12 On 2.0 litre engines remove the air cleaner assembly as described in Chapter 4A Section 5.
13 On 2.0 litre engines remove the alternator as described in Section 7.
14 On 2.0 litre engines remove the wiring plug from each of the four glow plugs **(see illustration)**.
15 On 2.2 litre engines remove the inlet manifold as described in Chapter 4A Section 16.
16 On 2.2 litre engines, if fitted, unscrew the nut and remove the washer securing each glow plug connector, then lift the wiring away from the plugs **(see illustration)**. Note that the wiring need not be removed completely for access to the plugs.
17 On all engines unscrew the glow plugs and remove them from the engine for inspection **(see illustration)**.

18 Inspect the glow plug stems for signs of damage. A badly burned or charred stem may be an indication of a faulty fuel injector – consult a diesel specialist for advice if necessary. Otherwise, if one plug is found to be faulty and the engine has completed a high mileage, it is probably worth renewing all four plugs as a set.

Refitting

19 Refitting is a reversal of removal, noting the following points:

a) *Apply a little anti-seize compound (or copper brake grease) to the glow plug threads.*

b) *Tighten the glow plugs to the specified torque.*

c) *Make sure when remaking the glow plug wiring connections that the contact surfaces are clean.*

d) *On 2.2 litre engines refit the inlet manifold as described in Chapter 4A Section 16.*

e) *On 2.0 litre engines refit the alternator as described in Section 7.*

f) *On 2.0 litre engines refit the air cleaner assembly as described in Chapter 4A Section 5.*

14.3 Release the clip and remove the plastic shield

14 Glow plug control module – removal and refitting

Removal

1 Disconnect the battery negative lead as described in Section 4.

2 Remove the left-hand headlight as described in Chapter 12 Section 11.

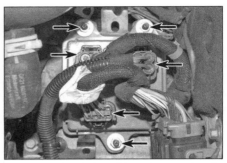

14.4 Disconnect the wiring plugs and undo the retaining nuts

3 Release the clip and remove the plastic shield above the control module **(see illustration)**.

4 Disconnect the wiring plugs, undo the 3 retaining nuts and remove the glow plug control module **(see illustration)**.

Refitting

5 Refitting is a reversal of removal.

Chapter 6
Clutch

Contents

Degrees of difficulty

Easy, suitable for novice with little experience	Fairly easy, suitable for beginner with some experience	Fairly difficult, suitable for competent DIY mechanic	Difficult, suitable for experienced DIY mechanic 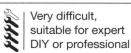	Very difficult, suitable for expert DIY or professional

Specifications

General

Type	Single dry plate, hydraulically operated with automatic adjustment
Disc diameter	258 mm
Lining thickness (approximate):	
New	9.0 mm
Minimum (worn)	6.0 mm

Torque wrench settings

	Nm	lbf ft
Clutch pressure plate-to-flywheel:		
Stage 1	6	4
Stage 2	25	18
Stage 3	30	22
Clutch master cylinder retaining bolts	9	7
Clutch release cylinder retaining bolts	11	8

1   General Information

1 The clutch consists of a friction disc, a pressure plate assembly, and the release mechanism; all of these components are contained in the large cast-aluminium alloy bellhousing, sandwiched between the engine and the transmission.

2 The friction disc is fitted between the engine flywheel and the clutch pressure plate, and is allowed to slide on the transmission input shaft splines.

3 The pressure plate assembly is bolted to the engine flywheel. When the engine is running, drive is transmitted from the crankshaft, via the flywheel, to the friction disc (these components being clamped securely together by the pressure plate assembly) and from the friction disc to the transmission input shaft.

4 To interrupt the drive, the pressure plate spring pressure must be relaxed. This is achieved using a hydraulic release mechanism which consists of a master cylinder, and a slave cylinder and release bearing, or a release cylinder. The release bearing is integral with the slave cylinder to form a single release cylinder assembly fitted concentrically around the transmission input shaft.

5 The clutch pedal is connected to the clutch master cylinder by a short pushrod. The master cylinder is mounted behind the clutch pedal and receives its hydraulic fluid supply from a separate chamber in the brake master cylinder reservoir. Depressing the clutch pedal moves the piston in the master cylinder forwards, so forcing hydraulic fluid through the clutch hydraulic pipe to the slave cylinder or release cylinder. In the externally mounted slave cylinder, the piston in the slave cylinder moves forward on the entry of the fluid and actuates the clutch release lever by means of a short pushrod. The release lever pivots on its mounting stud and presses the release bearing against the pressure plate spring fingers. This causes the springs to deform and releases the clamping force on the pressure plate. The piston in the release cylinder moves forward on the entry of the fluid and presses the integral release bearing directly against the pressure plate spring fingers.

6 On all models, the clutch operating mechanism is self-adjusting and no manual adjustment is required.

2 Clutch hydraulic system – bleeding

⚠️ **Warning: Hydraulic fluid is poisonous. Wash off immediately and thoroughly in the case of skin contact, and seek immediate medical advice if any fluid is swallowed or gets into the eyes. Certain types of hydraulic fluid are inflammable, and may ignite when allowed into contact with hot components. When servicing any hydraulic system, it is safest to assume that the fluid IS inflammable, and to take precautions against the risk of fire as though it is petrol that is being handled. Hydraulic fluid is also an effective paint stripper, and will attack plastics. If any is spilt, it should be washed off immediately, using copious quantities of clean water. When topping-up or renewing the fluid, always use the recommended type, and ensure that it comes from a freshly-opened sealed container.**

1 The clutch hydraulic system will not normally require bleeding, and this task should only be necessary when the system has been opened for repair work. However, as with the brake pedal, if the clutch pedal feels at all soggy or unresponsive in operation, this may indicate the need for bleeding.

2 The manufacturer recommends that the system should be bled by the 'back-bleeding' method using a hand pump kit – Ford tool 416-D001 (23-036A), or equivalent. This entails connecting the hand pump kit, containing fresh brake fluid, to the slave cylinder or release cylinder bleed screw. After syphoning some of the fluid out of the master cylinder reservoir, the bleed screw is opened, the pump is operated, and hydraulic fluid is delivered under pressure, backwards, to the reservoir.

3 In practice, this method would normally only be required if new hydraulic components have been fitted, or if the system has been completely drained of hydraulic fluid. If the system has only been disconnected to allow component removal and refitting procedures to be carried out, such as removal and refitting of the transmission (for example for clutch replacement) or engine removal and refitting,

2.9 Clutch release cylinder bleed screw

then it is quite likely that normal bleeding will be sufficient.

4 Our advice would therefore be as follows:

a) *If the hydraulic system has only been partially disconnected, and suitable precautions were taken to minimise fluid loss, try bleeding by the conventional method described in the relevant paragraphs below.*

b) *If conventional bleeding fails to produce a firm pedal on completion, it will be necessary to 'back-bleed' the system using the Ford hand-pump kit or suitable alternative equipment as described in the relevant paragraphs below.*

5 During the bleeding procedure, add only clean, unused hydraulic fluid of the recommended type; never re-use fluid that has already been bled from the system. Ensure that sufficient fluid is available before starting work.

6 If there is any possibility of incorrect fluid being already in the system, the hydraulic circuit must be flushed completely with uncontaminated fluid of the specified type (see *Lubricants and fluids*).

7 If hydraulic fluid has been lost from the system, or air has entered because of a leak, ensure that the fault is cured before continuing further.

8 The bleeding procedure varies slightly according to engine/transmission type. Proceed as described in the relevant sub-Section below.

Conventional method

9 The system bleed screw is located at the top of the transmission bellhousing (see illustration).

10 Obtain a clean jar, a suitable length of rubber or clear plastic tubing, which is a tight fit over the bleed screw on the clutch release cylinder, and a tin of the specified hydraulic fluid (see *Lubricants and fluids*). The help of an assistant will also be required.

11 Remove the filler cap from the brake master cylinder reservoir, and if necessary top-up the fluid. Keep the reservoir topped-up during subsequent operations.

12 Remove the bleed screw dust cap.

13 Connect one end of the bleed tube to the bleed screw, and insert the other end of the tube in the jar containing sufficient clean hydraulic fluid to keep the end of the tube submerged.

14 Open the bleed screw approximately half a turn.

15 Have your assistant depress the clutch pedal and then slowly release it. Continue this procedure until clean hydraulic fluid, free from air bubbles, emerges from the tube. Make sure that the brake master cylinder reservoir is checked frequently to ensure that the level does not drop too far, allowing air into the system. At the end of a downstroke, tighten the bleed screw.

16 Check the operation of the clutch pedal. After a few strokes, it should feel normal. Any sponginess would indicate air still present in the system.

17 On completion remove the bleed tube and

refit the dust cap. Top-up the master cylinder reservoir if necessary and refit the cap. Fluid expelled from the hydraulic system should now be discarded as it will be contaminated with moisture, air and dirt, making it unsuitable for further use.

'Back-bleeding' method

18 If conventional bleeding does not work, it may be necessary to 'back-bleed' the system using the hand pump kit described previously.

19 Syphon some of the fluid out of the master cylinder reservoir until the level is at the MIN mark.

20 Remove the bleed screw dust cap and connect the hose from the hand pump to the bleed screw. Fill the hand pump reservoir with new hydraulic fluid, open the bleed screw as previously described, and pump the fluid backwards through the system and up to the reservoir until it reaches its MAX mark.

21 On completion, tighten the bleed screw.

22 Remove the hand pump hose and refit the bleed screw dust cap. Top-up the master cylinder reservoir if necessary and refit the cap.

23 Depress the clutch pedal five to ten times to dispel any residual air still remaining in the system.

3 Clutch master cylinder – removal and refitting

Note: *Refer to the warning in Section 2 concerning the dangers of hydraulic fluid before proceeding.*

Removal

1 Before proceeding, anticipate some spillage of hydraulic (brake) fluid in the engine compartment. Place a good quantity of clean rags below the brake master cylinder hydraulic fluid reservoir and below the hydraulic hose connection on the clutch master cylinder.

2 Remove the clutch pedal position switch, if possible, as described in Chapter 4A Section 10.

Caution: If any brake fluid is spilt during this operation wash it away from the affected area with cold water.

3 Clamp the fluid supply hose from the hydraulic fluid reservoir (see illustration).

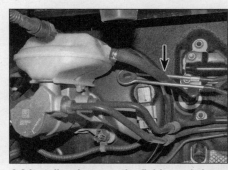
3.3 Install a clamp on the fluid supply hose from the hydraulic fluid reservoir

3.4 Pull out the retaining clip then pull the hydraulic pipe fitting out of the master cylinder

3.5 Remove the lower trim panel by pulling it away from the facia to release the retaining clips

3.6 Disconnect the clutch pedal position sensor wiring plug

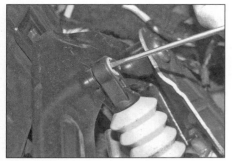

3.7 Extract the retaining clip and detach the master cylinder pushrod from the clutch pedal

3.8 Use a flat-bladed screwdriver to release the master cylinder hose clip

3.9 Undo the two bolts and disengage the two tabs securing the master cylinder to the pedal support bracket

4 Working in the engine bay, pull out the retaining clip, then pull the hydraulic pipe fitting out of the master cylinder **(see illustration)**. Again, plug or tape over the pipe end, to avoid losing fluid, and to prevent dirt entry.

5 From inside the cabin, remove the facia right-hand lower trim panel by pulling it away from the facia to release the retaining clips **(see illustration)**.

6 Working in the driver's footwell, disconnect the wiring plug from the clutch pedal position sensor **(see illustration)**.

7 Extract the retaining clip and detach the master cylinder pushrod from the clutch pedal **(see illustration)**.

8 Release the clip and detach the hose connected to the master cylinder. Be prepared for fluid to spill out **(see illustration)**.

9 Undo the two bolts securing the master cylinder to the pedal support bracket **(see illustration)**. Disengage the master cylinder locating tabs from the pedal support bracket and remove the master cylinder from the vehicle.

Refitting

10 Refitting is a reversal of removal, noting the following points:
a) Tighten the master cylinder retaining bolts to the specified torque.
b) Remove the hose clamp, and top-up the fluid level (see 'Weekly checks').
c) Refer to Section 2 and bleed the clutch hydraulic system.

4 Clutch release cylinder – removal, inspection and refitting

Note: *Refer to the warning in Section 2 concerning the dangers of hydraulic fluid before proceeding.*

Removal

1 The release bearing and slave cylinder are combined to form a release cylinder unit, which is located in the bellhousing of the transmission.

2 Remove the transmission as described in Chapter 2C Section 4.

3 Extract the retaining clip and withdraw the hydraulic pipe from the release cylinder and bellhousing **(see illustrations)**.

4 Undo the three mounting bolts, and withdraw the release cylinder from the transmission **(see illustration)**.

4.3a Extract the retaining clip...

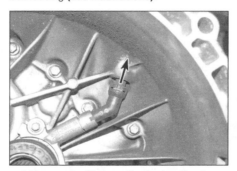

4.3b ...and withdraw the hydraulic pipe from the release cylinder and bellhousing

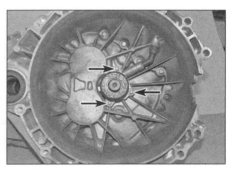

4.4 Release cylinder mounting bolts

6.3a Unscrew the clutch pressure plate retaining bolts...

6.3b ...using a home-made locking tool to hold the flywheel

Inspection

5 Check the release bearing for smoothness of operation and renew it if there is any sign of harshness or roughness as the bearing is spun. Do not attempt to dismantle, clean or lubricate the bearing.

6 Repair kits are not available from Ford. If a fault develops, the complete release cylinder must be renewed.

Refitting

7 Refitting is a reversal of the removal procedure, noting the following points:
a) Tighten the mounting bolts to the specified torque.
b) Refit the transmission as described in Chapter 2C Section 4.

5 Clutch pedal – removal and refitting

1 The clutch pedal is removed and refitted together with the brake pedal and pedal mounting bracket. Refer to the brake pedal removal and refitting procedures contained in Chapter 9 Section 11.

6 Clutch assembly – removal, inspection and refitting

⚠ **Warning: Dust created by clutch wear and deposited on the clutch components may contain**

6.12 Mount a large bolt and washer into a vice, then fit the pressure plate over it

hazardous material. DO NOT blow it out with compressed air, and do not inhale any of it. DO NOT use petrol or petroleum-based solvents to clean off the dust. Brake system cleaner or methylated spirit should be used to flush the dust into a suitable receptacle. After the clutch components are wiped clean with rags, dispose of the contaminated rags and cleaner in a sealed, marked container.

Removal

1 Unless the complete engine/transmission unit is to be removed from the vehicle and separated for major overhaul (see Chapter 2C Section 3, 4 or Chapter 2C Section 4), the clutch can be reached by removing the transmission as described in Chapter 7 Section 7.

2 Before disturbing the clutch, use a marker pen to mark the relationship of the pressure plate assembly to the flywheel.

3 Unscrew and remove the clutch pressure plate retaining bolts, working in a diagonal sequence, and slackening the bolts two turns at a time. The flywheel must be held stationary using a home-made locking tool **(see illustrations)** or a wide-bladed screwdriver, inserted in the teeth of the starter ring gear and resting against part of the cylinder block.

4 Ease the pressure plate off its locating dowels. Be prepared to catch the friction disc, which will drop out as the plate is removed. Note which way round the disc is fitted.

Inspection

5 The most common problem which occurs in the clutch is wear of the friction disc. However, all the clutch components should be inspected at this time, particularly if the engine has covered a high mileage. Unless the clutch components are known to be virtually new, it is worth renewing them all as a set (disc, pressure plate and release bearing/cylinder). Renewing a worn friction disc by itself is not always satisfactory, especially if the old disc was slipping and causing the pressure plate to overheat.

6 Examine the linings of the friction disc for wear, and the disc hub and rim for distortion, cracks, broken torsion springs, and worn splines. The surface of the friction linings

may be highly glazed, but as long as the friction material pattern can be clearly seen (and the thickness of the lining is within the specifications at the beginning of this Chapter) this is satisfactory. The disc must be renewed if the lining thickness has worn down to the minimum thickness given in the specifications.

7 If there is any sign of oil contamination, indicated by shiny black discoloration, the disc must be renewed, and the source of the contamination traced and rectified. This will be a leaking crankshaft oil seal or transmission input shaft oil seal. The renewal procedure for the former is given in Chapter 2A Section 15, Chapter 2B Section 15, as applicable. Renewal of the transmission input shaft oil seal is given in Chapter 7 Section 5.

8 Check the machined faces of the flywheel and pressure plate. If either is grooved or heavily scored, renewal is necessary. The pressure plate must also be renewed if any cracks are apparent, or if the diaphragm spring is damaged or its pressure suspect. Pay particular attention to the tips of the spring fingers, where the release bearing acts upon them.

9 With the transmission removed, it is also advisable to check the condition of the release bearing/release cylinder, as described in Section 4. Having got this far, it is almost certainly worth renewing it.

Refitting

10 The clutch pressure plate on certain engines is unusual, as it incorporates a pre-adjustment mechanism to compensate for wear in the friction disc. If the original pressure plate is to be refitted, this mechanism must be reset before refitting the pressure plate. A new plate may be supplied preset. Check if this is the case. If it is, this procedure can be ignored.

Original pressure plate refitment

11 Use a large diameter bolt (M14 at least) long enough to pass through the pressure plate, a matching nut, and several large diameter washers for this procedure. Mount the bolt head in the jaws of a sturdy bench vice, with one large washer fitted.

12 Offer the plate over the bolt, friction disc surface facing down, and locate it centrally over the bolt and washer or special tool – the washer should bear on the centre hub **(see illustration)**.

13 Fit several further large washers over the bolt, so that they bear on the ends of the spring fingers, then add the nut and tighten by hand to locate the washers **(see illustration)**.

14 The purpose of the procedure is to turn the plate's internal adjuster disc so that the small coil springs visible on the plate's outer surface are fully compressed. Tighten the nut just fitted until the adjuster disc is free to turn. Using a pair of thin-nosed, or circlip pliers, in

6.13 Fit large washers and a nut to the bolt and hand-tighten

6.14a Tighten the nut until the spring adjuster is free to turn...

6.14b ...then open up the jaws of suitable pliers to compress the springs

6.18 Transmission side 'GEARBOX-SIDE' marking on the clutch friction disc

6.22 Using a clutch alignment tool to centralise the clutch friction disc

6.26 Apply a little grease to the input shaft splines

one of the three windows in the top surface, open the jaws of the pliers to turn the adjuster disc anticlockwise, so that the springs are fully compressed **(see illustrations)**.

15 Hold the pliers in this position, then unscrew the centre nut. Once the nut is released, the adjuster disc will be gripped in position, and the pliers can be removed. Take the pressure plate from the vice – it is ready to fit.

New and original pressure plates

16 It is important that no oil or grease is allowed to come into contact with the friction material of the clutch disc or the pressure plate and flywheel faces. To ensure this, it is advisable to refit the clutch assembly with clean hands, and to wipe down the pressure plate and flywheel faces with a clean, dry rag before assembly begins.

17 Ford technicians use special tool 308-204 ('Aligner') for centralising the friction disc at this stage. The tool holds the disc centrally on the pressure plate and locates in the middle of

the diaphragm spring fingers. Aftermarket kits are also available.

18 Place the friction disc against the flywheel, ensuring that it is the right way round. It should be marked 'GEARBOX-SIDE', but if not, position it so that the raised hub with the cushion springs is facing away from the flywheel **(see illustration)**.

19 Place the clutch pressure plate over the dowels. Refit the retaining bolts, and tighten them finger-tight so that the friction disc is gripped lightly, but can still be moved.

20 If the Ford tool is not being used, the friction disc must now be centralised so that, when the engine and transmission are mated, the splines of the transmission input shaft will pass through the splines in the centre of the disc hub.

21 Centralisation can be carried out by inserting a round bar through the hole in the centre of the friction disc, so that the end of the bar rests in the spigot bearing in the rear end of the crankshaft. Move the bar sideways or up-and-down, to move the disc in whichever direction is necessary to achieve

centralisation. Centralisation can then be checked by removing the bar and viewing the friction disc hub in relation to the diaphragm spring fingers, and checking that the disc is central in relation to the outer edge of the pressure plate.

22 An alternative and more accurate method of centralisation is to use a commercially available clutch-alignment tool, obtainable from most accessory shops **(see illustration)**.

23 Once the clutch is centralised, progressively tighten the cover bolts in a diagonal sequence to the torque setting given in the Specifications.

24 Remove the centralisation tool.

25 Remove the flywheel locking tool.

26 Ensure that the input shaft splines, clutch disc splines and release bearing guide sleeve are clean. Apply a thin smear of high-melting-point grease to the input shaft splines **(see illustration)**. Ford recommend grease No. WSS-M1C273-A.

27 Refit the transmission to the engine as described in Chapter 7 Section 7.

Chapter 7
Manual transmission

Contents

Degrees of difficulty

Easy, suitable for novice with little experience	Fairly easy, suitable for beginner with some experience	Fairly difficult, suitable for competent DIY mechanic	Difficult, suitable for experienced DIY mechanic	Very difficult, suitable for expert DIY or professional

Specifications

General

Type . . . .   6 forward speeds and reverse. Synchromesh on all forward speeds and on reverse

Identification code VMT6

Lubrication

Lubricant type . . . .   See *Lubricants fluids and tyre pressures* on page 0•17
Lubricant capacity . . . .   See Chapter 1 Specifications

Torque wrench settings

	Nm	lbf ft
Engine/transmission rear mounting through-bolt: *		
M14x1.5	150	111
M14x2.0	175	129
Engine/transmission rear mounting-to-subframe*	133	98
Gearchange lever housing retaining bolts	9	7
Reversing light switch	20	15
Transmission-to-engine	40	30
Transmission oil drain plug	35	26
Transmission oil filler/level plug	35	26

Do not re-use

2.3 Prise out the locking slider from the selector cable end fitting

2.4a Angled adjustment slots in the gear lever housing (shown with shroud and gear lever removed)

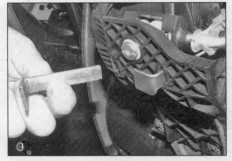

2.4b Insert the special tool or home-made alternative into the angled adjustment slots

1 General Information

1 The transmission is contained in a cast-aluminium alloy casing bolted to the engine's left-hand end, and consists of the gearbox and final drive differential.
2 Drive is transmitted from the crankshaft via the clutch to the input shaft, which has a splined extension to accept the clutch friction disc, and rotates in roller bearings at each end. From the input shaft, drive is transmitted to the output shaft, which also rotates in roller bearings at each end. From the output shaft, the drive is transmitted to the differential crown-wheel, which rotates with the differential case and planetary gears, thus driving the sun gears and driveshafts. The rotation of the planetary gears on their shaft allows the inner roadwheel to rotate at a slower speed than the outer roadwheel when the vehicle is cornering.
3 The input and output shafts are arranged side-by-side, parallel to the crankshaft and driveshafts, so that their gear pinion teeth are in constant mesh. In the neutral position, the output shaft gear pinions rotate freely, so that drive cannot be transmitted to the crownwheel.
4 Gear selection is via a facia-mounted lever and cable-operated selector linkage mechanism. The selector linkage causes the appropriate selector fork to move its

3.4 Separate the selector inner cable end fitting from the lever ball stud

respective synchro-sleeve along the shaft, to lock the gear pinion to the synchro-hub. Since the synchro-hubs are splined to the output shaft, this locks the pinion to the shaft, so that drive can be transmitted. To ensure that gearchanging can be made quickly and quietly, a synchromesh system is fitted to all gears, consisting of baulk rings and spring-loaded fingers, as well as the gear pinions and synchro-hubs. The synchromesh cones are formed on the mating faces of the baulk rings and gear pinions.
5 Because of the complexity, possible unavailability of parts and special tools necessary, internal repair procedures for the transmission are not recommended for the home mechanic. The bulk of the information in this Chapter is therefore devoted to removal and refitting procedures.

2 Gearchange cables – adjustment

Note: *Ford special tool 308-650 may be required to carry out the following adjustment. The tool locks the gear lever in the 3rd/4th gear position during adjustment. Before proceeding, either obtain the special tool or use the alternative described.*

 TOOL TiP *To make a gearchange cable adjustment tool, obtain a length of 3 mm thick steel strip, then cut it to a size of 65 mm x 13 mm*

1 Remove the facia lower panels beneath the steering wheel, the panel beneath the gear lever, the lower section of trim that joins with the centre console and the ventilation controls as described in Chapter 11 Section 24 and Chapter 3 Section 8.
2 Move the gear lever inside the vehicle to the 4th gear position and check that the transmission selector and shift levers are also in the 4th gear position.
3 Using a small screwdriver, disengage the locking slider from the selector cable end

fitting at the gear lever end of the cable **(see illustration)**.
4 With the gear lever still in the 4th gear position, insert the Ford special tool into the angled adjustment slots in the rear of the gear lever housing, at the base, to lock the lever in the 3rd/4th gear plane. If the Ford special tool is not available, a suitable alternative can easily be fabricated **(see illustrations and Tool Tip)**.
5 With the gear lever locked in the adjustment position and the transmission selector and shift levers in the 4th gear position, push the locking slider back into the cable end fitting.
6 Remove the special tool from the gear lever housing and check the operation of the gearchange mechanism.
7 Refit the facia lower centre panels as described in Chapter 11 Section 27.

3 Gearchange assembly – removal and refitting

Removal

1 Disconnect the battery negative terminal as described in Chapter 5 Section 4.
2 Remove the facia trim panels beneath the steering wheel and below the gearchange lever, which includes the shroud, as described in Chapter 11 Section 24.
3 Remove the heater controls panel as described in Chapter 3 Section 8.
Caution: Do not bend or kink the gearshift cables when disconnecting/reconnecting them.
4 Using a forked tool or pliers, lever the selector outer cable end fitting and slide the end fitting off the lever ball stud **(see illustration)**.
5 Pull back the retaining collar and detach the selector outer cable from the side of the gear lever housing **(see illustration)**.
6 Repeat paragraphs 4 and 5 to detach the inner shift cable from the gear lever housing.
7 Undo the four nuts and lift away the gear lever housing assembly **(see illustrations)**.

3.5 Pull back the retaining collar and detach the selector outer cable from the side of the gear lever housing

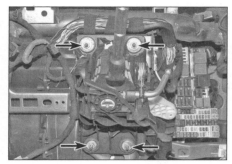

3.7a Undo the four retaining nuts...

3.7b ...and lift away the gear lever housing assembly

Refitting

8 Refitting is a reversal of removal. On completion, check the gearchange cable adjustment as described in Section 2.

4 Gearchange cables – removal and refitting

Removal

1 Disconnect the battery negative terminal as described in Chapter 5 Section 4.
2 Separate the selector inner cable end fitting from the transmission lever ball stud **(see illustration)**. Repeat this procedure with the shift cable.
3 Pull back the retaining collars and detach the selector and shift outer cables from the bracket on the transmission **(see illustration)**.
4 Disconnect the selector and shift cables from the gear lever as described in Section 3.
5 Remove the right-hand dashboard crossmember-to-floor mounting plate. First, undo the centre bottom facia panel's four screws and remove the panel. Then undo the four screws securing the crossmember floor mounting plate **(see illustrations)**.
6 Undo the two bolts securing the gearchange cable retaining plate to the floor **(see illustration)**. Note that it may

be necessary to cut through the sound insulation slightly to gain access to the right-hand bolt.
7 Note the routing and correct fitted position of the cables, then, with the help of an assistant, manoeuvre the cable assembly into the passenger compartment, then out of the vehicle.
Caution: Do not bend or kink the cables as damage may occur.

Refitting

8 Refitting is a reversal of removal, noting that the task will be made easier if you attach a pull cord to the selector lever cable. On completion, check the gearchange cable adjustment as described in Section 2.

4.2 Separate the selector inner cable end fitting from the the transmission lever

5 Oil seals – renewal

Differential oil seals

1 The differential oil seals are located at the sides of the transmission, where the driveshafts enter the transmission. If leakage at the seal is suspected, firmly apply the handbrake, then jack up the front of the vehicle and support it securely on axle stands (see *Jacking and vehicle support*). If the seal is leaking, oil will be found on the side of the transmission below the driveshaft.

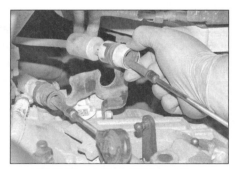

4.3 Pull back the retaining collars and detach the outer cables from the transmission bracket

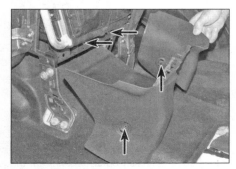

4.5a Undo the screw and remove the centre bottom facia panel...

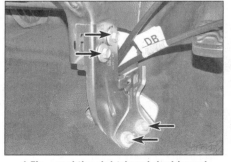

4.5b ...and the right-hand dashboard crossmember-to-floor mounting plate

4.6 Undo the two bolts securing the gearchange cable retaining plate to the floor

5.3 Prise out the oil seal with a suitable lever

5.6 Using a socket to drive in the new seal

5.10 Insert a self-tapping screw and pull the seal from its location

5.11 Drive the new seal squarely into place to its original depth

2 Remove the relevant driveshaft as described in Chapter 8 Section 2.
3 Using a large flat-bladed screwdriver or suitable lever, carefully prise the oil seal out of the transmission casing, taking care not to damage the casing **(see illustration)**.
4 Wipe clean the oil seal seating in the transmission casing.
5 Apply a small amount of general purpose grease to the new seal lips, then press it a little way into the casing by hand, making sure that it is square to its seating.
6 Using suitable tubing or a large socket, carefully drive the oil seal fully into position until it is flush with the casing edge **(see illustration)**.
7 Refit the driveshaft(s) as described in Chapter 8 Section 2.
8 Replenish the transmission oil as described in Section 9.

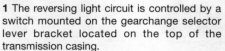

6.2 Disconnect the reversing light switch wiring plug

Input shaft oil seal

9 Remove the clutch release cylinder as described in Chapter 6 Section 4.
10 Note its fitted depth, then drill a small hole in the hard outer surface of the seal, insert a self-tapping screw, and use pliers to extract the seal **(see illustration)**.
11 Lubricate the new seal with grease and fit it to the bellhousing, lips pointing to the transmission side. Use a deep socket or suitable tubing to seat it (Ford recommends special service tool 307-032A and recommends temporarily using adhesive tape to cover the input shaft splines to prevent damaging the input shaft seal) **(see illustration)**.
12 Refit the clutch release cylinder as described in Chapter 6 Section 4.

6 Reversing light switch – removal and refitting

Removal

1 The reversing light circuit is controlled by a switch mounted on the gearchange selector lever bracket located on the top of the transmission casing.
2 Disconnect the wiring plug from the reversing light switch **(see illustration)**.
3 Unscrew the switch from the selector lever bracket on the transmission.

Refitting

4 Refitting is a reversal of the removal procedure. Tighten the switch to the specified torque.

7 Transmission – removal and refitting

Note: *Read through this procedure before starting work to see what is involved, particularly in terms of lifting equipment. Depending on the facilities available, the home mechanic may prefer to remove the engine and transmission together, then separate them on the bench, as described in Chapter 2C.*

Removal

1 Disconnect the battery negative terminal as described in Chapter 5 Section 4.
2 On 2.2 litre engines remove the air cleaner assembly as described in Chapter 4A Section 5.
3 Firmly apply the handbrake, then jack up the front of the vehicle and support it securely on axle stands (see *Jacking and vehicle support*). There must be sufficient clearance below the vehicle for the transmission to be lowered and removed. Remove both front roadwheels.
4 Drain the transmission oil as described in Section 9.
5 On 2.2 litre engines, lift off the heat shield, then disconnect the wiring plug from the crankshaft position sensor, located at the top of the bellhousing, to the rear.
6 On 2.2 litre engines undo the bolts and disconnect the catalytic converter from the turbo. Ensure that the flexible pipe is adequately supported.
7 Undo and discard the bolts securing the engine/transmission rear mounting to the front subframe and the through-bolt securing the mounting to the transmission as described in Chapter 2A Section 17 or Chapter 2B Section 17.
8 Remove the driveshafts as described in Chapter 8, Section 2.
9 Remove the starter motor as described in Chapter 5, Section 10.
10 Undo the two nuts and two bolts and remove the heater pipe retaining bracket from the transmission casing.
11 Disconnect the transmission ventilation hose from the transmission connector.
12 Disconnect the wiring from the reversing light switch on the top of the transmission.
13 Disconnect any remaining transmission wiring plugs or attachments, then detach the engine wiring harness from the support bracket.
14 Disconnect the gearchange cables as described in Section 4.
15 Pull back the retaining collars and detach the selector and shift outer cables from the bracket on the transmission **(see illustrations 4.2 and 4.3)**.
16 Using a small screwdriver, prise out

the retaining clip and disconnect the clutch hydraulic pipe from the transmission (use a suitable clamp on the hydraulic flexible hose to prevent leakage) **(see illustration)**. Cover both the union and the pipe ends to minimise fluid loss and prevent the entry of dirt into the hydraulic system.

Caution: While the hydraulic hose/pipe is disconnected, DO NOT depress the clutch pedal.

17 Release the clutch hydraulic pipe from the support bracket on the transmission.

18 Release the exhaust system rubber mountings from the underbody brackets and lower the system onto the rear axle.

19 The engine and transmission must now be supported, as the left-hand mounting must be disconnected. This can be done using a support bar which locates in the tops of the inner wing panels, and connected to the engine lifting eye at the left-hand end of the cylinder head – proprietary engine support bars are available from tool outlets.

20 If a support bar is not available, an engine hoist should be used. With an engine hoist, the engine/transmission can be manoeuvred more easily and safely; balancing the engine on a jack is not recommended.

21 Support the transmission with a trolley jack from below, then remove the engine/transmission left-hand mounting as described in Chapter 2A Section 17 or Chapter 2B Section 17.

22 Lower the engine/transmission assembly slightly on the left-hand side to provide sufficient clearance for removal of the transmission.

23 Working your way around the transmission casing, slacken and remove the transmission-to-engine securing bolts. Disconnect any wiring loom brackets, where applicable.

24 With the help of an assistant, withdraw the transmission squarely from the engine, taking care not to allow its weight to hang on the clutch friction disc. Once the transmission is free, lower the transmission on the jack and manoeuvre the unit out from under the vehicle.

25 The clutch components can now be inspected with reference to Chapter 6 Section 6, and renewed if necessary. Unless they are virtually new, it is worth renewing the clutch components as a matter of course, even if the transmission has been removed for some other reason.

Refitting

26 With the transmission secured on the trolley jack as on removal, raise it into position, and then carefully slide it onto the engine, at the same time engaging the input shaft with the clutch friction disc splines. Do not use excessive force to refit the transmission – if the input shaft does not slide into place easily, readjust the angle of the transmission so that it is level, and/or turn the input shaft so that the splines engage properly with the disc. If problems

7.16 Prise out the retaining clip and disconnect the clutch hydraulic pipe

are still experienced, check that the clutch friction disc is correctly centred (see Chapter 6 Section 6).

27 The remainder of refitting is a reversal of the removal procedure, bearing in mind the following points:
a) Use a new through-bolt when refitting the engine/transmission rear mounting.
b) Tighten all nuts and bolts to the specified torque.
c) If required, renew the differential oil seals as described in Section 5.
d) Refit the driveshafts as described in Chapter 8 Section 2.
e) Check and if necessary top-up the oil level in the transmission as described in Section 9.
f) If required, adjust the gearchange cables as described in Section 2.

28 Make a final check that all connections have been made, and all bolts tightened fully. Road test the vehicle to check for proper transmission operation, then check the transmission visually for leakage of oil.

8 Transmission overhaul – general information

1 Overhauling a manual transmission unit is a difficult and involved job for the DIY home mechanic. In addition to dismantling and reassembling many small parts, clearances must be precisely measured

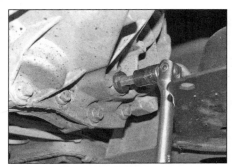

9.3 Transmission oil drain plug

and, if necessary, changed by selecting shims and spacers. Internal transmission components are also often difficult to obtain, and in many instances, extremely expensive. Because of this, if the transmission develops a fault or becomes noisy, the best course of action is to have the unit overhauled by a specialist repairer, or to obtain an exchange reconditioned unit.

2 Nevertheless, it is not impossible for the more experienced mechanic to overhaul the transmission, provided the special tools are available, and the job is done in a deliberate step-by-step manner, so that nothing is overlooked.

3 The tools necessary for an overhaul include internal and external circlip pliers, bearing pullers, a slide hammer, a set of pin punches, a dial test indicator and possibly a hydraulic press. In addition, a large, sturdy workbench and a vice will be required.

4 During dismantling of the transmission, make careful notes of how each component is fitted, to make reassembly easier and more accurate.

5 Before dismantling the transmission, it will help if you have some idea what area is malfunctioning. Certain problems can be closely related to specific areas in the transmission, which can make component examination and replacement easier. Refer to *Fault finding* at the end of this manual for more information.

9 Transmission oil – draining and refilling

Note: *Renewal of the transmission oil is not a service requirement and will normally only be necessary if the unit is removed for overhaul or renewal. However, if the vehicle has completed a high mileage, or is used under arduous conditions, it would be advisable to change the oil as a precaution, especially if the gearchange quality has deteriorated.*

Draining

1 Raise the vehicle and support it on axle stands (see *Jacking and vehicle support*). Ideally, the vehicle should be level to ensure accuracy.

2 Position a suitable container beneath the transmission.

3 The drain plug is located on the lower left-hand side of the differential casing. Unscrew and remove the drain plug and allow the oil to drain into the container **(see illustration)**. Check the condition of the drain plug sealing washer, where fitted, and renew if necessary.

4 When all the oil has drained, refit the drain plug and tighten it to the specified torque.

5 Dispose of the old oil safely in accordance with environmental regulations.

9.6 Transmission oil filler/level plug

Refilling

6 Unscrew the filler/level plug located on the front of the transmission casing **(see illustration)**.

7 Fill the transmission through the filler/level plug orifice with the correct type of oil (see *Lubricants and fluids*) until the oil level is approximately 20 mm below the lower edge of the filler/level plug hole. The best way to check the level is to use a 'dipstick' made up from a bent piece of wire. Put the wire in the hole (but don't drop it in) and check the level.

8 Refit the filler/level plug with a new seal (where fitted), and tighten it to the specified torque.

9 Lower the vehicle to the ground.

Chapter 8
Driveshafts and rear axle

Contents

Degrees of difficulty

Easy, suitable for novice with little experience	Fairly easy, suitable for beginner with some experience	Fairly difficult, suitable for competent DIY mechanic	Difficult, suitable for experienced DIY mechanic	Very difficult, suitable for expert DIY or professional

Specifications

Driveshafts

Type . . . . Solid steel shafts with inner and outer constant velocity (CV) joints.
Right-hand driveshaft incorporating intermediate shaft

Lubricant type/specification. . . . . Use only special grease supplied in sachets with gaiter kits – joints are otherwise pre-packed with grease and sealed

Rear axle

Type . . . . Beam axle supported on semi-eliptic single leaf springs

Torque wrench settings

	Nm	lbf ft
Driveshaft		
Driveshaft retaining nut: *		
Stage 1	Rotate the wheel hub 5 times	
Stage 2	250	185
Stage 3	Rotate the wheel hub 5 times	
Stage 4	500	369
Intermediate shaft support bearing retaining plate nuts*	25	19
Steering knuckle balljoint-to-lower suspension arm nut*	150	111
Track rod end balljoint retaining nut*	48	35
Rear axle		
Rear hub retaining nut: *		
45 mm flange diameter nut:		
Stage 1	Rotate the wheel hub 5 times	
Stage 2	200	148
Stage 3	Rotate the wheel hub 5 times	
Stage 4	300	221
Stage 5	Rotate the wheel hub 5 times	
51 mm flange diameter nut:		
Stage 1	Rotate the wheel hub 5 times	
Stage 2	200	148
Stage 3	Rotate the wheel hub 5 times	
Stage 4	420	310
Stage 5	Rotate the wheel hub 5 times	
Rear spring-to-axle U-bolt nuts: *		
Stage 1	25	19
Stage 2	50	37
Stage 3	75	55
Stage 4	100	74
Stage 5	125	92
Stage 6	150	111
Stage 7	175	129
Shock absorber lower mounting bolt nuts	110	81
Shock absorber upper mounting bolt nuts	175	129
Roadwheels		
Roadwheel nuts	200	148

*Do not re-use

1   General Information

Driveshafts

1 Drive is transmitted from the transmission differential to the front wheels by means of two, solid steel driveshafts, each incorporating two constant velocity (CV) joints. The right-hand driveshaft is in two sections, and incorporates a support bearing **(see illustration)**.

2 Each driveshaft consists of three main components: the sliding (tripod type) inner joint, the actual driveshaft, and the outer (fixed ball) joint. The inner (male) end of the left-hand tripod joint is secured in the differential side gear by the engagement of a circlip. The inner (female) end of the right-hand driveshaft is held on the intermediate shaft by the engagement of a circlip. The intermediate shaft is held in the transmission by the support bearing, which in turn is supported by a bracket bolted to the rear of the cylinder block. The outer CV joint on both driveshafts is of fixed ball-bearing type,

and is secured in the front hub by the hub nut. The outer CV joint must not be dismantled from the driveshaft because it is a press-fit.

Rear axle

3 The rear axle is a tubular steel beam axle supported on semi-elliptic single leaf springs. An elastic element supports the leaf springs in their function. Stub axles are bolted to the ends of the axle beam on each side and these carry the rear hub and bearing assemblies. Telescopic shock absorbers provide the damping for the axle assembly.

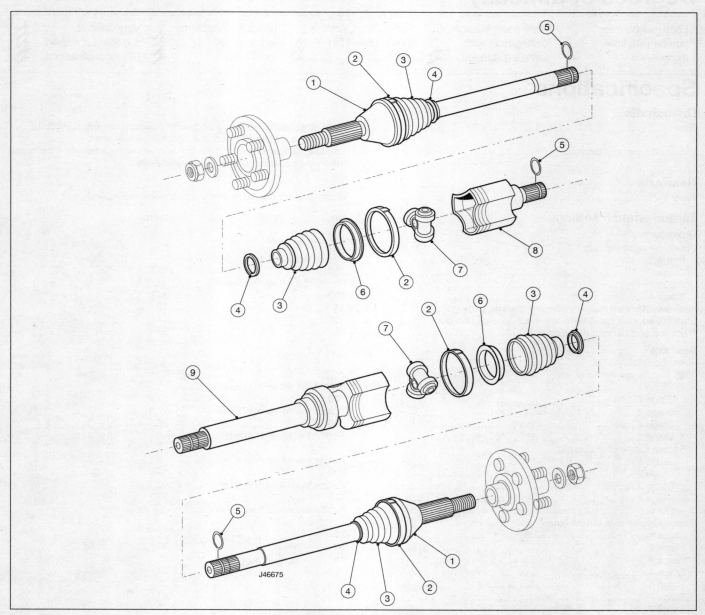

1.1 Exploded view of the driveshafts

1 Driveshaft with fixed outer CV joint	*4 Small gaiter retaining clamp*	*7 Inner joint tripod*
2 Large gaiter retaining clamp	*5 Circlip*	*8 Inner joint housing*
3 Gaiter	*6 Collar*	*9 Intermediate shaft*

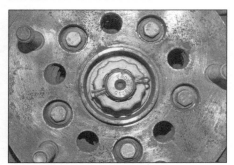
2.3a Bend up the split pin legs...

2.3b ...then extract the split pin...

2.3c ...and remove the retaining nut locking ring

2.4 Attach the holding tool to the wheel hub using two wheel nuts

2.5 Unscrew the retaining nut and remove the washer

2.6 Using a puller to release the track rod end balljoint shank from the steering arm

2 Driveshafts – removal and refitting

Removal

Caution: When removing the driveshafts, the inner CV joint must not be bent by more than 18° and the outer CV joint must not be bent by more than 45°.

Note: *A new driveshaft retaining nut and washer, split pin, steering knuckle balljoint retaining nut and track rod end retaining nut will be required for refitting. If working on the right-hand driveshaft, a new intermediate shaft support bearing retaining plate and nuts will also be required.*

1 Firmly apply the handbrake, then jack up the front of the vehicle and support it securely on axle stands (see *Jacking and vehicle support*). Remove the relevant front roadwheel.

2 Drain the transmission oil as described in Chapter 7 Section 9.
3 Extract the split pin from the driveshaft and remove the retaining nut locking ring **(see illustrations)**.
4 To prevent rotation of the wheel hub as the driveshaft retaining nut is slackened, make up a holding tool and attach the tool to the wheel hub using two wheel nuts **(see Tool Tip and illustration)**.

> **HAYNES HiNT** *A tool to hold the wheel hub stationary while the driveshaft retaining nut is slackened can be fabricated from two lengths of steel strip (one long, one short) and a nut and bolt; the nut and bolt forming the pivot of a forked tool.*

5 With the holding tool in place, unscrew

the driveshaft retaining nut, and remove the washer **(see illustration)**. Discard the nut and washer – new ones must be fitted.
6 Slacken the track rod end balljoint nut several turns, then use a balljoint separator tool or puller to release the balljoint shank from the steering arm **(see illustration)**. With the balljoint released, unscrew the nut and disconnect the balljoint from the steering arm. Discard the nut because a new one must be used for refitting.
7 Slacken the nut securing the steering knuckle balljoint to the lower suspension arm. Attach a two-legged puller to the lower suspension arm and tighten the puller to apply tension to the balljoint shank **(see illustrations)**. Strike the end of the lower suspension arm with a hammer a few times to release the balljoint shank taper.
8 Remove the puller and unscrew the balljoint retaining nut. A Torx key may be required to counterhold the nut **(see illustration)**.

2.7a Slacken the nut securing the steering knuckle balljoint to the lower suspension arm...

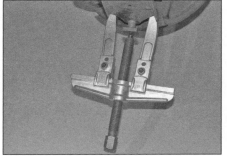
2.7b ...then release the balljoint using a two-legged puller

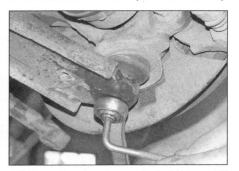
2.8 Use a Torx key to counterhold the nut if it rotates freely while being unscrewed

2.9 Push down on the suspension lower arm to disengage the balljoint from the arm

2.10 Using a puller to remove the outer end of the driveshaft from the front hub and steering knuckle

2.11 Unscrew the nuts and remove the intermediate shaft support bearing retaining plate

Measure the size of the balljoint retaining nut – they'll be either 24 mm or 30 mm. Discard the nut and obtain a new nut of the correct size for refitting.

9 Push down on the suspension lower arm to disengage the balljoint from the arm, then move the steering knuckle to one side and release the arm, taking care not to damage the balljoint rubber boot **(see illustration)**.

Right-hand driveshaft

10 Press the outer end of the driveshaft through the front hub and steering knuckle. If the end of the driveshaft is tight in the hub, temporarily refit the driveshaft retaining nut to protect the driveshaft threads, then tap the end of the driveshaft with a soft-faced hammer while pulling outwards on the steering knuckle **(see illustration)**. If the driveshaft is still reluctant, use a suitable puller.

11 Unscrew the nuts and remove the retaining plate securing the intermediate shaft support bearing to the cylinder block **(see illustration)**. A punch may be needed to loosen the plate once the nuts have been unscrewed. Note that Ford stipulate that new nuts and a new retaining plate will be required for refitting.

12 Pull the intermediate shaft out of the transmission. Be prepared for some oil spillage from the transmission.

13 Withdraw the driveshaft from under the vehicle.

14 Check the condition of the differential oil seal, and if necessary renew it as described

in Chapter 7 Section 5. Check the support bearing, and if necessary renew it as described in Section 5.

Left-hand driveshaft

15 Press the outer end of the driveshaft through the front hub and steering knuckle **(see illustration 2.10)**. If the end of the driveshaft is tight in the hub, temporarily refit the driveshaft retaining nut to protect the driveshaft threads, then tap the end of the driveshaft with a soft-faced hammer while pulling outwards on the steering knuckle.

16 Insert a lever between the inner driveshaft joint and the transmission case, with a thin piece of wood against the case. Prise free the inner joint from the differential **(see illustration)**. If it proves reluctant to move, strike the lever firmly with the palm of the hand. Be careful not to damage adjacent components, and in particular, make sure that the driveshaft oil seal in the differential is not damaged. Be prepared for some oil spillage from the transmission. Support the inner end of the driveshaft on an axle stand, if necessary.

17 Withdraw the driveshaft from under the vehicle.

18 Extract the circlip from the groove on the inner end of the driveshaft, and obtain a new one **(see illustration)**.

19 Check the condition of the differential oil seal, and if necessary renew it as described in Chapter 7 Section 5.

Refitting

Right-hand driveshaft

20 Insert the inner end of the intermediate shaft into the transmission and engage it with the splines on the differential sun gear, taking care not to damage the oil seal. Locate the intermediate shaft support bearing in position, fit the new retaining plate, and tighten the new retaining nuts to the specified torque.

21 Pull the knuckle outwards, and insert the outer end of the driveshaft through the hub. Turn the driveshaft as necessary to engage the splines in the hub, and fully push on the hub. If necessary, use a wooden mallet to tap the hub fully onto the driveshaft splines.

Left-hand driveshaft

22 Fit the new circlip to the groove on the inner end of the driveshaft, making sure it is correctly seated.

23 Keeping the driveshaft level, insert the splined inner end into the transmission and engage it with the splines in the differential sun gear. Take care not to damage the transmission oil seal. Press in the driveshaft until the circlip is fully engaged.

24 Pull the knuckle outwards, and insert the outer end of the driveshaft through the hub. Turn the driveshaft as necessary to engage the splines in the hub, and fully push on the hub. If necessary, use a wooden mallet to tap the hub fully onto the driveshaft splines.

Both driveshafts

25 Push down on the lower suspension arm and engage the steering knuckle balljoint with the arm. Fit the new balljoint retaining nut and tighten the nut to the specified torque.

26 Locate the track rod end balljoint on the steering arm. Screw on a new nut and tighten it to the specified torque. If the balljoint shank is hollow, a 5 mm Allen key can be used to prevent the balljoint from rotating as the nut is tightened. If the shank is solid, use a stout bar to lever up on the underside of the track rod end. This will lock the balljoint shank taper in the steering arm and prevent rotation as the nut is tightened.

27 Place the new washer over the end of the driveshaft and screw on the new retaining nut. Tighten the driveshaft retaining nut to

2,16 Using a lever to remove the left-hand driveshaft from the transmission

2.18 Circlip on the inner end of the left-hand driveshaft

the specified torque in the four stages given in the Specifications. Prevent the driveshaft from rotating as the nut is tightened using the method employed for removal.

28 Refit the driveshaft retaining nut locking ring, aligning the slots with the split pin hole in the driveshaft. Insert a new split pin and bend over the split pin legs to secure.

29 Refit the roadwheel and tighten the wheel nuts to the specified torque.

30 Refill the transmission with oil as described in Chapter 7 Section 9.

3 Driveshaft inner CV joint gaiter – renewal

Note: *If both the inner and outer gaiters are being renewed at the same time, the outer gaiter is removed from the inner end of the driveshaft.*

1 Remove the driveshaft as described in Section 2, and mount it in a vice.

2 Mark the driveshaft in relation to the joint housing, to ensure correct refitting.

3 Release and discard the two retaining clips from the gaiter, and slide the gaiter back along the driveshaft a little way **(see illustrations)**.

4 Withdraw the inner joint housing from the tripod and scoop out the grease from the joint and gaiter **(see illustration)**. You may need to tap the joint housing with a soft-faced mallet and rotate it to be able to free it.

5 Check that the inner end of the driveshaft is marked in relation to the splined tripod hub. If not, carefully centre-punch the two items, to ensure correct refitting. Alternatively, use dabs of paint on the driveshaft and one end of the tripod.

6 Extract the circlip retaining the tripod on the driveshaft and discard it **(see illustration)**.

7 Using a puller, remove the tripod from the end of the driveshaft, and slide off the gaiter **(see illustration)**.

8 If the outer gaiter is also to be renewed, remove it and fit the new one with reference to Section 4.

9 Clean the driveshaft, and obtain a new joint retaining circlip. The gaiter retaining clips must also be renewed.

10 Slide the new gaiter on the driveshaft, together with the new small diameter clip **(see illustrations)**. Make sure that the gaiter is located in the special groove in the driveshaft, then tighten the retaining clip. If possible, use a gaiter retaining clip tightening tool to tighten the clip. Otherwise, use pincers.

11 Refit the tripod on the driveshaft splines, if necessary using a soft-faced mallet and a suitable metal tube to drive it fully onto the splines. It must be fitted with the chamfered edge leading (towards the driveshaft), and with the previously-made marks aligned. Secure it in position using a new circlip. Ensure that the circlip is fully engaged in its groove.

3.3a Remove the inner joint gaiter large clip...

3.3b ...and small clip

3.4 Withdraw the inner joint housing from the tripod and scoop out the grease

3.6 Extract the circlip retaining the tripod on the driveshaft

12 Pack the joint with the grease supplied in the repair kit **(see illustration)**. Work the grease well into the tripod and joint housing and fill the rubber gaiter with any excess.

13 Guide the joint housing onto the tripod fully, and locate the gaiter in position, ensuring it is not twisted or distorted **(see illustrations)**.

3.7 Using a puller, remove the tripod from the end of the driveshaft

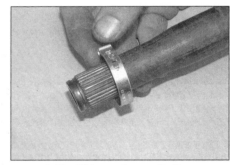
3.10a Slide on the small clip...

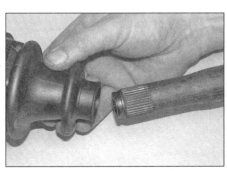
3.10b ...followed by the gaiter

3.12 Pack the specified amount of CV joint grease into the tripod and joint housing

3.13a Guide the joint housing onto the tripod fully...

14 Insert a small screwdriver under the lip of the gaiter at the housing end. This will allow trapped air to escape, then position the joint housing so that the distance from the inner end of the gaiter to the outer end is 90.0 mm.

15 Fit and tighten the new large diameter retaining clip. If possible, use the special tool to tighten the clip, otherwise, use pincers.

16 Refit the driveshaft as described in Section 2.

4 Driveshaft outer CV joint gaiter – renewal

Note: *The outer CV joint is pressed onto the driveshaft and must not be removed.*

1 The outer CV joint gaiter is removed by first detaching the inner gaiter as described in Section 3.

2 Clean the exposed part of the driveshaft to facilitate removal of the outer gaiter.

3 Release and discard the outer gaiter retaining clips. Slip the gaiter off the outer CV joint, then slide it off the inner end of the driveshaft together with the clips **(see illustrations)**. Scoop out the grease from the outer CV joint.

4 Slide the new gaiter, together with the new clips, onto the driveshaft until it is near the outer CV joint.

5 Pack the joint with the grease supplied in the repair kit. Work the grease well into the bearing tracks while twisting the joint, and fill the rubber gaiter with any excess.

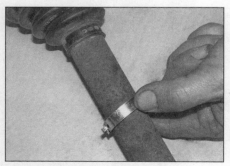

4.3a Remove the small clip...

3.13b ...and locate the gaiter in position

6 Slide the gaiter fully into position on the driveshaft and CV joint housing. Ensure the gaiter is not twisted or distorted.

7 Make sure that the gaiter is located in the special groove in the driveshaft, then fit and tighten the new small diameter retaining clip. If possible, use a gaiter retaining clip tightening tool to tighten the clip. Otherwise use pincers.

8 Insert a small screwdriver under the lip of the gaiter at the housing end. This will allow trapped air to escape, then position the joint housing so that the distance from the inner end of the gaiter to the outer end is approximately 110 mm.

9 Fit and tighten the new large diameter retaining clip. If possible, use the special tool to tighten the clip, otherwise, use pincers.

10 Refit the inner gaiter with reference to Section 3.

5 Intermediate shaft support bearing – renewal

1 Remove the right-hand driveshaft as described in Section 2, then remove the inner CV joint gaiter as described in Section 3.

2 Using a press or suitable puller, draw the bearing off the end of the intermediate shaft.

3 Drive or press on the new bearing, applying the pressure to the inner race only.

4 Refit (or renew) the inner CV joint gaiter as described in Section 3, then refit the driveshaft as described in Section 2.

4.3b ...and large clip from the outer joint...

6 Driveshafts – inspection and joint renewal

1 Road test the vehicle, and listen for a metallic clicking from the front as the vehicle is driven slowly in a circle on full-lock. If a clicking noise is heard, this indicates wear in the outer constant velocity joint, which means that the driveshaft and outer joint must be renewed. It is not possible to renew the joint separately.

2 If vibration, consistent with road speed, is felt through the vehicle when accelerating, there is a possibility of wear in the inner constant velocity joints. To renew an inner joint, remove the driveshaft as described in Section 2, then separate the joint from the driveshaft with reference to Section 3.

3 Continual noise from the right-hand driveshaft, increasing with road speed, may indicate wear in the intermediate shaft support bearing. Renewal procedures for the support bearing are contained in Section 5.

7 Rear axle – removal and refitting

Note: *The rear axle removal/refitting details described below are for the removal of the unit on its own. If required, it can be removed together with the roadwheels and rear leaf springs as a combined unit, although this method requires the vehicle to be raised and supported at a greater height (to allow the roadwheels to clear the body during withdrawal of the unit). If the latter method is used, follow the instructions given, but ignore the references to removal of the roadwheels and detaching the springs from the axle. Refer to Chapter 10 Section 12 for details on detaching the springs from the underbody.*

Note: *New spring-to-axle U-bolt retaining nuts will be required for refitting.*

Removal

1 Chock the front wheels then jack up the rear of the vehicle and securely support it on axle stands positioned beneath the underframe

4.3c ...then slide the gaiter off the inner end of the driveshaft

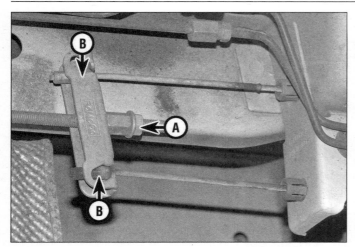

7.8 Slacken the handbrake cable adjustment nut (A), then slip the handbrake inner cable ends (B) out of the slots in the equaliser

7.10 Undo the retaining bolt on each side and release the handbrake cable supports from the underbody

side members in front of the rear springs (see *Jacking and vehicle support*). Remove the rear roadwheels on both sides.

2 If a new axle is being fitted, remove the wheel bearing and wheel hub as described in Section 8.

3 Support the weight of the rear axle with a trolley jack positioned beneath the centre of the axle beam.

4 Using two brake hose clamps, clamp the flexible hydraulic hoses leading to the rear axle.

5 Undo the two bolts securing the brake caliper mounting bracket to the rear axle. Slide the caliper and mounting bracket, complete with brake pads, off the disc and suspend the assembly from the rear spring using a cable tie.

6 Unscrew the union nuts and disconnect the rear brake hydraulic pipes from the flexible hoses at the support bracket on the rear axle. Be prepared for some loss of brake fluid, and plug or tape over the ends of the pipes and hoses to prevent entry of dust and dirt.

7 Undo the retaining bolt and lift the flexible hydraulic hose support bracket off the rear axle.

8 Slacken the handbrake cable adjustment nut until there is sufficient slack to enable the handbrake inner cable ends to be slipped out of the slots in the equaliser **(see illustration)**.

9 Depress the tabs on the end fittings, and withdraw the handbrake cables from the abutment bracket.

10 Undo the bolt each side securing the handbrake cable supports to the underbody **(see illustration)**. Release the cables from any additional clips so that both cables are free to be removed with the axle.

11 On vehicles equipped with a load apportioning valve in the brake hydraulic circuit, undo the retaining bolt and detach the load apportioning valve operating rod from the rear axle bracket.

12 Disconnect the wheel speed sensor wiring at the chassis side member.

13 Undo the retaining nuts and bolts, and detach the rear shock absorbers from the axle **(see illustration)**.

14 Check that the axle unit is securely supported in the centre by the jack. Have an assistant available, to steady the axle each side as it is lowered from the vehicle.

15 Undo and discard the four retaining nuts, and remove the spring-to-axle U-bolts and fittings each side **(see illustration)**. Check that the various axle fittings and attachments are disconnected and out of the way, then carefully lower the axle unit and withdraw it from under the vehicle.

Refitting

16 Refitting is a reversal of the removal procedure, noting the following points:
a) Tighten all retaining nuts and bolts to the specified torque (where given).
b) Use new retaining nuts on the spring-to-axle U-bolts.
c) Final tightening of the rear axle U-bolt nuts and shock absorber mounting nuts should be carried out with the weight of the vehicle resting on the roadwheels.
d) Referring to the procedures contained in Chapter 9 Section 2, top-up and bleed the brake hydraulic system, then adjust

the handbrake as described in Chapter 1 Section 22.

8 Rear hub and bearing – removal, overhaul and refitting

Removal

Caution: Due to the extremely high tightening torque of the rear hub retaining nut take great care when removing and refitting the nut. Use only the correct sockets and make sure you have a suitable extension bar for removal, and a torque wrench capable of tightening the nut to the correct setting (see Specifications) for refitting. Entrust this work to a dealer or suitably equipped garage if in doubt about the procedure, or if the required tools are not available.

Note: *A new rear hub retaining nut will be required for refitting.*

1 Chock the front wheels then jack up the rear of the vehicle and securely support it on axle stands (see *Jacking and vehicle support*).

2 Remove the appropriate rear wheel and release the handbrake.

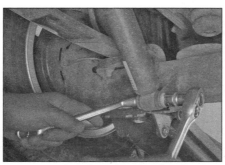

7.13 Undo the nuts, remove the bolts and detach the rear shock absorbers from the axle

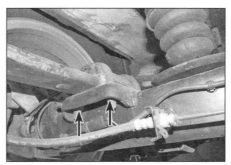

7.15 Undo the retaining nuts (two of four shown) and remove the spring-to-axle U-bolts and fittings each side

8.3 Slide the brake caliper and mounting bracket, complete with brake pads, off the disc

8.4a Unscrew the rear hub retaining nut...

8.4b ...collect the washer...

8.4c ...then withdraw the brake disc and rear hub, as an assembly, off the stub axle

3 Undo the two bolts securing the brake caliper mounting bracket to the rear axle. Slide the caliper and mounting bracket, complete with brake pads, off the disc and suspend the

assembly from the rear spring using a cable tie **(see illustration)**.

4 Unscrew the rear hub retaining nut, collect the washer, then withdraw the brake disc and

rear hub as an assembly off the stub axle **(see illustrations)**.

5 Measure the diameter of the hub retaining nut flange. Obtain a new hub retaining nut of the appropriate size for refitting.

6 If necessary, separate the brake disc from the hub as described in Chapter 9 Section 8.

Overhaul

7 Wipe clean all the components, then carefully examine each item for damage and deterioration. Check the bearing for wear by spinning the inner track and checking for any roughness. Similarly, attempt to move the inner track laterally. Excessive movement is an indication of wear.

8 If the bearing is worn or damaged, it will be necessary to obtain a complete rear hub and bearing assembly. Seek the advice of a Ford dealer regarding parts availability.

Refitting

9 Slide the hub and disc assembly into position over the stub axle. Fit the washer and a new hub retaining nut, then tighten the nut to the specified torque in the five stages given in the Specifications.

10 Slide the brake caliper assembly over the disc and into position on the rear axle. Refit the two mounting bracket retaining bolts and tighten them to the specified torque.

11 Check and, if necessary, adjust the hand-brake as described in Chapter 1 Section 22.

12 Refit the roadwheel, then lower the vehicle to the ground and tighten the roadwheel nuts to the specified torque.

Chapter 9
Braking system

Contents

Degrees of difficulty

Easy, suitable for novice with little experience	Fairly easy, suitable for beginner with some experience	Fairly difficult, suitable for competent DIY mechanic	Difficult, suitable for experienced DIY mechanic	Very difficult, suitable for expert DIY or professional

Specifications

Front brakes

Type	Ventilated disc, with twin-piston sliding caliper
Brake pad friction material minimum thickness.	1.5 mm
Disc diameter	288.0 or 308.0 mm according to model
Disc thickness:	
New	33.0 mm
Minimum.	30.0 mm
Maximum disc run-out	0.10 mm
Maximum disc thickness variation	0.02 mm

Rear disc brakes

Type	Solid disc, with single-piston sliding caliper
Brake pad friction material minimum thickness.	1.5 mm
Disc diameter	288.0 or 308.0 according to model
Disc thickness:	
New	16.0 mm
Minimum.	13.0 mm
Maximum disc run-out	0.10 mm
Maximum disc thickness variation	0.02 mm

Torque wrench settings

	Nm	lbf ft
ABS hydraulic modulator-to-mounting bracket	20	15
ABS wheel speed sensor retaining bolts	11	8
ABS ECU retaining bolts:		
Stage 1	2	1
Stage 2	3	2
Brake fluid pipe unions:		
ABS hydraulic moderator	18	13
Flexible pipe to caliper	17	13
Flexible pipe to rigid pipe	15	11
Brake pedal mounting bracket nuts	20	15
Clutch master cylinder retaining bolts	9	7
Driveshaft retaining nut: *		
Stage 1	Rotate the wheel hub 5 times	
Stage 2	250	185
Stage 3	Rotate the wheel hub 5 times	
Stage 4	500	369
Front brake caliper guide pin bolts.	60	44
Front brake caliper mounting bracket bolts	270	200
Front brake disc-to-hub flange bolts: *		
Stage 1	30	22
Stage 2	Angle-tighten a further 90°	
Front hub assembly-to-steering knuckle bolts*	53	39
Handbrake lever retaining nuts	22	16
Master cylinder retaining nuts	25	18
Rear brake caliper guide pin bolts	31	23
Rear brake caliper mounting bracket bolts	115	85
Rear brake disc-to-hub flange bolts*	72	53
Rear hub retaining nut: *		
44 mm flange diameter nut:		
Stage 1	Rotate the wheel hub 5 times	
Stage 2	200	148
Stage 3	Rotate the wheel hub 5 times	
Stage 4	300	221
Stage 5	Rotate the wheel hub 5 times	
51 mm flange diameter nut:		
Stage 1	Rotate the wheel hub 5 times	
Stage 2	200	148
Stage 3	Rotate the wheel hub 5 times	
Stage 4	420	310
Stage 5	Rotate the wheel hub 5 times	
Roadwheel nuts	200	148
Vacuum pump-to-cylinder head bolts:		
2.0 litre engines:		
Stage 1	5	4
Stage 2	10	7
2.2 litre engines	10	7
Vacuum servo unit mounting nuts	24	18

* Do not re-use

1 General Information

1 The braking system is of servo-assisted, dual-circuit hydraulic type split diagonally. The arrangement of the hydraulic system is such that each circuit operates one front and one rear brake from a tandem master cylinder. Under normal circumstances, both circuits operate in unison. However, in the event of hydraulic failure in one circuit, full braking force will still be available at two wheels.

2 All models are fitted with front disc brakes. Depending on vehicle specification, either rear disc brakes or rear drum brakes may be fitted. An Anti-lock Braking System (ABS) is fitted as standard to all vehicles covered in this manual. Refer to Section 19 for further information on ABS operation.

3 The front brake discs are of the ventilated type and are fitted with twin-piston sliding pin type brake calipers.

4 The rear brake discs are of the solid type and are fitted with single-piston sliding pin type brake calipers.

5 The cable-operated handbrake provides an independent mechanical means of rear brake application.

6 A vacuum servo unit is fitted between the master cylinder and the bulkhead, its function being to reduce the amount of pedal pressure required to operate the brakes. Since there is no throttling as such of the inlet manifold on diesel engines, the manifold is not a suitable source of vacuum to operate the vacuum servo unit. The servo unit is therefore connected to a separate engine-mounted vacuum pump. The pump is bolted to the cylinder head and driven by the exhaust camshaft.

7 The braking force available at the rear wheels is controlled by the ABS hydraulic modulator under all driving conditions.

 Warning: When servicing any part of the system, work carefully and methodically; also observe scrupulous cleanliness when overhauling any part of the hydraulic system. Always renew components (in axle sets, where applicable) if in doubt about their condition, and use only genuine Ford replacement parts, or at least those of known good

quality. Note the warnings given in 'Safety first!' and at relevant points in this Chapter concerning the dangers of dust and hydraulic fluid.

2 Hydraulic system – bleeding

⚠ *Warning: Hydraulic fluid is poisonous. Always wear gloves but wash off immediately and thoroughly in the case of skin contact, and seek immediate medical advice if any fluid is swallowed or gets into the eyes. Certain types of hydraulic fluid are inflammable, and may ignite when allowed into contact with hot components. When servicing any hydraulic system, it is safest to assume that the fluid is inflammable, and to take precautions against the risk of fire as though it is petrol that is being handled. Hydraulic fluid is also an effective paint stripper, and will attack plastics; if any is spilt, it should be washed off immediately, using copious quantities of fresh water. Finally, it is hygroscopic (it absorbs moisture from the air) therefore old fluid may be contaminated and unfit for further use. When topping-up or renewing the fluid, always use the recommended type, and ensure that it comes from a freshly opened sealed container.*

Note: *This procedure applies only to vehicles not fitted with stability assist. For vehicles with stability assist use the BleedMASTER function in the diagnostic tool. Consult a dealer for more information.*

General

1 The correct operation of any hydraulic system is only possible after removing all air from the components and circuit; this is achieved by bleeding the system.

2 During the bleeding procedure, add only clean, unused hydraulic fluid of the recommended type; never re-use fluid that has already been bled from the system. Ensure that sufficient fluid is available before starting work.

3 If there is any possibility of incorrect fluid being already in the system, the brake components and circuit must be flushed completely with uncontaminated, correct fluid, and new seals should be fitted to the various components.

4 If hydraulic fluid has been lost from the system, or air has entered because of a leak, ensure that the fault is cured before proceeding further.

5 When bleeding the brakes on vehicles with a load-apportioning valve in the rear brake hydraulic circuit, it is important to note that the vehicle must be standing on its wheels. If the rear of the vehicle is jacked up and the axle is in a 'wheel free' state, the load-apportioning valve will prevent complete bleeding of the system.

6 Check that all pipes and hoses are secure, unions tight and bleed screws closed. Clean any dirt from around the bleed screws.

7 Unscrew the master cylinder reservoir cap and top-up the master cylinder reservoir to the MAX level line. Refit the cap loosely, and remember to maintain the fluid level at least above the MIN level line throughout the procedure, otherwise there is a risk of further air entering the system.

8 There are a number of one-man, do-it-yourself brake bleeding kits currently available from motor accessory shops. It is recommended that one of these kits is used whenever possible, as they greatly simplify the bleeding operation, and also reduce the risk of expelled air and fluid being drawn back into the system. If such a kit is not available, the basic (two-man) method must be used, which is described in detail below.

9 If a kit is to be used, prepare the vehicle as described previously, and follow the kit manufacturer's instructions, as the procedure may vary slightly according to the type being used, Generally, they are as outlined below in the relevant sub-Section.

10 If the system has been only partially disconnected, and suitable precautions were taken to minimise fluid loss, it should only be necessary to bleed that part of the system (ie, the primary or secondary circuit). If the master cylinder or main brake lines have been disconnected, then the complete system must be bled.

Bleeding

Basic (two-man) method

11 Collect together a clean glass jar, a suitable length of plastic or rubber tubing which is a tight fit over the bleed screw, and a ring spanner to fit the screw. The help of an assistant will also be required.

12 Remove the dust cap from the bleed screw at the wheel to be bled **(see illustrations)**. Fit the spanner and tube to the screw, place the other end of the tube in the jar, and pour in sufficient fluid to cover the end of the tube.

13 Ensure that the master cylinder reservoir fluid level is maintained at least above the MIN level line throughout the procedure.

14 Have the assistant fully depress the brake pedal several times to build-up pressure, then maintain it on the final downstroke.

15 While pedal pressure is maintained, unscrew the bleed screw (approximately one turn) and allow the compressed fluid and air to flow into the jar. The assistant should maintain pedal pressure, following it down to the floor if necessary, and should not release it until instructed to do so. When the flow stops, tighten the bleed screw again, have the assistant release the pedal slowly, and recheck the reservoir fluid level.

16 Repeat the steps given in paragraphs 14 and 15 until the fluid emerging from the bleed screw is free from air bubbles. If the master cylinder has been drained and refilled, and air is being bled from the first bleed screw, allow approximately five seconds between cycles for the master cylinder passages to refill.

17 When no more air bubbles appear, securely tighten the bleed screw, remove the tube and spanner, and refit the dust cap. Do not overtighten the bleed screw.

18 Repeat the procedure on the remaining bleed screws, until all air is removed from the system and the brake pedal feels firm again.

Using a one-way valve kit

19 As the name implies, these kits consist of a length of tubing with a one-way valve fitted, to prevent expelled air and fluid being drawn back into the system. Some kits include a translucent container, which can be positioned so that the air bubbles can be more easily seen flowing from the end of the tube.

20 The kit is connected to the bleed screw, which is then opened. The user returns to the driver's seat, depresses the brake pedal with a smooth, steady stroke, and slowly releases it; this is repeated until the expelled fluid is clear of air bubbles.

21 Note that these kits simplify work so much that it is easy to forget the master cylinder reservoir fluid level. So ensure that this is maintained at least above the MIN level line at all times.

Using a pressure-bleeding kit

22 These kits are usually operated by a reservoir of pressurised air contained in the spare tyre. However, note that it will probably be necessary to reduce the pressure to a lower level than normal. Refer to the instructions supplied with the kit.

23 By connecting a pressurised, fluid-filled

2.12a Front caliper bleed screw...

2.12b ...and rear caliper bleed screw...

container to the master cylinder reservoir, bleeding can be carried out simply by opening each bleed screw in turn, and allowing the fluid to flow out until no more air bubbles can be seen in the expelled fluid.

24 This method has the advantage that the large reservoir of fluid provides an additional safeguard against air being drawn into the system during bleeding.

25 Pressure-bleeding is particularly effective when bleeding 'difficult' systems, or when bleeding the complete system at the time of routine fluid renewal.

All methods

26 When bleeding is complete, and firm pedal feel is restored, wash off any spilt fluid, securely tighten the bleed screws, and refit the dust caps.

27 Check the hydraulic fluid level in the master cylinder reservoir, and top-up if necessary (see *Weekly Checks*).

28 Discard any hydraulic fluid that has been bled from the system because it will not be fit for re-use.

29 Check the feel of the brake pedal. If it feels at all spongy, air is still present in the system, and further bleeding is required. Failure to bleed satisfactorily after a reasonable repetition of the bleeding procedure may be due to worn master cylinder seals.

3 Hydraulic pipes and hoses – renewal

Note: *Before starting work, refer to the note at the beginning of Section 2 concerning the dangers of hydraulic fluid.*

1 If any pipe or hose is to be renewed, minimise fluid loss by first removing the master cylinder reservoir cap and screwing it down onto a piece of polythene. Alternatively, flexible hoses can be sealed, if required, using a proprietary brake hose clamp. Metal brake pipe unions can be plugged (if care is taken not to allow dirt into the system) or capped immediately they are disconnected. Place a wad of rag under any union that is to be disconnected, to catch any spilt fluid.

2 If a flexible hose is to be disconnected,

3.2 Front flexible brake hose retaining clip

unscrew the brake pipe union nut(s) before removing the spring clip or retaining bolt which secures the hose to its mounting bracket **(see illustration)**. Where applicable, unscrew the union nut securing the hose to the caliper.

3 To unscrew union nuts, it is preferable to obtain a brake pipe spanner of the correct size; these are available from most motor accessory shops. Failing this, a close-fitting open-ended spanner will be required, though if the nuts are tight or corroded, their flats may be rounded-off if the spanner slips. In such a case, a self-locking wrench is often the only way to unscrew a stubborn union, but it follows that the pipe and the damaged nuts must be renewed on reassembly. Always clean a union and surrounding area before disconnecting it. If disconnecting a component with more than one union, make a careful note of the connections before disturbing any of them.

4 If a brake pipe is to be renewed, it can be obtained, cut to length and with the union nuts and end flares in place, from Ford dealers. All that is then necessary is to bend it to shape, following the line of the original, before fitting it to the vehicle. Alternatively, most motor accessory shops can make up brake pipes from kits, but this requires very careful measurement of the original, to ensure that the replacement is of the correct length. The safest answer is usually to take the original to the shop as a pattern.

5 On refitting, do not overtighten the union nuts.

6 When refitting hoses to the front calipers, make sure that the hoses are positioned so that they will not touch surrounding bodywork or the roadwheels.

7 Ensure that the pipes and hoses are correctly routed, with no kinks, and that they are secured in the clips or brackets provided. After fitting, remove the polythene from the reservoir, and bleed the hydraulic system as described in Section 2. Wash off any spilt fluid and check carefully for fluid leaks.

4 Front brake pads – renewal

⚠️ *Warning: Renew BOTH sets of front brake pads at the same time – NEVER renew the pads on only one wheel, as uneven braking may result. Note that the dust created by wear of the pads is a health hazard. Never blow it out with compressed air, and do not inhale any of it. An approved filtering mask should be worn when working on the brakes. DO NOT use petroleum-based solvents to clean brake parts – use brake cleaner or methylated spirit only.*

1 Apply the handbrake, then jack up the front of the vehicle and support it on axle stands (see *Jacking and vehicle support*). Remove the front roadwheels.

2 Follow the accompanying photos **(illustrations 4.2a to 4.2r)** for the actual pad renewal procedure, bearing in mind the additional points given in the following paragraphs. Be sure to stay in order and read the caption under each illustration. Note that if the old pads are to be refitted, ensure that they are identified so that they can be returned to their original positions.

3 If the original brake pads are still serviceable, carefully clean them using a clean, fine wire brush or similar, paying particular attention to the sides and back of the metal backing plate. Clean out the grooves in the friction material, and pick out any large embedded particles of dirt or debris. Carefully clean the pad locations in the caliper mounting bracket.

4.2a If required, slightly lever back the caliper to release the pads

4.2b Unscrew the lower guide pin bolt while counter-holding the guide pin with a second spanner.

4.2c Lift the caliper up to gain access to the brake pads...

4.2d ...and secure it in the raised position using wire or a cable tie

4.2e If fitted, disconnect the brake pad wear indicator wiring plug at the back of the caliper before lifting out the inner brake pad...

4.2f ...and the outer brake pad

4.2g Remove the four anti-rattle springs from the caliper upper and lower mounting brackets, noting their fitted positions

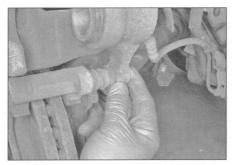

4.2h Check the upper and lower guide pins to make sure they slide freely. If not, remove and lubricate with a high-temperature grease

4.2i Measure the thickness of the pad friction material. If any are worn down to the specified minimum, all four pads must be renewed

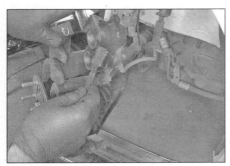

4.2j Clean the dust and dirt from the caliper piston and mounting bracket using aerosol brake cleaner and a brush

4.2k If new pads are to be fitted, push back the caliper piston, ideally with a piston retraction tool....

4.2l ...and keep an eye on the level in the brake fluid reservoir, removing any surplus with a syringe or similar

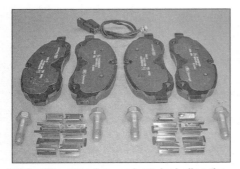

4.2m The complete pad set, including the brake pad wear indicator wiring, if required

4.2n Fit the four new spring steel shims to the caliper bracket

4.2o Install the outer pad...

4.2p ...and the inner pad, making sure the friction material on both pads is facing the brake disc

4.2q Reconnect the brake pad wear indicator wiring plug, if fitted. Lower the caliper back into position over the brake pads

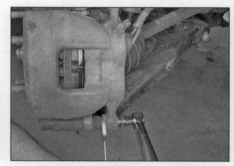

4.2r Install the lower guide pin bolt, tightening it to the specified torque

4 Prior to fitting the pads, check that the guide pins are a snug fit in the caliper mounting bracket. Inspect the dust seals around the pistons for damage, and the pistons for evidence of fluid leaks, corrosion or damage. If attention to any of these components is necessary, refer to Section 6.

5 If new brake pads are to be fitted, the caliper pistons must be pushed back into the cylinder to allow for the extra pad thickness. Either use a G-clamp or similar tool, or use suitable pieces of wood as levers. Clamp off the flexible brake hose leading to the caliper then connect a brake bleeding kit to the caliper bleed screw. Open the bleed screw as the pistons are retracted, the surplus brake fluid will then be collected in the bleed kit vessel. Close the bleed screw just before the caliper pistons are pushed fully into the caliper. This should ensure no air enters the hydraulic system.

Note: *The ABS unit contains hydraulic components that are very sensitive to impurities in the brake fluid. Even the smallest particles can cause the system to fail through blockage. The pad retraction method described here prevents any debris in the brake fluid expelled from the caliper from being passed back to the ABS hydraulic unit, as well as preventing any chance of damage to the master cylinder seals.*

6 With the brake pads installed, depress the brake pedal repeatedly, until normal (non-assisted) pedal pressure is restored, and the pads are pressed into firm contact with the brake disc.

7 Repeat the above procedure on the remaining front brake caliper.

8 Refit the roadwheels, then lower the vehicle to the ground and tighten the roadwheel nuts to the specified torque setting.

9 Check the hydraulic fluid level as described in *Weekly checks*.

Caution: New pads will not give full braking efficiency until they have bedded-in. Be prepared for this, and avoid hard braking as far as possible for the first hundred miles or so after pad renewal.

5 Front brake disc – inspection, removal and refitting

Note: *Before starting work, refer to the warning at the beginning of Section 4 concerning the dangers of dust. If either disc requires renewal, both should be renewed at the same time together with new pads, to ensure even and consistent braking.*

Inspection

1 Firmly apply the handbrake, then jack up the front of the vehicle and support it securely on axle stands (see *Jacking and vehicle support*). Remove the roadwheel.

2 If fitted, disconnect the brake pad wear indicator wiring plug at the rear of the caliper.

3 Unscrew the bolts securing the brake caliper mounting bracket to the steering knuckle then slide the caliper/bracket

assembly from the steering knuckle and brake disc (there is no need to remove the brake pads) **(see illustration)**. Suspend the caliper/bracket assembly from the strut coil spring using wire or a cable tie – do not allow the caliper to hang on the brake hose.

4 Temporarily refit two of the wheel nuts to diagonally opposite studs, with the flat sides of the nuts against the disc. Tighten the nuts progressively, to hold the disc firmly.

5 Scrape any corrosion from the disc. Rotate the disc, and examine it for deep scoring, grooving or cracks. Using a micrometer, measure the thickness of the disc in several places **(see illustration)**. The minimum thickness is given in the Specifications. Light wear and scoring is normal, but if excessive, the disc should be removed, and either reground by a specialist, or renewed. If regrinding is undertaken, the minimum thickness must be maintained. Obviously, if the disc is cracked, it must be renewed.

6 Using a dial gauge or a flat metal block and feeler gauges, check that the disc run-out 10 mm from the outer edge does not exceed the limit given in the Specifications. To do this, fix the measuring equipment, and rotate the disc, noting the variation in measurement as the disc is rotated **(see illustration)**. The difference between the minimum and maximum measurements recorded is the disc run-out.

7 If the run-out is greater than the specified amount, check for variations of the disc thickness as follows. Mark the disc at eight positions 45° apart then, using a micrometer,

5.3 Slide the caliper and mounting bracket, complete with brake pads, off the disc

5.5 Using a micrometer to measure the thickness of the brake disc

5.6 Measuring the disc run-out with a dial gauge

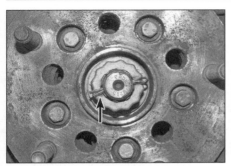

5.10a Bend up the split pin legs...

5.10b ...then extract the split pin...

5.10c ...and remove the retaining nut locking ring

5.11 Attach the holding tool to the wheel hub using the two wheel nuts

5.12 Unscrew the retaining nut, and remove the washer

5.14 Hub assembly-to-steering knuckle retaining bolts

measure the disc thickness at the eight positions, 15 mm in from the outer edge. If the variation between the minimum and maximum readings is greater than the specified amount, the disc should be renewed.

8 To remove a disc, proceed as follows.

Removal

Caution: Due to the extremely high tightening torque of the driveshaft/wheel spindle retaining nut, take great care when removing and refitting the nut. Use only the correct sockets and make sure you have a suitable extension bar for removal, and a torque wrench capable of tightening the nut to the correct setting (see Specifications) for refitting. Entrust this work to a dealer or suitably equipped garage if in doubt about the procedure, or if the required tools are not available.

Note: *A new driveshaft/wheel spindle retaining nut, washer and split pin, together with new brake disc and hub assembly retaining bolts will be required for refitting.*

9 Firmly apply the handbrake, then jack up the front of the vehicle and support it securely on axle stands (see *Jacking and vehicle support*). Remove the relevant front roadwheel.

10 Extract the split pin from the driveshaft and remove the retaining nut locking ring **(see illustrations)**.

11 To prevent rotation of the wheel hub as the driveshaft/wheel spindle retaining nut is slackened, make up a holding tool and attach the tool to the wheel hub using two wheel nuts **(see Tool Tip and illustration)**.

TOOL TiP *A tool to hold the wheel hub stationary while the driveshaft retaining nut is slackened can be fabricated from two lengths of steel strip (one long, one short) and a nut and bolt; the nut and bolt forming the pivot of a forked tool.*

12 With the holding tool in place, unscrew the retaining nut and remove the washer **(see illustration)**. Discard the nut and washer as new components must be used on refitting.

13 If not already done, undo the two bolts securing the brake caliper mounting bracket to the steering knuckle. Slide the caliper and mounting bracket, complete with brake pads, off the disc and suspend the assembly from the coil spring using a cable tie **(see illustration 5.3)**.

14 Using a long socket bit inserted through the holes in the hub flange, undo the five bolts securing the hub assembly to the steering knuckle **(see illustration)**. Note that new bolts will be required for refitting.

15 Withdraw the hub assembly and brake disc from the steering knuckle. If necessary, tap the rear of the brake disc with a soft faced mallet to free the hub assembly from the knuckle.

16 With the hub assembly on the bench, undo the five bolts securing the brake disc to the hub flange, then turn the assembly over and lift off the disc **(see illustrations)**. Note that new bolts will be required for refitting. If the original disc is to be refitted, make alignment marks on the hub flange and disc prior to separation to ensure correct reassembly.

Refitting

17 Thoroughly clean the mating surfaces of

5.16a Undo the bolts securing the brake disc to the hub flange...

5.16b ...then turn the assembly over and lift off the disc

6.3 Front brake caliper brake hose pipe union

the brake disc and hub flange ensuring that all traces of dirt and corrosion are removed.

18 Place the disc in position on the hub flange, aligning the marks made on removal if the original disc is being refitted. Fit the five new disc retaining bolts and tighten them in a progressive diagonal sequence to the specified torque.

19 Clean the mating faces of the hub assembly and steering knuckle, then locate the hub assembly in position on the knuckle. Fit the five new hub assembly retaining bolts and tighten them in a progressive diagonal sequence to the specified torque.

20 Place the new washer over the end of the driveshaft/wheel spindle and screw on the new retaining nut. Only tighten the nut finger tight at this stage.

21 Slide the brake caliper assembly over the disc and into position on the steering knuckle. Refit the two mounting bracket retaining bolts and tighten them to the specified torque.

22 Tighten the driveshaft/wheel spindle retaining nut to the specified torque in the four stages given in the Specifications. Prevent the driveshaft/wheel spindle from rotating as the nut is tightened, using the method employed for removal.

23 Refit the retaining nut locking ring, aligning the slots with the split pin hole in the driveshaft/wheel spindle. Insert a new split pin and bend over the split pin legs to secure.

24 Refit the roadwheel, tighten the wheel nuts to the specified torque, then lower the vehicle to the ground.

6.13 Check the condition of the guide pins and dust covers in the caliper mounting bracket

6 Front brake caliper – removal, overhaul and refitting

Note: *A new brake caliper upper guide pin bolt will be required when refitting. Before starting work, refer to the note at the beginning of Section 2 concerning the dangers of hydraulic fluid, and to the warning at the beginning of Section 4 concerning the dangers of dust.*

Removal

1 Apply the handbrake, then jack up the front of the vehicle and support it on axle stands (see *Jacking and vehicle support*). Remove the roadwheel.

2 Minimise fluid loss by first removing the master cylinder reservoir cap and screwing it down onto a piece of polythene. Alternatively, use a brake hose clamp to clamp the flexible hose leading to the brake caliper.

3 Clean the area around the caliper brake hose pipe union **(see illustration)**. Unscrew and remove the pipe union and withdraw the pipe from the caliper. Suitably plug the pipe end and caliper hole, to minimise fluid loss and prevent the ingress of dust and dirt into the hydraulic system.

4 Remove the brake pads as described in Section 4.

5 Unscrew the caliper upper guide pin bolt while counterholding the guide pin with a spanner, then lift the caliper off the mounting bracket.

Overhaul

Note: *Before starting work, check on the availability of parts (caliper overhaul kit/ seals).*

6 With the caliper on the bench, brush away any traces if dust and dirt, but take care not to inhale any of the dust because it may be harmful to your health.

7 Carefully remove the dust seals from the two pistons and the caliper body.

8 Using a G-clamp or similar tool, or suitable pieces of wood, retain one of the pistons in the fully retracted position.

9 Apply compressed air to the brake hose union hole to push out the remaining piston approximately half way out of its bore. Only low pressure should be required, such as is generated by a foot pump.

10 Retain the partially ejected piston in position using the G-clamp or similar tool, or suitable pieces of wood. Again, using compressed air, push out the other piston approximately half way out of its bore. The two partially ejected pistons can now be removed by hand from the caliper body. Suitably identify the two pistons so that they can be refitted to their original bores in the caliper.

11 Using a small screwdriver, carefully remove the piston seals from the grooves in the caliper, taking care not to mark the bore.

12 Thoroughly clean all components with clean hydraulic fluid. Never use mineral-based solvents such as petrol or paraffin, which will attack the rubber components of the hydraulic system. Dry the components using compressed air or a clean, lint-free cloth. If available, use compressed air to blow clear the fluid passages.

⚠ *Warning: Wear eye protection when using compressed air.*

13 Check all components and renew any that are worn or damaged. If the pistons and/ or caliper bore are scratched excessively, renew the complete caliper body. Similarly check the condition of the guide pins and dust covers in the caliper mounting bracket **(see illustration)**. The bushes and guide pins should be undamaged and (when cleaned) the pins should be a reasonably tight sliding fit. If there is any doubt about the condition of any component, renew it.

14 If the caliper is fit for further use, obtain the necessary components from your Ford dealer. Renew the caliper seals and dust covers as a matter of course since these should never be re-used.

15 On reassembly, ensure that all components are absolutely clean and dry.

16 Dip the first piston and the new piston seal in clean hydraulic fluid and smear clean fluid on the caliper bore surface.

17 Locate the new seal in the caliper bore groove, using only the fingers to manipulate it into position.

18 Fit the new dust seal to the piston, then insert the piston into the cylinder bore using a twisting motion to ensure it enters the seal correctly. Locate the dust seal in the body groove, and push the piston fully into the caliper bore.

19 Repeat paragraphs 17 to 19 to reassemble the remaining piston.

Refitting

20 Place the caliper in position on the mounting bracket and fit the new upper guide pin bolt. Tighten the upper guide pin bolt to the specified torque while counterholding the guide pin with a spanner.

21 Refit the brake pads as described in Section 4.

22 Reconnect the caliper brake hose pipe union ensuring that it locates correctly on the caliper. Tighten the union nut to the specified torque.

23 Remove the brake hose clamp or polythene, and bleed the hydraulic system as described in Section 2. Note that, providing the precautions described were taken to minimise brake fluid loss, it should only be necessary to bleed the relevant front brake circuit.

24 Refit the roadwheel, then lower the vehicle to the ground and tighten the roadwheel nuts to the specified torque.

7 Rear brake pads – renewal

Warning: Renew BOTH sets of rear brake pads at the same time – NEVER renew the pads on only one wheel, as uneven braking may result. Note that the dust created by wear of the pads is a health hazard. Never blow it out with compressed air, and do not inhale any of it. An approved filtering mask should be worn when working on the brakes. DO NOT use petroleum-based solvents to clean brake parts – use brake cleaner or methylated spirit only.

1 Slacken the rear roadwheel nuts, then chock the front wheels then jack up the rear of the vehicle and securely support it on axle stands (see *Jacking and vehicle support*).

2 Fully undo the nuts and remove the rear roadwheels.

3 Follow the accompanying photos **(illustrations 7.3a to 7.3q)** for the actual pad renewal procedure, bearing in mind the additional points given in the following paragraphs. Be sure to stay in order and read the caption under each illustration. Note that if the old pads are to be refitted, ensure that they are identified so that they can be returned to their original positions.

4 If the original brake pads are still serviceable, carefully clean them using a clean, fine wire brush or similar, paying particular attention to the sides and back of the metal backing plate. Clean out the grooves in the friction material, and pick out any large embedded particles of dirt or debris. Carefully clean the pad locations in the caliper body/mounting bracket.

5 Prior to fitting the pads, check that the guide pins are a snug fit in the caliper mounting bracket. Brush the dust and dirt from the caliper and piston, but do not inhale it, as it is injurious to health. Inspect the dust seal around the piston for damage, and the piston for evidence of fluid leaks, corrosion or damage. If attention to any of these components is necessary, refer to Section 9.

6 If new brake pads are to be fitted, it will be necessary to retract the piston fully into the caliper bore by rotating it and at the same time pushing it in very firmly. Retract the piston on the left-hand side caliper by turning it anti-clockwise. Retract the piston on the right-hand side caliper by turning it clockwise. The pistons can be rotated using sturdy circlip pliers, however special tools are readily available to achieve this with less effort. While the caliper is being retracted, clamp off the flexible brake hose leading to the caliper then connect a brake bleeding kit to the caliper bleed screw. Open the bleed screw as the piston is retracted, the surplus brake fluid will then be collected in the bleed kit vessel. Close the bleed screw just before the caliper piston is pushed fully into the caliper. This should ensure no air enters the hydraulic system.

Note: *The ABS unit contains hydraulic components that are very sensitive to*

7.3a Remove the brake pad wear sensor plug from the back of the caliper, if fitted. Unscrew and remove the upper guide pin bolt while counterholding the guide pin with a second spanner...

impurities in the brake fluid. Even the smallest particles can cause the system to fail through blockage. The pad retraction method described here prevents any debris in the brake fluid expelled from the caliper from being passed back to the ABS hydraulic unit, as well as preventing any chance of damage to the master cylinder seals.

7 With the brake pads installed, depress the brake pedal repeatedly, until normal (non-assisted) pedal pressure is restored, and the pads are pressed into firm contact with the brake disc.

8 Repeat the above procedure on the remaining rear brake caliper.

9 Refit the roadwheels, then lower the vehicle

7.3b ...and unscrew and remove the lower guide pin bolt in the same manner

7.3c Lift the caliper off the mounting bracket...

7.3d ...and suspend it from rear spring using wire or a cable tie

7.3e Remove the outer pad...

7.3f ...and inner pad from the caliper mounting bracket

7.3g Remove and discard the four anti-rattle springs from the caliper mounting bracket, noting their fitted position

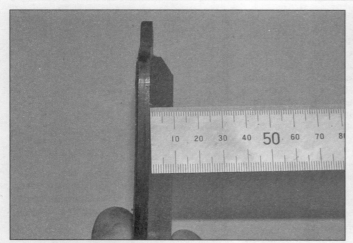

7.3h Measure the thickness of the pad friction material. If any are worn down to the specified minimum, all four pads must be renewed

7.3i Using a caliper retracting tool to retract the caliper piston. For vehicles made from 03/09/2012 to 28/5/2016 the piston on the left-hand wheel should be turned anti-clockwise and the piston on the right-hand wheel should be turned clockwise. On vehicles made from 29/5/2016 the left-hand side wheel piston should be turned clockwise and the right-hand side wheel piston anti-clockwise

7.3j Check the brake fluid level in the reservoir and draw some off if necessary

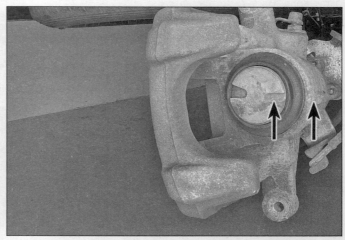

7.3k Once the piston is fully retracted, unscrew it slightly until the cut-outs are in this position, slightly off horizontal and matching up with the raised mark on the caliper body

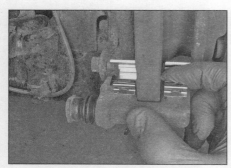

7.3l Refit the lower anti-rattle springs to the caliper mounting bracket...

7.3m ...and the upper anti-rattle springs to the caliper mounting bracket

7.3n If present, remove the protective backing from the rear of the brake pads. Place the outer pad in position...

7.3o ...followed by the inner pad, then reconnect the brake pad wear indicator wiring, if fitted

7.3p Slide the caliper into position in the mounting bracket, making sure the lug on the inner pad engages with the slot in the piston

7.3q Fit the upper and lower guide pin bolts and tighten them both to the specified torque

to the ground and tighten the wheel nuts to the specified torque.

10 Check the hydraulic fluid level as described in *Weekly checks*.

Caution: New pads will not give full braking efficiency until they have bedded-in. Be prepared for this, and avoid hard braking as far as possible for the first hundred miles or so after pad renewal.

---

8 Rear brake disc –
inspection, removal and refitting 🔧

Note: *Before starting work, refer to the warning at the beginning of Section 7 concerning the dangers of dust. If either disc requires renewal, both should be renewed at the same time together with new pads, to ensure even and consistent braking.*

Inspection

1 Chock the front wheels then jack up the rear of the vehicle and securely support it on axle stands (see *Jacking and vehicle support*). Remove the relevant rear roadwheel.

2 Scrape any corrosion from the disc. Rotate the disc, and examine it for deep scoring, grooving or cracks. Using a micrometer, measure the thickness of the disc in several places. The minimum thickness is given in the

Specifications. Light wear and scoring is normal, but if excessive, the disc should be removed, and either reground by a specialist, or renewed. If regrinding is undertaken, the minimum thickness must be maintained. Obviously, if the disc is cracked, it must be renewed.

3 Using a dial gauge or a flat metal block and feeler gauges, check that the disc run-out 10 mm from the outer edge does not exceed the limit given in the Specifications. To do this, fix the measuring equipment, and rotate the disc, noting the variation in measurement as the disc is rotated. The difference between the minimum and maximum measurements recorded is the disc run-out.

4 If the run-out is greater than the specified amount, check for variations of the disc thickness as follows. Mark the disc at eight positions 45° apart then, using a micrometer, measure the disc thickness at the eight positions, 15 mm in from the outer edge. If the variation between the minimum and maximum readings is greater than the specified amount, the disc should be renewed.

Removal

5 Remove the relevant rear hub and bearing as described in Chapter 8 Section 8.

6 With the hub assembly on the bench, undo the five bolts securing the brake disc to the hub flange **(see illustration)**. Note that new bolts will be required for refitting. If the original

8.6 Undo the five bolts securing the rear brake disc to the hub flange

disc is to be refitted, make alignment marks on the hub flange and disc prior to separation to ensure correct reassembly.

7 Support the brake disc with the hub assembly facing downward and apply liberal amounts of penetrating oil to the contact area of the disc and hub **(see illustration)**. The hub is flanged into the brake disc by approximately 20 mm and is likely to be extremely tight; particularly on older vehicles where the effects of corrosion will be a factor.

8 Using a hammer and suitable mandrels, drive the hub assembly out of the disc **(see illustration)**. In extreme cases of disc-to-hub corrosion, it may be necessary to use a hydraulic press to press the hub out of the disc.

8.7 Apply liberal amounts of penetrating oil to the contact area of the disc and hub (shown with disc separated from the hub)

8.8 Using a hammer and suitable mandrels, drive the hub assembly out of the disc

8.10a Place the hub assembly in position on the brake disc...

8.10b ...fit the five new disc retaining bolts...

8.10c ...and tighten them in a progressive diagonal sequence to the specified torque

Refitting

9 Thoroughly clean the mating surfaces of the brake disc and hub flange ensuring that all traces of dirt and corrosion are removed.

10 Place the hub assembly in position on the brake disc, aligning the marks made on removal if the original disc is being refitted. Fit the five new disc retaining bolts and tighten them in a progressive diagonal sequence to the specified torque **(see illustrations)**.

11 Refit the rear hub and bearing as described in Chapter 8 Section 8.

9 Rear brake caliper – removal, overhaul and refitting

Removal

Note: *Before starting work, refer to the note*

at the beginning of Section 2 concerning the dangers of hydraulic fluid, and to the warning at the beginning of Section 7 concerning the dangers of dust.

1 Chock the front wheels, then jack up the rear of the vehicle and support on axle stands (see *Jacking and vehicle support*). Remove the relevant rear roadwheel, then make sure that the handbrake is fully released.

2 Move the handbrake operating lever on the caliper upwards and detach the handbrake inner cable end fitting from the lever **(see illustration)**.

3 Using pliers, compress the tabs on the handbrake outer cable collar and withdraw the cable from the mounting bracket **(see illustration)**.

4 Minimise fluid loss by first removing the master cylinder reservoir cap and screwing it down onto a piece of polythene. Alternatively, use a brake hose clamp to clamp the flexible hose leading to the brake caliper.

5 Clean the area around the caliper brake hose union. Slacken (but do not completely unscrew) the union on the caliper end of the flexible hose.

6 Unscrew the caliper upper and lower guide pin bolts while counterholding the guide pins with a second spanner, then slide the caliper off the mounting bracket **(see illustrations)**.

7 Support the caliper in one hand, and prevent the flexible hose from turning with the other hand. Unscrew the caliper from the hose, making sure that the hose is not twisted unduly or strained. Once the caliper is detached, plug the open hydraulic unions in the caliper and hose, to keep out dust and dirt.

8 If necessary, remove the brake pads with reference to Section 7, then undo the two retaining bolts and remove the caliper mounting bracket **(see illustrations)**.

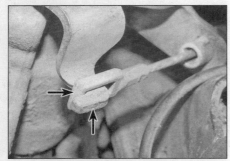

9.2 Detach the handbrake inner cable end fitting from the caliper lever

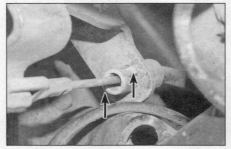

9.3 Compress the tabs on the handbrake outer cable collar and withdraw the cable from the mounting bracket

9.6a Unscrew the caliper upper and lower guide pin bolts...

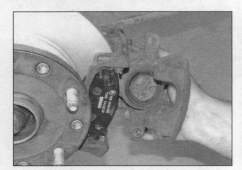

9.6b ...then slide the caliper off the mounting bracket

9.8a Undo the two retaining bolts...

9.8b ...and remove the caliper mounting bracket

Overhaul

9 No overhaul procedures, or parts, were available at the time of writing. Check the availability of spares before dismantling the caliper. Do not attempt to dismantle the handbrake mechanism inside the caliper; if the mechanism is faulty, the complete caliper assembly must be renewed.

Refitting

10 Refit the caliper by reversing the removal operations. Make sure that the flexible brake hose is not twisted. Tighten the mounting bolts and wheel nuts to the specified torque.

11 Bleed the brake circuit according to the procedure given in Section 2, remembering to remove the brake hose clamp (where applicable) from the flexible hose. Make sure there are no leaks from the hose connections. Test the brakes carefully before returning the vehicle to normal service.

10 Master cylinder –
removal, overhaul and refitting

Note: *Before starting work, refer to the warning at the beginning of Section 2 concerning the dangers of hydraulic fluid.*

Removal

1 Undo the upper master cylinder reservoir retaining screws, release the reservoir, undo the cap and empty the fluid into a container **(see illustration)**.

2 Disconnect the hose linking the upper and lower reservoirs by releasing the fastener at the lower reservoir end **(see illustration)**.

3 Depress the tab and disconnect the wiring plug from the brake fluid level sensor on the lower reservoir **(see illustration)**.

4 Release the clip and disconnect the clutch hydraulic hose from the lower fluid reservoir **(see illustration)**. Be prepared for some fluid loss. Tape over or plug the outlet.

5 Place rags beneath the master cylinder to collect escaping brake fluid. Identify the brake pipes for position, then unscrew the union nuts and move the pipes to one side **(see illustration)**. Plug or tape over the pipe ends to prevent dirt entry. Be prepared for fluid loss.

6 Unclip any associated wiring clips, unscrew the two mounting nuts and withdraw the master cylinder from the vacuum servo unit **(see illustration)**. Take care not to spill fluid on the vehicle paintwork. Recover the master cylinder-to-servo unit seal.

7 If required, the fluid reservoir can be removed from the master cylinder by undoing the retaining bolt and pulling the reservoir up and off the mounting seals.

Overhaul

8 The master cylinder comes as one unit, so servicing is not possible. The only parts

10.1 Undo the reservoir screws (one of two shown)

10.3 Disconnect the wiring plug from the brake fluid level sensor

10.2 Press the buttons and release the hose linking the reservoirs

10.4 Release the clip and disconnect the clutch hydraulic hose from the fluid reservoir

available individually are the fluid reservoirs and their mounting seals, and the filler cap.

9 If the master cylinder is worn excessively, it must be renewed.

10 If new reservoir seals are to be fitted, extract the old seals from the cylinder body, lubricate the new seals with clean brake hydraulic fluid and push the seals into position.

Refitting

11 Where applicable, refit the fluid reservoir to the master cylinder body and secure with the retaining bolt.

12 Place the master cylinder-to-servo unit seal in position, then fit the master cylinder to the servo unit. Ensure that the servo unit pushrod enters the master cylinder piston centrally.

Fit the retaining nuts and tighten them to the specified torque.

13 Refit the brake pipes and tighten the union nuts securely.

14 Reconnect the clutch hydraulic hose to the lower fluid reservoir.

15 Reconnect the wiring plug to the brake fluid level sensor.

16 Remove the upper reservoir filler cap, then top-up the reservoir with fresh hydraulic fluid to the MAX mark (see Weekly checks 0 Section 5).

17 Bleed the brake and clutch hydraulic systems as described in Section 2 and Chapter 6 Section 2 then refit the filler cap. Thoroughly check the operation of the brakes and clutch before using the vehicle on the road.

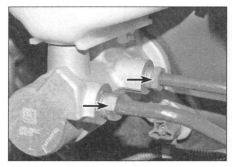

10.5 Unscrew the union nuts and move the brake pipes to one side

10.6 Master cylinder mounting nuts

11.7 Extract the locking plate and retaining clip then slide the servo unit pushrod off the stud on the brake pedal

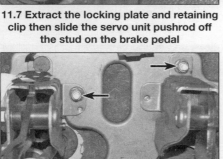

11.9a Undo the three bracket retaining nuts from inside the vehicle…

11.8 Brake servo retaining nuts

11.9b …and the two from within the engine compartment

11 Brake pedal –
removed and refitting

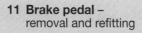

Note: *This Section includes the removal and refitting of the brake pedal and clutch pedal as an assembly.*

Removal

1 Disconnect the battery negative terminal as described in Chapter 5 Section 4.
2 Remove the steering column as described in Chapter 10 Section 17.
3 Remove the clutch master cylinder, as described in Chapter 6 Section 3.
4 Remove the brake stop-light switch, as described in Chapter 12 Section 5.
5 Remove the clutch pedal position sensor, if possible, as described in Chapter 4A

12.5 Remove the hose from the servo unit, leaving the grommet in place

Section 10, or, if it is integral with the pedal, disconnect the wiring plug.
6 Release the wiring retaining clips from the pedal mounting bracket.
7 Slide off the retaining clip, then slide the servo unit pushrod off the stud on the brake pedal **(see illustration)**.
8 Undo the four nuts securing the brake servo unit to the bulkhead **(see illustration)**. Make sure the servo unit is supported from within the engine bay.
9 Undo the three remaining nuts on the drivers side of the bulkhead and two nuts on the engine compartment side, then remove the pedals and mounting bracket assembly from the vehicle **(see illustrations)**.
10 Check the pedals and mounting bracket for excessive wear and damage. It is not possible to renew the pedal pivot bushes separately, so if they are worn, the complete assembly must be renewed.

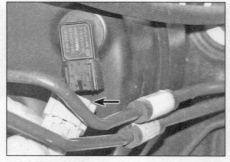

12.6 If fitted, remove the wiring plug from the servo housing

Refitting

11 Manoeuvre the pedal and mounting bracket assembly into place making sure the brake servo pushrod fits correctly over the brake pedal.
12 Refit the pedal mounting bracket nuts and tighten to the specified torque.
13 With the servo unit pushrod engaged with the stud on the brake pedal, refit the retaining clip and locking plate.
14 Refit the clutch master cylinder to the pedal mounting bracket and secure with the two bolts, tightened securely.
15 Engage the clutch master cylinder pushrod with the clutch pedal, then refit the retaining clip.
16 Reattach the wiring harness to the support clips on the pedal mounting bracket.
17 Hold the brake pedal and clutch pedal in the raised position and insert the stop-light switch and clutch pedal position switch (if removed) into the holes in the pedal mounting bracket. Push the switches down to depress the plungers, then turn the switches to lock them in position. Reconnect the wiring plugs to the switches.
18 Refit the steering column as described in Chapter 10 Section 17.
19 Reconnect the battery negative terminal on completion.

12 Vacuum servo unit –
testing, removal and refitting

Testing

1 To test the operation of the servo unit, with the engine switched off, depress the footbrake pedal several times to exhaust the vacuum. Now start the engine, keeping the pedal firmly depressed. As the engine starts, there should be a noticeable 'give' in the brake pedal as the vacuum builds-up. Allow the engine to run for at least two minutes, then switch it off. The brake pedal should now feel normal, but further applications should result in the pedal feeling firmer, the pedal stroke decreasing with each application.
2 If the servo does not operate as described, first inspect the servo unit check valve as described in Section 13.
3 If the servo unit still fails to operate satisfactorily, the fault lies within the unit itself. Repairs to the unit are not possible; if faulty, the servo unit must be renewed.

Removal

4 Remove the brake master cylinder as described in Section 10.
5 Carefully ease the vacuum hose out of the servo unit, taking care not to displace the sealing grommet **(see illustration)**.
6 Disconnect the wiring plug from the servo housing **(see illustration)**.

7 From inside the cabin, remove the facia right-hand lower trim panel by pulling it away from the facia to release the retaining clips **(see illustration)**.

8 Extract the locking plate and retaining clip, then slide the servo unit pushrod off the stud on the brake pedal **(see illustration 11.7)**.

9 Undo the four nuts securing the servo unit and pedal mounting bracket to the bulkhead **(see illustration 11.8)**.

10 Return to the engine compartment and lift the servo unit out of position. Recover the servo unit-to-bulkhead gasket.

Refitting

11 Refit the gasket, then locate the vacuum servo unit in position on the bulkhead. Refit the four nuts and tighten them to the specified torque.

12 With the servo unit pushrod engaged with the stud on the brake pedal, refit the retaining clip and locking plate.

13 Refit the facia right-hand lower trim panel.

14 Refit the vacuum hose to the servo grommet, ensuring that the hose is correctly seated.

15 Refit the brake master cylinder as described in Section 10.

13 Vacuum servo unit check valve and hose – removal, testing and refitting

Removal

1 Carefully ease the vacuum hose out of the servo unit, taking care not to displace the sealing grommet.

2 Unscrew the union nut, or disconnect the quick-release fitting (as applicable) and remove the vacuum hose from the vacuum pump.

3 Unclip the vacuum hose from its supports, then remove the hose and check valve from the vehicle.

Testing

4 Examine the check valve and hose for signs of damage, and renew if necessary. The valve may be tested by blowing through it in both directions. Air should flow through the valve in one direction only – when blown through from the servo unit end. If air flows in both directions, or not at all, renew the valve and hose as an assembly.

5 Examine the check valve rubber sealing grommet for signs of damage or deterioration, and renew as necessary.

Refitting

6 Refitting is a reversal of removal, ensuring that the hose is correctly seated in the servo grommet.

7 On completion, start the engine and check there are no air leaks.

12.7 Remove the facia trim panel by pulling it away to release the retaining clips

14 Vacuum pump – removal and refitting

Removal

1 Disconnect the battery negative terminal as described in Chapter 5 Section 4.

2 On 2.2 litre engines drain the cooling system as described in Chapter 1 Section 32.

3 Refer to Chapter 4A Section 5 and remove the air cleaner assembly and air ducts.

4 On 2.0 litre engines, undo the fasteners and remove the fuel regulator assembly above the vacuum pump. There is no need to disconnect any pipes.

5 Undo the retaining nut and release the

wiring harness and hose support bracket from the vacuum pump stud.

6 On 2.2 litre models, unbolt the thermostat housing from the vacuum pump and recover the seal. Note that a new seal will be required for refitting.

7 Disconnect the vacuum hoses from the vacuum pump. Note the different connections **(see illustration)**.

8 Unscrew the mounting bolts, withdraw the vacuum pump from the end of the cylinder head and recover the gasket and seal **(see illustrations)**. Note that a new gasket and seal, if fitted, will be required for refitting.

9 Thoroughly clean the mating surfaces of the vacuum pump, cylinder head and thermostat housing.

Refitting

10 Locate a new seal on the end of the cylinder head and place a new gasket on the vacuum pump. Refit the pump to the cylinder head, making sure that the drive dog engages correctly with the end of the camshaft **(see illustration)**. Insert the mounting bolts and tighten them to the specified torque.

11 Refit the thermostat housing to the vacuum pump using a new O-ring seal and tighten the mounting bolt to the specified torque.

12 Reconnect the vacuum hose to the rear of the vacuum pump.

13 Reconnect the coolant hoses to the thermostat housing and the expansion tank hose to the vacuum pump.

14 Refit the wiring harness and hose support

14.7 Disconnect the hose(s) from the vacuum pump

14.8b ...and recover the gasket and seal, if fitted

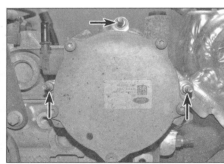

14.8a Unscrew the mounting bolts and remove the vacuum pump...

14.10 Vacuum pump drive dog on the end of the camshaft

15.3 Handbrake cable adjuster nut

15.5 Disconnect the warning light switch wiring plug

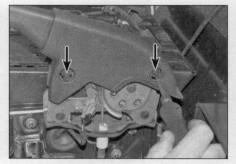

15.6 Undo the screws and remove the covers

15.7a Detach the inner cable...

15.7b ...then squeeze together the tabs and release the outer cable

15.8 Remove the battery box

bracket to the vacuum pump stud and tighten the retaining nut securely.

15 Refit the air ducts and air cleaner assembly as described in Chapter 4A Section 5.

16 Reconnect the battery negative terminal, then refill the cooling system as described in Chapter 1 Section 32.

15 Handbrake lever – removal and refitting

Removal

1 Disconnect and remove the battery as described in Chapter 5 Section 4.

2 Chock the front wheels then jack up the rear of the vehicle and securely support it on axle stands (see *Jacking and vehicle support*). Ensure that the handbrake lever is released.

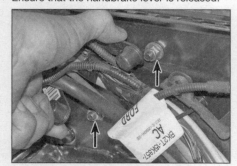

15.9a Battery compartment-side nuts (driver's seat removed for clarity)...

3 From under the vehicle, unscrew the locknut, then slacken the handbrake cable adjuster nut at the cable compensator plate (see illustration).

4 Release the handbrake lever gaiters by releasing the clips and sliding them up and off the lever.

5 Disconnect the wiring plug from the handbrake lever warning light switch (see illustration).

6 Remove the covers from the lever mechanism by removing the two screws – the cover is in two halves (see illustration).

7 Detach the handbrake inner cable from the lever, then release the outer cable from the bracket on the side of the lever base (see illustrations).

8 Move the driver's seat fully forward and remove the battery box (see illustration).

9 Undo the nuts securing the handbrake lever assembly to the side of the battery box and

15.9b ...and handbrake lever-side retaining nut

remove the lever assembly from the vehicle (see illustrations).

Refitting

10 Refitting is the reverse of removal, bearing in mind the following points:

a) *Lubricate the exposed end of the handbrake cable and the cable attachment on the lever with molybdenum disulphide grease.*

b) *Adjust the handbrake as described in Chapter 1 Section 22 on completion.*

16 Handbrake cables – removal and refitting

Removal

1 The handbrake cable consists of three sections, a front cable which connects the handbrake lever to the intermediate cable, an intermediate cable or rod which links the front cable to the compensator plate, and the rear cables which link the compensator plate to the rear brake pads. Each section can be removed individually as follows.

Front cable

2 Chock the front wheels then jack up the rear of the vehicle and securely support it on axle stands (see *Jacking and vehicle support*). Ensure that the handbrake lever is released.

3 From under the vehicle, unscrew the locknut, then slacken the handbrake cable adjuster nut at the cable compensator plate (see illustration 15.3).

4 Release the handbrake lever rubber gaiter from the floor and slide it up and off the lever.

5 Detach the handbrake inner cable from the lever, then release the outer cable from the bracket on the side of the lever base **(see illustrations 15.7a and 15.7b)**.

6 Disconnect the front cable from the connector joining the front cable to the intermediate or rod **(see illustration)**.

7 Detach the front cable from the abutment bracket on the underbody.

8 From inside the vehicle, lift up the floor covering below the handbrake lever and prise out the handbrake cable grommet from the floor.

9 Remove the cable from under the vehicle.

Intermediate cable/rod

10 Chock the front wheels then jack up the rear of the vehicle and securely support it on axle stands (see *Jacking and vehicle support*). Ensure that the handbrake lever is released.

11 From under the vehicle, unscrew and remove the handbrake cable locknut and adjuster nut at the cable compensator plate and withdraw the intermediate rod from the compensator **(see illustration 15.3)**.

12 Disconnect the intermediate rod from the connector joining the intermediate cable/rod to the front cable, then remove the rod from under the vehicle **(see illustration 16.6)**.

Rear cables

Note: *There is a separate cable for each rear brake.*

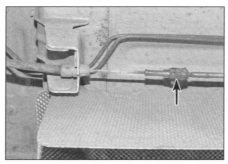

16.6 Disconnect the front handbrake cable at the rod connector

13 Chock the front wheels then jack up the rear of the vehicle and securely support it on axle stands (see *Jacking and vehicle support*). Ensure that the handbrake lever is released.

14 From under the vehicle, unscrew the locknut, then slacken the handbrake cable adjuster nut at the cable compensator plate **(see illustration 15.3)**.

15 Move the handbrake operating lever on the brake caliper upwards and detach the handbrake inner cable end fitting from the lever **(see illustration)**.

16 Using pliers, compress the tabs on the handbrake outer cable collar and withdraw the cable from the mounting bracket **(see illustration)**.

17 Open up the retaining bracket or drill out the rivet and release the cable from the guide

plate on the left-hand side of the rear axle **(see illustration)**.

18 Undo the retaining bolt and release the cable support bracket from the underbody **(see illustration)**.

19 Slip the inner cable end out of the slot in the compensator **(see illustration)**.

20 Compress the tabs on the outer cable end fitting and withdraw the cable from the abutment bracket on the underbody **(see illustration)**. Remove the cable from under the vehicle.

Refitting

21 Refitting is a reversal of the removal procedure, but adjust the handbrake as described in Chapter 1 Section 22.

---

17 Stop-light switch – removal, refitting and adjustment

Removal

1 The stop-light switch is located on the brake pedal mounting bracket in the driver's footwell.

2 Remove the facia right-hand lower trim panel by pulling it away from the facia to release the retaining clips **(see illustration 12.7)**.

3 Disconnect the wiring plug from the stop-light switch **(see illustration)**.

4 Rotate the stop-light switch clockwise by a

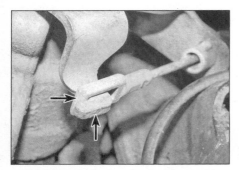

16.15 Detach the handbrake inner cable end fitting from the lever

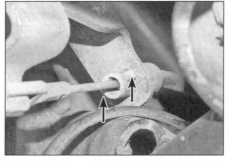

16.16 Compress the tabs on the handbrake outer cable collar

16.17 Drill out the rivet or open the bracket to release the cable

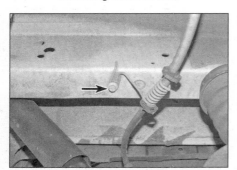

16.18 Undo the retaining bolt and release the cable support bracket from the underbody

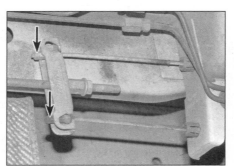

16.19 Slip the inner cable end out of the relevant slot in the compensator

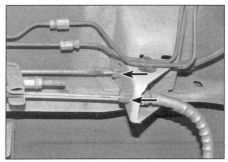

16.20 Withdraw the relevant cable from the abutment bracket on the underbody

17.3 Disconnect the stop-light switch wiring plug

17.4 Rotate the switch clockwise to remove it

quarter-turn and remove the switch from the pedal mounting bracket. Do not depress the brake pedal during the removal or refitting procedure – the pedal must be 'at rest' **(see illustration)**.

Refitting and adjustment

5 With the ignition key in the 'off' position, depress the brake pedal 10 times. Allow the pedal to return to its rest position and refit the stop-light switch, reversing the removal procedure. Do not raise or depress the pedal while refitting the switch.

18 Handbrake warning light switch – removal and refitting

Removal

1 Release the handbrake lever rubber gaiter from the floor and slide it up and off the lever.
2 Disconnect the wiring plug from the warning light switch on the side of the handbrake lever **(see illustration 15.5)**.
3 Undo the screws and remove the switch from the handbrake lever bracket.

Refitting

4 Refitting is a reversal of removal.

19 Anti-lock braking and stability control systems – general information

1 ABS is fitted as standard on all models and incorporates traction control and an electronic stability program (ESP) as additional safety features.
2 The ABS system comprises a hydraulic modulator and electronic control unit together with four wheel speed sensors. The hydraulic modulator contains the electronic control unit (ECU), the hydraulic solenoid valves (one set for each brake) and the electrically-driven pump. The purpose of the system is to prevent the wheel(s) locking during heavy braking. This is achieved by automatic release of the brake on the relevant wheel, followed by re-application of the brake.

3 The solenoid valves are controlled by the ECU, which itself receives signals from the four wheel speed sensors which monitor the speed of rotation of each wheel. By comparing these signals, the ECU can determine the speed at which the vehicle is travelling. It can then use this speed to determine when a wheel is decelerating at an abnormal rate, compared to the speed of the vehicle, and therefore predicts when a wheel is about to lock. During normal operation, the system functions in the same way as a conventional braking system.
4 If the ECU senses that a wheel is about to lock, it operates the relevant solenoid valve(s) in the hydraulic unit, which then isolates from the master cylinder the relevant brake(s) on the wheel(s) which is/ are about to lock, effectively sealing-in the hydraulic pressure.
5 If the speed of rotation of the wheel continues to decrease at an abnormal rate, the ECU operates the electrically-driven pump which pumps the hydraulic fluid back into the master cylinder, releasing the brake. Once the speed of rotation of the wheel returns to an acceptable rate, the pump stops, and the solenoid valves switch again, allowing the hydraulic master cylinder pressure to return to the caliper, which then re-applies the brake. This cycle can be carried out many times a second.
6 The action of the solenoid valves and return pump creates pulses in the hydraulic circuit. When the ABS system is functioning, these pulses can be felt through the brake pedal.
7 On models with traction control, the ABS hydraulic modulator incorporates an additional set of solenoid valves which operate the traction control system. The system operates at speeds up to approximately 25 mph (40 km/h) using the signals supplied by the wheel speed sensors. If the ECU senses that a driving wheel is about to lose traction, it prevents this by momentarily applying the relevant front brake. In certain conditions, such as deep mud or snow, turning off the system will allow the wheels to spin with full engine power, which may be beneficial.
8 The electronic stability program (ESP) is a

further development of the ABS and traction control systems. Using additional sensors to monitor steering wheel position, vehicle yaw rate, acceleration and deceleration, in conjunction with the ABS sensors, the ECU can intervene under conditions of vehicle instability and/or traction loss. Using the signals from the various sensors, the ECU can determine driver intent (steering wheel position, throttle position, vehicle speed and engine speed). From the sensor inputs from the wheel speed sensors, yaw rate sensors and acceleration sensors the ECU can calculate whether the vehicle is responding to driver input, or whether an unstable driving situation is occurring. If instability is detected, the ECU will intervene by applying or releasing the relevant front or rear brake, in conjunction with a power reduction, until vehicle stability returns.
9 The operation of the ABS, traction control and ESP is entirely dependent on electrical signals. To prevent the system responding to any inaccurate signals, a built-in safety circuit monitors all signals received by the ECU. If an inaccurate signal or low battery voltage is detected, the system is automatically shut down, and the relevant warning light on the instrument panel is illuminated, to inform the driver that the system is not operational. Normal braking is still available, however.
10 If a fault develops in the system, the vehicle must be taken to a Ford dealer or diagnostic specialist for fault diagnosis and repair.

20 Anti-lock braking and stability control components – removal and refitting

Note: *Faults on the ABS system can only be diagnosed using Ford diagnostic equipment or compatible alternative equipment.*
Note: *Before starting work, refer to the note at the beginning of Section 2 concerning the dangers of hydraulic fluid.*

Hydraulic modulator and ECU/ESP module

Removal

1 Disconnect the battery negative lead as described in Chapter 5 Section 4.
2 Remove the master cylinder reservoir cap, and syphon the hydraulic fluid from the reservoir. Alternatively, open the front brake caliper bleed screws, one at a time, and gently pump the brake pedal to expel the fluid through a plastic tube connected to the screw (see Section 2).

 Warning: Do not syphon the fluid by mouth – it is poisonous. Use a syringe or an old hydrometer.

3 Remove the left-hand headlight unit as described in Chapter 12 Section 11.
4 Note and record the fitted position of the brake pipes at the modulator, then unscrew the union nuts and release the pipes **(see**

20.4 Note the fitted positions of the brake pipes

20.5 Disconnect the wiring harness plug from the ABS ECU on the side of the modulator

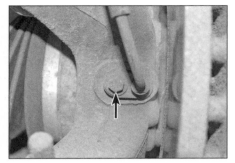

20.18 Front wheel speed sensor retaining bolt

20.19 Disconnect the wheel speed sensor wiring plug on the suspension strut

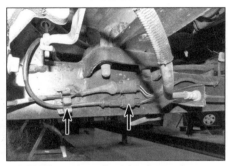

20.22 Disconnect the wheel speed sensor wiring and release the retaining clip

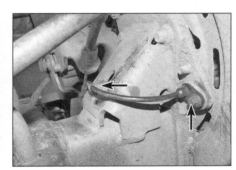

20.23 Undo the sensor retaining bolt and unclip the wiring

illustration). As a precaution, place absorbent rags beneath the brake pipe unions when unscrewing them. Suitably plug or cap the disconnected unions to prevent dirt entry and fluid loss.

5 Pull out the locking bar and disconnect the wiring harness plug from the ECU on the side of the modulator **(see illustration)**.

6 Release the wiring harness from the clip on the modulator mounting bracket.

7 Undo the two bolts securing the modulator mounting bracket to the engine compartment side panel, then manipulate the modulator and mounting bracket assembly out from its location in the engine compartment.

8 If required, undo the three nuts and remove the modulator from the mounting bracket.

Refitting

9 Refitting is the reverse of the removal procedure, noting the following points:
Refit the brake pipes to their respective locations and tighten the union nuts securely.
Ensure that the wiring is correctly routed, and that the ECU wiring harness plug is firmly pressed into position and locked.
On completion, bleed the complete hydraulic system as described in Section 2.

Electronic control unit (ECU)

Removal

Note: *If a new ECU is to be fitted, this work*

must be entrusted to a Ford dealer or suitably-equipped specialist as it is necessary to program the new ECU after installation. This work requires the use of dedicated Ford diagnostic equipment or a compatible alternative.

10 Remove the hydraulic modulator as described previously in this Section.

11 Thoroughly clean the area around the ECU and hydraulic modulator and exercise extreme cleanliness during the following operations.

12 Undo the four retaining bolts and carefully withdraw the ECU from the base of the hydraulic modulator.

13 Thoroughly clean the mating face of the hydraulic modulator.

Refitting

14 Ensuring that the seal is correctly located, carefully place the ECU in position, keeping it square and level.

15 Fit and moderately tighten the four retaining bolts in a diagonal sequence to the specified torque.

16 On completion, refit the hydraulic modulator as described previously in this Section.

Front wheel speed sensor

Removal

17 Firmly apply the handbrake, then jack

up the front of the vehicle and support it securely on axle stands (see *Jacking and vehicle support*). Remove the right-hand side roadwheel.

18 Undo the retaining bolt and withdraw the sensor from the steering knuckle **(see illustration)**.

19 Disconnect the sensor wiring plug mounted on the suspension strut **(see illustration)**.

Refitting

20 Refitting is the reverse of the removal procedure, tightening the sensor retaining bolt to the specified torque.

Rear wheel speed sensor

Removal

21 Chock the front wheels then jack up the rear of the vehicle and securely support it on axle stands (see *Jacking and vehicle support*). Remove the left-hand rear roadwheel.

22 Disconnect the wiring plug and release the wiring from the clips on the rear and top of the axle **(see illustration)**.

23 Undo the retaining bolt and withdraw the sensor from the rear axle **(see illustration)**.

Refitting

24 Refitting is the reverse of the removal procedure, tightening the sensor retaining bolt to the specified torque.

Chapter 10
Suspension and steering

Contents

Degrees of difficulty

| Easy, suitable for novice with little experience | Fairly easy, suitable for beginner with some experience | Fairly difficult, suitable for competent DIY mechanic | Difficult, suitable for experienced DIY mechanic | Very difficult, suitable for expert DIY or professional |

Specifications

Front suspension
Type . . . . . Independent with MacPherson struts, gas-filled shock absorbers and anti-roll bar

Rear suspension
Type . . . . . Beam axle supported on semi-elliptic single leaf springs

Steering
Type . . . . . Hydraulic power-assisted rack and pinion
Fluid type . . . . . See *Lubricants fluids and tyre pressures* on page 0•17

Wheel alignment and steering angles
Front wheel:
  Camber angle . . . . . -0.5° ± 0.5°
  Castor angle . . . . . 2.00° ± 0.6°
  Toe setting . . . . . 0.27° ± 0.25° toe-in
Rear wheel:
  Camber angle . . . . . -1.00° ± 0.5°
  Toe setting . . . . . 0.20° ± 0.4° toe-in

Torque wrench settings

	Nm	lbf ft
Front suspension		
ABS wheel speed sensor retaining bolts	11	8
ABS wiring harness support bracket-to-strut nut	25	18
Anti-roll bar-to-subframe-clamp bolts	63	46
Anti-roll bar connecting link nut	55	41
Brake caliper mounting bracket bolts	270	200
Brake disc-to-hub flange bolts: *		
Stage 1	30	22
Stage 2	Angle-tighten a further 90°	
Driveshaft retaining nut: *		
Stage 1	Rotate the wheel hub 5 times	
Stage 2	250	185
Stage 3	Rotate the wheel hub 5 times	
Stage 4	500	369
Steering knuckle balljoint-to-lower suspension arm nut: *		
Ball joint secured with a circlip	150	111
Ball joint secured with bolts	215	159
Subframe mountings:		
Mounting-to-subframe	133	98
Mounting through-bolt:		
M14x1.5	150	111
M14x2.0	175	129
Suspension lower arm mounting bolts	275	203
Suspension strut piston rod retaining nut	70	52
Suspension strut-to-steering knuckle pinch-bolt: *		
Stage 1	100	74
Stage 2	Angle-tighten a further 180°	
Suspension strut upper mounting retaining nuts	30	22
Do not re-use		
Rear suspension		
Anti-roll bar connecting link nuts*	70	52
Anti-roll bar clamp bolts*	70	52
Leaf spring front mounting bolt nuts	275	203
Leaf spring rear mounting bolt nuts	175	129
Spring-to-axle U-bolt nuts:		
Stage 1	25	18
Stage 2	50	37
Stage 3	75	55
Stage 4	100	74
Stage 5	125	92
Stage 6	150	111
Stage 7	175	129
Shock absorber lower mounting bolt nuts	110	81
Shock absorber upper mounting bolt nuts	175	129
Do not re-use		
Steering		
Power steering fluid cooler retaining bracket bolts	11	8
Power steering pump attachments:		
High-pressure pipe union	25	18
Mounting bolts	24	18
Coolant pump retaining bolts	23	18
Steering column intermediate shaft pinch-connecting bolt	28	21
Steering column retaining nuts	20	15
Steering gear-to-front subframe	115	85
Steering wheel retaining bolt	48	35
Track rod end balljoint nut*	48	35
Do not re-use		
Roadwheels		
Roadwheel nuts	200	148

1 General Information

1 The independent front suspension is of the MacPherson strut type, incorporating coil springs and integral telescopic shock absorbers. The MacPherson struts are located by transverse lower suspension arms, connected to the front subframe by rubber mounting bushes, and to the steering knuckles via a balljoint. The front steering knuckles, which carry the hub bearings, brake calipers and disc assemblies, are bolted to the MacPherson struts, and connected to the lower arms via the balljoints. A front anti-roll bar is fitted, which has link rods at each end to connect it to the suspension strut. Some models also have a rear anti-roll bar, fitted to the rear axle.

2 The rear axle is a tubular steel beam axle supported on semi-elliptic single leaf springs. An elastic element supports the leaf springs in their function. Stub axles are bolted to the ends of the axle beam on each side and these carry the rear hub and bearing assemblies. Telescopic shock absorbers provide the damping for the axle assembly.

3 On all models, further information and procedures relating to the rear axle assembly are contained in Chapter 8.

4 The steering column incorporates an intermediate shaft with a universal joint at the upper end. The lower end of the shaft is connected to the steering gear pinion shaft by means of a flexible coupling.

5 The steering gear is mounted on the front subframe. It is connected by two track rods and track rod ends to the steering arms projecting rearwards from the steering knuckles. The track rod ends are threaded to enable wheel alignment adjustment.

6 Hydraulic power steering is fitted to all models, with the power steering pump being belt-driven from the crankshaft pulley.

2 Front hub carrier – removal and refitting

Caution: Due to the extremely high tightening torque of the driveshaft/ wheel spindle retaining nut, take great care when removing and refitting the nut. Use only the correct sockets and make sure you have a suitable extension bar for removal, and a torque wrench capable of tightening the nut to the correct setting (see Specifications) for refitting. Entrust this work to a dealer or suitably equipped garage if in doubt about the procedure, or if the required tools are not available.

Removal

Note: *A new driveshaft/wheel spindle retaining nut, washer and split pin, together with new brake disc and hub assembly retaining bolts will be required for refitting.*

1 Firmly apply the handbrake, then jack up the front of the vehicle and support it securely on axle stands (see *Jacking and vehicle support*). Remove the relevant front roadwheel.

2 Extract the split pin from the driveshaft and remove the retaining nut locking ring **(see illustrations)**.

3 To prevent rotation of the wheel hub as the driveshaft/wheel spindle retaining nut is slackened, make up a holding tool and attach the tool to the wheel hub using two wheel nuts **(see Tool Tip and illustration)**.

> **TOOL TiP** *A tool to hold the wheel hub stationary while the driveshaft retaining nut is slackened can be fabricated from two lengths of steel strip (one long, one short) and a nut and bolt; the nut and bolt forming the pivot of a forked tool.*

4 With the holding tool in place, unscrew the driveshaft/wheel spindle retaining nut, and remove the washer **(see illustration)**. Discard the nut and washer as new components must be used on refitting.

5 Undo the two bolts securing the brake caliper mounting bracket to the steering knuckle. Slide the caliper and mounting bracket, complete with brake pads, off the disc and suspend the assembly from the coil spring using a cable tie **(see illustration)**.

6 Using a long socket bit inserted through the holes in the hub flange, undo the five bolts securing the hub assembly to the steering

2.2a Bend up the split pin legs...

2.2b ...then extract the split pin...

2.2c ...and remove the retaining nut locking ring

2.3 Attach the holding tool to the wheel hub using two wheel nuts

2.4 Unscrew the retaining nut, and remove the washer

2.5 Slide the caliper and mounting bracket, complete with brake pads, off the disc

2.6 Hub assembly-to-steering knuckle retaining bolts

2.8a Undo the bolts securing the brake disc to the hub flange...

2.8b ...then turn the assembly over and lift off the disc

knuckle **(see illustration)**. Note that new bolts will be required for refitting.

7 Withdraw the hub assembly and brake disc from the steering knuckle. If necessary, tap the rear of the brake disc with a soft-faced mallet to free the hub assembly from the knuckle.

8 With the hub assembly on the bench, undo the five bolts securing the brake disc to the hub flange, then turn the assembly over and lift off the disc **(see illustrations)**. Note that new bolts will be required for refitting. Make alignment marks on the hub flange and disc prior to separation to ensure correct reassembly.

Refitting

9 Thoroughly clean the mating surfaces of the brake disc and hub flange ensuring that all traces of dirt and corrosion are removed.

10 Place the disc in position on the hub flange, aligning the marks made on removal. Fit the five new disc retaining bolts and tighten them in a progressive diagonal sequence to the specified torque.

11 Clean the mating faces of the hub assembly and steering knuckle, then locate the hub assembly in position on the knuckle. Fit the five new hub assembly retaining bolts and tighten them in a progressive diagonal sequence to the specified torque.

12 Slide the brake caliper assembly over the disc and into position on the steering knuckle. Refit the two mounting bracket retaining bolts and tighten them to the specified torque.

13 Place the new washer over the end of the driveshaft/wheel spindle and screw on

the new retaining nut. Tighten the retaining nut to the specified torque in the four stages given in the Specifications. Prevent the hub from rotating as the nut is tightened, using the method employed for removal.

14 Refit the driveshaft/wheel spindle retaining nut locking ring, aligning the slots with the split pin hole in the driveshaft/wheel spindle. Insert a new split pin and bend over the split pin legs to secure.

15 Refit the roadwheel, tighten the wheel nuts to the specified torque, then lower the vehicle to the ground.

3 Front hub bearings – inspection and renewal

Inspection

1 The front hub bearings are of sealed, pre-adjusted and prelubricated, double-row roller type, and are intended to last the vehicle's entire service life without maintenance or attention. The bearings are integral with the front hub assembly and if renewal is necessary a complete hub assembly must be obtained. The actual bearings are not available separately.

2 To check the bearings for excessive wear, firmly apply the handbrake, then jack up the front of the vehicle and support it securely on axle stands (see *Jacking and vehicle support*).

3 Grip the front wheel at the top and bottom and attempt to rock it. If excessive movement

is noted, it may be that the hub bearings are worn. Do not confuse wear in the front suspension lower arm balljoint with wear in the bearings. Hub bearing wear will show up as roughness or vibration when the wheel is spun; it will also be noticeable as a rumbling or growling noise when driving.

Renewal

Note: *A press will be required to dismantle and rebuild the assembly. The bearing's inner races are an interference fit on the hub flange and the outer bearing inner race will remain on the hub flange when the flange is pressed out of the hub assembly. A knife-edged bearing puller will be required to remove it.*

4 Remove the steering knuckle as described in Section 2.

5 Securely support the outer face of the hub assembly on the press bed, with the hub flange facing downward. Using a tubular spacer (or suitable socket) which bears only on the inner end of the hub flange, press the hub flange out of the hub assembly **(see illustration)**.

6 With the hub flange removed from hub assembly, lift off the outer bearing rollers. Remove the outer bearing inner race by supporting the race and pressing the hub flange down through it. Alternatively, use a bearing puller to remove it **(see illustrations)**.

7 Thoroughly clean the hub flange, removing all traces of dirt and grease, and polish away any burrs or raised edges which might hinder reassembly. Obtain a new hub assembly (complete with new bearings) for reassembly.

3.5 Using a tubular spacer which bears only on the inner end of the hub flange press the flange out of the hub assembly

3.6a Using a bearing puller...

3.6b ...to remove the outer bearing inner race from the hub flange

8 Support the hub flange on the press bed with the wheel studs facing downwards, and place the new hub assembly on the hub flange. Using a tubular spacer (or suitable socket) which bears only on the inner bearing inner race, press the hub assembly onto the hub flange approximately one third of the way. Make sure that the hub assembly remains square when pressing it on and doesn't bind on the hub flange.

9 Rotate the hub assembly a minimum of five turns, then continue to press it onto the hub flange approximately half way. Rotate the hub assembly a minimum of five turns again, then continue to press it onto the hub flange until it is fully home. Finally, rotate the hub assembly a minimum of five turns again then remove it from the press bed.

10 Refit the brake disc, then refit the hub assembly to the steering knuckle as described in Section 2.

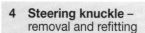

4   Steering knuckle –
   removal and refitting

Removal

1 Remove the front hub assembly as described in Section 2.

2 Undo the retaining bolt and withdraw the wheel speed sensor from the steering knuckle **(see illustration)**.

3 Slacken the track rod end balljoint nut several turns, then use a balljoint separator tool to release the balljoint shank from the steering knuckle **(see illustration)**. With the balljoint released, unscrew the nut and disconnect the balljoint from the steering arm. Discard the nut as a new one must be used for refitting.

4 Slacken the nut securing the steering knuckle balljoint to the lower suspension arm. Attach a two-legged puller to the lower suspension arm and tighten the puller to apply tension to the balljoint shank **(see illustrations)**. Strike the end of the lower suspension arm with a hammer a few times to release the balljoint shank taper.

5 Remove the puller and unscrew the balljoint retaining nut. Discard the nut and obtain a new nut for refitting.

6 Push or pull down on the suspension lower arm to disengage the balljoint from the arm, then move the steering knuckle to one side and release the arm, taking care not to damage the balljoint rubber boot **(see illustration)**. It is advisable to place a protective cover over the rubber boot such as the plastic cap from an aerosol can, suitably cut to fit.

7 Unscrew and remove the pinch-bolt and nut securing the steering knuckle assembly to the front suspension strut **(see illustration)**. Discard the nut and bolt as new ones must be used for refitting. Prise open the clamp using a wedge-shaped tool and release the

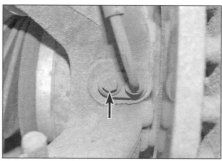

4.2 Front wheel speed sensor retaining bolt

4.4a Slacken the nut securing the steering knuckle balljoint to the lower suspension arm...

4.3 Using a balljoint separator tool to release the track rod end balljoint

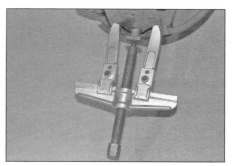

4.4b ...then release the balljoint using a two-legged puller

knuckle from the strut. If necessary, tap the knuckle downwards with a soft-headed mallet to separate the two components. Remove the knuckle from the vehicle.

Refitting

8 Thoroughly clean the bottom end of the suspension strut and its location in the steering knuckle. Locate the knuckle onto the strut and over the tab, then insert the pinch-bolt and tighten it to the specified torque.

9 Push down on the lower suspension arm and engage the steering knuckle balljoint with the arm. Fit the new balljoint retaining nut and tighten the nut to the specified torque.

Note: *The new balljoint retaining nut torque specifications will vary depending on whether*

the lower arm balljoint is secured with a Circlip or with two bolts.

10 Locate the track rod end balljoint on the steering arm. Screw on a new nut and tighten it to the specified torque. If the balljoint shank is hollow, a 5 mm Allen key can be used to prevent the balljoint from rotating as the nut is tightened. If the shank is solid, use a stout bar to lever up on the underside of the track rod end. This will lock the balljoint shank taper in the steering arm and prevent rotation as the nut is tightened.

11 Refit the wheel speed sensor to the steering knuckle and secure with the retaining bolt, tightened to the specified torque.

12 Refit the front hub carrier as described in Section 2.

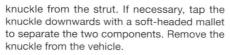

4.6 Lower the suspension arm and disengage the balljoint

4.7 Unscrew the pinch-bolt securing the steering knuckle to the front suspension strut

5.3 Undo the retaining nut and release the ABS wiring harness support bracket

5.4 Unscrew the nut and detach the anti-roll bar

5.5a Remove the pinch bolt and discard it

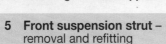

5 Front suspension strut – removal and refitting

Removal

1 Disconnect the battery as described in Chapter 5 Section 4.

2 Firmly apply the handbrake, then jack up the front of the vehicle and support it securely on axle stands (see *Jacking and vehicle support*). Remove the roadwheel.

3 Undo the retaining nut and release the ABS wiring harness support bracket from the strut **(see illustration)**.

4 Unscrew the nut and detach the anti-roll bar connecting link from the strut bracket **(see illustration)**. If necessary, use an Allen key to hold the spindle while the nut is unscrewed.

5 Unscrew and remove the pinch-bolt securing the steering knuckle assembly to the front suspension strut. Discard the bolt as a new one must be used for refitting. Prise open the clamp using a wedge-shaped tool and release the knuckle from the strut. If necessary, tap the knuckle downwards with a soft-headed mallet to separate the two components **(see illustrations)**. If necessary, use a lever and chain around the lower arm, and force the steering knuckle and arm downwards.

Right-hand suspension strut

6 From inside the vehicle, remove the two lower facia panels from beneath the steering wheel, the right-hand cupholder assembly (removing the cupholder to access the screw beneath) and undo the screws and remove the right-hand side facia mounting bracket, as described in Chapter 11 Section 27.

7 Unclip (but don't disconnect) the wiring plug to access the bolt at the bottom right-hand side and undo the nuts at the front, and move the fusebox and mounting bracket to one side. There is no need to disconnect any wiring plugs but access is limited **(see illustrations)**. To improve access, undo the 2 nuts and move the 16-pin diagnostic socket to one side.

8 Pull back the carpet and lift out the sound insulation material above the shock absorber mountings.

Left-hand suspension strut

9 Fully open the glovebox, unclip the bottle holder.

10 Undo the retaining bolts, disconnect the wiring plug and position it to one side **(see illustration)**.

11 Unclip the wiring loom and remove the support bracket **(see illustrations)**. There's no need to disconnect the wiring plug.

5.5b A chisel can be used to wedge open the clamp to free the knuckle from the strut

5.7a Undo the bolt…

5.7b …undo the fusebox mounting fasteners at the front and rear…

5.7c …and lift the sound insulation material from above the shock mountings

5.10 Undo the bolts and disconnect the wiring plug

5.11a Unclip the wiring loom…

12 Remove the sound insulation material from above the shock absorber mountings.

Both suspension struts

13 Have an assistant support the strut from under the wheel arch. Undo the three upper mounting nuts, then lower the strut and remove it from under the vehicle **(see illustration)**.

Refitting

14 With the help of an assistant, lift the suspension strut into position and insert the upper mounting studs through the holes in the body.
15 Screw on the upper mounting retaining nuts and tighten them to the specified torque.
16 Refit the dashboard trim removed earlier.
17 Thoroughly clean the bottom end of the suspension strut and its location in the steering knuckle. Locate the strut onto the knuckle and over the tab, then insert the pinch-bolt and tighten it to the specified torque.
18 Slide the brake caliper assembly over the disc and into position on the steering knuckle. Insert the new mounting bracket retaining bolts and tighten them to the specified torque.
19 Refit the ABS wiring harness support bracket to the strut and securely tighten the retaining nut. Attach the anti-roll bar connecting link to the strut bracket and tighten the retaining nut to the specified torque. If necessary, use a 5 mm Allen key to hold the spindle while the nut is tightened.
20 Refit the roadwheel, then lower the vehicle to the ground and tighten the roadwheel nuts to the specified torque.

5.11b ...and remove its support bracket

5.13 Undo the upper mounting nuts before removing the strut from under the vehicle

6 Front suspension strut – overhaul

Warning: Before attempting to dismantle the suspension strut, a suitable tool to hold the coil spring in compression must be obtained. Adjustable coil spring compressors which can be positively secured to the spring coils are readily available, and are recommended for this operation. Any attempt to dismantle the strut without such a tool is likely to result in damage or personal injury.

1 If the front suspension struts exhibit signs of wear (leaking fluid, loss of damping capability, sagging or cracked coil springs) then they should be dismantled and overhauled as necessary. The struts themselves cannot be serviced, and should be renewed if faulty, but the springs and related components can be renewed. To maintain balanced characteristics on both sides of the vehicle, the components on both sides should be renewed at the same time.
2 With the strut removed from the vehicle as described in Section 5, clean away all external dirt, then carefully mount it in a vice.
3 Fit the coil spring compressor tools (ensuring they are fully engaged) and compress the spring until all tension is relieved from the upper mounting.
4 Hold the strut piston with an Allen key, and unscrew the piston rod retaining nut with a ring spanner **(see illustration)**.
5 Remove the piston rod retaining nut, upper mounting, thrust bearing, bump stop and upper spring seat, gaiter and coil spring **(see illustrations)**.

6.4 Hold the strut piston with an Allen key while unscrewing the rod retaining nut

6.5a Remove the nut...

6.5b ...followed by the top mounting...

6.5c ...thrust bearing...

6.5d ...bump stop and upper spring seat...

6.5e ...gaiter...

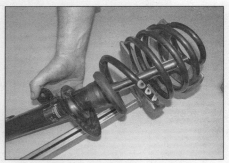

6.5f ...and coil spring (with compressor tool)

6 If a new spring is to be fitted, the original spring must now be carefully released from the compressor. If it is to be re-used, it can be left in compression.

7 With the strut assembly now completely dismantled, examine all the components for wear or damage, and check the thrust bearing for smoothness of operation. Renew components as necessary.

8 Examine the strut for signs of fluid leakage. Check the strut piston for signs of pitting along its entire length, and check the strut body for signs of damage.

9 Test the operation of the strut, while holding it in an upright position, by moving the piston rod through a full stroke and then through short strokes of 50 to 100 mm. In both cases the resistance felt should be smooth and continuous. If the resistance is jerky, or uneven, or if there is any visible sign of wear or damage to the strut, renewal is necessary.

7.5a Lower arm front mounting bolts...

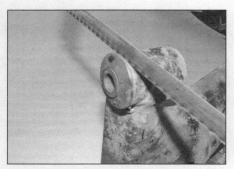

8.2a If the suspension lower arm bush is being renewed, first cut off the bush lips

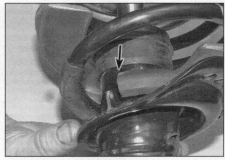

6.10 Make sure that the coil spring ends are located against the spring seats

10 Reassembly is a reversal of dismantling, noting the following points:
a) *Make sure that the coil spring ends are correctly located in the upper and lower seats before releasing the spring compressor* **(see illustration)**.
b) *Check that the thrust bearing is correctly fitted to the upper mounting.*
c) *Tighten the piston rod retaining nut to the specified torque.*

7 Front suspension lower arm – removal and refitting

Removal

1 Firmly apply the handbrake, then jack up the front of the vehicle and support it securely on axle stands (see *Jacking and vehicle support*). Remove the roadwheel.

7.5b ...and rear mounting bolts

8.2b Fit a commercially available bush renewal tool to the suspension lower arm...

2 Slacken the nut securing the steering knuckle balljoint to the suspension lower arm. Attach a two-legged puller to the lower arm and tighten the puller to apply tension to the balljoint shank **(see illustrations 4.4a and 4.4b)**. Strike the end of the lower arm with a hammer a few times to release the balljoint shank taper.

3 Remove the puller and unscrew the balljoint retaining nut. Discard the nut and obtain a new nut of the correct diameter for refitting.

4 Push down on the suspension lower arm to disengage the balljoint from the arm, then move the steering knuckle to one side and release the arm, taking care not to damage the balljoint rubber boot **(see illustration 4.6)**. It is advisable to place a protective cover over the rubber boot such as the plastic cap from an aerosol can, suitably cut to fit.

5 Unscrew the lower arm front and rear mounting bolts/nuts and remove the lower arm from the subframe **(see illustrations)**.

Refitting

6 Locate the lower arm in position in the subframe and refit the front mounting bolt and nut. Only loosely tighten the mounting nut at this stage.

7 Position a trolley jack under the outer end of the lower arm and raise the arm until it is in approximately a horizontal position.

8 Refit the rear mounting bolt, then tighten the front and rear mounting bolts/nuts to the specified torque. Remove the trolley jack.

9 Push down on the suspension lower arm and engage the steering knuckle balljoint with the arm. Fit the new balljoint retaining nut and tighten the nut to the specified torque. The retaining nut torque specifications will vary depending on whether the lower arm balljoint is secured with a circlip or with two bolts.

10 Refit the roadwheel, then lower the vehicle to the ground and tighten the roadwheel nuts to the specified torque.

8 Front suspension lower arm bushes – renewal

Note: *A commercially available bush renewal tool will be required for this operation.*

1 Remove the front suspension lower arm as described in Section 7.

2 If the suspension arm bushes are worn or perished, they can be withdrawn from the suspension arm using a commercially available bush renewal tool. Alternatively (and preferably), if a press is at hand, the bushes can be pushed out using a suitable rod or a length of tube of suitable diameter. If the horizontal bush is being renewed, first cut off the bush lips using a sharp knife or a hacksaw **(see illustrations)**.

3 To ease the fitting of the new bushes into the suspension arm, lubricate the relevant bush and the eye in the arm with multi-purpose grease, then press or draw (as applicable) the

bush into the arm so that the bush lips are seated correctly **(see illustration)**.

4 Wipe off any excess grease, then refit the front suspension lower arm as described in Section 7.

9 Steering knuckle balljoint – renewal

1 Remove the steering knuckle as described in Section 4.

2 On vehicles where the balljoint is secured to the steering knuckle with a circlip, extract the circlip securing the balljoint to the knuckle using circlip pliers.

3 On vehicles where the balljoint is secured to the steering knuckle with two bolts, undo and remove the bolts.

4 Mount a G-clamp or similar tool over the balljoint, with suitable spacers above, and a tube of a diameter to allow the balljoint to pass through, below.

5 Tighten the G-clamp to press the balljoint down and out of the steering knuckle.

6 Clean the balljoint locating area in the knuckle and remove any burrs that might hinder refitting.

7 Lubricate the balljoint locating area in the knuckle with multi-purpose grease and place the balljoint in position.

8 Using the G-clamp with suitable spacers and a tube of suitable diameter, press the new balljoint back into position in the steering knuckle.

9 Refit the circlip, or the two bolts, as applicable to secure the balljoint in position. Tighten the bolts to the specified torque.

10 Refit the steering knuckle as described in Section 4.

10 Front anti-roll bar – removal and refitting

Removal

1 Firmly apply the handbrake, then jack up the front of the vehicle and support it securely on axle stands (see *Jacking and vehicle support*). Remove the front roadwheels.

2 Unscrew the nut and detach the anti-roll bar connecting link from the anti-roll bar on each side. If necessary, use a 5 mm Allen key to hold the connecting link spindle while the nut is unscrewed.

3 Undo the two bolts each side securing the anti-roll bar clamps to the subframe **(see illustration)**.

4 Manipulate the anti-roll bar out from the side of the vehicle to remove.

5 With the anti-roll bar removed, check the condition of the mounting bushes and renew as necessary.

Refitting

6 Refitting is a reversal of removal, tightening all fastenings to the specified torque.

8.2c ...and draw out the lower arm bushes

11 Front subframe – removal and refitting

Removal

1 Firmly apply the handbrake, then jack up the front of the vehicle and support it securely on axle stands (see *Jacking and vehicle support*). Set the front wheels in the straight-ahead position, then remove the ignition key to lock the column in position.

2 Remove the front anti-roll bar as described in Section 10, then disconnect the steering knuckle balljoint from the lower suspension arm on each side as described in Section 9.

3 Undo the retaining clamp bolt and release the power steering fluid pipes from the front subframe.

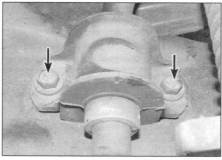

10.3 Undo the clamp-retaining bolts

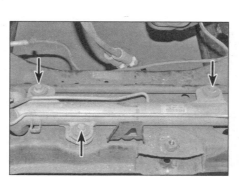

11.6 Steering gear retaining bolts

8.3 Assemble the renewal tool and draw the new bush into the lower arm

4 According to equipment fitted, work around the subframe and release the wiring harness, fuel hoses and emission system pipes from their retaining clips.

5 Undo the single bolt securing the engine/transmission rear mounting to the subframe. Undo the through-bolt securing the mounting to the transmission and remove the mounting from under the vehicle **(see illustration)**. Note that a new through-bolt will be required for refitting.

6 Undo the three bolts securing the steering gear to the front subframe **(see illustration)**. Using cable ties, support the steering gear clear of the subframe.

7 Suitably support the subframe on a trolley jack and engage the help of an assistant to steady the subframe as it is removed.

8 Undo the bolt and nut each side securing the front subframe to the underbody **(see illustration)**. Lower the jack and remove the subframe from under the vehicle.

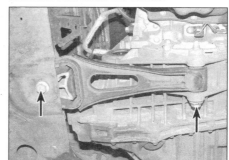

11.5 Rear mounting retaining bolts

11.8 Front subframe retaining nut

12.3 Undo the four retaining nuts (two of four shown) and remove the spring-to-axle U-bolts and fittings each side

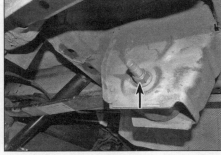

12.4a Spring front mounting bolt nut...

12.4b ...and rear mounting bolt nut

12.6 Use a bush extraction kit or a threaded rod and suitable spacers to remove the bush

Refitting

9 Refitting is a reversal of removal, using new nuts/bolts where applicable, and tightening all fastenings to the specified torque. Note that the through-bolt securing the mounting to the transmission will be either an M14x1.5 or an M14x2.0 – both have different torque ratings.

12 Rear axle leaf spring – removal and refitting

Removal

1 Chock the front wheels then jack up the rear of the vehicle and securely support it on axle stands (see *Jacking and vehicle*

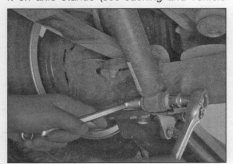

13.3 Rear shock absorber lower mounting bolt retaining nut...

support). Remove the roadwheel on the side concerned.

2 Support the rear of the body with axle stands.

3 Undo the retaining nuts, and remove the spring-to-axle U-bolts and fittings each side **(see illustration)**.

4 Unscrew and remove the front and rear leaf mounting retaining nuts and, if required, drive out the mounting bolts with a soft metal drift **(see illustrations)**.

5 The rear spring can now be lifted from the rear axle and withdrawn from beneath the vehicle.

6 Examine the front and rear mounting bushes, and check the condition of the spring leaves; renew any faulty components. The rear spring hanger bush consists of two parts, while the bushes that locate within the springs are single pieces **(see illustration)**.

13.4 ...and upper mounting bolt

Refitting

7 Refitting is a reversal of removal, but note the following additional points:
a) *Tighten all nuts and bolts to the specified torque, noting that the mounting bolt nuts must not be fully tightened until after the vehicle is lowered to the ground.*
b) *Tighten the U-bolt nuts evenly. The difference in length of exposed thread on the same bolt must not exceed 3 mm.*

13 Rear shock absorber – removal and refitting

Removal

1 Chock the front wheels then jack up the rear of the vehicle and securely support it on axle stands (see *Jacking and vehicle support*).

2 Support the rear axle with a trolley jack.

3 Undo the retaining nut, and withdraw the shock absorber lower mounting bolt **(see illustration)**.

4 Unscrew the upper mounting bolt and remove the shock absorber **(see illustration)**.

5 To test the shock absorber for efficiency, grip the upper or lower mounting eye in a vice, and then pump the piston repeatedly through its full stroke. If the resistance is weak or is felt to be uneven, the shock absorber is defective and must be renewed. It must also be renewed if it is leaking fluid. It is advisable to renew both rear shock absorbers at the same time, or the handling characteristics of the vehicle could be adversely affected.

Refitting

6 Refitting is a reversal of removal. Ensure that the mounting bolts are tightened to the specified torque.

14 Rear anti-roll bar – removal and refitting

Removal

Note: *A rear anti-roll bar is not fitted to all models.*
Caution: Avoid using power tools to remove or install the stabiliser bar link nuts because you risk damaging the stabiliser bar link ball joints and boots.

1 Firmly apply the handbrake, then jack up the front of the vehicle and support it securely on axle stands (see *Jacking and vehicle support*).

2 Support the rear axle with a trolley jack.

3 Unscrew the nut each side and detach the anti-roll bar connecting links from the anti-roll bar. If necessary, use a 5 mm Allen key to hold the spindles while the nuts are unscrewed. Discard the nuts because new ones must be used for refitting.

4 Undo the retaining nuts, and withdraw the

14.5 Undo the two bolts each side and release the anti-roll bar clamps from the rear axle

15.3 Disconnect the wiring plug from the airbag rotary connector

15.4 Unscrew the retaining bolt securing the steering wheel to the column

shock absorber lower mounting bolts **(see illustration 13.3)**.

5 Undo the two bolts each side and release the anti-roll bar clamps from the rear axle **(see illustration)**. Discard the bolts because new ones must be used for refitting.

Refitting

6 Refitting is a reversal of removal. Stabiliser bar bushings must be installed with the slits facing the front of the vehicle – replace them with new bushings if they are worn. Wetting the brackets with water will make installation easier. Tighten all nuts and bolts to the specified torque, and use new nuts to secure the anti-roll bar connecting links and the anti-roll bar clamps.

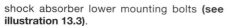

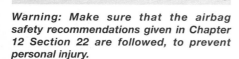

15 Steering wheel – removal and refitting

Warning: Make sure that the airbag safety recommendations given in Chapter 12 Section 22 are followed, to prevent personal injury.

Removal

1 Remove the driver's airbag as described in Chapter 12 Section 23.
2 Set the front road wheels in the straight-ahead position, then remove the ignition key to lock the column in position.
3 Disconnect the horn switch wiring plug from the airbag rotary connector **(see illustration)**.
4 Prevent the steering wheel turning by grasping the rim firmly, then unscrew and remove the steering wheel securing bolt **(see illustration)**. Do not rely on the steering column lock to prevent the wheel turning because this may damage the lock; an extra pair of hands would be helpful at this point.
5 Grip the steering wheel with both hands and carefully rock it from side-to-side to release it from the taper on the steering column. As the steering wheel is being removed, guide the wiring for the airbag through the aperture in the wheel, taking care not to damage the wiring plugs **(see illustration)**.
6 Place adhesive tape across the airbag

15.5 Guide the wiring for the airbag through the aperture in the steering wheel

rotary connector to avoid accidental rotation while the steering wheel is removed **(see illustration)**.

Refitting

7 Make sure that the front road wheels are pointing in the straight-ahead position, then remove the adhesive tape from the airbag rotary connector.
8 Refit the steering wheel, routing the airbag wiring plug through the steering wheel aperture.
Note: *Make sure the lugs on the airbag rotary connector locate correctly with the opening on the steering wheel, and that the two arrows on the rotary connector are aligned. If necessary, refer to the procedures contained in Chapter 12 Section 23 and centralise the*

16.4 Disconnect the PATS wiring plug

15.6 Apply adhesive tape to prevent the rotary connector being moved out of position

rotary connector if there is any doubt about its position.
9 Refit the steering wheel securing bolt and tighten to the specified torque – again, do not rely on the steering column lock to hold the wheel as the bolt is tightened.
10 Reconnect the wiring plug for the horn.
11 Release the steering lock and refit the airbag as described in Chapter 12 Section 23.

16 Steering column lock/ Ignition switch – removal and refitting

Removal

1 Disconnect the battery negative terminal as described in Chapter 5 Section 4.
2 Remove the steering column shrouds as described in Chapter 11 Section 27.
3 Remove the steering wheel as described in Section 15.

Steering column lock cylinder

4 Disconnect the wiring plug from the Passive Anti-Theft System (PATS) transceiver **(see illustration)**.
5 Spread the upper and lower retaining tabs and remove the PATS transceiver from the lock cylinder **(see illustration)**.
6 Insert the ignition key into the ignition switch/lock, and turn it to position 1.
7 Insert a thin screwdriver into the hole under the lock housing, press the screwdriver to

16.5 Spread the upper and lower retaining tabs and remove the PATS transceiver from the lock cylinder

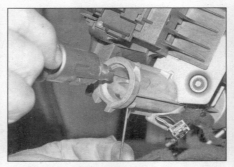

16.7 Insert a thin screwdriver into the hole in the top of the lock housing and pull out the lock cylinder using the key

16.8 Depress the locking tang and disconnect the ignition switch wiring plug

16.9a Depress the upper and lower retaining tabs...

16.9b ...and remove the ignition switch

release the detent buttons and pull out the lock cylinder using the key **(see illustration).**

Ignition switch

Caution: Do not remove the ignition switch

17.4 Undo the bolt and detach the steering column lower coupling from the bulkhead

while the steering column lock cylinder is removed.

8 Depress the locking tang and disconnect the ignition switch wiring plug **(see illustration).**

17.6a Undo the top two screws...

17.5 Disconnect the switchgear wiring plugs

17.6b ...and those at the rear, and remove the mounting assembly

9 Using two small screwdrivers, depress the upper and lower retaining tabs and remove the ignition switch **(see illustrations).**

Refitting

10 Refitting is a reversal of removal.

17 Steering column – removal and refitting

Removal

1 Disconnect the battery negative terminal as described in Chapter 5 Section 4.
2 Remove the steering column shrouds as described in Chapter 11 Section 27.
3 Remove the steering wheel as described in Section 15.
Note: *The steering column must be handled with care. Do not knock it or drop it because this may impair its ability to absorb energy in an impact.*
4 Undo the bolt and detach the steering column lower coupling from the bulkhead **(see illustration)**.
5 Disconnect the wiring plugs for the Passive Anti-Theft System (PATS) transceiver, windscreen wiper/washer switch, horn switch, ignition switch and direction indicator switch. Release the wiring harness from the retaining clips on the steering column and move the harness to one side. **(see illustration)**.
6 Although not essential for this procedure, removing the mounting assembly for the column switchgear/airbag clockspring/steering column lock will make removal of the steering column easier. The assembly is retained by two screws at the top and two at the rear **(see illustrations)**.
7 Undo the four steering column retaining nuts and carefully manoeuvre the column from vehicle **(see illustration)**.

Refitting

8 Refitting is a reversal of removal, but note the following additional points:
a) *Ensure that both the steering column and roadwheels are centralised when refitting the intermediate shaft to the flexible coupling, and secure with a new pinch-bolt.*

b) *Tighten all fastenings to the specified torque.*
c) *Ensure that all wiring is securely connected and correctly routed.*

18 Steering gear – removal and refitting

Removal

1 Disconnect the battery negative terminal as described in Chapter 5, Section 4
2 Set the front roadwheels in the straight-ahead position, then remove the ignition key to lock the column in position.
3 Undo the bolt and detach the steering column lower bearing from the bulkhead (see illustration 17.4).
4 Undo the bolts and remove the plastic column fitting from the bulkhead (see illustration).
5 Firmly apply the handbrake, then jack up the front of the vehicle and support it securely on axle stands (see *Jacking and vehicle support*). Remove both front roadwheels.
6 From under the vehicle, undo the nut and remove the lower pinch-bolt securing the steering column intermediate shaft flexible coupling to the steering gear pinion shaft. Note that a new pinch-bolt and nut will be required for refitting. Slide the flexible coupling up and off the steering gear pinion shaft.
7 Remove the shield from over the steering gear (see illustration).
8 Remove the flexible rubber mounting from the base of the steering column and unclip the power steering fluid pipes from the front subframe. Move the pipes to one side.
9 Working on one side of the vehicle at a time, slacken the track rod end balljoint nut several turns, then use a balljoint separator tool to release the balljoint shank from the steering knuckle (see illustration 4.3). With the balljoint released, unscrew the nut and disconnect the balljoint. Discard the nut as a new one must be used for refitting.
10 Unclip any wiring retainers from the steering gear and move the wiring to one side.
11 Undo the two bolts and remove the bracket and hydraulic pipes from the rear of the steering gear.

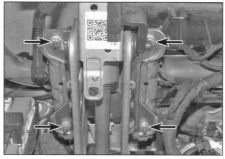

17.7 Steering column retaining nuts

12 Disconnect the rear engine mounting as described in Chapter 2A Section 17 or Chapter 2B Section 17.
13 Unscrew the nut and detach the anti-roll bar connecting link from the anti-roll bar on each side. If necessary, use a 5 mm Allen key to hold the connecting link spindle while the nut is unscrewed. Support the anti-roll bar with a cable tie (see illustration).
14 Use a transmission jack to support the subframe.
15 Undo and remove the front subframe bolts and then the rear subframe bolts (see illustration).
16 Undo the three bolts securing the steering gear to the front subframe and remove the steering gear through the driver's side wheel arch (see illustration).

Refitting

17 Refitting is a reversal of removal, but note the following additional points:

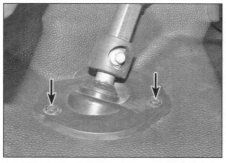

18.4 Undo the bolts and remove the plastic fitting

a) *Ensure that both the steering wheel and steering gear are centralised when refitting the intermediate shaft flexible coupling to the steering gear pinion.*
b) *If a new steering gear unit is being fitted, the straight-ahead position can be ascertained by halving the number of turns necessary to move the rack from lock-to-lock.*
c) *Use new nuts/bolts when refitting the intermediate shaft flexible coupling and track rod end balljoints.*
d) *Fit new O-rings to the fluid pipes.*
e) *Tighten all fastenings to the specified torque.*
f) *Fill and bleed the power steering hydraulic system as described in Section 23.*
g) *Have the front wheel toe-setting checked and adjusted at the earliest opportunity.*

19 Steering gear rubber gaiters – renewal

1 Remove the track rod end as described in Section 20.
2 Note the position of the track rod end locknut by counting the number of threads from the nut face to the end of the track rod, or take a photo with your phone. Then unscrew and remove the locknut.
3 Remove the clips, and slide the gaiter from the track rod and steering gear housing (see illustration).
4 Slide the new gaiter over the track rod, and onto the steering gear. Where applicable,

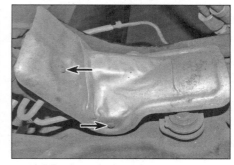

18.7 Remove the steering gear shield

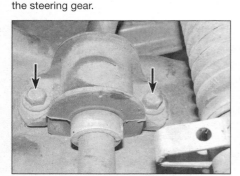

18.13 Undo the nuts and support the anti-roll bar with a cable tie

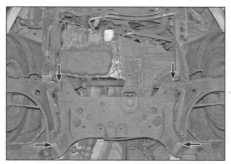

18.15 Undo and remove the front and rear subframe bolts

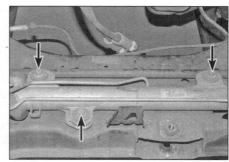

18.16 Undo the bolts and manoeuvre the steering gear out through the wheel arch

19.3 Use a flat-bladed screwdriver to release the gaiter clips

make sure that the gaiter locates in the cut-outs provided in the track rod and steering gear housing.

5 Fit and secure the clips, ensuring that the gaiter is not twisted.

6 Screw the track rod end locknut onto the track rod, and position it with the exact number of threads exposed as noted during removal.

7 Refit the track rod end as described in Section 20.

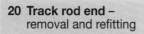
20 Track rod end – removal and refitting

Removal

1 Firmly apply the handbrake, then jack up the

21.3 Slacken the retaining clip and disconnect the fluid return hose

21.4b Remove the teflon seal from the pipe union (2.2 litre engine shown)

20.2 Loosen the track rod end locknut on the track rod a quarter turn

front of the vehicle and support it securely on axle stands (see *Jacking and vehicle support*). Remove the relevant front roadwheel.

2 Loosen the track rod end securing locknut on the track rod a quarter turn, while holding the track rod stationary with a second spanner on the flats provided **(see illustration)**. If necessary, use a wire brush to remove rust from the nut and threads and lubricate the threads with penetrating oil before unscrewing the nut. As an additional check, measure the visible amount of threads on the track rod using vernier calipers. This will ensure the track rod end is refitted in the same position.

3 Slacken the track rod end balljoint nut several turns, then use a balljoint separator tool to release the balljoint shank from the steering arm **(see illustration 4.3)**. With the balljoint released, unscrew the nut and disconnect the balljoint from the steering arm.

21.4a High-pressure pipe retaining bolt (2.0 litre engine shown). Plug the opening to prevent contamination

21.5 Undo the three bolts securing the coolant pump to the power steering pump

Discard the nut because a new one must be used for refitting.

4 Unscrew the track rod end from the track rod, counting the number of turns necessary to remove it and taking care not to disturb the locknut.

Refitting

5 Screw the new track rod end onto the track rod the exact number of turns as noted during removal.

6 Engage the track rod end balljoint shank in the steering arm, and screw on the new retaining nut. Tighten the nut to the specified torque.

7 Tighten the track rod end locknut.

8 Refit the roadwheel, then lower the vehicle to the ground, and tighten the roadwheel nuts to the specified torque.

9 Have the front wheel alignment checked and adjusted at the earliest opportunity.

21 Power steering pump – removal and refitting

Removal

1 Disconnect the battery negative terminal as described in Chapter 5 Section 4.

2 On the 2.0 litre engine, slacken and lock the main drivebelt tensioner, and remove the belt from the power steering pump pulley, leaving the coolant pump stretch belt in place. On the 2.2 litre engine remove the stretch belt. Both procedures are described in Chapter 1 Section 33.

3 Position a suitable container beneath the power steering pump, then slacken the retaining clip and disconnect the fluid return hose from the top of the pump **(see illustration)**. Allow the fluid to drain into the container. Cover the hose end and pump orifice after disconnection, to prevent the ingress of foreign matter.

4 Slacken the high-pressure pipe support bracket bolt, then unscrew the union nut and disconnect the high-pressure pipe from the front of the pump on 2.0 litre engines or the bottom of the pump on 2.2 litre engines. If fitted, remove the Teflon seal from the pipe union and discard it; a new one must be used for refitting **(see illustrations)**. Cover the pipe end and pump orifice after disconnection, to prevent the ingress of foreign matter.

5 On 2.2 litre engines, suitably support the coolant pump, then working through the holes in the power steering pump pulley, undo the three bolts securing the coolant pump to the power steering pump **(see illustration)**.

6 On 2.2 litre engines, using a large screwdriver, ease the coolant pump drive coupling away from the drive dog on the power steering pump shaft. Disengage the drive coupling then move the coolant pump clear of the power steering pump **(see illustrations)**.

7 On the 2.0 litre engine, undo the three bolts securing the power steering pump to the cylinder block and remove the pump from the engine **(see illustration)**.

Refitting

8 If removed, fit a new Teflon seal to the high-pressure pipe union. Ideally, the special Ford fitting sleeve (211-188) should be used to expand the seal and allow it to pass over the union threads. In the absence of the fitting sleeve a suitable alternative can be made out of conical plastic tubing or by wrapping suitable tape over the threads **(see illustration)**.

9 On all engines, locate the power steering pump on the cylinder block, refit the three retaining bolts and tighten them to the specified torque.

10 On 2.2 litre engines, engage the coolant pump drive coupling with the power steering pump drive dog, then place the coolant pump in position on the power steering pump. Insert the three retaining bolts and tighten them to the specified torque.

11 On all engines, reconnect the high-pressure pipe to the pump and tighten the pipe union to the specified torque.

12 Refit and securely tighten the high-pressure pipe support bracket bolt.

13 Reconnect the fluid return hose to the pump and tighten the retaining clip.

14 Refit the power steering pump/auxiliary drivebelt as described in Chapter 1 Section 33.

15 Reconnect the battery, then fill and bleed the power steering hydraulic system as described in Section 23.

22 Power steering fluid cooler – removal and refitting

Removal

1 Remove the intercooler as described in Chapter 4A Section 18.

2 Wearing gloves, remove the power steering fluid reservoir cap and remove all of the fluid with a syringe or similar.

3 Undo the two fluid cooler bracket mounting bolts and lower the unit from its location.

4 Position a suitable container beneath the fluid cooler, then clamp the two fluid hoses using brake hose clamps or similar tools.

5 Release the retaining clips and disconnect the fluid hoses from the cooler. Allow the surplus fluid to drain into the container. Cover the hose ends and fluid cooler orifices after disconnection, to prevent the ingress of foreign matter.

Refitting

6 Refitting is a reversal of removal. On completion, fill and bleed the power steering hydraulic system as described in Section 23.

21.6a On 2.2 engines, ease the coolant pump drive coupling away from the power steering pump drive dog...

21.6b ...then disengage the drive coupling and move the coolant pump clear of the power steering pump

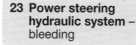

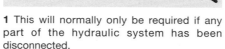

21.7 Undo the bolts securing the power steering pump to the cylinder block

21.8 Using a conical sleeve to aid fitting of a new teflon seal to the high-pressure pipe union (2.2 litre engines)

23 Power steering hydraulic system – bleeding

1 This will normally only be required if any part of the hydraulic system has been disconnected.

2 Referring to *Weekly checks*, remove the fluid reservoir filler cap and top-up with the specified fluid to the maximum level mark.

3 Firmly apply the handbrake, then jack up the front of the vehicle and support it securely on axle stands (see *Jacking and vehicle support*).

4 With the engine switched on, slowly turn the steering wheel from lock-to-lock several times, adding fluid to the reservoir as necessary. Continue turning the steering wheel from lock-to-lock until the fluid level in the reservoir stops dropping.

Note: *Make sure the fluid level doesn't drop below the 'MIN' level in the reservoir.*

5 Turn off the engine and lower the vehicle to the ground. Top up the fluid reservoir, restart the engine and allow it to idle. Turn the steering wheel to full left, or full right lock and hold it there for two or three seconds. Now turn the steering to full lock in the other direction and again hold it there for a few seconds. Repeat this procedure several times, adding fluid to the reservoir as necessary, until the fluid level in the reservoir stops dropping.

6 Stop the engine and re-check the fluid level. Top-up the fluid if necessary.

24 Wheel alignment and steering angles – general information

Definitions

1 A vehicle's steering and suspension geometry is defined in four basic settings **(see illustration)** – all angles are expressed in degrees (toe settings are also expressed as a measurement); the steering axis is defined as an imaginary line drawn through the axis of the suspension strut, extended where necessary to contact the ground.

2 Camber is the angle between each roadwheel and a vertical line drawn through its centre and tyre contact patch, when viewed from the front or rear of the vehicle. Positive camber is when the roadwheels are tilted outwards from the vertical at the top; negative camber is when they are tilted inwards. The camber angle is not adjustable.

3 Castor is the angle between the steering axis and a vertical line drawn through each roadwheel's centre and tyre contact patch, when viewed from the side of the vehicle. Positive castor is when the steering axis is tilted so that it contacts the ground ahead of the vertical; negative castor is when it contacts the ground behind the vertical. The castor angle is not adjustable.

4 Toe is the difference, viewed from above, between lines drawn through the roadwheel centres and the vehicle's centre-line. 'Toe-in'

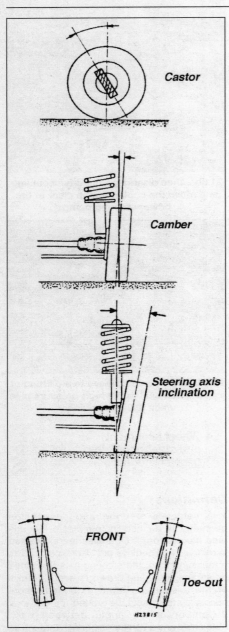

24.1 Wheel alignment and steering angles

is when the roadwheels point inwards, towards each other at the front, while 'toe-out' is when they splay outwards from each other at the front.

5 The front wheel toe setting is adjusted by screwing the track rod in or out of its track rod ends, to alter the effective length of the track rod assembly. The rear wheel toe setting is not adjustable.

Checking and adjustment

6 Due to the special measuring equipment necessary to check the wheel alignment and steering angles, and the skill required to use it properly, the checking and adjustment of these settings is best left to a Ford dealer or a tyre-fitting shop with the necessary checking equipment.

Chapter 11
Bodywork and fittings

Contents

Degrees of difficulty

Easy, suitable for novice with little experience	Fairly easy, suitable for beginner with some experience	Fairly difficult, suitable for competent DIY mechanic	Difficult, suitable for experienced DIY mechanic	Very difficult, suitable for expert DIY or professional

Specifications

Torque wrench settings	Nm	lbf ft
Driver's seat retaining bolts	25	18
Bench seat retaining bolts	48	35
Seat belt mounting bolts	40	30

1 General Information

1 The body and chassis on all versions of the Transit is of all-steel construction. Two basic chassis types are available: L1 and L2 (L1 – short wheelbase, L2 – long wheelbase).
2 The main body types are Van, Crewbus ("Double Cab in Van"), Kombi (9 seats) and Tourneo Custom (8/9-seat minibus) with low or high roof (H1 or H2). Twin opening rear doors or a tailgate are fitted and, on some models, side opening door(s) are available.
3 Extensive use is made of plastic materials, mainly on the interior, but also in exterior components. The front and rear bumper covers are injection-moulded from a synthetic material which is very strong and yet light. Plastic components such as wheel arch liners may be fitted to the underside of the vehicle, to improve the body's resistance to corrosion.
4 Due to the large number of specialist applications of this vehicle range, information contained in this Chapter is given on parts found to be common on the popular factory-produced versions. No information is provided on special body versions.

2 Maintenance – bodywork and underframe

1 The general condition of a vehicle's bodywork is the one thing that significantly affects its value. Maintenance is easy, but needs to be regular. Neglect, particularly after minor damage, can lead quickly to further

deterioration and costly repair bills. It is important also to keep watch on those parts of the vehicle not immediately visible, for instance the underside, inside all the wheel arches, and the lower part of the engine compartment.

2 The basic maintenance routine for the bodywork is washing – preferably with a lot of water, from a hose. This will remove all the loose solids which may have stuck to the vehicle. It is important to flush these off in such a way as to prevent grit from scratching the finish. The wheel arches and underframe need washing in the same way, to remove any accumulated mud, which will retain moisture and tend to encourage rust. Paradoxically enough, the best time to clean the underframe and wheel arches is in wet weather, when the mud is thoroughly wet and soft. In very wet weather, the underframe is usually cleaned of large accumulations automatically, and this is a good time for inspection.

3 Periodically, except on vehicles with a wax-based underbody protective coating, it is a good idea to have the whole of the underframe of the vehicle steam-cleaned, engine compartment included, so that a thorough inspection can be carried out to see what minor repairs and renovations are necessary. Steam-cleaning is available at many garages, and is necessary for the removal of the accumulation of oily grime, which sometimes is allowed to become thick in certain areas. If steam-cleaning facilities are not available, there are some excellent grease solvents available which can be brush-applied; the dirt can then be simply hosed off. Note that these methods should not be used on vehicles with wax-based underbody protective coating, or the coating will be removed. Such vehicles should be inspected annually, preferably just prior to Winter, when the underbody should be washed down, and any damage to the wax coating repaired. Ideally, a completely fresh coat should be applied. It would also be worth considering the use of such wax-based protection for injection into door panels, sills, box sections, etc, as an additional safeguard against rust damage, where such protection is not provided by the vehicle manufacturer.

4 After washing paintwork, wipe off with a chamois leather to give an unspotted clear finish. A coat of clear protective wax polish will give added protection against chemical pollutants in the air. If the paintwork sheen has dulled or oxidised, use a cleaner/polisher combination to restore the brilliance of the shine. This requires a little effort, but such dulling is usually caused because regular washing has been neglected. Care needs to be taken with metallic paintwork, as special non-abrasive cleaner/polisher is required to avoid damage to the finish. Always check that the door and ventilator opening drain holes and pipes are completely clear, so that water can be drained out. Brightwork should be treated in the same way as paintwork.

Windscreens and windows can be kept clear of the smeary film which often appears, by the use of proprietary glass cleaner. Never use any form of wax or other body or chromium polish on glass.

3 Maintenance – upholstery and carpets

1 Mats and carpets should be brushed or vacuum-cleaned regularly, to keep them free of grit. If they are badly stained, remove them from the vehicle for scrubbing or sponging, and make quite sure they are dry before refitting. Seats and interior trim panels can be kept clean by wiping with a damp cloth. If they do become stained (which can be more apparent on light-coloured upholstery), use a little liquid detergent and a soft nail brush to scour the grime out of the grain of the material. Do not forget to keep the headlining clean in the same way as the upholstery. When using liquid cleaners inside the vehicle, do not over-wet the surfaces being cleaned. Excessive damp could get into the seams and padded interior, causing stains, offensive odours or even rot.

4 Minor body damage – repair

Minor scratches

1 If the scratch is very superficial, and does not penetrate to the metal of the bodywork, repair is very simple. Lightly rub the area of the scratch with a paintwork renovator, or a very fine cutting paste, to remove loose paint from the scratch, and to clear the surrounding bodywork of wax polish. Rinse the area with clean water.

2 Apply touch-up paint to the scratch using a fine paint brush; continue to apply fine layers of paint until the surface of the paint in the scratch is level with the surrounding paintwork. Allow the new paint at least two weeks to harden, then blend it into the surrounding paintwork by rubbing the scratch area with a paintwork renovator or a very fine cutting paste. Finally, apply wax polish.

3 Where the scratch has penetrated right through to the metal of the bodywork, causing the metal to rust, a different repair technique is required. Remove any loose rust from the bottom of the scratch with a penknife, then apply rust-inhibiting paint to prevent the formation of rust in the future. Using a rubber or nylon applicator, fill the scratch with bodystopper paste. If required, this paste can be mixed with cellulose thinners to provide a very thin paste which is ideal for filling narrow scratches. Before the stopper-paste in the scratch hardens, wrap a piece of smooth cotton rag around the top of a finger. Dip the

finger in cellulose thinners and quickly sweep it across the surface of the stopper-paste in the scratch; this will ensure that the surface of the stopper-paste is slightly hollowed. The scratch can now be painted over as described earlier in this Section.

Dents

4 When deep denting of the vehicle's bodywork has taken place, the first task is to pull the dent out, until the affected bodywork almost attains its original shape. There is little point in trying to restore the original shape completely, as the metal in the damaged area will have stretched on impact, and cannot be reshaped fully to its original contour. It is better to bring the level of the dent up to a point which is about 3 mm below the level of the surrounding bodywork. In cases where the dent is very shallow anyway, it is not worth trying to pull it out at all. If the underside of the dent is accessible, it can be hammered out gently from behind, using a mallet with a wooden or plastic head. While doing this, hold a suitable block of wood firmly against the outside of the panel, to absorb the impact from the hammer blows and thus prevent a large area of the bodywork from being 'belled-out'.

5 Should the dent be in a section of the bodywork which has a double skin, or some other factor making it inaccessible from behind, a different technique is called for. Drill several small holes through the metal inside the area – particularly in the deeper section. Then screw long self-tapping screws into the holes, just sufficiently for them to gain a good purchase in the metal. Now the dent can be pulled out by pulling on the protruding heads of the screws with a pair of pliers.

6 The next stage of the repair is the removal of the paint from the damaged area, and from an inch or so of the surrounding 'sound' bodywork. This is accomplished most easily by using a wire brush or abrasive pad on a power drill, although it can be done just as effectively by hand, using sheets of abrasive paper. To complete the preparation for filling, score the surface of the bare metal with a screwdriver or the tang of a file, or alternatively, drill small holes in the affected area. This will provide a really good 'key' for the filler paste.

7 To complete the repair, see the Section on filling and respraying.

Rust holes or gashes

8 Remove all paint from the affected area, and from an inch or so of the surrounding 'sound' bodywork, using an abrasive pad or a wire brush on a power drill. If these are not available, a few sheets of abrasive paper will do the job most effectively. With the paint removed, you will be able to judge the severity of the corrosion, and therefore decide whether to renew the whole panel (if this is possible) or to repair the affected area. New body panels are not as expensive as most people think, and it is often quicker and more satisfactory to fit a new panel than to attempt to repair large areas of corrosion.

9 Remove all fittings from the affected area, except those which will act as a guide to the original shape of the damaged bodywork (eg headlight shells etc). Then, using tin snips or a hacksaw blade, remove all loose metal and any other metal badly affected by corrosion. Hammer the edges of the hole inwards, in order to create a slight depression for the filler paste.

10 Wire-brush the affected area to remove the powdery rust from the surface of the remaining metal. Paint the affected area with rust-inhibiting paint, if the back of the rusted area is accessible, treat this also.

11 Before filling can take place, it will be necessary to block the hole in some way. This can be achieved by the use of aluminium or plastic mesh, or aluminium tape.

12 Aluminium or plastic mesh, or glass-fibre matting, is probably the best material to use for a large hole. Cut a piece to the approximate size and shape of the hole to be filled, then position it in the hole so that its edges are below the level of the surrounding bodywork. It can be retained in position by several blobs of filler paste around its periphery.

13 Aluminium tape should be used for small or very narrow holes. Pull a piece off the roll, trim it to the approximate size and shape required, then pull off the backing paper (if used) and stick the tape over the hole; it can be overlapped if the thickness of one piece is insufficient. Burnish down the edges of the tape with the handle of a screwdriver or similar, to ensure that the tape is securely attached to the metal underneath.

Filling and respraying

14 Before using this Section, see the Sections on dent, deep scratch, rust holes and gash repairs.

15 Many types of bodyfiller are available, but generally speaking, those proprietary kits which contain a tin of filler paste and a tube of resin hardener are best for this type of repair. A wide, flexible plastic or nylon applicator will be found invaluable for imparting a smooth and well-contoured finish to the surface of the filler.

16 Mix up a little filler on a clean piece of card or board – measure the hardener carefully (follow the maker's instructions on the pack), otherwise the filler will set too rapidly or too slowly. Using the applicator, apply the filler paste to the prepared area; draw the applicator across the surface of the filler to achieve the correct contour and to level the surface. As soon as a contour that approximates to the correct one is achieved, stop working the paste – if you carry on too long, the paste will become sticky and begin to 'pick-up' on the applicator. Continue to add thin layers of filler paste at 20-minute intervals, until the level of the filler is just proud of the surrounding bodywork.

17 Once the filler has hardened, the excess can be removed using a metal plane or file. From then on, progressively-finer grades of abrasive paper should be used, starting with a 40-grade production paper, and finishing with a 400-grade wet-and-dry paper. Always wrap the abrasive paper around a flat rubber, cork, or wooden block – otherwise the surface of the filler will not be completely flat. During the smoothing of the filler surface, the wet-and-dry paper should be periodically rinsed in water. This will ensure that a very smooth finish is imparted to the filler at the final stage.

18 At this stage, the 'dent' should be surrounded by a ring of bare metal, which in turn should be encircled by the finely 'feathered' edge of the good paintwork. Rinse the repair area with clean water, until all of the dust produced by the rubbing-down operation has gone.

19 Spray the whole area with a light coat of primer – this will show up any imperfections in the surface of the filler. Repair these imperfections with fresh filler paste or bodystopper, and once more smooth the surface with abrasive paper. Repeat this spray-and-repair procedure until you are satisfied that the surface of the filler, and the feathered edge of the paintwork, are perfect. Clean the repair area with clean water, and allow to dry fully.

20 The repair area is now ready for final spraying. Paint spraying must be carried out in a warm, dry, windless and dust-free atmosphere. This condition can be created artificially if you have access to a large indoor working area, but if you are forced to work in the open, you will have to pick your day very carefully. If you are working indoors, dousing the floor in the work area with water will help to settle the dust which would otherwise be in the atmosphere. If the repair area is confined to one body panel, mask off the surrounding panels; this will help to minimise the effects of a slight mis-match in paint colours. Bodywork fittings (eg chrome strips, door handles etc) will also need to be masked off. Use genuine masking tape, and several thicknesses of newspaper, for the masking operations.

21 Before commencing to spray, agitate the aerosol can thoroughly, then spray a test area (an old tin, or similar) until the technique is mastered. Cover the repair area with a thick coat of primer; the thickness should be built up using several thin layers of paint, rather than one thick one. Using 400-grade wet-and-dry paper, rub down the surface of the primer until it is really smooth. While doing this, the work area should be thoroughly doused with water, and the wet-and-dry paper periodically rinsed in water. Allow to dry before spraying on more paint.

22 Spray on the top coat, again building up the thickness by using several thin layers of paint. Start spraying at one edge of the repair area, and then, using a side-to-side motion, work until the whole repair area and about 2 inches of the surrounding original paintwork is covered. Remove all masking material 10 to 15 minutes after spraying on the final coat of paint.

23 Allow the new paint at least two weeks to harden, then, using a paintwork renovator, or a very fine cutting paste, blend the edges of the paint into the existing paintwork. Finally, apply wax polish.

Plastic components

24 With the use of more and more plastic body components by the vehicle manufacturers (eg bumpers. spoilers, and in some cases major body panels), rectification of more serious damage to such items has become a matter of either entrusting repair work to a specialist in this field, or renewing complete components. Repair of such damage by the DIY owner is not really feasible, owing to the cost of the equipment and materials required for effecting such repairs. The basic technique involves making a groove along the line of the crack in the plastic, using a rotary burr in a power drill. The damaged part is then welded back together, using a hot-air gun to heat up and fuse a plastic filler rod into the groove. Any excess plastic is then removed, and the area rubbed down to a smooth finish. It is important that a filler rod of the correct plastic is used, as body components can be made of a variety of different types (eg polycarbonate, ABS, polypropylene).

25 Damage of a less serious nature (abrasions, minor cracks etc) can be repaired by the DIY owner using a two-part epoxy filler repair material. Once mixed in equal proportions, this is used in similar fashion to the bodywork filler used on metal panels. The filler is usually cured in 20 to 30 minutes, ready for sanding and painting.

26 If the owner is renewing a complete component himself, or if he has repaired it with epoxy filler, he will be left with the problem of finding a suitable paint for finishing which is compatible with the type of plastic used. At one time, the use of a universal paint was not possible, owing to the complex range of plastics encountered in body component applications. Standard paints, generally speaking, will not bond to plastic or rubber satisfactorily. However, it is now possible to obtain a plastic body parts finishing kit which consists of a pre-primer treatment, a primer and coloured top coat. Full instructions are normally supplied with a kit, but basically, the method of use is to first apply the pre-primer to the component concerned, and allow it to dry for up to 30 minutes. Then the primer is applied, and left to dry for about an hour before finally applying the special-coloured top coat. The result is a correctly coloured component, where the paint will flex with the plastic or rubber, a property that standard paint does not normally possess.

6.2 Prise out the clips and remove the sound insulation from the bonnet

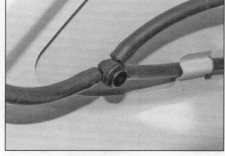

6.3 Disconnect the hose from the under-bonnet junction

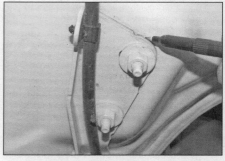

6.4 Make alignment marks to aid refitment

5 Major body damage – repair

1 The chassis members are spot-welded to the underbody, and in this respect can be termed of being monocoque or unit construction. Major damage repairs to this type of body combination must of necessity be carried out by body shops with welding and hydraulic straightening facilities.
2 Extensive damage to the body may distort the chassis, and result in unstable and dangerous handling, as well as excessive wear to tyres and suspension or steering components. It is recommended that checking of the chassis alignment be entrusted to a Ford agent or accident repair specialist with special checking jigs.

6 Bonnet – removal, refitting and adjustment

Removal

1 Open the bonnet, and support it with its prop.
2 Prise out the clips and remove the sound insulation material **(see illustration)**.
3 Disconnect the washer jet hose from the junction on the underside of the bonnet **(see illustration)**.
4 Mark around the bonnet hinges, to show the outline of their fitted positions for correct realignment on assembly **(see illustration)**.
5 Have an assistant support the bonnet while you unscrew and remove the hinge-retaining nuts, then lift the bonnet clear.

Refitting

6 Refitting is a reversal of removal. Tighten the hinge nuts fully when bonnet alignment is satisfactory.

Adjustment

7 Further adjustment of the bonnet fit is available by loosening the hinges and the locknuts of the bump stops on the radiator grille opening panel. The bonnet can now be adjusted to give an even clearance between its outer edges and the surrounding panels. Adjust the front bump stops to align the edges of the bonnet with the front wing panels, then retighten the locknuts and hinge bolts.

7 Bonnet lock – removal and refitting

Removal

1 Remove the front bumper cover as described in Section 22.
2 If fitted, remove the Torx screws holding the bonnet lock cover in place **(see illustration)**.
3 Use a flat-bladed screwdriver to remove the spring clip, remove the rubber shroud and pull the barrel lock out **(see illustration)**.
4 To remove the rest of the mechanism unclip the cables, undo the retaining bolts and lift out the assembly **(see illustration)**.

Refitting

5 Refit the spring clip first before fitting the shroud to the barrel and then inserting the barrel into the assembly.

8 Door trim panels – removal and refitting

Front doors

Removal

1 Carefully prise the trim cap, then undo the retaining screw on the outside edge of the door trim on both doors **(see illustration)**.

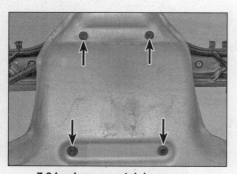

7.2 Lock cover retaining screws

7.3 Remove the spring clip and pull out the bonnet lock

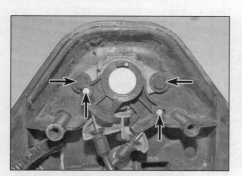

7.4 Release the cables and undo the bolts to remove the bonnet lock assembly

8.1 Lift off the trim cap and undo the retaining screw

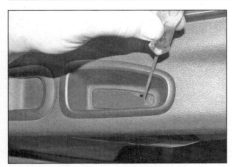

8.2a Remove the blanking panel...

8.2b ...and undo the screw

8.3 Remove the reflector and undo the screw beneath

2 Remove the blanking panel in the base of each door pull recess, and undo the retaining screw **(see illustrations)**.

3 Carefully prise the reflector from the door trim and undo the screw beneath **(see illustration)**.

4 Using a trim removal tool, lift off the trim cap in the lower storage compartment then undo the retaining screw **(see illustration)**.

5 Prise out the trim in the interior door release handle recess, and undo the retaining screw **(see illustration)**.

6 Carefully prise off the door pull handle trim and undo the two screws beneath **(see illustrations)**.

7 Undo the two retaining screws at the base of the door trim **(see illustration)**.

8 Carefully prise the electric windows control module from the top of the door trim; use a trim removal tool or similar to raise the rear of the module, then disconnect the wiring

8.4 Undo the screw in the lower storage compartment

plugs. Undo the retaining screw exposed **(see illustrations)**.

9 Carefully prise the central locking switch from the trim, and disconnect the wiring plug **(see illustration)**.

8.5 Remove the door release handle trim and undo the screw

10 Carefully remove the door trim panel, prising with a suitable tool between the panel around its outer and lower edges. Disconnect any wiring plugs as the door trim panel is withdrawn **(see illustrations)**.

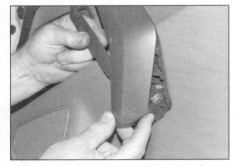

8.6a Prise off the door pull handle trim...

8.6b ...and undo the screws

8.7 Undo the two screws at the base of the door

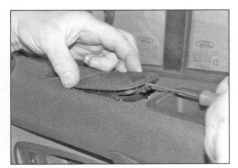

8.8a Raise the rear of the windows control module before removing it from the door...

8.8b ...and undo the retaining screw beneath the electric window controls

8.9 Remove the central locking switch and disconnect the plug

8.10a Carefully prise free the door trim panel to release the retaining clips and remove the panel

8.10b Disconnect and wiring plugs...

8.10c ...and disconnect the interior door handle cable before removing the panel

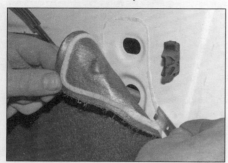

8.11 Take care when removing the insulation sheet

8.13 Prise out the centre pin and remove the expansion rivet

8.15 Remove the clips on each panel

11 If the panel has been removed for access to the door internal components, the plastic insulation sheet will have to be locally removed for access. To do this, cut through the adhesive securing the plastic sheet to the door using a sharp knife, and carefully peel back the insulation sheet as necessary **(see illustration)**. Do not attempt to peel back the sheet without first cutting through the adhesive, and take care not to touch the adhesive after the sheet has been removed. If care is taken, the existing adhesive will re-bond the sheet on completion.

Refitting

12 Refitting is a reversal of removal, taking care not to damage any plastic clips or retainers.

Rear doors and tailgate

Removal

13 Eight retaining clips hold each trim cover

to each rear door. Prise out the centre pin and lever out the expansion rivets, then detach the cover **(see illustration)**. Carefully peel back the membrane.

Refitting

14 Refitting is a reversal of removal. Align the panel and press the clips into position.

Sliding side door

Removal

15 Working from the inside of the van, with the door closed, prise out the centre pins and lever out the expansion rivets **(see illustration)**. Remove each of these with a flat-bladed screwdriver and detach the cover. Carefully peel back membrane. If the membrane is damaged, a new one may be required.

Refitting

16 Refitting is a reversal of removal.

9 Front door handle and lock components – removal and refitting

Exterior handle

Removal

1 Remove the plastic trim on the rear edge of the door that covers the door handle retaining screw. Rotate the screw approximately eight times until it is possible to remove the bezel **(see illustrations)**.

2 Withdraw the handle to the rear before removing it **(see illustration)**.

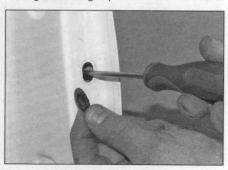

9.1a Rotate the retaining screw anticlockwise...

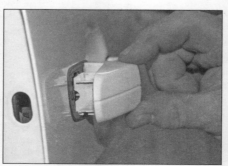

9.1b ...until the bezel can be removed

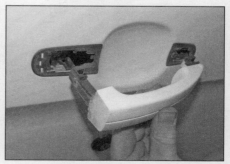

9.2 Pull out the rear of the exterior handle, then slide it rearwards

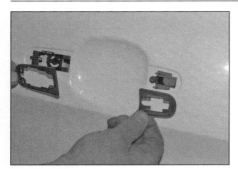

9.3 Remove the two gaskets

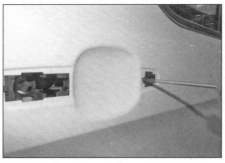

9.4 Undo the screw before sliding the door handle frame out

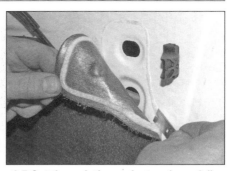

9.7 Cut through the sealant and carefully peel away the waterproof inner membrane

3 Remove the rubber gaskets **(see illustration)**.

4 If required, undo the screw, release the clips and slide the door handle frame out **(see illustration)**.

Refitting

5 Refitting is a reversal of removal.

Door lock cylinder

Removal

6 Remove the front door trim panel as described in Section 8.

7 Remove the waterproof inner membrane covering the door lock and electric window mechanism **(see illustration)**.

8 Disconnect the door lock wiring plug **(see illustration)**.

9 Extract the lock cylinder retaining clip **(see illustration)**.

10 Insert the ignition key into the lock cylinder and turn it clockwise.

11 Using a flat-bladed screwdriver, depress the tang on the cylinder body, turn the key anticlockwise and withdraw the cylinder from the door **(see illustrations)**.

Refitting

12 Refitting is a reversal of removal, noting that the door key must be removed from the lock prior to refitting the cylinder retaining clip.

Door lock unit

Removal

13 Remove the front door trim panel as described in Section 8.

9.8 Disconnect the door lock wiring plug

14 Remove the front door exterior handle as described previously.

15 If required, remove the door lock cylinder as described previously.

16 Undo the retaining screws and remove the

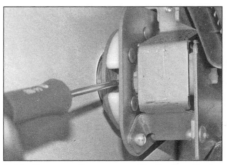

9.11a Depress the tang on the lock cylinder body...

9.9 Slide out the door lock cylinder retaining clip

door window glass rear guide channel **(see illustrations)**.

17 Undo the Torx screw in the door handle aperture **(see illustration)**.

18 Undo the door lock retaining

9.11b ...turn the key anticlockwise, then withdraw the cylinder from the door

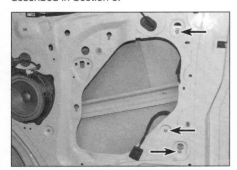

9.16a Undo the screws...

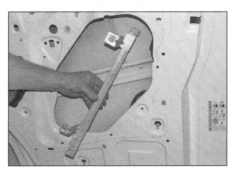

9.16b ...and remove the window glass guide channel

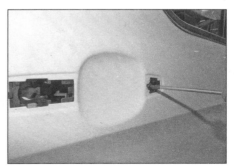

9.17 Undo the Torx screw

9.18 Door lock retaining screws

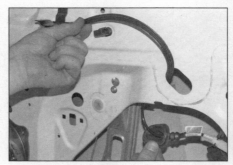

9.19 Unclip the cable and grommet, then feed the cable into the door

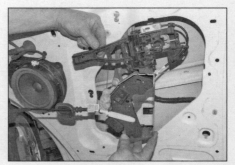

9.20 Remove the door lock unit

9.21a Disconnect the outer handle cable...

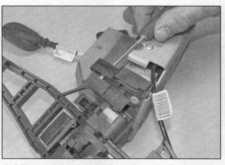

9.21b ...and release the clips and separate the bracket from the lock assembly

9.22 Detach the interior release handle cable

screws at the door rear edge (see illustration).

19 Unclip the door pull cable, release the cable grommet and feed the cable into the door (see illustration).

20 Manoeuvre the lock unit from place (see illustration).

21 If required, the door handle bracket can be separated from the door lock unit by disconnecting the outer handle operating

cable from the bracket and releasing the clips (see illustrations).

22 Unclip the interior release handle operating cable from the bracket, if required (see illustration).

Refitting

23 Refitting is a reversal of removal.

---

10 Front door – removal, refitting and adjustment

Removal

1 Disconnect the battery negative terminal as described in Chapter 5 Section 4.

2 Carefully prise off the trim in front of the door mirror (see illustration).

3 Open the door, and position a suitable padded jack or support blocks underneath it; don't lift the door, just take its weight.

4 Undo the Torx screw and remove the door check strap bracket from the body pillar (see illustration).

5 Disconnect the door wiring harness plug from the vehicle body. First, remove the cable grommet. Raise the exposed wiring plug to disengage the lower clip before using a flat-bladed screwdriver to release the upper clip. Pull out the wiring plug from the wing aperture, then use the screwdriver to release the two vehicle-side plugs that connect to the door-side plug (see illustrations).

6 With the help of an assistant, undo the upper and lower hinge nuts and lift the door off the hinges (see illustrations).

10.2 Prise off the trim in front of the door mirror

10.4 Undo the screw and remove the door check strap bracket from the body pillar

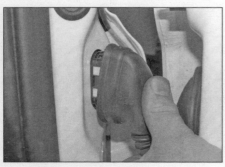

10.5a Remove the cable grommet...

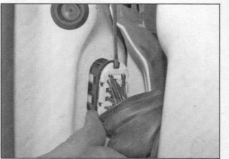

10.5b ...lift the plug and release the upper clip with a screwdriver...

Refitting and adjustment

7 Refitting is a reversal of removal. After fitting, open and shut the door to ensure that it does not bind with the body aperture at any point. Adjust the door striker plate if necessary. Also make sure the cable grommet is fitted correctly.

---

11 Sliding side door handle and lock components – removal and refitting

---

Exterior handle

Removal

1 Remove the door inner trim panel as described in Section 8.
2 Undo the handle-retaining screw on the inside of the door **(see illustration)**.
3 Pull off the bezel and then pull out the rear of the handle and slide it rearwards **(see illustrations)**.
4 If required, remove the rubber gaskets, undo the screw, release the clips and slide the door handle frame out **(see illustrations)**. Peel back the plastic insulation to access the handle frame.

Refitting

5 Refitting is a reversal of removal.

Door lock unit

Removal

6 Remove the door inner trim panel as described in Section 8.

7 Undo the three bolts securing the lock to the door **(see illustration)**.
8 Prise away the access panel from the inside of the door **(see illustration)**.

9 Withdraw the lock unit from its location and disconnect the wiring plug **(see illustrations)**. Unclip any cable tidies as necessary to remove the lock unit.

10.5c ...then pull out the wiring plug and release the vehicle-side wiring plugs...

10.5d ...and pull out the plugs

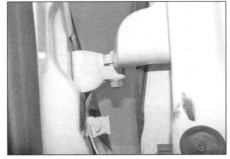

10.6a Undo the upper...

10.6b ...and lower hinge nut and lift the door off the hinges

11.2 Remove the screw on the inside of the door

11.3a Pull off the bezel...

11.3b ...before sliding the handle rearwards and removing it

11.4a Undo the screw...

11.4b ...and remove the inner door handle frame

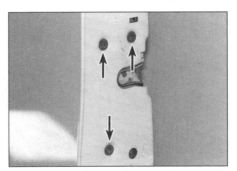

11.7 Undo the three bolts securing the lock to the door

11.8 Remove the access panel

11.9a Withdraw the lock unit from its location...

11.9b ...and disconnect the wiring plug

11.10a Undo the screws...

11.10b ...and remove the security shield

Refitting

13 Refitting is a reversal of removal.

Interior release handle

Removal

14 Remove the door inner trim panel as described in Section 8.

15 Remove the plastic caps and undo the nuts securing the handle cover **(see illustrations)**.

16 Release the two cables from the retaining clips on the inside of the door **(see illustration)**.

17 Disconnect the cable end from the mechanism **(see illustration)**.

18 Lift up the handle and remove it and the operating cables from the door **(see illustration)**.

10 Undo the two screws and remove the security shield **(see illustrations)**.
11 Note the fitted position of the cables and remove them as necessary **(see illustrations)**.
12 Remove the lock unit from the vehicle.

11.11a Note the fitted position of the cables...

11.11b ...before removing them

11.15a Undo the nuts securing the handle cover...

11.15b ...and remove the cover

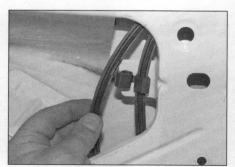

11.16 Release the cables

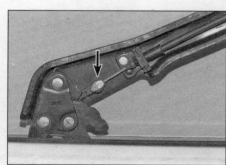

11.17 Disconnect the cable end

11.18 Remove the handle and operating cable from the door

11.19 Detach the cables from the handle

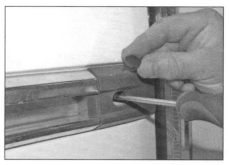

12.1 Undo the retaining bolt from the end stop

19 Remove the attached cables, if necessary **(see illustration)**.

Refitting

20 Refitting is a reversal of removal.

12 Sliding side door – removal, refitting and adjustment

Removal

Note: *Before slackening any retaining bolts, make alignment marks on the guide supports to aid alignment when refitting.*

1 Remove the cover, undo the retaining bolt and remove the end stop from the centre rail **(see illustration)**.

2 Slide the door open, prise off the plastic caps where fitted and undo the two nuts securing the door lower guide

bracket. Slide the arm out of the slot **(see illustrations)**.

3 Enlist the aid of an assistant to support the weight of the door on the centre rail, then slide the upper guide support out of its track.

4 Support the door at each end, slide it to the rear, and remove it from the vehicle.

Refitting

5 Refitting is a reversal of removal. Align the door and engage it onto the centre track, then reconnect the fittings.

Adjustment

6 Check the door for satisfactory adjustment. Adjust if necessary by loosening off the lower support bolts to reposition the door as required, then tighten them and recheck the fitting.

7 To adjust the height, loosen off the upper support locknut, turn the adjuster bolt as required, then retighten the locknut to secure.

8 When fitted, and in the closed position, the door should be aligned flush to the surrounding body, and should close securely. If required, adjust the striker plate position to suit.

13 Rear door handle and lock components – removal and refitting

Exterior handle

Removal

1 Remove the plastic cover from the door's edge and slacken the screw approximately eight turns **(see illustration)**.

2 Remove the rear section of the exterior handle, then slide the rest of the handle to the left-hand side and remove it **(see illustrations)**.

3 Remove the rubber gaskets **(see illustration)**.

12.2a Unscrew the bolts, remove the bracket...

12.2b ...and slide the arm out of the slot

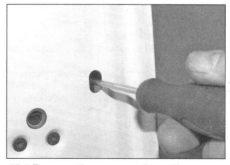

13.1 Remove the cover and turn the screw anticlockwise

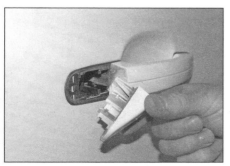

13.2a Remove the bezel...

13.2b ...before sliding the handle to the left to release it

13.3 Remove the rubber gaskets

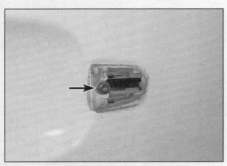

13.7 Slacken the Torx screw in the handle aperture

13.8 Lock retaining screws

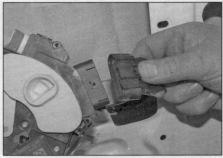

13.9 Disconnect the lock wiring plug

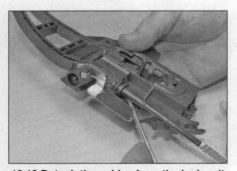

13.10 Detach the cables from the lock unit

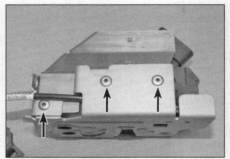

13.11 Drill out the rivets and undo the Torx screw if necessary

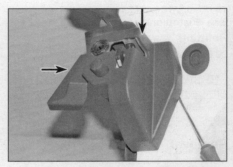

13.13 Use a trim removal tool to release the clips

Refitting

4   Refitting is a reversal of removal.

Door lock unit

Removal

5   Remove the door inner trim panel as described in Section 8.
6   Remove the exterior door handle as described in this Section.
7   Slacken the Torx screw **(see illustration)**.
8   Undo the three Torx screws on the door's edge, securing the lock unit **(see illustration)**.
9   Disconnect the wiring plug from the lock unit **(see illustration)**.
10   If required, detach the operating cables from the lock unit **(see illustration)**.
11   The exterior handle operating cable is available separately. Drill out the three rivets,

undo the Torx screw and remove the security shield **(see illustration)**.

Refitting

12   Refitting is a reversal of removal.

Lock upper latch

Removal

13   Prise open the rear edge then release the clips and pull the plastic trim rearwards **(see illustration)**.
14   Undo the three Torx bolts and pull the latch away from the door **(see illustration)**.
15   Using a pair of thin-nosed pliers, compress the clips, detach the outer cable from the bracket and then disengage the cable end fitting from the operating lever **(see illustration)**.

Refitting

16   Refitting is a reversal of removal. Align the latch with the striker before tightening the three bolts **(see illustration)**.

Lock lower latch

Removal

17   Remove the door inner trim panel as described in Section 8.
18   Remove the plastic guard from the latch **(see illustration)**.
19   Undo the three retaining bolts securing the latch to the door **(see illustration)**.
20   Pull out the latch and detach the latch operating cable from the bracket, then detach the inner cable end fitting from the latch lever **(see illustration)**. Remove the lower latch from the door.

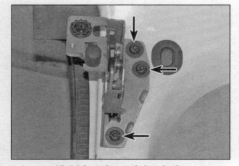

13.14 Latch retaining bolts

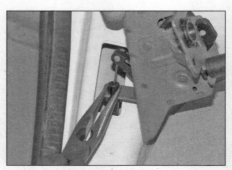

13.15 Detach the cable from the bracket

13.16 Align the latch with the striker before tightening the bolts

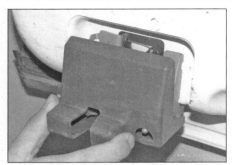

13.18 Unclip the guard from the latch

13.19 Lower latch retaining screws

13.20 Disconnect the operating cable from the latch

13.21 Align the latch with the striker before tightening the bolts

13.23 Undo the release lever screw

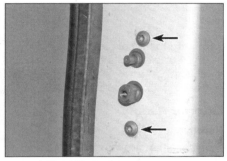

13.24 Undo the two screws

Refitting

21 Refitting is a reversal of removal. Align the latch with the striker before tightening the three bolts **(see illustration)**.

Latch release lever

Removal

22 Remove the door inner trim panel as described in Section 8.
23 Undo the release lever Torx screw **(see illustration)**.
24 Undo the two screws and withdraw the latch release mechanism into the door **(see illustration)**.
25 Release the two operating cables with thin-nosed pliers **(see illustration)**.

Refitting

26 Refitting is a reversal of removal.

| 14 Rear doors – |
| removal, refitting |
| and adjustment |

Removal

1 Open the rear doors. Remove the inner trim panels (Section 8).
2 Disconnect the relevant wiring plugs, release the rubber grommet and withdraw the loom from the door **(see illustration)**.
3 Undo the two bolts securing the check strap to the door **(see illustration)**.
4 To aid refitting, make alignment marks around the door hinge. Have an assistant support the

door, undo three retaining bolts from each hinge and withdraw the door **(see illustration)**.

Refitting and adjustment

5 Refitting is a reversal of removal. Align the

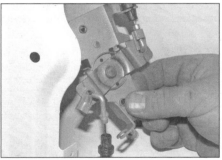

13.25 Release the cables from the latch release mechanism

14.3 Check strap retaining bolts

hinges with the previously-made marks, then tighten the bolts.
6 Open and shut the doors, and ensure that they don't bind with the body aperture at any point. Adjust the door hinges and striker plate

14.2 Disconnect the rubber grommet

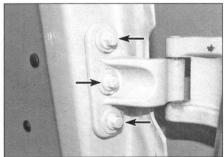

14.4 Undo the rear door hinge retaining bolts

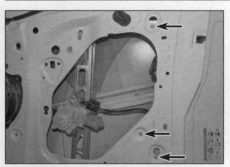

17.4 Rear guide channel retaining screws

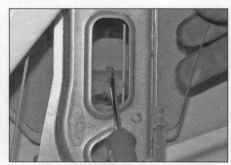

17.5 Press out the clamping peg

if necessary, to provide an even clearance all round.

15 Tailgate handle and lock – removal and refitting

Exterior handle

Removal

1 Remove the tailgate inner trim panel as described in Section 8.
2 Disconnect the wiring plug from the number plate bulb holders/door latch mechanism.
3 Undo the four nuts securing the exterior handle to the tailgate. Remove it from the tailgate.

Refitting

4 Refitting is a reversal of removal.

Tailgate lock unit

Removal

5 Remove the tailgate inner trim panel as described in Section 8.
6 Remove the plastic guard from the lock unit.
7 Undo the three retaining bolts and lift out the lock unit.
8 Disconnect the wiring plug from the central locking actuator.

Refitting

9 Refitting is a reversal of removal.

16 Tailgate – removal, refitting and adjustment

Removal

1 The aid of two assistants will be required to support the tailgate as it is removed. First open the tailgate, then support it in the open position and detach the wiring harness at the multi-plug connectors in the body. Pull the wiring loom through the body, and leave it attached to the tailgate.
2 Where applicable, disconnect the rear window washer hose.
3 Prise up the retaining clips (take care not to lift the clips by more than 4 mm) and pull the gas struts from the balljoint on the door. Swing the struts down and out of the way.
4 Loosen off and remove the tailgate hinge bolts (two on each side), and have the two assistants support the weight of the tailgate as it is removed.

Refitting

5 Refit the tailgate in the reverse order of removal. Press the struts' balljoints onto their studs, using hand pressure only. Note that the struts are gas-filled, and therefore cannot be repaired. If renewing, be sure to obtain the correct replacements.

Adjustment

6 When the tailgate is refitted, check its

adjustment and if necessary re-adjust as follows.

Height adjustment

7 Loosen off the hinge retaining bolts, and reset the tailgate at the required height to suit the latch/striker engagement and the body aperture, then fully retighten the bolts.

Side clearance adjustment

8 Loosen off the tailgate side bump guides, the striker plate and the hinge bolts. Centralise the tailgate in its aperture, then retighten the hinge bolts. If required, re-adjust the position of the striker plate so that the tailgate closes securely. Now adjust the position of the side bump guides so that they only just contact the D-pillar bumpers when the tailgate is set at the safety catch position, and only make full contact when the tailgate is closed.

17 Front door window glass – removal and refitting

Note: *To improve access, remove the door speaker as described in Chapter 12 Section 20.*

Removal

1 Lower the window approximately 180 mm.
2 Disconnect the battery negative lead as described in Chapter 5 Section 4.
3 Remove the door inner trim panel and waterproof inner membrane as described in Section 8.
4 Undo the three screws and remove the door window glass rear guide channel **(see illustration)**. Unclip any wiring loom as necessary.
5 Carefully press out the clamping peg slightly and slide the window to the top of the frame **(see illustration)**.
6 Undo the retaining bolts, disconnect the wiring plug and remove the front door glass window regulator as described in Section 18.
7 Lower the glass into the door.
8 Undo the two retaining screws, and lower and manoeuvre the front window guide from the door **(see illustrations)**.
9 Carefully lift the window glass up and out from the inside of the door **(see illustration)**.

17.8a Undo the upper...

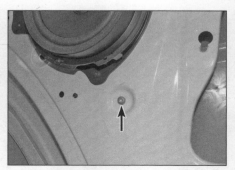

17.8b ...and lower retaining screw before removing the front window guide

17.9 Carefully lift the window glass up and out towards the inside of the door

Refitting

10 Refitting is a reversal of removal. Removal of the door speaker, as described in Chapter 12 Section 20, will improve access for raising the glass **(see illustration)**. When refitting the weatherstrip, engage the front lower corner first, then work round ensuring correct seating. Before refitting the door trim panel, raise and lower the window to ensure that it operates in a satisfactory manner.

18 Front door electric window regulator – removal and refitting

Removal

1 Follow the front door window glass procedure as described in Section 17. There is no need to completely remove the glass. Slide it to the top of the door frame and secure it with a length of adhesive tape.
2 Disconnect the regulator motor wiring plug **(see illustration)**.
3 Undo the three screws securing the window regulator to the door **(see illustration)**.
4 Manipulate the regulator assembly out through the door aperture **(see illustration)**.
5 If required, undo the three retaining screws and detach the motor from the regulator assembly **(see illustration)**.

Refitting

6 Refitting is a reversal of removal.

19 Front door quarter glass – removal and refitting

Removal

1 Remove the front door window glass as described in Section 17.
2 Gently pull the glass rearwards to release it from the weatherstrip **(see illustration)**.

Refitting

3 Refitting is the reversal of removal.

20 Windscreen/tailgate and fixed/sliding windows – removal and refitting

1 These areas of glass are secured by the tight fit of the weatherseal in the body aperture, and are bonded in position with a special adhesive. Renewal of such fixed glass is a difficult, messy and time-consuming task, which is considered beyond the scope of the home mechanic. It is difficult, unless one has plenty of practice, to obtain a secure, waterproof fit. Furthermore, the task carries a high risk of breakage; this applies especially to the laminated glass windscreen. In view of this, owners are strongly advised to have this sort of work carried out by one of the many specialist windscreen fitters.

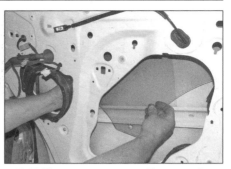

17.10 The aperture created by removing the door speaker makes it easier to handle the window glass

21 Exterior mirrors – removal and refitting

Door mirror glass

1 Adjust the glass electrically or manually by hand so that the outer edge is as far rearwards as possible. With the careful use of a wedge tool, lever the glass off its mount and disconnect any electrical plugs from the mirror glass as it's withdrawn **(see illustration)**. Refitting is the reverse of removal, ensuring the glass is securely attached.

Door mirror

2 Remove the door interior trim panel as described in Section 8.

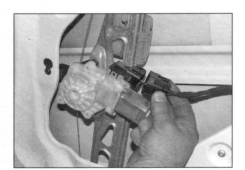

18.2 Disconnect the wiring plug

18.3 Front door window regulator retaining screws

18.4 Remove the assembly through the door aperture

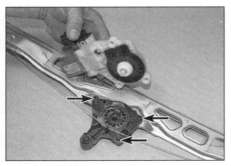

18.5 Motor retaining screws

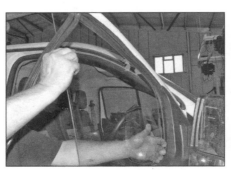

19.2 Ease the quarter glass from the weatherstrip, taking care not to damage it

21.1 Use a wedge tool to remove the mirror glass

21.4 Disconnect the wiring plug and release the cable-retaining clip

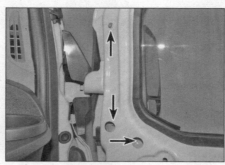

21.5a Undo the three retaining bolts…

6 Refitting is a reversal of removal.

Door mirror cover

7 Use a trim removal tool or similar to gently lever the cover from the mirror unit **(see illustration)**.

8 Refitting is a reversal of removal.

---

22 Front bumper – removal and refitting

Removal

1 Apply the handbrake, then jack up the front of the vehicle and support it on axle stands (see *Jacking and vehicle support*). Remove the front roadwheels for improved access.

2 Remove the headlights as described in Chapter 12 Section 11.

3 Undo the retaining screws and remove the front number plate, and the undo the two bumper retaining screws **(see illustration)**.

4 Prise up the centre pins and remove the plastic expansion rivets at the rear of the bonnet slam panel **(see illustration)**.

5 Undo the three bolts along the bonnet slam panel **(see illustration)**.

6 Undo the Torx screws securing the air deflector to the lower front edge of the bumper **(see illustration)**.

7 Undo the two screws on each side of the rear edge of the lower bumper **(see illustration)**.

8 Gently pull the rear edges of the bumper from the fasteners on the inner wing panel **(see illustration)**.

21.5b …and remove the mirror assembly

21.7 Use a trim removal tool to release the clips retaining the mirror cover

3 Remove the door speaker as described in Section 12 Section 20.

4 Working inside the door recess, disconnect the mirror wiring plug and release the cable-retaining clip **(see illustration)**.

5 Remove the two grommets covering the lower bolts, then support the mirror and undo the three bolts securing the mirror housing **(see illustrations)**. Carefully manoeuvre the mirror assembly from place.

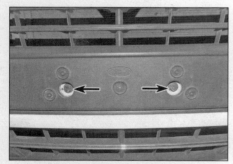

22.3 Undo the two bumper retaining screws behind the number plate

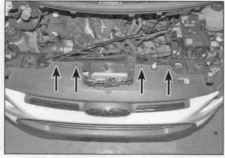

22.4 Remove the plastic expansion rivets

22.5 Remove the three bolts along the front edge of the slam panel

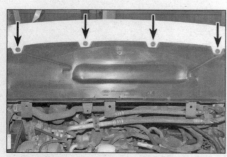

22.6 Undo the screws securing the air deflector to the lower front edge of the bumper

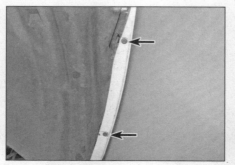

22.7 Undo the Torx screws in the wheelarch apertures

22.8 Detach the bumper from the inner wing panel

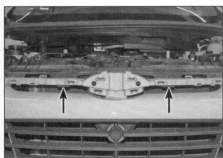

22.9 Release the two clips securing the upper section

22.10 Release the clips securing the lower section

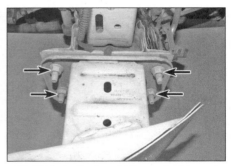

22.13 Undo the four bolts each side and remove the bumper brace

9 Release the two clips either side of the upper grille badge that secure the top section of the bumper cover **(see illustration)**.
10 Release the clip at the base of each headlight aperture **(see illustration)**.
11 With the help of an assistant, the bumper can now be removed from the vehicle. Disconnect any wiring plugs as the bumper is removed.
12 If required, undo the single fastener securing the plastic wind deflector to each end of the bumper brace and remove the deflectors.
13 Release the clips retaining the ambient temperature sensor, undo the four bolts each side and remove the bumper brace from the vehicle **(see illustration)**.

Refitting
14 Refitting is a reversal of removal.

23 Rear bumper – removal and refitting

Removal
1 Raise the rear of the vehicle and support it on axle stands (see *Jacking and vehicle support*) and remove the rear wheels.
2 Using a forked tool, remove the six

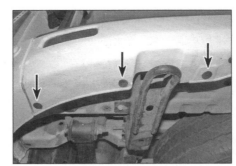

23.2 Prise out the six fasteners on the underside (left-hand fasteners arrowed)

fasteners securing the bumper cover to the underside of the vehicle **(see illustration)**.
3 Undo the five Torx screws securing the upper edge of the bumper centre section to the body **(see illustration)**.
4 On vehicles with rear parking sensors, disconnect the wiring plug under the right-hand edge of the bumper cover.
5 Remove the fastener on each side of the rear door recess and, on vehicles with parking sensors, unplug each sensor from behind the bumper cover **(see illustration)**.
6 Now remove the centre bumper cover by pulling it rearwards.

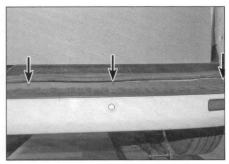

23.3 Undo the Torx screws securing the upper edge of the bumper (right-hand screws arrowed)

7 Gently pull the bumper cover outer sections out to remove them. Disconnect any wiring plugs as necessary.
8 If required, unclip the parking sensors from the bumper cover **(see illustration)**. Note that not all sensors are fitted in the same way
9 If required, undo the two nuts each side and remove the bumper brace from the vehicle, unclipping any associated wiring **(see illustration)**.

Refitting
10 Refitting is a reversal of removal, using new pop rivets.

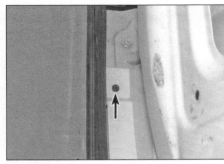

23.5 Remove the fastener on each side of the rear door recess (right-hand side shown)

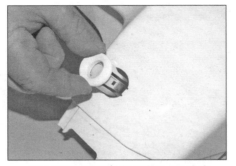

23.8 Unclip the wiring plug, expand the tabs and push the sensor out of its housing and compress the white collar's clips and push the housing out of the bumper cover

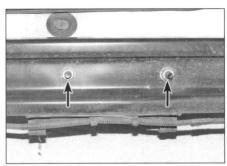

23.9 Two nuts retain the bumper brace at each side

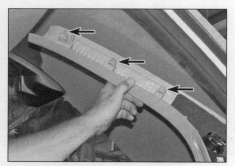

24.2a Pull the upper edge of the trim away from the A-pillar...

24.2b ...and disconnect the speaker wiring plug

24.3 Depress the tangs and withdraw the tweeter speaker from the A-pillar trim

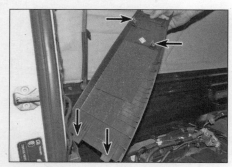

24.5 Pull the centre section inwards, then upwards

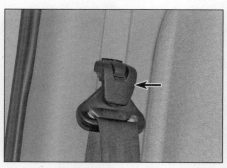

24.6a Lift the plastic cover off the seat belt upper mounting...

24.6b ...then unscrew the upper mounting bolt

24 Interior trim – removal and refitting

Door trim panels

1 Refer to the procedures contained in Section 8.

A-pillar trim

Removal

2 Pull the upper edge of the trim away from the pillar to disengage the three retaining clips, then lift the trim up to disengage the lower lugs from the facia (see illustrations). The uppermost metal clip is likely to break so a new one will be needed for refitting.

Disconnect the plug for the tweeter speaker as you remove the trim.
3 If required, depress the three tangs and remove the tweeter speaker (see illustration).

Refitting

4 Refitting is a reversal of removal. You will need a new uppermost retaining clip.

B-pillar trim

Removal

5 Pull the centre section of the pillar trim inwards to release the two fasteners and lift the trim panel upwards (see illustration).
6 Gently pull the plastic cover off the seat belt upper mounting, then unscrew the upper mounting bolt and move the upper mounting and belt to one side (see illustrations).
7 Gently prise inwards the lower section of

trim taking care to avoid breaking the clips (see illustration).
8 Undo the screw, then pull the upper section of the trim inwards to release the clips (see illustration).

Refitting

9 Refitting is a reversal of removal, ensuring that the seat belt mountings are tightened to the specified torque.

Grab handle

10 Prise open the access flaps, undo the retaining screws and remove the handle (see illustration).
11 Refitting is a reversal of removal.

Sun visor

12 The sun visor mounting bracket is retained by two screws. Use a small screwdriver to

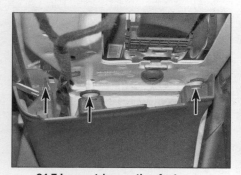

24.7 Lower trim section fasteners

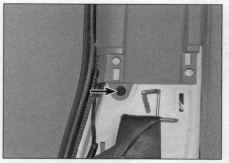

24.8 Undo the screw and disengage the clips, and remove the upper section of trim

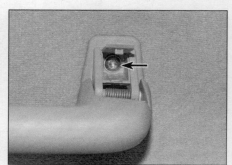

24.10 Undo the screws and remove the grab handle

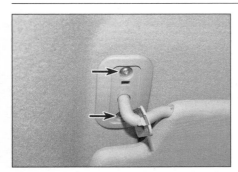

24.12 Undo the screws, release the bracket and remove the sun visor

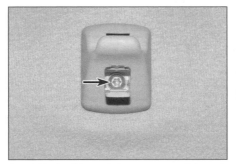

24.13 Undo the retaining screw and detach the sun visor clip

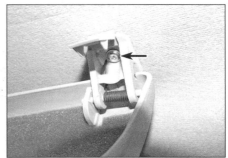

24.14 Undo the screws and remove the glasses holder

remove the plastic cover and access the screws. Undo the screws, unclip the other end of the sun visor and remove it (see illustration).

13 The sun visor clip is retained by one screw. Open the access flap with a small screwdriver, undo the screw and remove the clip (see illustration).

Glasses holder

14 The glasses holder is located above the driver's seat. Open the access flap, undo the retaining screws and remove it (see illustration).

15 Refitting is a reversal of removal.

Overhead storage bin

16 The storage bin is mounted to the roof between the front seats.

17 With the front courtesy light removed, as described in Chapter 12 Section 10, reach into the light aperture and push the storage bin plastic insert to the rear to release and remove it. Undo the retaining screw at the top of the aperture revealed by removing the bin, use a flat-bladed screwdriver to release the two clips at the top of the rear edge of the assembly and pull it to the rear. Release any wiring clips as the storage bin frame is withdrawn (see illustrations).

18 Refitting is a reversal of removal.

Coat hooks

19 Open the access flap with a small screwdriver and undo the screw (see illustration).

Loadspace trim

20 Refer to the procedures contained in Section 8

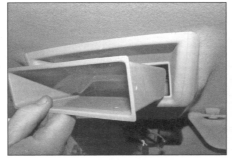

24.17a Push/pull the bin unit from the assembly...

Removal

1 Disconnect the battery negative terminal as described in Chapter 5 Section 4. On models equipped with side airbags, wait a minimum of 3 minutes before proceeding.

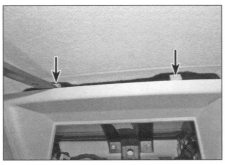

24.17c ...release the tabs and pull the unit rearwards to remove it

24.17b ...undo the retaining screw...

Driver's seat

2 Remove the cover and undo the seatbelt lower retaining bolt (see illustrations).

3 Where fitted, on the driver's seat, remove the cover at the base of the rear of the seat,

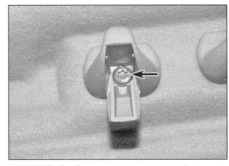

24.19 Undo the screw to remove the coat hook

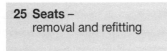

25 Seats –
removal and refitting

Warning: Some models may be equipped with side airbags built into the outer sides of the front seats. Refer to Chapter 12 Section 22 for the precautions which should be observed when dealing with an airbag system.

25.2a Remove the cover from the side of the driver's seat...

25.2b ...and undo the retaining bolt

25.3 Remove the fasteners and battery compartment cover

25.4 Driver's seat front seat rail retaining bolt

25.5 Undo the bolt and disconnect the plug beneath the the seat

remove the fasteners and remove the battery compartment cover **(see illustration)**.

4 Move the seat fully to the rear and undo the two front seat rail retaining bolts **(see illustration)**.

5 Undo the retaining bolt and disconnect the wiring plug from beneath the seat, releasing the wiring retaining clips **(see illustration)**.

6 Move the seat fully to the front and undo the rear seat rail retaining bolt each side **(see illustration)**.

7 The seat can now be removed from the vehicle. Take care when storing the seat to avoid damage to any fitted components that protrude beneath the rails.

Caution: The seats are very heavy!

Bench seat

8 Remove the cover and undo the seatbelt lower retaining bolt **(see illustration)**.

9 Flip up the seat base and disconnect the wiring plug on the inner right-hand side of the

seat frame, releasing the wiring retaing clip **(see illustration)**.

10 Unclip the fasteners and remove the trim on the left-hand edge to provide better access to the seat retaining bolts **(see illustration)**.

11 Undo the bench seat retaining nuts and bolts **(see illustrations)**.

12 The bench seat can now be removed from the vehicle. Take care when storing the seat to avoid damage to any components that protrude beneath the rails.

Refitting

13 Refitting is a reversal of removal.

Rear seats

14 Various combinations of rear seats may be fitted, according to vehicle type and specification. The removal and refitting procedures are essentially the same as those described previously for the front seats.

26 Seat belt components – removal and refitting

Front seat belt

Removal

1 Disconnect the battery negative terminal as described in Chapter 5 Section 4.

⚠️ *Warning: Seat belt tensioners are incorporated in the inertia reel of the driver's seat belt and also into the inertia reel of the passenger's seat belt. Before proceeding, wait a minimum of 3 minutes, as a precaution against accidental firing of the seat belt tensioners. This period ensures that any residual electrical energy is dissipated.*

25.6 Driver's seat rear seat rail retaining bolt

25.8 The seatbelt retaining bolt is behind a cover

25.9 Disconnect the wiring plug

25.10 Remove the trim to improve access to the bench seat bolts

25.11a Bench seat retaining nut and bolt (right-hand side)…

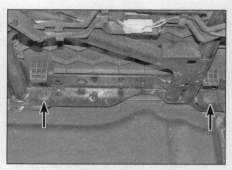

25.11b …and bench seat retaining bolts (left-hand side)

26.3a Release the clip and disconnect the wiring plug…

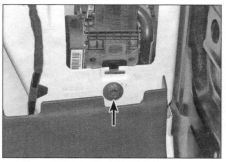

26.3b …undo the retaining bolt and remove the front seat belt inertia reel from the B-pillar

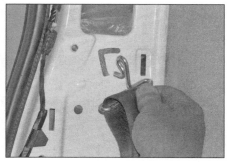

26.4 The seatbelt guide unhooks from the B-pillar frame

⚠️ *Warning: There is a potential risk of the seat belt tensioning device firing during removal, so it should be handled carefully. Once removed, treat it with care – do not allow chemicals on or near it, and do not expose it to high temperatures, or it may detonate.*

2 Remove the B-pillar trim as described in Section 24, taking note that only the upper part of the lower section of trim needs to be removed.

3 Disconnect the inertia reel wiring plug, unscrew the mounting bolt and lift the reel to remove it from the base of the pillar (**see illustrations**).

4 Unhook the seatbelt guide and remove it (**see illustration**).

5 If required, undo the seatbelt height adjuster retaining bolts and remove it (**see illustration**).

Refitting

6 Refitting is a reversal of removal, ensuring that the tag on the inertia reel engages correctly in the B-pillar. Tighten the retaining bolts to the specified torque.

Front centre seat belt

Removal

Note: *On vehicles equipped with a double front passenger's seat, the seat belt inertia reel is fitted internally within the seat.*

7 Remove the bench seat as described in Section 25. Remove the headrests.

8 Remove the headrest guides by using an Allen key to gently compress the plastic clip and pull the guide out (**see illustration**). Take care not to damage the clips.

9 Undo the outer seatbelt lower retaining bolt (**see illustration 25.8**).

10 Flip up the outer seat base and undo the seatbelt lower anchorage/lower stalk bolt (**see illustration**).

11 Remove the plastic cover and undo the bolts securing the seatbelt guide (**see illustration**).

12 Depress the tabs and pull off the front and rear seatbelt guide covers (**see illustrations**).

13 Separate the seat back cover from the front by releasing the two fasteners (one for each seat) at the base of the bench (**see illustration**).

14 Reach up under the rear of the seat trim and depress the clips to release the mounting panel for the arm rest/cupholder. Manoeuvre the panel from place (**see illustration**).

15 Feed the seatbelt through the slot in the top of the seatbelt guide and carefully feed the belt and buckle assembly through the

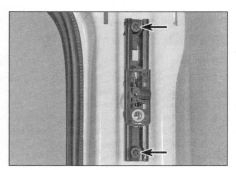

26.5 Undo the bolts and remove the seatbelt height adjuster

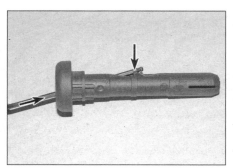

26.8 Use an Allen key to depress the clip and extract the guide

26.10 Undo the bolt and remove the lower anchoring point

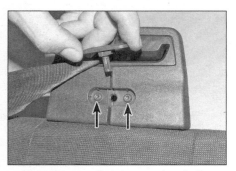

26.11 Remove the cover and undo the seatbelt guide-retaining bolts

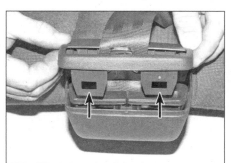

26.12a Press the two tabs and remove the guide front cover…

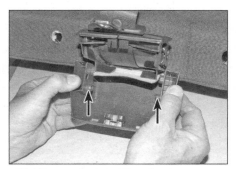

26.12b …and spread the clips to remove the rear cover

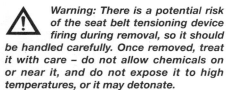

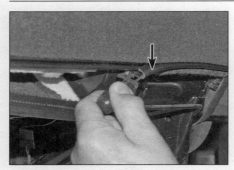

26.13 Disengage the fasteners to separate the seat trim

26.14 Arm rest/cupholder mounting panel clips

26.15 Feed the belt and buckle down through the back of the seat

26.16 Undo the bolt and remove the inertia reel and belt assembly from beneath the seat

26.17 Ensure the belt is installed into the guide channel

26.18 Open the plastic cover and undo the retaining nut to remove the seat belt stalk

aperture in the top of the seat, taking care not to damage the material **(see illustration)**.

16 Undo the retaining bolt, lift the inertia reel out of its bracket and manoeuvre it and the belt and buckle assembly out from under the seat **(see illustration)**.

Refitting

17 Refitting is a reversal of removal, ensuring that the seatbelt is correctly fitted into the guide channel that runs up the inside of the back of the seat back trim **(see illustration)**. Tighten the retaining bolts to the specified torque.

Seat belt stalks

18 Various combinations of seat belt stalks may be fitted, according to vehicle type and specification. The removal and refitting procedures are essentially self-explanatory,

but it may be necessary in some instances to remove certain interior trim panels for access. Ensure that all attachment bolts are tightened to the specified torque when refitting **(see illustration)**.

27 Facia panel components – removal and refitting

1 Remove the A-pillar trim panel as described in Section 24 before dismantling the dashboard.

Glovebox

Removal

2 Open the glovebox, then press in the tab at each upper side of the lid and lower the lid fully **(see illustration)**.

3 Disengage the hinge pins at the base of the glovebox lid by using a flat-bladed screwdriver to slide them inwards. Then remove the lid **(see illustration)**.

Refitting

4 Refitting is a reversal of removal.

Side bottle holders

Removal

5 Remove the glovebox (left-hand side) or right-hand lower trim panel (right-hand side), as described elsewhere in this Section.

6 Using a trim removal tool, prise the bottle holder shroud from the facia, then remove the bottle holder **(see illustrations)**.

Refitting

7 Refitting is a reversal of removal.

27.2 Press in the tab at each upper side of the glovebox lid (one shown) and lower the lid fully

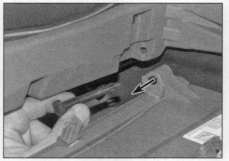

27.3 Disengage the hinges at the base of the glovebox lid and remove the lid

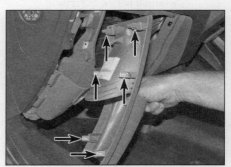

27.6a Release the shroud retaining clips...

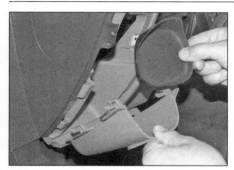

27.6b ...then remove the bottle holder

27.8 Remove the facia lower trim panel, including bottle holder, by pulling it away to release the retaining clips

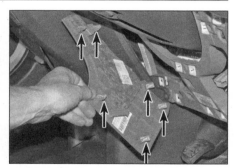

27.9 Pull off the inner right-hand lower panel, noting the location of the clips

Right-hand lower trim panels

Removal

8 Use a trim removal tool to prise the bottle holder shroud and panel **(see illustration)**.
9 Remove the facia inner right-hand lower trim panel beneath the steering wheel by pulling it away from the facia to release the retaining clips **(see illustration)**.

Refitting

10 Refitting is a reversal of removal.

Side cup holders

Removal

11 Each of the side cupholders is held in place by five clips and two screws, one of which is accessed beneath the top cup moulding. Pull the moulding upwards from place.
12 Undo the screws and release the clips, then pull the cupholder from the facia **(see illustrations)**.

Refitting

13 Refitting is a reversal of removal.

Lower centre trim panel

Removal

14 Remove the glovebox, the left-hand lower trim panel, the ventilation controls surround as described in Chapter 12 Section 5 and inner right-hand lower trim panel as described previously.
15 Pull up the gearlever gaiter to release its retaining clips.
16 Undo the three screws securing the lower centre trim panel to the facia. Carefully prise the panel away from the facia to release the retaining clips **(see illustrations)**.

Refitting

17 Refitting is a reversal of removal.

Facia mounting frames

Right-hand side

18 The right-hand frame is in two parts. The outer part is retained by five screws and the left-hand frame is retained by six screws.
19 Undo the screws, disconnect any attached wiring plug clips and manoeuvre the frames out of the vehicle **(see illustration)**.

27.12a Undo the screw beneath the cup moulding

Left-hand side

20 The left-hand frame is retained by six screws and two clips.

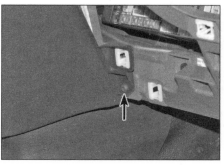

27.16a Undo the one screw on the right-hand side...

27.16c ...before carefully prising the panel away from the facia

27.12b Undo the remaining screw halfway down, then release the clips

21 Undo the screws and manoeuvre the frame out of the vehicle **(see illustration)**.

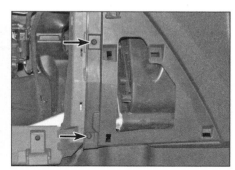

27.16b ...the two screws on the left...

27.19 Undo the screws and remove the right-hand side frames

27.21 Undo the screws and release the two clips at the top

27.22a Undo the two screws…

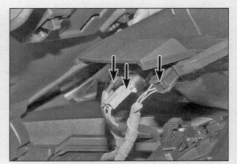

27.22b …disconnect the aux, 12V and USB plugs then withdraw the base of the compartment

Upper right-hand storage compartment

22 Open the storage compartment lid, undo the two retaining screws and remove the base of the compartment, disconnecting the wiring plugs as it is removed **(see illustrations)**.
23 Use a flat-bladed screwdriver to slide the hinge pins inward **(see illustration)**. Squeeze the hinges inwards to release the compartment lid.
24 Refitting is a reversal of removal.

Steering column shrouds

25 Turn the steering wheel clockwise 90° from the straight ahead position and, using a small screwdriver, depress the tab securing the right-hand side of the upper shroud to the lower shroud and lift the upper shroud upward on that side. Now turn the steering wheel 180°

anticlockwise and repeat the procedure to remove the left side **(see illustration)**.
26 Use a trim removal tool to release the front edge of the shroud. The entire upper shroud can now be removed **(see illustration)**.
27 Undo the two screws securing the lower shroud to the steering column and remove it **(see illustration)**.
28 Refitting is a reversal of removal.

Instrument cluster

Removal

29 Remove the upper right-hand storage compartment and the steering column shrouds as described previously.
30 Undo the two upper and two lower screws, then manoeuvre the instrument cluster rearwards, and disconnect the wiring plug **(see illustrations)**.

Refitting

31 Refitting is a reversal of removal.

Complete facia

Removal

32 Disconnect the battery negative lead as described in Chapter 5 Section 4.
33 Remove the A-pillar trim panels on both sides as described in Section 24.
34 Remove the following facia panels detailed previously in this Section and listed in order of removal below, with the following additions:
35 Glovebox, left-hand side bottle holder, right-hand lower trim panel, right-hand side bottle holder, side cup holders.
36 Remove the lower centre left panel **(see illustration)**.

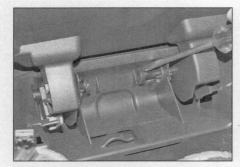

27.23 Slide the hinge pins in to release the lid

27.25 Use a screwdriver to depress the tab to release rear edges of the upper shroud

27.26 Free the front edge of the shroud and remove it

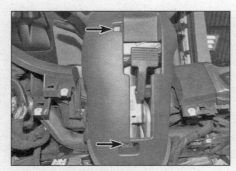

27.27 Undo the two screws securing the lower shroud

27.30a Remove the upper…

27.30b …and lower screws

27.36 Use a trim removal tool to remove the lower centre left panel

27.39a Unscrew the gearshift lever anticlockwise...

27.39b ...and unclip the gearshift gaiter

37 Remove the ventilation controls as described in Chapter 3 Section 8.
38 Remove the lower centre trim panel, facia mounting frame (right-hand side), as described previously in this Section.
39 Remove the gearshift knob by unscrewing it anticlockwise, and remove the gearshift gaiter by releasing its lower fastenings **(see illustrations)**.
40 Remove the facia mounting frame (left-hand side), infotainment screen and shroud, infotainment centre panel switches and audio unit as described in Chapter 12 Section 18, Chapter 12 Section 5 and Chapter 12 Section 19.
41 Remove the upper right-hand storage compartment, steering column shrouds and instrument cluster, as described earlier in this Section, then the instrument binnacle switches and headlights switch, as described in Chapter 12 Section 5.
42 Reach into the glovebox aperture and undo the two screws retaining the module and disconnect the wiring plug **(see illustration)**.
43 Working in the glovebox aperture, undo the two airbag retaining nuts and disconnect the wiring plug **(see illustration)**.
44 Unclip the wire-retaining clips in the infotainment console recess/screen

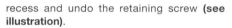
27.42 Remove the control module in the glovebox recess

27.43 Undo the nuts and disconnect the wiring plug for the airbag

recess and undo the retaining screw **(see illustration)**.
Note: *Make sure that all wiring attached to equipment below the facia can pass safely through facia apertures before you undo the final fasteners. Pay particular attention to the wiring plugs at the base of the A-pillars, some of which need to be disconnected.*
Caution: An assistant will be required to help remove the heavy facia from the vehicle.
45 Undo the three screws on each side of the facia and the two screws at bottom

centre. Adjust the steering wheel so it is fully rearwards and downwards; the facia can be removed with the wheel in place but clearance is limited. There are additional clips that retain the facia – pull it rearwards and up, checking that all wiring plugs and clips are released as it is manoeuvred out of the vehicle **(see illustrations)**.

Refitting

46 Refitting is a reversal of removal ensuring that all air ducts and wiring are correctly reconnected and all mountings securely tightened.

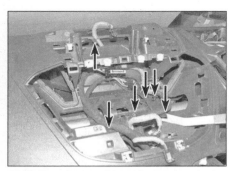
27.44 Detach the wiring clips and undo the screw

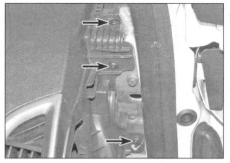
27.45a Undo the three screws at each side of the facia...

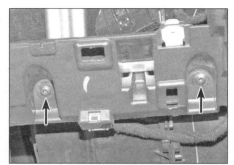
27.45b ...and the two screws at the centre before removing the facia

Chapter 12
Body electrical systems

Contents

Degrees of difficulty

Easy, suitable for novice with little experience	Fairly easy, suitable for beginner with some experience	Fairly difficult, suitable for competent DIY mechanic	Difficult, suitable for experienced DIY mechanic	Very difficult, suitable for expert DIY or professional

Specifications

Fuses and relays

Refer to the labels on the fuse/relay box covers and to the wiring diagrams at the end of this Chapter

Bulbs	Wattage	Type
Courtesy lights	10	W5W
Direction indicator lights	21	PY21W
Direction indicator side repeater lights	5	WY5W
Front foglights	55	H11
Headlights	55	H7/H15
High-level stop-light	16	W16W
Illuminated stepwell light	10	
Number plate light	5	W5W
Reading lights	10	
Rear foglights	21	P21W
Reversing lights	16	W16W
Sidelights	5	W5W
Side marker lights	3	
Stop/tail lights (Van and Bus models)	21/5	P21/5W

Torque wrench settings	Nm	lbf ft
Passenger airbag lower mounting bracket retaining nuts:		
Upper nuts (4)	4	3
Lower nuts (2)	25	18
Tailgate/rear window wiper arm nut	15	11
Windscreen wiper arm nuts	22	16
Windscreen wiper motor mounting bolts	10	7

1 General information and precautions

⚠️ **Warning: Before carrying out any work on the electrical system, read through the precautions given in 'Safety first!' at the beginning of this manual, and in Chapter 5 Section 1.**

1 The electrical system is of the 12 volt negative earth type. Power for the lights and all electrical accessories is supplied by a silver-calcium type battery, which is charged by the engine-driven alternator.

2 This Chapter covers repair and service procedures for the various electrical components not associated with the engine. Information on the battery, alternator and starter motor can be found in Chapter 5.

3 It should be noted that, prior to working on any component in the electrical system, the battery negative terminal should first be disconnected, to prevent the possibility of electrical short-circuits and/or fires.

Caution: Before proceeding, refer to Section.

2 Electrical fault finding – general information

Note: *Refer to the precautions given in 'Safety first!' and in Section 1 of this Chapter before starting work. The following tests relate to testing of the main electrical circuits, and should not be used to test delicate electronic circuits, particularly where an electronic control module is used.*

General

1 A typical electrical circuit consists of an electrical component, any switches, relays, motors, fuses, fusible links or circuit breakers related to that component, and the wiring and plugs which link the component to both the battery and the chassis. To help to pinpoint a problem in an electrical circuit, wiring diagrams are included at the end of this Chapter.

2 Before attempting to diagnose an electrical fault, first study the appropriate wiring diagram, to obtain a complete understanding of the components included in the particular circuit concerned. The possible sources of a fault can be narrowed down by noting if other components related to the circuit are operating properly. If several components or circuits fail at one time, the problem is likely to be related to a shared fuse or earth connection.

3 Electrical problems usually stem from simple causes, such as loose or corroded connections, a faulty earth connection, a blown fuse, a melted fusible link, or a faulty relay (refer to Section 3 for details of testing relays). Visually inspect the condition of all fuses, wires and connections in a problem circuit before testing the components. Use the wiring diagrams to determine which terminal connections will need to be checked in order to pinpoint the trouble-spot.

4 The basic tools required for electrical fault-finding include a circuit tester or voltmeter (a 12-volt bulb with a set of test leads can also be used for certain tests); an ohmmeter (to measure resistance and check for continuity); a battery and set of test leads; and a jumper wire, preferably with a circuit breaker or fuse incorporated, which can be used to bypass suspect wires or electrical components. Before attempting to locate a problem with test instruments, use the wiring diagram to determine where to make the connections.

5 To find the source of an intermittent wiring fault (usually due to a poor or dirty connection, or damaged wiring insulation), a 'wiggle' test can be performed on the wiring. This involves wiggling the wiring by hand to see if the fault occurs as the wiring is moved. It should be possible to narrow down the source of the fault to a particular section of wiring. This method of testing can be used in conjunction with any of the tests described in the following sub-Sections.

6 Apart from problems due to poor connections, two basic types of fault can occur in an electrical circuit – open-circuit, or short-circuit.

7 Open-circuit faults are caused by a break somewhere in the circuit, which prevents current from flowing. An open-circuit fault will prevent a component from working.

8 Short-circuit faults are caused by a 'short' somewhere in the circuit, which allows the current flowing in the circuit to 'escape' along an alternative route, usually to earth. Short-circuit faults are normally caused by a breakdown in wiring insulation, which allows a feed wire to touch either another wire, or an earthed component such as the bodyshell. A short-circuit fault will normally cause the relevant circuit fuse to blow.

Finding an open-circuit

9 To check for an open-circuit, connect one lead of a circuit tester or the negative lead of a voltmeter either to the battery negative terminal or to a known good earth.

10 Connect the other lead to a plug in the circuit being tested, preferably nearest to the battery or fuse. At this point, battery voltage should be present, unless the lead from the battery or the fuse itself is faulty (bearing in mind that some circuits are live only when the ignition switch is moved to a particular position).

11 Switch on the circuit, then connect the tester lead to the plug nearest the circuit switch on the component side.

12 If voltage is present (indicated either by the tester bulb lighting or a voltmeter reading, as applicable), this means that the section of the circuit between the relevant plug and the switch is problem-free.

13 Continue to check the remainder of the circuit in the same fashion.

14 When a point is reached at which no voltage is present, the problem must lie between that point and the previous test point with voltage. Most problems can be traced to a broken, corroded or loose connection.

Finding a short-circuit

15 To check for a short-circuit, first disconnect the load(s) from the circuit (loads are the components which draw current from a circuit, such as bulbs, motors, heating elements, etc).

16 Remove the relevant fuse from the circuit, and connect a circuit tester or voltmeter to the fuse connections.

17 Switch on the circuit, bearing in mind that some circuits are live only when the ignition switch is moved to a particular position.

18 If voltage is present (indicated either by the tester bulb lighting or a voltmeter reading, as applicable), this means that there is a short-circuit.

19 If no voltage is present during this test, but the fuse still blows with the load(s) reconnected, this indicates an internal fault in the load(s).

Finding an earth fault

20 The battery negative terminal is connected to 'earth' – the metal of the engine/transmission and the vehicle body – and many systems are wired so that they only receive a positive feed, the current returning via the metal of the vehicle body. This means that the component mounting and the body form part of that circuit. Loose or corroded mountings can therefore cause a range of electrical faults, ranging from total failure of a circuit, to a puzzling partial failure. In particular, lights may shine dimly (especially when another circuit sharing the same earth point is in operation), motors (eg wiper motors or the heater blower motor) may run slowly, and the operation of one circuit may have an apparently-unrelated effect on another. Note that on many vehicles, earth straps are used between certain components, such as the engine/transmission and the body, usually where there is no metal-to-metal contact between components, due to flexible rubber mountings, etc.

21 To check whether a component is properly earthed, disconnect the battery and connect one lead of an ohmmeter to a known good earth point. Connect the other lead to the wire or earth connection being tested. The resistance reading should be zero; if not, check the connection as follows.

22 If an earth connection is thought to be faulty, dismantle the connection, and clean both the bodyshell and the wire terminal (or the component earth connection mating surface) back to bare metal. Be careful to remove all traces of dirt and corrosion, then use a knife to trim away any paint, so that a clean metal-to-metal joint is made. On reassembly, tighten the joint fasteners securely; if a wire terminal

is being refitted, use serrated washers between the terminal and the bodyshell, to ensure a clean and secure connection. When the connection is remade, prevent the onset of corrosion in the future by applying a coat of petroleum jelly or silicone-based grease, or by spraying on (at regular intervals) a proprietary water-dispersant lubricant **(see illustrations)**.

3 Fuses and relays – general information

Fuses

1 Four separate fuse/relay boxes are used on Transit vehicles. One is located on the left-hand side of the engine compartment, two more are located inside the vehicle beneath the steering wheel, and another is located under the driver's seat.
2 To gain access to the engine compartment fuses, lift the retaining tab and remove the fuse/relay box cover **(see illustration)**. Tweezers may be stored on the inside of the lid for fuse replacement.
3 To gain access to the fuse/relay boxes located inside the vehicle, remove the trim panels beneath the steering wheel as described in Chapter 11 Section 24 **(see illustrations)**.
4 Access to the pre-fuses under the driver's seat is gained by moving the driver's seat fully forward, opening the battery box cover and lifting off the fuse/relay box cover **(see illustration)**.

2.22a The main earth strap is between the battery negative terminal and the vehicle body

5 The respective fuses and relays are identified on the diagram on the inside surface of the fuse/relay box cover or lid. Each fuse is also marked with its rating.
6 To remove a fuse, pull it out of the holder, preferably using the tweezers, then slide the fuse sideways from the tweezers. The wire within the fuse is clearly visible, and it will be broken if the fuse is blown **(see illustrations)**.
7 Always renew a fuse with one of an identical rating; never use a fuse with a different rating from the original, nor substitute anything else. Never renew a fuse more than once without tracing the source of the trouble. The fuse rating is stamped on top of the fuse; note that the fuses are also colour-coded for easy recognition.
8 If a new fuse blows immediately, find the cause before renewing it again; a short to earth as a result of faulty insulation is most

2.22b Other earth connections can be found at various points in the engine bay

likely. Where a fuse protects more than one circuit, try to isolate the defect by switching on each circuit in turn (if possible) until the fuse blows again. Always carry a supply of spare fuses of each relevant rating on the vehicle, a spare of each rating should be clipped into the fuse/relay box cover.

Relays

9 The relays are located in most of the fuse/relay boxes.
10 If a circuit or system controlled by a relay develops a fault and the relay is suspect, operate the system; if the relay is functioning, it should be possible to hear it click as it is energised. If this is the case, the fault lies with the components or wiring of the system. If the relay is not being energised, then either the relay is not receiving a main supply or a switching voltage, or the relay itself is faulty.

3.2 Lift the retaining tab and remove the engine compartment fuse/relay box cover

3.3a Left-hand side fuse box...

3.3b ...right-hand side fuse box

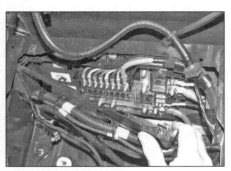

3.4 The pre-fusebox at the rear of the battery box

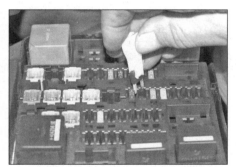

3.6a To remove a fuse, pull it out of the holder, preferably using the tweezers

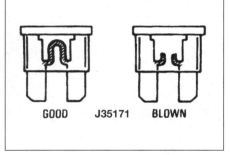

3.6b The fuses can be checked visually to determine if they are blown

4.5a Most electrical connectors have a single release tab that you depress to release the plug

4.5b Some electrical connectors have a retaining tab which must be pried up to free the plug

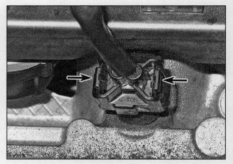

4.5c Some connectors have two release tabs that you must squeeze to release the plug

4.5d Some connectors use wire retainers that you squeeze to release the plug

4.5e Critical connectors often employ a sliding lock (1) that you must pull out before you can depress the release tab (2)

4.5f Here's another sliding-lock style connector, with the lock (1) and the release tab (2) on the side of the plug

Testing is by the substitution of a known good unit, but be careful; while some relays are identical in appearance and in operation, others look similar but perform different functions.

11 To renew a relay, first ensure that the ignition switch is off. The relay can then simply be pulled out from the socket and the new relay pressed in.

4 Electrical connectors – general information

1 Most electrical connections on these

vehicles are made with multiwire plastic plugs. The mating halves of many connectors are secured with locking clips molded into the plastic connector shells. The mating halves of some large connectors, such as some of those under the instrument panel, are held together by a bolt through the centre of the connector.

2 To separate a plug with locking clips, use a small screwdriver to pry the clips apart carefully, then separate the plug halves. Pull only on the shell, never pull on the wiring harness, as you may damage the individual wires and terminals inside the plugs. Look at the plug closely before trying to separate the halves. Often the locking clips are

engaged in a way that is not immediately clear. Additionally, many plugs have more than one set of clips.

3 Each pair of plug terminals has a male half and a female half. When you look at the end view of a connector in a diagram, be sure to understand whether the view shows the harness side or the component side of the plug. Plug halves are mirror images of each other, and a terminal shown on the right side end-view of one half will be on the left side end-view of the other half.

4 It is often necessary to take circuit voltage measurements with a plug connected. Whenever possible, carefully insert a small straight pin (not your meter probe) into the rear of the plug shell to contact the terminal inside, then clip your meter lead to the pin. This kind of connection is called "backprobing." When inserting a test probe into a terminal, be careful not to distort the terminal opening. Doing so can lead to a poor connection and corrosion at that terminal later. Using the small straight pin instead of a meter probe results in less chance of deforming the terminal connector. "T" pins are a good choice as temporary meter connections. They allow for a larger surface area to attach the meter leads too.

4.5g On some connectors the lock (1) must be pulled out to the side and removed before you can lift the release tab (2)

4.5h Some critical connectors, such as the multi-pin connectors at the Electronic Control Module, employ pivoting locks that must be flipped open

Electrical connectors

5 Typical electrical connectors:

5.4a Undo the Torx screws...

5.4b ...depress the tabs and pull out the multi-function switch

5.7a Remove the exterior light switch from the facia...

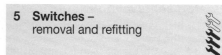

5 Switches – removal and refitting

Note: *Disconnect the battery negative terminal (see 'Disconnecting the battery' in Chapter 5, Section 4) before removing any switch, and reconnect the terminal after refitting.*

Ignition switch/ steering column lock

1 Refer to Chapter 10 Section 16.

Steering column multi-function switch

2 The steering column multi-function switch consists of left-hand and right-hand assemblies. The left-hand switch assembly comprises the headlight dip/flasher switch and the direction indicator switch; the right-hand switch assembly comprises the wiper/washer switch. The two halves can be removed and refitted independently of each other as follows.
3 Remove the steering column shrouds as described in Chapter 11 Section 27.
4 Undo the two Torx screws, depress the tabs and slide the relevant switch out of the housing **(see illustrations)**.
5 Refitting is a reversal of removal.

Exterior lights switch

6 Remove the side bottle holder and side cup holder as described in Chapter 11 Section 27.
7 Reach into the aperture and push the light switch from the facia, and disconnect the wiring plug **(see illustrations)**.
8 Refitting is a reversal of removal.

Infotainment console

9 Remove the infotainment screen shroud as described in Section 18.

10 Undo the two screws at the top of the console and use a trim removal tool to carefully lever the panel away, and release the four retaining clips. Disconnect the plugs as the console is removed **(see illustrations)**.
11 If required, undo the four retaining screws at the rear and remove the panel **(see illustration)**.
12 The hazard lights switch is removed by depressing the tangs from inside the infotainment console **(see illustration)**.
13 Refitting is a reversal of removal.

Stop-lights switch

14 Refer to Chapter 9 Section 17.

Handbrake warning light switch

15 Refer to Chapter 9 Section 18.

Electric window switch

16 Using a plastic spatula or similar tool, carefully prise up the rear of the electric

5.7b ...and disconnect the wiring plug

5.10a Undo the screws from the top...

5.10b ...before levering the console out and removing the wiring plugs

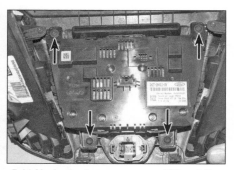

5.11 Undo the four screws and lift out the panel

5.12 Push the hazard lights switch out from the console

5.16 Remove window switch and disconnect the wiring plugs

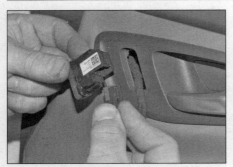

5.18 Remove the central locking switch and disconnect the wiring plug

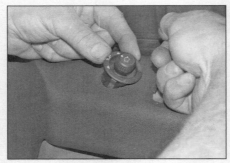

5.21 Push the mirror control switch up from the panel

5.23 Pull the light switch from place

windows switch housing from the top of the door trim, and disconnect the wiring plugs **(see illustration)**.

17 Refitting is a reversal of removal.

Central locking switch

18 Use a trim removal tool to prise the switch from the door trim and disconnect the wiring plug **(see illustration)**.

19 Refitting is a reversal of removal.

Door mirror control switch

20 Remove the electric window switch removal procedure, as described earlier in this section.

21 Reach into the window switch aperture and push the mirror control switch up, disconnecting the wiring plug as it is removed **(see illustration)**.

22 Refitting is a reversal of removal.

Loadspace light switch

23 The light switch is located in the pillar ahead of the left rear wheel arch, to the rear of the sliding door. Disconnect the wiring plug and pull the switch from position **(see illustration)**.

24 Refitting is a reversal of removal.

Heating/ventilation/air conditioning system switches

25 The switches are all an integral part of the heating/ventilation control unit, and cannot be individually removed. Should a switch become faulty, the complete control unit assembly must be renewed (see Chapter 3 Section 8).

Heated seats switch

26 The heated seat switches are mounted beneath the driver's and outer passenger's seat bases. On the passenger's seat, lift up the seat base and disconnect the wiring plug to the switch. Depress the tangs and push the switch out of the seat base. On the driver's seat, depress the tangs and push the switch out of the seat base before disconnecting the wiring plug **(see illustrations)**.

Instrument binnacle switches

27 Remove the instrument binnacle as described in Chapter 11 Section 27.

28 Use a trim removal tool, reach in and push the switches out from inside the housing. Disconnect the wiring plugs from the rear **(see illustration)**.

29 Refitting is a reversal of removal.

Steering wheel switches

30 Use a trim plastic removal tool to lever the chrome-effect plastic trim housing the steering wheel switches from the frame **(see illustration)**.

31 Undo the wiring retaining clips from the top side of the steering wheel **(see illustration)**.

32 Disconnect the wiring plug(s) at the relevant switch **(see illustration)**.

33 Undo the retaining screws and remove the switches **(see illustration)**.

34 On some models, the cruise control

5.26a Disconnect the wiring plug...

5.26b ...and squeeze the clips to extract the clip (passenger seat)

5.28 Reach in and push the binnacle switches from the housing

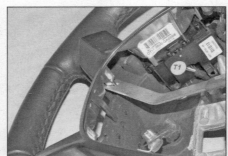

5.30 Some of the switches are housed within the chrome-effect trim

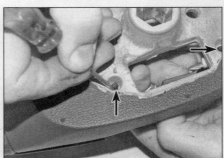

5.31 Release the wiring from the clips on the reverse of the steering wheel

5.32 Depress the clips and disconnect the relevant wiring plug

5.33 Undo the Torx screws and remove the switch

5.34 Undo the screws and remove the switch

and voice control switches are mounted lower down on the steering wheel. Undo the retaining screws and disconnect the wiring plug **(see illustration)**.

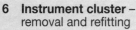

6 Instrument cluster – removal and refitting

1 The instrument cluster/binnacle is removed as described in Chapter 11 Section 27.

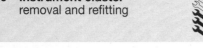

7 Tachograph – removal and refitting

Removal

Note: *Ford recommends that any vehicle requiring a tachograph replacement is sent to an authorised VDO Tachograph Service Centre for system installation and calibration.*
Note: *Special service tool 415-001 (two pieces), obtainable from most car accessory shops, is required for removal. Alternatively, suitable tools can be fabricated from 3 mm diameter wire, such as welding rod.*
1 If fitted, the tachograph is located in the overhead storage bin.
2 Insert the special tools into the holes on the front of the unit, and push them until they snap into place. The tachograph can then be slid out of the facia.
3 Disconnect the wiring plugs at the rear of the unit, and remove the unit from the vehicle.

9.3 Remove the cover to access the main beam bulb

4 Remove the special tools.

Refitting

5 To refit the tachograph, reconnect the wiring and simply push the unit into the facia until the retaining lugs snap into place, then close the tachograph display.

8 Headlight/foglight beam alignment – general information

1 Accurate adjustment of the headlight/foglight beam is only possible using optical beam-setting equipment, and this work should therefore be carried out by a Ford dealer or suitably equipped workshop.
2 An electrically operated headlight beam adjustment system is fitted, controlled via a switch in the middle of the headlight switch. With the vehicle unladen, the switch should be set in position '0'. With the vehicle partially or fully loaded, set the switch position to provide adequate illumination without dazzling oncoming drivers.

9 Bulbs (exterior lights) – renewal

General

1 Whenever a bulb is renewed, note the following points:
a) Make sure the switch is in the OFF

9.4a Twist the bulbholder anticlockwise...

position, for the respective bulb you are working on.
b) Remember that if the bulb being removed is still operational, and it has just been used, it might be extremely hot.
c) Always check the bulb contacts and holder, ensuring that there is clean metal-to-metal contact between the bulb and its live(s) and earth. Clean off any corrosion or dirt before fitting a new bulb.
d) Wherever bayonet-type bulbs are fitted, ensure that the live contact(s) bear firmly against the bulb contact.
e) Always ensure that the new bulb is of the correct rating, and that it is completely clean before fitting it; this applies particularly to headlight/foglight bulbs.

Headlight

Main beam

2 Remove the headlight unit as described in Section 11.
3 Release the rubber cover at the rear of the headlight unit **(see illustration)**.
4 Twist the bulb holder anticlockwise, withdraw the holder and disconnect the wiring plug from the rear of the holder **(see illustrations)**.
5 The bulb is integral with the holder and must be renewed as a complete unit. When handling the new bulb, use a tissue or clean cloth to avoid touching the glass with the fingers; moisture and grease from the skin can cause blackening and rapid failure of this type of bulb. If the glass is accidentally touched, wipe it clean using methylated spirit.

9.4b ...withdraw the holder and disconnect the wiring plug

9.9 Remove the dipped beam bulb rubber cover

9.10 Disconnect the wiring plug from the back of the bulb

9.11a Compress the leg of the retaining spring clip and pivot the clip away from the bulb...

9.11b ...and then lift the bulb out of the light unit

9.16 Pull the sidelight bulbholder from the rear of the headlight

9.20 Remove the cover to access the front cornering light bulb

6 Reconnect the wiring plug, refit the bulbholder to the headlight unit and turn it clockwise to lock it in position.

7 Refit the cover to the rear of the headlight unit, then refit the headlight unit as described in Section 11. Check for satisfactory operation on completion.

Dipped beam

8 Remove the headlight unit as described in Section 11.

9 Release the rubber cover at the rear of the headlight unit (see illustration).

10 Pull the wiring plug from the bulb (see illustration).

11 Compress the leg of the retaining spring clip and pivot the clip away from the bulb. Lift the bulb out of the light unit (see illustrations). When handling the new bulb, use a tissue or clean cloth to avoid touching the glass with

the fingers; moisture and grease from the skin can cause blackening and rapid failure of this type of bulb. If the glass is accidentally touched, wipe it clean using methylated spirit.

12 Fit the new bulb to the headlight unit and secure with the spring clip. Reconnect the wiring plug.

13 Refit the cover to the rear of the headlight unit, then refit the headlight unit as described in Section 11. Check for satisfactory operation on completion.

Front sidelight

14 Remove the headlight unit as described in Section 11.

15 Remove the main beam bulb cover (see illustration 9.3).

16 Pull the sidelight bulbholder from the rear of the headlight, then pull the capless bulb from the holder (see illustration).

17 Fit the new bulb using a reversal of the removal procedure. Check for satisfactory operation on completion.

18 Refit the cover to the rear of the headlight unit, then refit the headlight unit as described in Section 11. Check for satisfactory operation on completion.

Front cornering light

19 Remove the headlight unit as described in Section 11.

20 Remove the cornering light bulb cover, located on the edge of the headlight unit (see illustration).

21 Disconnect the wiring plug from the bulb (see illustration).

22 Compress the leg of the retaining spring clip and pivot the clip away from the bulb. Lift the bulb out of the light unit (see illustrations). When handling the new bulb, use a tissue or

9.21 Disconnect the wiring plug from the bulb

9.22a Compress the leg of the retaining spring clip and pivot the clip away from the bulb...

9.22b ...and then lift the bulb out of the light unit

9.26 Twist the indicator bulbholder anti-clockwise

9.27 Remove the bulb from the holder

9.30 Remove the small Torx screw

9.32a Release the clip and pull the light unit from the mirror

9.32b Pull the bulbholder from the lamp

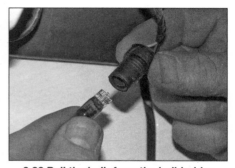

9.33 Pull the bulb from the bulbholder

clean cloth to avoid touching the glass with the fingers; moisture and grease from the skin can cause blackening and rapid failure of this type of bulb. If the glass is accidentally touched, wipe it clean using methylated spirit.
23 Fit the new bulb to the headlight unit and secure with the spring clip. Reconnect the wiring plug.
24 Refit the cover to the rear of the headlight unit, then refit the headlight unit as described in Section 11. Check for satisfactory operation on completion.

Front direction indicator

25 Remove the headlight unit as described in Section 11.
26 Twist the indicator bulbholder anti-clockwise, and remove it from the rear of the headlight unit (see illustration).
27 The bulb is a bayonet fit in the holder, and

can be removed by pressing it and twisting in an anti-clockwise direction (see illustration).
28 Fit the new bulb using a reversal of the removal procedure. Check for satisfactory operation on completion.

Front direction indicator side repeater

29 Fold the door mirror to its fully forward position.
30 Remove the Torx screw (see illustration).
31 Fold the door mirror back to its 'closed' position.
32 Use a small flat-bladed screwdriver to release the clip and pull the light unit from the mirror, noting its fitted position as you do so (see illustrations).
33 Remove the push-fit bulb from the bulbholder (see illustration).
34 Fit the new bulb using a reversal of the

removal procedure. Check for satisfactory operation on completion.

Front foglight

35 From under the front bumper, disconnect the wiring plug from the bulbholder (see illustration).
36 Turn the bulbholder anticlockwise and remove it. The bulb is integral with the holder (see illustration).
37 When handling the new bulb, use a tissue or clean cloth to avoid touching the glass with the fingers; moisture and grease from the skin can cause blackening and rapid failure of this type of bulb. If the glass is accidentally touched, wipe it clean using methylated spirit.
38 Fit the new bulbholder using a reversal of the removal procedure. Check for satisfactory operation on completion.
39 If desired, undo the retaining screws and remove the foglight unit (see illustration).

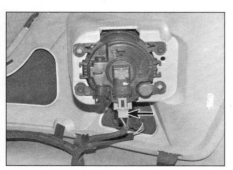

9.35 Disconnect the wiring plug from the bulbholder

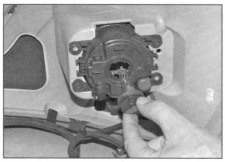

9.36 Twist the bulbholder anticlockwise to remove it

9.39 Undo the two Torx screws and remove the foglight unit from the bumper cover

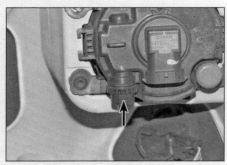

9.40 Foglight aim adjustment control

9.42 Undo the rear light cluster retaining nut

9.43a Undo the upper…

9.43b Centre and lower screws…

9.43c …withdraw the light cluster…

9.43d …and disconnect the wiring plug

40 The foglight beam can be adjusted via the aim adjuster (**see illustration**).

Rear light cluster

41 Open the rear door, unclipping the door stay and folding the door back to its fullest extent.

42 Unscrew the rear light cluster retaining nut from the inside of the vehicle (**see illustration**).

43 Remove the upper, centre and lower screws and pull the rear light cluster from the vehicle, disconnect the wiring plug (**see illustrations**).

44 Release the eight clips and separate the bulbholder from the light cluster. The bulbs are a bayonet fit in the bulbholder, and can be removed by pressing in and twisting in an anti-clockwise direction (**see illustrations**).

45 Fit the new bulb(s) using a reversal of the removal procedure. Check for satisfactory operation on completion.

Rear number plate light

46 Prise the lens from place using a suitable screwdriver, remove the bulbholder by turning it anticlockwise then pull the bulb out (**see illustrations**).

47 Fit the new bulb using a reversal of the removal procedure. Check for satisfactory operation on completion.

9.44b …and separate the bulbholder from the light cluster

9.44c Press and untwist the bulb to remove it from its holder

9.46a Release the number plate light cap using a suitable screwdriver…

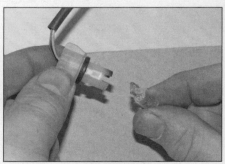

9.46b …then remove the bulb from its holder by pulling it free

9.44a Compress the retaining clips…

High-level brake-light

Note: *The high-level brake-light is equipped with LEDs. If defective, the complete unit will need to be replaced.*

48 If fitted, remove the interior trim panel from around the top of the rear window/aperture by releasing the four clips.

49 Remove the rubber grommets and use a flat-bladed screwdriver to release the two clips in the holes uncovered by the trim removal **(see illustrations)**.

50 Disconnect the wiring plug from the light unit.

---

10 Bulbs
(interior lights) –
renewal

General

1 Refer to Section 9, paragraph 1.

Front courtesy lights

Front ceiling-mounted light unit

2 The forward-mounted light unit contains a festoon bulb and two capless bulbs, used for the reading lights. Unclip the lens with a small screwdriver and pull the interior light festoon type bulb from the contacts **(see illustrations)**.

3 The capless bulbs are difficult to extract from below, so remove the light unit by releasing the clip on the front side. Disconnect the wiring plugs as the unit is extracted. Use a small screwdriver to release the tabs and remove the module from the top of the light unit. Turn the capless bulb holder anticlockwise to release it. The bulb pulls straight out of the holder **(see illustrations)**.

Rear ceiling-mounted light unit

4 Use a small screwdriver to release the clip on the front edge of the light unit. Withdraw the unit and twist the bulb holder to remove it. Pull the capless bulb(s) from the holder(s) **(see illustrations)**.

5 Fit the new bulbs using a reversal of the removal procedure. Check for satisfactory operation on completion.

10.3c ...and turn the capless bulb holder anti-clockwise to remove it

9.49a Use a screwdriver to release the clips...

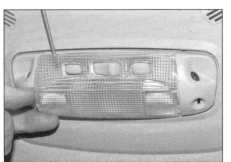

10.2a Unclip the interior light lens...

Sun visor lights

6 Carefully prise the light unit from its location with a small screwdriver **(see illustration)**.

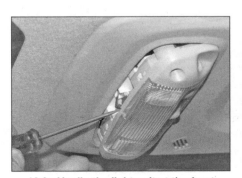

10.3a Unclip the light unit at the front edge...

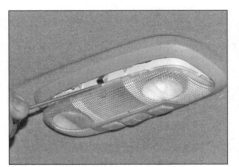

10.4a Release the clip on the front edge...

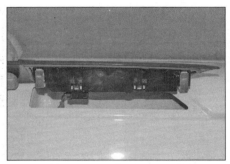

9.49b ...and unclip the stop-light

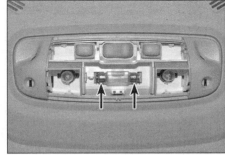

10.2b ...and pull the festoon type bulb from the contacts

7 Pull out the capless bulb and press a new one into place **(see illustration)**.

8 Fit the new bulb using a reversal of the

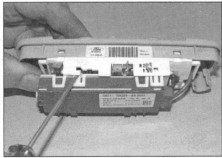

10.3b ...release the clips to remove the module...

10.4b ...and twist the bulb holder to release it

10.6 Use a small screwdriver to remove the sun visor light unit

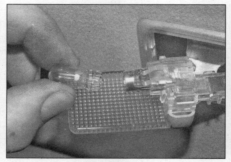

10.7 Pull out the capless bulb from the bulbholder

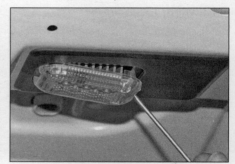

10.9 Carefully prise the light unit from place

removal procedure. Check for satisfactory operation on completion.

Rear loadspace lights

9 Insert a small screwdriver blade into the indents either side of the light unit and carefully prise it from place **(see illustration)**.
10 The light is equipped with LED. If defective the complete assembly must be replaced.
11 Fitting is a reversal of the removal procedure. Check for satisfactory operation on completion.

Heater control illumination

12 The heater controls are not serviceable and have to be replaced as one unit. Remove the control panel as described in Chapter 3 Section 8.

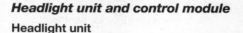

11 Exterior light units –
removal and refitting

Note: *Move the driver's seat fully forward, open the battery box cover and disconnect the battery negative terminal (refer to Disconnecting the battery) before removing any light unit. Reconnect the terminal after refitting.*

Headlight unit and control module

Headlight unit

Caution: Take extra care not to damage the fixings when handling the headlight unit.
1 Undo the two screws securing the headlight to the body panel **(see illustrations)**.

2 Push the headlight back and up to disengage the upper retainer. Withdraw the headlight unit from its location, and disconnect the wiring plugs **(see illustration)**.
3 Refit in the reverse order of removal. Refer to Section 8 for details on headlight beam alignment. Check the headlights, sidelights and indicators for satisfactory operation on completion.

Control module

4 The headlight unit control module is mounted to the in-vehicle crossbeam and is accessed from within the aperture once the glovebox has been removed, as described in Chapter 11 Section 27.
5 Undo the two Torx screws beneath the module casing, disconnect the plug and withdraw the module **(see illustration)**.

Direction indicator side repeater

6 Removal and refitting of the light unit is part of the bulb renewal procedure. Refer to the procedures contained in Section 9.

Front foglight

7 Removal and refitting of the light unit is part of the bulb renewal procedure. Refer to the procedures contained in Section 9.

Rear light cluster

8 Open the rear door, unclip the door stay and folding the door back to its fullest extent.
9 Unscrew the rear light cluster retaining nut from the inside of the vehicle **(see illustration)**.

11.1a Undo the inner retaining screw...

11.1b ...and the rear retaining screw securing the headlight to the body panel

11.2 Disconnect the wiring plugs

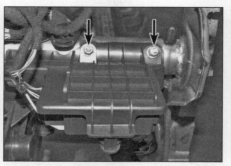

11.5 Undo the Torx screws and remove the module from the casing (viewed upside down with crossbeam out of the vehicle)

11.9 Undo the rear light cluster retaining nut

10 Remove the upper, centre and lower screws and pull the rear light cluster from the vehicle, then disconnect the wiring plug (see illustrations).

Rear number plate light

11 Removal and refitting of the light unit is part of the bulb renewal procedure. Refer to the procedures contained in Section 9.

High-level stop-light

12 Removal and refitting of the light unit is part of the bulb renewal procedure. Refer to the procedures contained in Section 9.

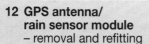

12 GPS antenna/ rain sensor module – removal and refitting

Removal

1 The GPS antenna/rain sensor module is fixed to the underside of the facia, on the front left-hand side, ahead of the passenger airbag.
2 Remove the complete facia assembly as described in Chapter 11 Section 27.
3 With the assembly turned upside down on the bench release the clips and withdraw the module (see illustration).

Refitting

4 Refit in the reverse order of removal. Check for satisfactory operation on completion.

13 Horn – removal and refitting

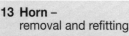

Removal

1 The horn is located in the engine compartment on the left-hand side, at the front.
2 Disconnect the wiring plug from the horn, then unscrew the two retaining bolts and remove the horn from the mounting bracket. The horn cannot be adjusted or repaired, and therefore if defective, it must be renewed.

Refitting

3 Refit in the reverse order of removal. Check for satisfactory operation on completion.

14 Wiper arms – removal and refitting

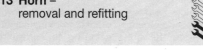

Removal

1 With the wipers 'parked' (ie, in the normal at-rest position), check for blade alignment marks on the windscreen (see illustration). If no marks are visible, mark the position of the blades on the windscreen/rear window, using a wax crayon or strips of masking tape.
2 Prise up the cap from the wiper arm, then

11.10a Undo the upper...

11.10b ...centre and lower screws...

11.10c ...withdraw the light cluster...

11.10d ...and disconnect the wiring plug

unscrew the retaining nut and remove the washer (see illustration).
3 Lift the wiper arm and release it from the

taper on the spindle by easing it from side to side (see illustration). If the arm is reluctant to release, use a suitable puller.

12.3 Release the clips and withdraw the GPS antenna/rain sensor module

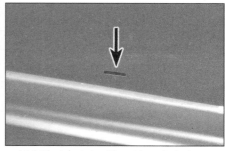

14.1 Marks etched into the windscreen glass indicate the parked position of the wiper blades

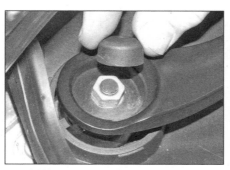

14.2 Lift up the plastic cap and unscrew the wiper arm retaining nut

14.3 A puller may be needed to release the wiper arm from the taper on the spindle

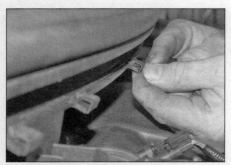

15.3 Remove the clips from the cowl panel

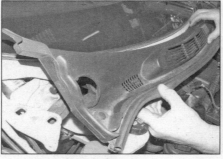

15.4 Lift off the upper panel

15.5 Undo the bolts and remove the motor

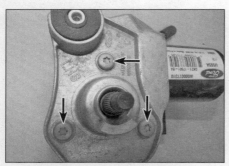

15.6 Undo the three retaining bolts and remove the motor from the mounting bracket

15.9a Carefully lever the moulding away from the windscreen…

15.9b …then disconnect the wiring plug(s) and the sensor bracket(s)

Refitting

4 Refitting is a reversal of removal. Ensure each arm is refitted to the spindle it was removed from. Also make sure the arm is fitted in its previously noted position before tightening the nut to the specified torque.

15 Windscreen wiper components – removal and refitting

Wiper motors

1 Disconnect the battery negative terminal as described in Chapter 5 Section 4.
2 Remove the wiper arms as described in Section 14.
3 Prise out the clips at the front edge of the upper cowl panel **(see illustration)**.
4 Lift off the upper cowl panel, releasing it from the lower edge of the windscreen **(see illustration)**.
5 Undo the two bolts and remove the wiper motor(s) **(see illustration)**. Disconnect the wiring plug as the motor(s) are withdrawn.
6 Undo the three retaining Torx bolts and remove the motor from the mounting bracket **(see illustration)**.
7 Refitting is a reversal of removal.

Rain/light sensor

Caution: Take extra care not to damage the windscreen when removing/installing the sensor assembly.
8 The sensor(s) is mounted on the inside

of the windscreen, at the top, behind a moulding.
9 Use a trim removal tool to carefully ease the moulding away from the plastic mounting attached to the windscreen glass. Disconnect the sensor wiring plug, unclip the mounting bracket either side and remove the sensor **(see illustrations)**.
10 When refitting, make sure the contact surface is clean before mounting the sensor.

16 Tailgate/rear door wiper motor – removal and refitting

Removal

1 Disconnect the battery negative terminal as described in Chapter 5 Section 4.

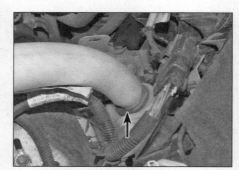

17.3a Unclip the washer reservoir filler neck…

2 Remove the wiper arm.
3 Remove the tailgate/rear door trim panel as described in Chapter 11 Section 24.
4 Disconnect the wiper motor wiring plug and washer hose.
5 Undo the three bolts and remove the wiper motor and mounting bracket from the tailgate.
6 Undo the bolts securing the motor to the mounting bracket. Lift off the motor and recover the spacers, noting their fitted position.

Refitting

7 Refitting is a reversal of removal, using new pop rivets (where applicable). Check for satisfactory operation on completion.

17 Windscreen/tailgate washer system components – removal and refitting

Reservoir and pump

Removal

1 Remove the right-hand headlight as described in Section 11.
2 Remove the front bumper cover as described in Chapter 11 Section 22.
3 Detach the reservoir filler neck from the reservoir, and release it from the retaining clip in the engine compartment **(see illustrations)**.
4 Disconnect the wiring plug and pull the level sensor from the grommet **(see illustration)**. Be prepared for fluid spillage.

17.3b ...and release the release the retaining clip

17.4 Remove the sensor

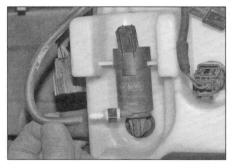

17.5 Disconnect the connections to the reservoir pump

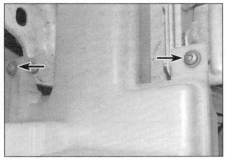

17.7 Remove the bolts and extract the reservoir from under the vehicle

17.10 Prise out the clips using a forked tool

17.11 Depress the clip and push the jet from place

5 Disconnect the wiring plug and washer hose from the reservoir pump. If required, pull the pump from the reservoir **(see illustration)**.
6 Detach the wiring loom and hose(s) from the side of the reservoir.
7 Undo the retaining bolts and remove the reservoir **(see illustration)**.

Refitting

8 Refitting is a reversal of removal. Lubricate the pump seal (if removed) with a little washing-up liquid, to ease fitting.
9 On completion, top-up the reservoir with the required water/washer solution mix, and check for leaks and satisfactory operation.

Washer jets

Removal

10 Prise out the clips and remove the bonnet insulation material **(see illustration)**.

11 Disconnect the hose, depress the clip and push the jet from the bonnet **(see illustration)**.

Refitting

12 Refitting is a reversal of removal. Note that the aim of the jet is not adjustable.

18 Infotainment screen – removal and refitting

1 Disconnect the battery negative terminal as described in Chapter 5 Section 4.
2 Using a trim removal tool, gently ease the shroud from around the screen **(see illustration)**.
3 Undo the two retaining screws, lift the unit and disconnect the wiring plug **(see illustrations)**.
4 Refitting is a reversal of removal.

19 Audio unit – removal and refitting

Removal

Note: *This Section applies only to standard-fit audio equipment.*
Note: *If a new audio unit is to be fitted, it must be configured using Ford diagnostic equipment. Entrust this task to a Ford dealer or suitably equipped specialist.*

1 Disconnect the battery negative terminal as described in Chapter 5 Section 4.
2 Remove the infotainment screen as described in Section 18.
3 Remove the infotainment console as described in Section 5.
4 Undo the two screws retaining the

18.2 Gently prise the shroud from the screen

18.3a Undo the screws, lift the unit...

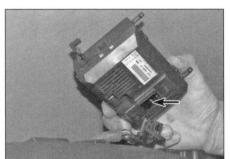

18.3b ...and disconnect the plug

19.4 Undo the screws and ease the audio unit rearwards

audio unit and gently pull it rearward **(see illustration)**.

5 Disconnect the wiring and aerial plugs at the rear of the unit, and remove the unit from the vehicle **(see illustration)**.

Refitting

6 Refitting is a reversal of removal, ensuring that the aerial and wiring plugs are properly connected before reinstalling the unit.

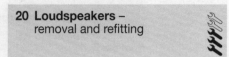

20 Loudspeakers – removal and refitting

1 Refer to Chapter 11 Section 24 for details of the tweeter speaker removal in the A-pillar trim.

Removal

2 Remove the appropriate door trim panel for access to the speaker, as described in Chapter 11 Section 24.

3 Disconnect the wiring plug, undo the retaining screws and withdraw the speaker unit **(see illustrations)**.

Refitting

4 Refitting is a reversal of removal.

21 Anti-theft alarm system and engine immobiliser – general information

1 An anti-theft alarm and immobiliser system is fitted as standard equipment. Should the

20.3a Disconnect the wiring plug...

19.5 Disconnect the two wiring plugs and the aerial plug

system become faulty, the vehicle should be taken to a Ford dealer or specialist for examination. They will have access to a special diagnostic tester which will quickly trace any fault present in the system.

22 Airbag system – general information and precautions

General information

1 The driver's airbag is located in the steering wheel centre pad. The passenger's airbag is located in the facia and protects both front passenger seats, if fitted. Side airbags fire from modules built into the front seats, while side curtain airbags fire from modules above the front side windows.

2 The system is armed only when the ignition is switched on however, a reserve power source maintains a power supply to the system in the event of a break in the main electrical supply. The system is activated by a 'g' sensor (deceleration sensor), incorporated at the front of the vehicle and by side impact sensors located at the base of the B-pillars. Note that the restraints control module also controls the front seat belt tensioners, which are fitted to all models.

3 The airbags are inflated by gas generators, which force the bags out from their locations. Although these are safety items, their deployment is violently rapid, and this may cause injury if they are triggered unintentionally.

20.3b ...undo the retaining screws and withdraw the speaker unit

Precautions

⚠️ **Warning: The following precautions must be observed when working on vehicles equipped with an airbag system, to prevent the possibility of personal injury.**

General precautions

4 The following precautions must be observed when carrying out work on a vehicle equipped with an airbag:

a) Do not disconnect the battery with the engine running.

b) Before carrying out any work in the vicinity of the airbag, removal of any of the airbag components, or any welding work on the vehicle, de-activate the system as described later in this Section.

c) Do not attempt to test any of the airbag system circuits using test meters or any other test equipment.

d) If the airbag warning light comes on, or any fault in the system is suspected, consult a Ford dealer without delay.

e) Do not attempt to carry out fault diagnosis, or any dismantling of the components.

Precautions when handling an airbag

a) Transport the airbag by itself, bag upward.

b) Do not put your arms around the airbag.

c) Carry the airbag close to the body, bag outward.

d) Do not drop the airbag or expose it to impacts.

e) Do not attempt to dismantle the airbag unit.

f) Do not connect any form of electrical equipment to any part of the airbag circuit.

Precautions when storing an airbag

a) Store the unit in a cupboard with the airbag upward.

b) Do not expose the airbag to temperatures above 80°C.

c) Do not expose the airbag to flames.

d) Do not attempt to dispose of the airbag – consult a Ford dealer.

e) Never refit an airbag which is known to be faulty or damaged.

De-activation of airbag system

5 The system must be de-activated before carrying out any work on the airbag components or surrounding area:

a) Switch on the ignition and check the operation of the airbag warning light on the instrument panel. The light should illuminate when the ignition is switched on, then extinguish.

b) Switch off the ignition.

c) Remove the ignition key.

d) Switch off all electrical equipment.

e) Disconnect the battery negative terminal as described in Chapter 5 Section 4.

f) Insulate the battery negative terminal and the end of the battery negative lead to prevent any possibility of contact.

g) Wait for at least 3 minutes before carrying out any further work. Wait at least 10

23.4 Airbag retaining wire spring access holes in the rear of the steering wheel

23.6a Withdraw the airbag from the steering wheel and disconnect the main wiring plug...

23.6b ...and the lower leads

minutes if the airbag warning light did not operate correctly.

Activation of airbag system

6 To activate the system on completion of any work, proceed as follows:
a) *Ensure that there are no occupants in the vehicle, and that there are no loose objects around the vicinity of the steering wheel.*
b) *Ensure that the ignition is switched off then reconnect the battery negative terminal.*
c) *Open the driver's door and switch on the ignition, without reaching in front of the steering wheel. Check that the airbag warning light illuminates briefly then extinguishes.*
d) *Switch off the ignition.*
e) *If the airbag warning light does not operate as described in paragraph c), consult a Ford dealer before driving the vehicle.*

23 Airbag system components
– removal and refitting

⚠️ *Warning: See 'Precautions' given in Section 22 before attempting work on the airbag components.*

Driver's airbag

Removal

1 De-activate the airbag system as described in Section 22. The airbag unit is an integral part of the steering wheel centre pad.
2 Remove the steering column shrouds as described in Chapter 11 Section 27.
3 If not already done, adjust the steering wheel reach and rake so it is out and down as far as it will go.
4 Insert a small screwdriver into one of the two access holes in the reverse of the steering wheel, with the screwdriver engaged under the airbag retaining wire spring **(see illustration)**.
5 Move the end of the screwdriver to release the wire spring from the lug on the steering wheel, while at the same time pulling the side of the airbag away from the steering wheel.

Release the other wire spring on the opposite side in the same way.
6 Once the airbag retaining wire springs have been released, withdraw the airbag from the steering wheel and disconnect the main wiring plug and the two earth leads **(see illustrations)**. Remove the airbag and store it in a safe place, with reference to the precautions in Section 22.

Refitting

7 Refitting is a reversal of removal, noting the following points:
a) *The battery must still be disconnected when reconnecting the airbag wiring.*
b) *Ensure that the airbag wiring plug is securely reconnected.*
c) *The airbag must be firmly pressed into place to secure the retaining wire spring.*

Passenger's airbag

Removal

8 De-activate the airbag system as described in Section 22.
9 Remove the glovebox as described in Chapter 11 Section 27.
10 Disconnect the wiring plugs from the module beneath the airbag assembly then undo the two nuts securing the module to the support bar and remove it **(see illustration)**.
11 Undo the six nuts securing the airbag mounting bracket **(see illustration)**.
12 Undo the four nuts securing the upper edge of the airbag to the facia and remove the wiring plug.

23.10 Unplug the module and undo the two retaining nuts before removing it

13 Using a plastic spatula or similar tool, carefully prise free the airbag facia from the dashboard and withdraw it. Remove the airbag and store it in a safe place, with reference to the precautions in Section 22.

Refitting

14 Refitting is a reversal of removal, bearing in mind the following points:
a) *The battery must still be disconnected when reconnecting the airbag wiring.*
b) *Make sure that the wiring plug is securely reconnected.*
c) *Tighten the mounting nuts securely.*

Side airbags

15 The side airbags are located internally within the front seat backrest, and no attempt should be made to remove them. Any suspected problems with the side airbag system should be referred to a Ford dealer.

Airbag clockspring (rotary connector)

Removal

16 De-activate the airbag system as described in Section 22.
17 Remove the steering wheel as described in Chapter 10 Section 15.
18 Remove the steering column shrouds as described in Chapter 11 Section 27.
19 Remove the steering column multi-function switches as described in Section 5.
20 Disconnect the clockspring wiring plug

23.11 Undo the six nuts (four shown) securing the passenger airbag bracket

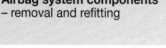

23.20 Disconnect the clockspring wiring plug from the base of the steering column

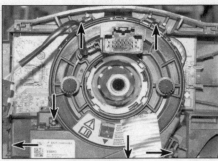

23.21a Free the retaining clips...

23.21b ...and remove the clockspring from the steering column

23.26 Turn the clockspring rotor clockwise until the arrow on the rotor is aligned with the 'V' marked on the clockspring body

from the base of the steering column **(see illustration)**.

21 Undo the clips and remove the clockspring from the steering column **(see illustrations)**.

Refitting

22 Refitting is a reversal of removal.

23 Before refitting the steering column shrouds and steering wheel, the clockspring unit should be centralised (unless it is known absolutely that the steering wheel was centralised before removal, and that the clockspring has not been turned during or since its removal).

24 The procedure for centralising should be written on the clockspring itself. If this procedure conflicts significantly with what appears below, consult a Ford dealer for the latest information.

25 First, turn the clockspring rotor anti-clockwise gently, until resistance is felt.

26 Turn the clockspring rotor clockwise until the arrow marked on the clockspring rotor is aligned with the raised 'V' marked on the clockspring body **(see illustration)**.

27 Refit the steering column shrouds as described in Chapter 11 Section 27.

28 Refit the steering wheel as described in Chapter 10 Section 15.

Restraints control module

29 The restraints control module is located beneath the facia between the front seats and no attempt should be made to remove it. Any suspected problems with the control module should be referred to a Ford dealer.

AUXILIARY JUNCTION BOX (AJB) 2.0 L

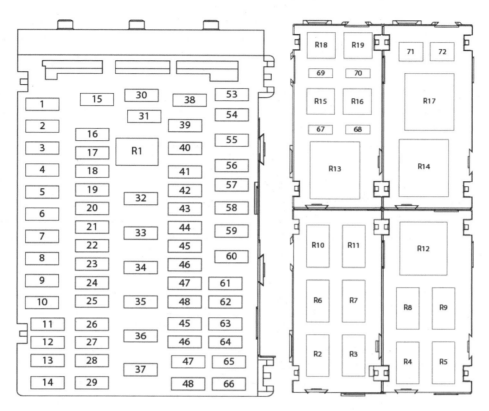

FUSE/RELAY	VALUE	DESCRIPTION	OEM NAME
1	60 A	Front wiper relay	F1
2	40 A	Blower motor relay	F2
3	-	Not used	F3
4	40 A	Heated rear window relay	F4
5	40 A	Trailer module	F5
6	40 A	Auxiliary power point relay	F6
7	40 A	Power point relay	F7
8	20 A	Horn relay	F8
9	15 A	Rear washer relay	F9
10	10 A	Horn relay, Blower motor relay, Power point relay, Auxiliary power point relay, Front wiper relay	F10
11	-	Not used	F11
12	-	Not used	F12
13	20 A	Auxiliary power point	F13
14	20 A	Front power outlet socket	F14
15	50 A	Low voltage Direct Current/Direct Current (DC/DC) converter, Body Control Module (BCM) - F12, F13, F32, F33	F15
16	25 A	Anti-lock Brake System	F16
17	5 A	Fuel pump relay, Powertrain Control Module (PCM) power relay	F17
18	10 A	Brake Pedal Position (BPP) switch	F18
19	15 A	External locking relay	F19
20	5 A	Fuel fired booster heater control module	F20
21	15 A	Transmission Control Module (TCM)	F21

Fuses and relays - 2.0 litre models

22	25 A	Transmission auxiliary oil pump	F22
23	-	Not used	F23
24	10 A	Exterior mirror LH, Exterior mirror RH	F24
25	7.5 A	Driver door latch	F25
26	7.5 A	Passenger door latch	F26
27	-	Not used	F27
28	-	Not used	F28
29	40 A	Auxiliary blower motor relay	F29
30	20 A	Rear passenger power outlet socket	F30
31	30 A	Heated rear window element	F31
32	60 A	Run/start relay	F32
33	60 A	Fuel pump relay	F33
34	40 A	Heated windshield element LH relay	F34
35	40 A	Heated windshield element RH relay	F35
36	50 A	Body Control Module (BCM)	F36
37	50 A	Body Control Module (BCM) - F1	F37
38	-	Not used	F38
39	20 A	Heated front seat switch	F39
40	5 A	Glow plug module, Powertrain Control Module (PCM)	F40
41	5 A	Fuel fired booster heater relay	F41
42	5 A	Headlamp assembly LH, Headlamp assembly RH, Headlamp switch	F42
43	5 A	Transmission Control Module (TCM), Transmission auxiliary oil pump	F43
44	10 A	Low voltage Direct Current/Direct Current (DC/DC) converter, Vehicle Dynamics Module (VDM), Proximity warning radar unit, Auxiliary blower motor switch, Rear parking aid camera	F44
45	20 A	Adaptive front lighting module	F45
46	5 A	Auxiliary blower motor relay, Heated windshield element LH relay, Heated windshield element RH relay, Heated rear window relay	F46
47	5 A	Anti-lock Brake System (ABS) module	F47
48	10 A	Customer access	F48
49	20 A	Rear window wiper motor	F49
50	5 A	Rear washer relay, Autolamp and rain sensor	F50
51	25 A	Windshield wiper motor - LHD, Auxiliary windshield wiper motor - RHD	F51
52	25 A	Windshield wiper motor - RHD, Auxiliary windshield wiper motor - LHD	F52
53	40 A	Rear air suspension relay	F53
54	15 A	Vehicle Dynamics Module (VDM)	F54
55	40 A	Anti-lock Brake System (ABS) module	F55
56	-	Not used	F56
57	30 A	Front seat control switch	F57
58	-	Not used	F58
59	30 A	Starter relay	F59
60	15 A	Trailer module	F60
61	15 A	Driver door latch - LHD, Passenger door latch - RHD, Sliding door contact plate LH	F61
62	15 A	Rear door latch, Passenger door latch - LHD, Driver door latch - RHD, Sliding door contact plate RH	F62
63	15 A	Driver door latch - LHD, Passenger door latch - RHD, Sliding door contact plate LH	F63
64	15 A	Rear door latch, Passenger door latch - LHD, Driver door latch - RHD, Sliding door contact plate RH	F64
65	20 A	Fuel pump control module	F65
66	40 A	Fuel filter heater/water-in-fuel sensor	F66
67	-	Not used	F67

Fuses and relays - 2.0 litre models (continued)

68	-	Not used	F68
69	7.5 A	Tachograph	F69
70	-	Not used	F70
71	40 A	Direct Current/Alternating Current (DC/AC) inverter	F71
72	30 A	Trailer socket	F72
R1	-	Horn relay	R1
R2	-	Heated rear window relay	R2
R3	-	Auxiliary blower motor relay	R3
R4	-	Auxiliary power point relay	R4
R5	-	Power point relay	R5
R6	-	Heated windshield element LH relay	R6
R7	-	Heated windshield element RH relay	R7
R8	-	Rear washer relay	R8
R9	-	Fuel fired booster heater relay	R9
R10	-	Blower motor relay	R10
R11	-	External locking relay	R11
R12	-	Fold mirror module relay	R12
R13	-	Run/start relay	R13
R14	-	Fuel pump relay	R14
R15	-	Not used	R15
R16	-	Not used	R16
R17	-	Front wiper relay	R17
R18	-	Not used	R18
R19	-	Not used	R19

BATTERY JUNCTION BOX (BJB) 2.0 L

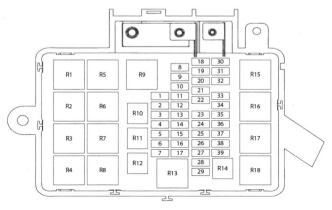

FUSE/RELAY	VALUE	DESCRIPTION	OEM NAME
1	5 A	Audio front Control Module (ACM)	F1
2	-	Not used	F2
3	-	Not used	F3
4	-	Not used	F4
5	-	Not used	F5
6	-	Not used	F6
7	-	Not used	F7
8	20 A	Cooling fan relay	F8
9	-	Not used	F9
10	-	Not used	F10

Fuses and relays - 2.0 litre models (continued)

11	-	Not used	F11
12	-	Not used	F12
13	-	Not used	F13
14	-	Not used	F14
15	-	Not used	F15
16	-	Not used	F16
17	-	Not used	F17
18	40 A	Cooling fan relay	F18
19	60 A	Low speed cooling fan relay, High speed cooling fan relay (Twin fans)	F19
	40 A	Low speed cooling fan relay (Twin fans)	
20	40 A	Reductant heater relay	F20
21	40 A	Glow plug module	F21
22	40 A	Glow plug module	F22
23	10 A	Air Conditioning (A/C) clutch relay	F23
24	-	Not used	F24
25	-	Not used	F25
26	-	Not used	F26
27	-	Not used	F27
28	5 A	Positive Crankcase Ventilation (PCV) valve heater element	F28
29	15 A	Coolant water pump	F29
30	60 A	Powertrain Control Module (PCM) power relay	F30
31	-	Not used	F31
32	20 A	Auxiliary Heater Control Module (AHCM)	F32
33	-	Not used	F33
34	-	Not used	F34
35	20 A	Powertrain Control Module (PCM)	F35
36	20 A	Battery Junction Box (BJB) - F28, F29	F36
37	15 A	Reductant tank, Universal Heated Oxygen Sensor (HO2S), Exhaust Gas Recirculation (EGR) cooler bypass valve solenoid	F37
38	10 A	High speed cooling fan relay, Cooling fan relay, Air Conditioning (A/C) clutch relay, Low speed cooling fan relay	F38
39	10 A	Glow plug module, NOx sensor module	F39
R1	-	High speed cooling fan relay	R1
R2	-	Not used	R2
R3	-	Rear window wiper relay	R3
R4	-	Rear air suspension relay	R4
R5	-	Cooling fan relay	R5
R6	-	Not used	R6
R7	-	Not used	R7
R8	-	Not used	R8
R9	-	Starter relay	R9
R10	-	Air Conditioning (A/C) clutch relay	R10
R11	-	Not used	R11
R12	-	Not used	R12
R13	-	Reductant heater relay	R13
R14	-	Not used	R14
R15	-	Low speed cooling fan relay	R15
R16	-	Not used	R16
R17	-	Not used	R17
R18	-	Powertrain Control Module (PCM) power relay	R18

Fuses and relays - 2.0 litre models (continued)

BODY CONTROL MODULE 2.0 L

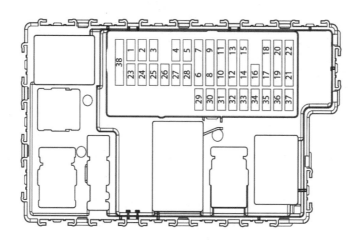

FUSE	VALUE	DESCRIPTION	OEM NAME
1	10 A	Third row interior lamp, Fourth row interior lamp, Front interior lamp, Vanity mirror lamp RH, Vanity mirror lamp LH	F1
2	7.5 A	Fold mirror module relay, Driver door window control switch, Exterior mirror control switch	F2
3	20 A	Auxiliary Junction Box (AJB) - F25, F26	F3
4	-	Not used	F4
5	-	Not used	F5
6	-	Not used	F6
7	-	Not used	F7
8	10 A	Anti-theft alarm horn LH, Anti-theft alarm horn RH	F8
9	-	Not used	F9
10	-	Not used	F10
11	5 A	Auxiliary blower motor switch, Intrusion sensor	F11
12	7.5 A	Heating, Ventilation and Air Conditioning (HVAC) control module	F12
13	7.5 A	Instrument Panel Cluster (IPC), Steering Column Control Module (SCCM), Gateway Module A (GWM)	F13
14	-	Not used	F14
15	10 A	Gateway Module A (GWM)	F15
16	15 A	Sliding door contact plate LH, Sliding door contact plate RH	F16
17	5 A	Anti-theft alarm horn with integral battery	F17
18	5 A	Ignition switch	F18
19	5 A	Message center switch	F19
20	5 A	Tachograph	F20
21	5 A	Electric booster heater	F21
22	-	Not used	F22
23	10 A	Audio front Control Module (ACM), Direct Current/Alternating Current (DC/AC) inverter	F23
24	30 A	Auxiliary Junction Box (AJB) - F61, F62, F63, F64	F24
25	-	Not used	F25
26	-	Not used	F26
27	-	Not used	F27
28	-	Not used	F28
29	-	Not used	F29
30	-	Not used	F30
31	-	Not used	F31

Fuses and relays - 2.0 litre models (continued)

32	10 A	Radio Frequency (RF) receiver, Front Control/Display Interface Module (FCDIM), SYNC module (APIM), Global Positioning System Module (GPSM), Message center switch	F32
33	20 A	Audio front Control Module (ACM)	F33
34	30 A	Body Control Module (BCM) - F19, F20, F21, F23, F35, F36	F34
35	5 A	Restraints Control Module (RCM)	F35
36	15 A	Steering Column Control Module (SCCM), Auto-dimming interior mirror, Parking Assist control Module (PAM)	F36
37	-	Not used	F37
38	30 A	Driver door window control switch, Passenger door window control switch	F38

HIGH CURRENT BATTERY JUNCTION BOX (BJB) 2.0 L

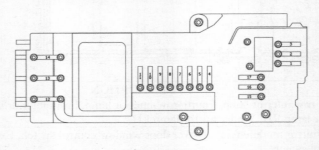

FUSE/RELAY	VALUE	DESCRIPTION	OEM NAME
1	470 A	Generator, Starter motor, Battery Junction Box (BJB) - F18, F19, F20, F21, F22, F23	F1
2	100 A	Body Control Module (BCM) - F2, F3, F8, F11, F15, F16, F17, F18, F24, F34, F38	F2
3	40 A	Auxiliary Junction Box (AJB) - F71	F3
4	200 A	Auxiliary Junction Box (AJB) - F53, F54, F55, F57, F59, F60	F4
5	100 A	Auxiliary Junction Box (AJB) - F15, F16, F17, F18, F19, F20, F21, F22	F5
6	100 A	Electric booster heater	F6
7	80 A	Auxiliary Junction Box (AJB) - F34, F35	F7
8	100 A	Auxiliary Junction Box (AJB) - F36, F37	F8
9	100 A	Auxiliary Junction Box (AJB)- F1, F2, F4, F5, F6, F7, F8, F9, F10	F9
10	100 A	Auxiliary Junction Box (AJB) - F32, F33	F10
11	100 A	Battery Junction Box (BJB) - F30, F32	F11
12	60 A	Customer access	F12
13	60 A	Customer access	F13
14	60 A	Customer access	F14
15	60 A	Auxiliary Junction Box (AJB) - F29	F15
16	-	Not used	F16
17	60 A	Customer access	F17

FUSE COLOR CODE INDEX

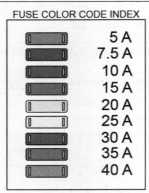

Fuses and relays - 2.0 litre models (continued)

AUXILIARY JUNCTION BOX (AJB) 2.2 L

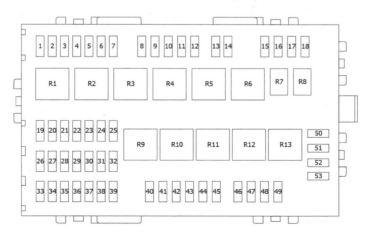

FUSE/RELAY	VALUE	DESCRIPTION	OEM NAME
1	10 A	Restraints Control Module (RCM)	F1
2	-	Not used	F2
3	10 A	Exterior mirrors	F3
4	-	Not used	F4
5	20 A	Auxiliary Heater Control, Module (AHCM)	F5
6	5 A	Tachograph	F6
7	-	Not used	F7
8	40 A	Direct Current/ Alternating Current (DC/AC) inverter	F8
9	-	Not used	F9
10	30 A	Front seat control switch	F10
11	-	Not used	F11
12	-	Not used	F12
13	-	Not used	F13
14	5 A	Powertrain Control Module (PCM) relay	F14
15	40 A	Powertrain Control Module (PCM) relay	F15
16	40 A	Body Control Module (BCM) - F1, F2, F3	F16
17	-	Not used	F17
18	-	Not used	F18
19	5 A	Tachograph	F19
20	5 A	Heated rear window relay, Heated windshield element LH relay, Heated windshield element RH relay, Direct Current/Alternating Current (DC/AC) inverter	F20
21	10 A	Customer access	F21
22	15 A	Body Control Module (BCM) - F4, F5	F22
23	7.5 A	Fuel fired booster heater relay, Auxiliary blower motor switch, Electric booster heater, Blower motor switch, Message center switch	F23
24	5 A	Headlamp assemblies	F24
25	7.5 A	Interior lamps	F25
26	-	Not used	F26
27	20 A	Heated front seat switch	F27
28	20 A	Adaptive front lighting module	F28
29	10 A	Image Processing Module B (IPMB), Auto-dimming interior mirror, Steering Column Control Module (SCCM), Image Processing Module A (IPMA)	F29
30	-	Not used	F30
31	-	Not used	F31

Fuses and relays - 2.2 litre models

32	10 A	Interior lamps	F32
33	-	Not used	F33
34	20 A	Rear window wiper relay, Rear window wiper motors	F34
35	5 A	Driver door window control switch, Exterior mirror control switch	F35
36	20 A	Horn relay	F36
37	7.5 A	SYNC module (APIM), Global Positioning System Module (GPSM)	F37
38	5 A	Rear window wiper relay, Horn relay, Blower motor relay	F38
39	7.5 A	Auxiliary blower motor switch, Radio Frequency (RF) receiver, Intrusion sensor	F39
40	40 A	Blower motor relay	F40
41	40 A	Auxiliary blower motor relay	F41
42	30 A	Heated rear window relay	F42
43	30 A	Trailer module, Trailer socket	F43
44	60 A	Auxiliary power point relay	F44
45	-	Not used	F45
46	30 A	Driver door window control switch, Passenger door window control switch	F46
47	20 A	Auxiliary power point	F47
48	20 A	Rear passenger power outlet socket	F48
49	20 A	Front power outlet socket	F49
50	60 A	Auxiliary ignition relay 1	F50
51	60 A	Auxiliary ignition relay 2	F51
52	40 A	Heated windshield element LH relay	F52
53	40 A	Heated windshield element RH relay	F53
R1	-	Fuel fired booster heater relay	R1
R2	-	Auxiliary power point relay	R2
R3	-	Not used	R3
R4	-	Auxiliary ignition relay 2	R4
R5	-	Not used	R5
R6	-	Auxiliary ignition relay 1	R6
R7	-	Horn relay	R7
R8	-	Not used	R8
R9	-	Blower motor relay	R9
R10	-	Auxiliary blower motor relay	R10
R11	-	Heated rear window relay	R11
R12	-	Heated windshield element RH relay	R12
R13	-	Heated windshield element LH relay	R13

Fuses and relays - 2.2 litre models (continued)

BATTERY JUNCTION BOX (BJB) 2.2 L

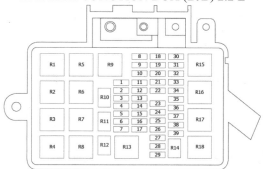

FUSE/RELAY	VALUE	DESCRIPTION	OEM NAME
1	-	Not used	F1
2	-	Not used	F2
3	-	Not used	F3
4	-	Not used	F4
5	5 A	Powertrain Control Module (PCM)	F5
6	5 A	Anti-lock Brake System	F6
7	7.5 A	Glow plug module, Powertrain Control Module (PCM)	F7
8	-	Not used	F8
9	30 A	Windshield wiper motor	F9
10	30 A	Auxiliary windshield wiper motor	F10
11	10 A	Air Conditioning (A/C) clutch relay	F11
12	20 A	Glow plug relay	F12
13	-	Not used	F13
14	-	Not used	F14
15	-	Not used	F15
16	-	Not used	F16
17	-	Not used	F17
18	40 A	Anti-lock Brake System	F18
19	30 A	Starter relay	F19
20	60 A	Glow plug module	F20
21	60 A	Ignition relay	F21
22	-	Not used	F22
23	25 A	Anti-lock Brake System	F23
24	7.5 A	Fuel pump relay	F24
25	-	Not used	F25
26	5 A	Econetic coolant valve relay	F26
27	-	Not used	F27
28	-	Not used	F28
29	3 A	Econetic coolant valve relay	F29
30	60 A	Low speed cooling fan relay, High speed cooling fan relay	F30
31	-	Not used	F31
32	60 A	Windshield wiper motor relay	F32
33	-	Not used	F33
34	-	Not used	F34
35	15 A	Powertrain Control Module (PCM)	F35
36	7.5 A	Mass Air Flow (MAF) sensor	F36
37	7.5 A	Fuel metering valve	F37
38	7.5 A	Air Conditioning (A/C) clutch relay	F38

Fuses and relays - 2.2 litre models (continued)

39	15 A	Low speed cooling fan relay, High speed cooling fan relay, Glow plug relay, Fuel vaporizer system fuel pump, Heated Oxygen Sensor (HO2S), Econetic coolant valve relay	F39
R1	-	Ignition relay	R1
R2	-	Starter relay (Early production)	R2
R3	-	Rear window wiper relay	R3
R4	-	Windshield wiper motor relay	R4
R5	-	Not used	R5
R6	-	Not used	R6
R7	-	Not used	R7
R8	-	Not used	R8
R9	-	Starter relay (Late production)	R9
R10	-	Air Conditioning (A/C) clutch relay	R10
R11	-	Glow plug relay	R11
R12	-	Fuel pump relay	R12
R13	-	Not used	R13
R14	-	Econetic coolant valve relay	R14
R15	-	Low speed cooling fan relay	R15
R16	-	Not used	R16
R17	-	Powertrain Control Module (PCM) relay	R17
R18	-	High speed cooling fan relay	R18

BODY CONTROL MODULE 2.2 L

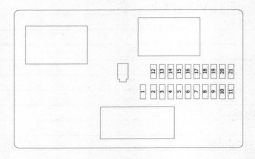

FUSE	VALUE	DESCRIPTION	OEM NAME
1	15 A	Passenger door latch, Sliding door contact plate LH, Sliding door contact plate RH, Rear door latch	F1
2	15 A	Driver door latch, Passenger door latch, Sliding door contact plate LH, Sliding door contact plate RH, Rear door latch, Liftgate latch	F2
3	15 A	Ignition switch, Auxiliary battery relay	F3
4	5 A	Parking Assist Control	F4
5	5 A	Autolamp and rain sensor	F5
6	15 A	Windshield washer pump	F6
7	7.5 A	Exterior mirrors	F7
8	15 A	Front fog lamps	F8
9	10 A	Headlamp assembly RH	F9
10	10 A	Headlamp assembly LH	F10
11	25 A	Headlamp assembly RH, Rear lamp assembly LH, Rear lamp assembly RH, Auto-dimming interior mirror	F11
12	20 A	Anti-theft alarm horn with integral battery, Anti-theft alarm horn LH, Anti-theft alarm horn RH	F12

Fuses and relays - 2.2 litre models (continued)

13	15 A	Data Link Connector (DLC), Glove compartment lamp, Auxiliary power point relay, Luggage compartment lamps, Interior lamps, Illuminated vanity mirror lamps, Footwell lamps	F13
14	25 A	Headlamp assemblies, Rear lamp assemblies, Exterior mirrors	F14
15	25 A	Headlamp assembly LH, Rear lamp assembly LH, License plate lamps, Trailer module, Illumination lamps	F15
16	20 A	Audio front Control Module (ACM)	F16
17	7.5 A	Instrument Panel Cluster (IPC), Blower motor switch	F17
18	10 A	Headlamp switch, Brake Pedal Position (BPP) switch, Steering Column Control Module (SCCM)	F18
19	5 A	Front Control/Display Interface, Module (FCDIM), Message center switch	F19
20	5 A	Passive Anti-theft System (PATS) transceiver	F20
21	5 A	Audio front Control Module (ACM)	F21

AUXILIARY FUSE AND RELAY PANEL 2.2 L

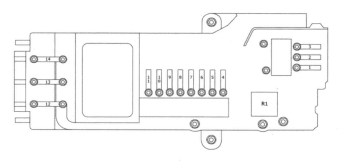

FUSE/RELAY	VALUE	DESCRIPTION	OEM NAME
1	350 A	Generator, Starter motor, Battery Junction Box (BJB) - F18, F19, F20, F21, F23, F24, F26	F1; C
2	100 A	Auxiliary Junction Box (AJB) - F14, F15, F16	F2; D
3	-	Not used	F3; E
4	200 A	Auxiliary Junction Box (AJB) - F35, F36, F37, F38, F39, F40, F41, F42, F43, F44	F4; F
5	100 A	Auxiliary Junction Box (AJB) - F5, F6, F8, F10	F5; G
6	80 A	Electric booster heater	F6; H
7	80 A	Auxiliary Junction Box (AJB) - F52, F53	F7; J
8	100 A	Battery Junction Box (BJB) - F30, F32	F8; K
9	100 A	Auxiliary Junction Box (AJB) - F50, F51	F9; L
10	60 A	Body Control Module (BCM) - F6, F7, F8, F9, F10, F11	F10; M
11	60 A	Body Control Module (BCM) - F12, F13, F14, F15, F16, F17, F18, F19	F11; N
12	60 A	Customer access	F12; P
13	-	Not used	F13; R
14	60 A	Customer access	F14; S
R1	-	Auxiliary battery relay	-

Fuses and relays - 2.2 litre models (continued)

AUXILIARY FUSE AND RELAY PANEL 2.2 L

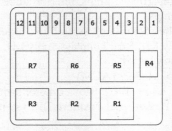

FUSE/RELAY	VALUE	DESCRIPTION	OEM NAME
1	3 A	Beacon switch, Water heater switch, Auxiliary switch 1, Auxiliary switch 2	F1
2	-	Not used	F2
3	20 A	Beacon relay	F3
4	20 A	Ignition relay	F4
5	15 A	Water heater relay, Auxiliary relay 2	F5
6	15 A	Work lamp relay	F6
7	15 A	Turn signal relay LH, Turn signal relay RH, Auxiliary relay 1	F7
8	10 A	Interior lamp relay	F8
9	20 A	2 way radio	F9
10	-	Not used	F10
11	-	Not used	F11
12	-	Not used	F12
R1	-	Beacon relay	R1
R2	-	Ignition relay	R2
R3	-	Water heater relay- auxiliary heater or Auxiliary relay 2 - utility package	R3
R4	-	Work lamp relay	R4
R5	-	Turn signal relay LH - roof mounted turn signals or Auxiliary relay 1 - utility package	R5
R6	-	Turn signal relay RH	R6
R7	-	Interior lamp relay	R7

Fuses and relays - 2.2 litre models (continued)

SUPPLEMENTARY FUSE BOX 2.2 L

FUSE	VALUE	DESCRIPTION	OEM NAME
1	-	Not used	F1
2	-	Not used	F2
3	-	Not used	F3
4	-	Not used	F4
5	-	Not used	F5
6	-	Not used	F6
7	-	Not used	F7
8	-	Not used	F8
9	-	Not used	F9
10	-	Not used	F10
11	-	Not used	F11
12	-	Not used	F12
13	20 A	Roof mounted indicators LH, Roof mounted indicators RH	F13
14	-	Not used	F14
15	-	Not used	F15
16	-	Not used	F16
17	-	Not used	F17
18	-	Not used	F18

FUSE COLOR CODE INDEX

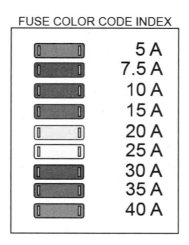

Fuses and relays - 2.2 litre models (continued)

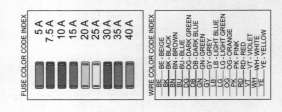

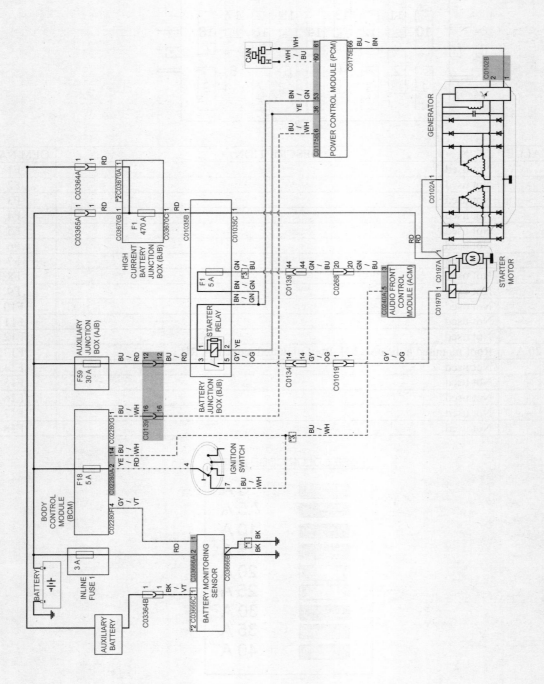

Starting and charging - 2.0 litre models

*1 Right Hand Drive
*2 Dual Battery
*3 Without multi-function display

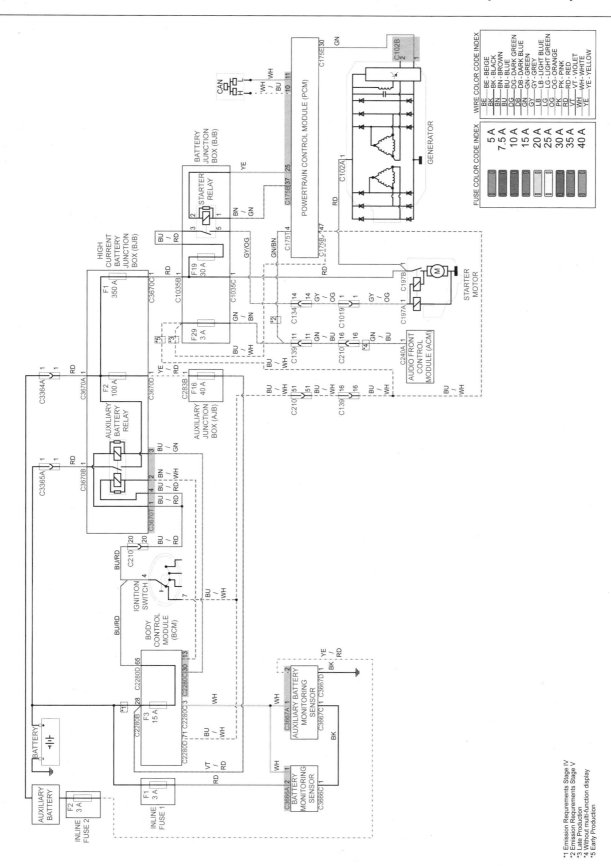

Starting and charging - 2.2 litre models

*1 Emission Requirements Stage IV
*2 Emission Requirements Stage V
*3 Late Production
*4 Without multi-function display
*5 Early Production

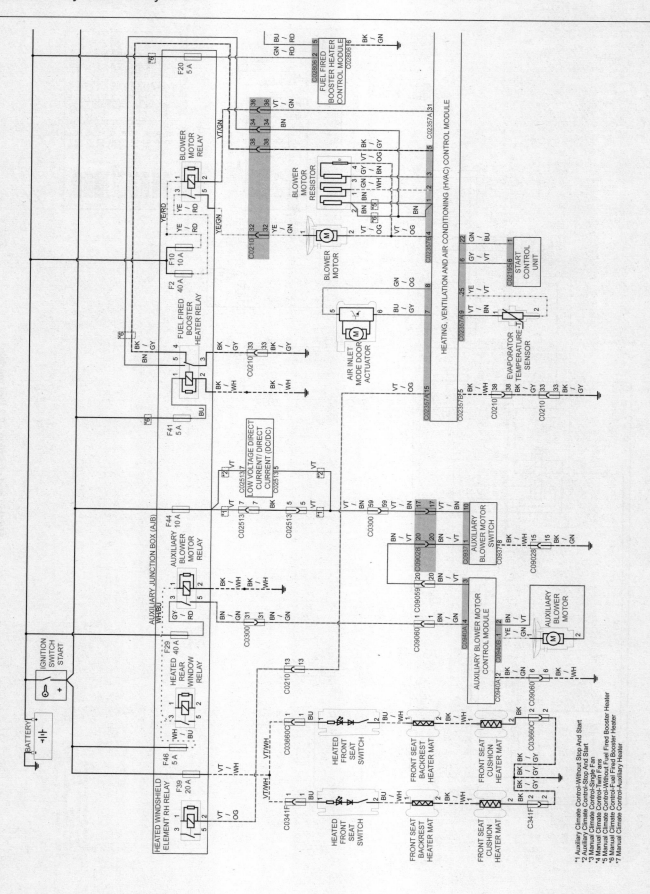

Air conditioning, heating and cooling - 2.0 litre models - Part 1

*1 Auxiliary Climate Control-Without Stop And Start
*2 Auxiliary Climate Control-Stop And Start
*3 Manual Climate Control-Single Fan
*4 Manual Climate Control-Twin Fans
*5 Manual Climate Control-Without Fuel Fired Booster Heater
*6 Manual Climate Control-Fuel Fired Booster Heater
*7 Manual Climate Control-Auxiliary Heater

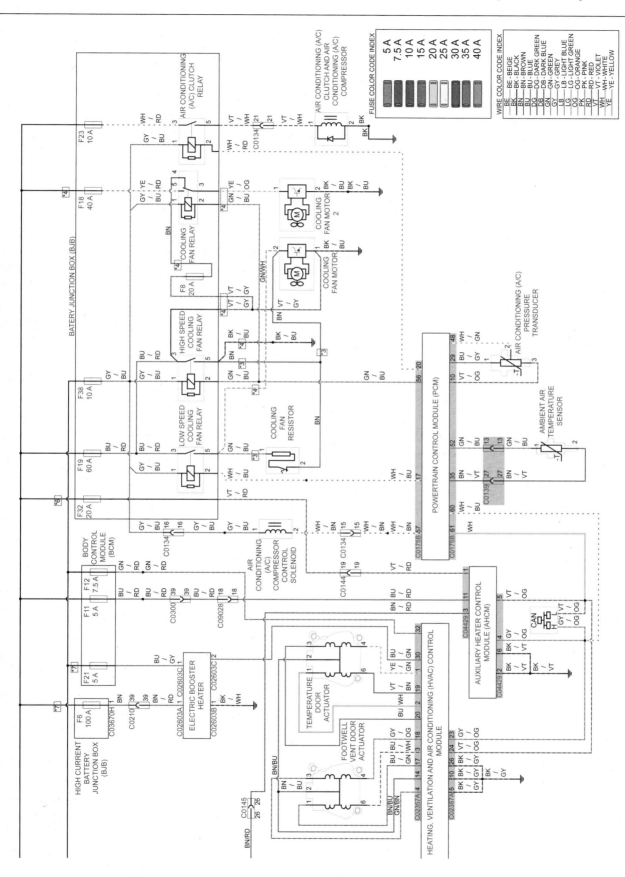

Air conditioning, heating and cooling - 2.0 litre models - Part 2

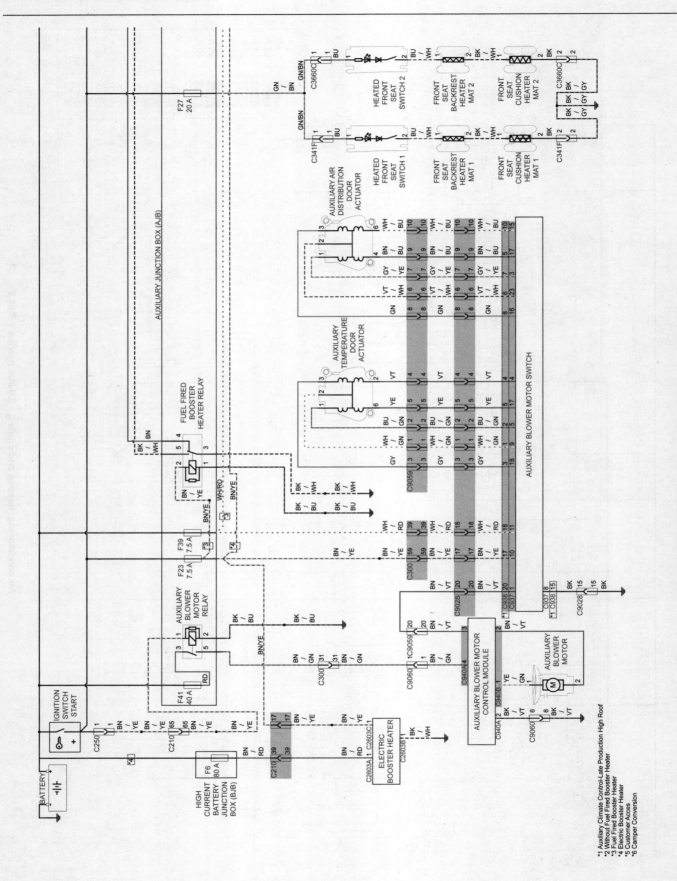

Air conditioning, heating and cooling - 2.2 litre models - Part 1

*1 Auxiliary Climate Control-Late Production High Roof
*2 Without Fuel Fired Booster Heater
*3 Fuel Fired Booster Heater
*4 Electric Booster Heater
*5 Customer Acces
*6 Camper Conversion

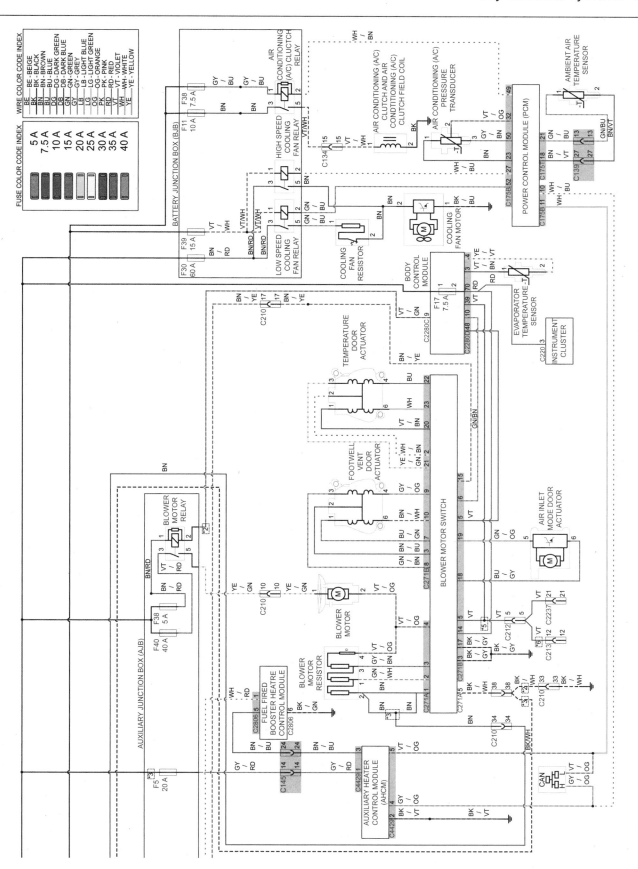

Air conditioning, heating and cooling - 2.2 litre models - Part 2

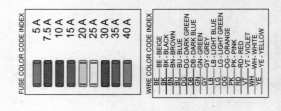

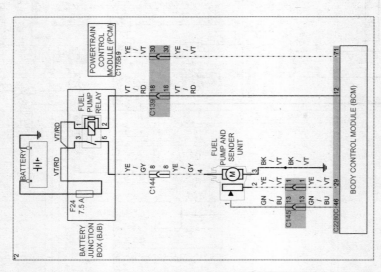

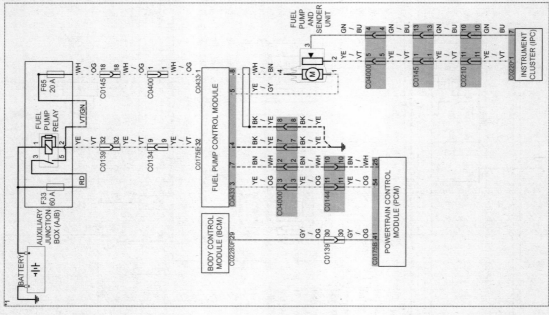

Fuel pump

*1 Engine: 2.0 L diesel
*2 Engine: 2.2 L diesel

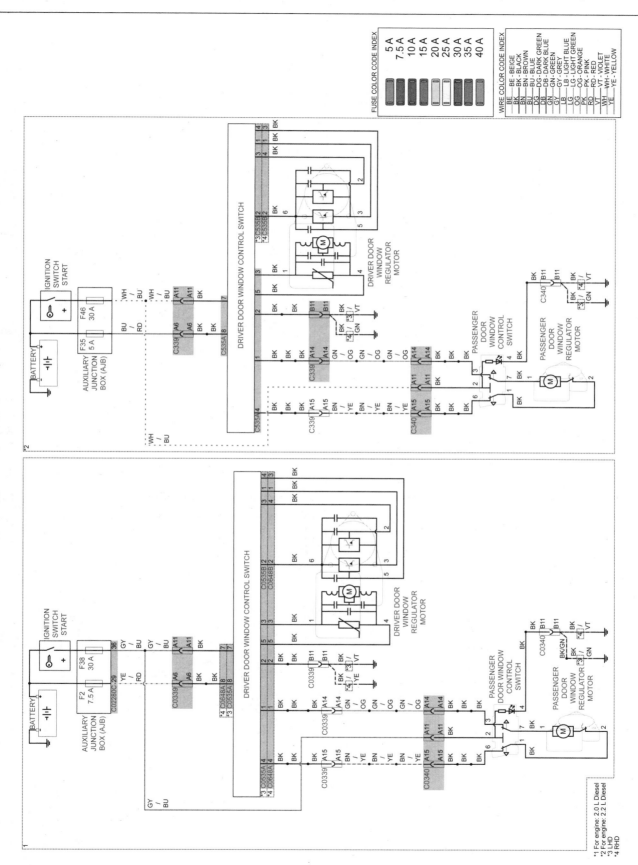

Electric windows

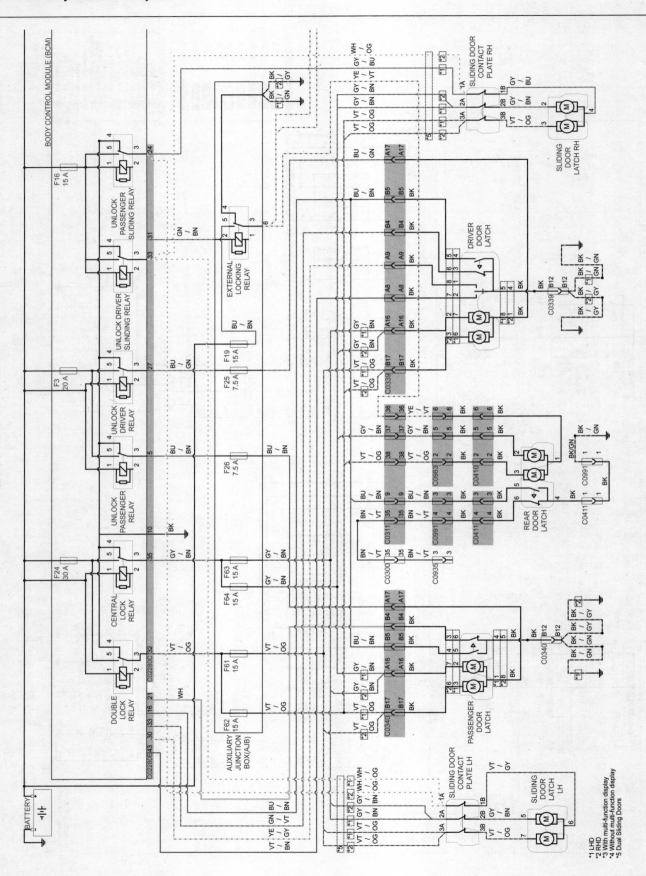

Central locking - 2.0 litre models - Part 1

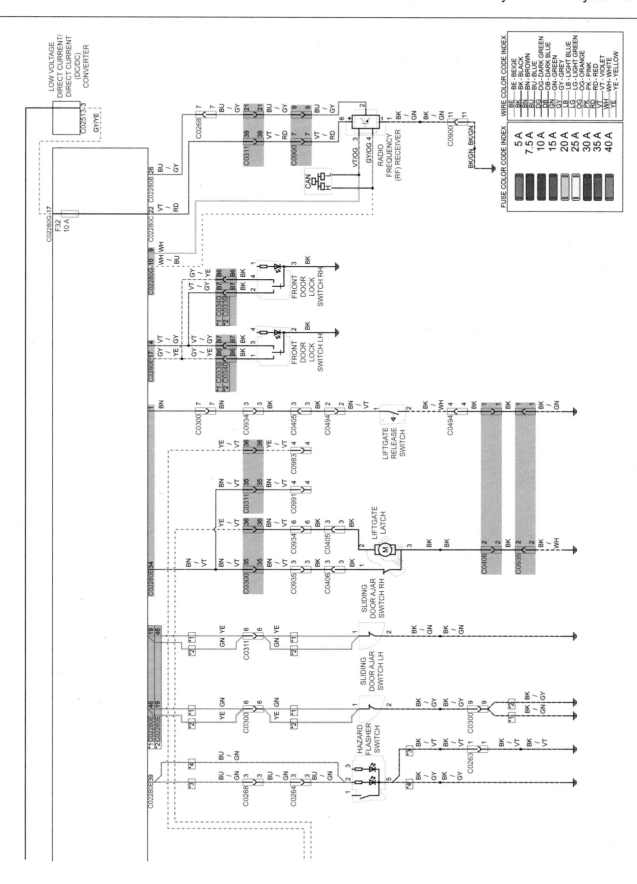

Central locking - 2.0 litre models - Part 2

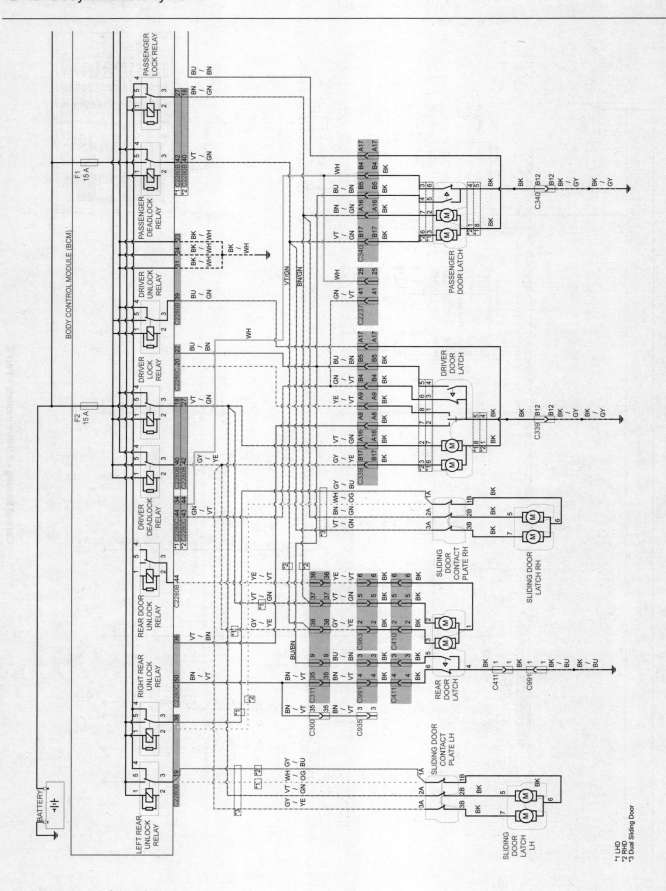

Central locking - 2.2 litre models - Part 1

Central locking - 2.2 litre models - Part 2

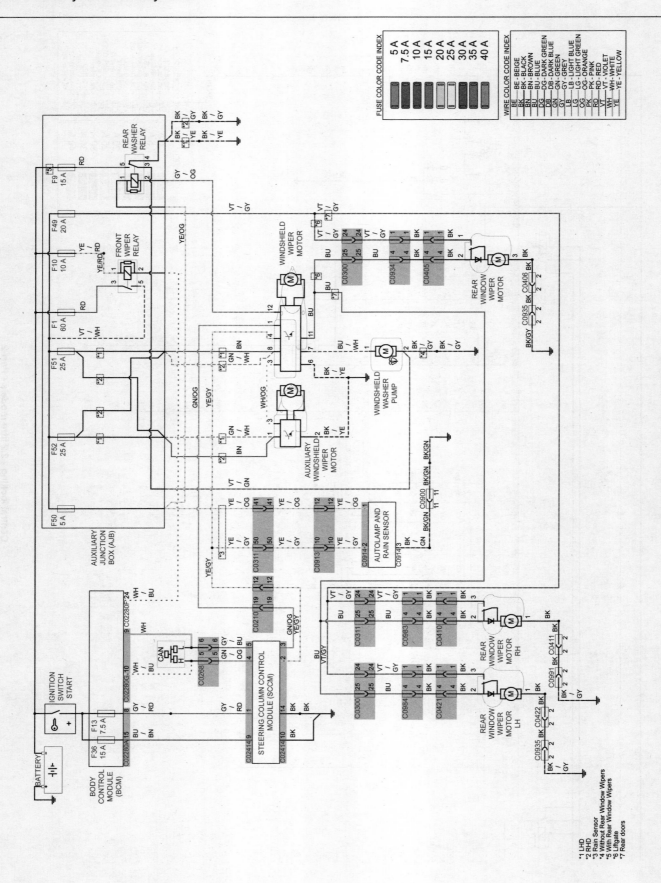

Washers and wipers - 2.0 litre models

*1 LHD
*2 RHD
*3 Rain Sensor
*4 Without Rear Window Wipers
*5 With Rear Window Wipers
*6 Liftgate
*7 Rear doors

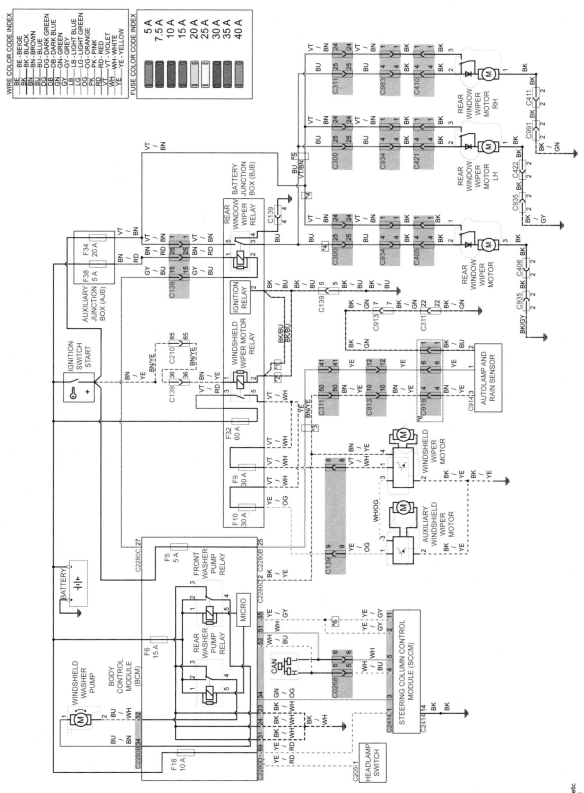

Washers and wipers - 2.2 litre models

*1 Without Econetic
*2 With Econetic
*3 Rain Sensor
*4 Liftgate
*5 Rear doors
*6 Lane Departure Warning

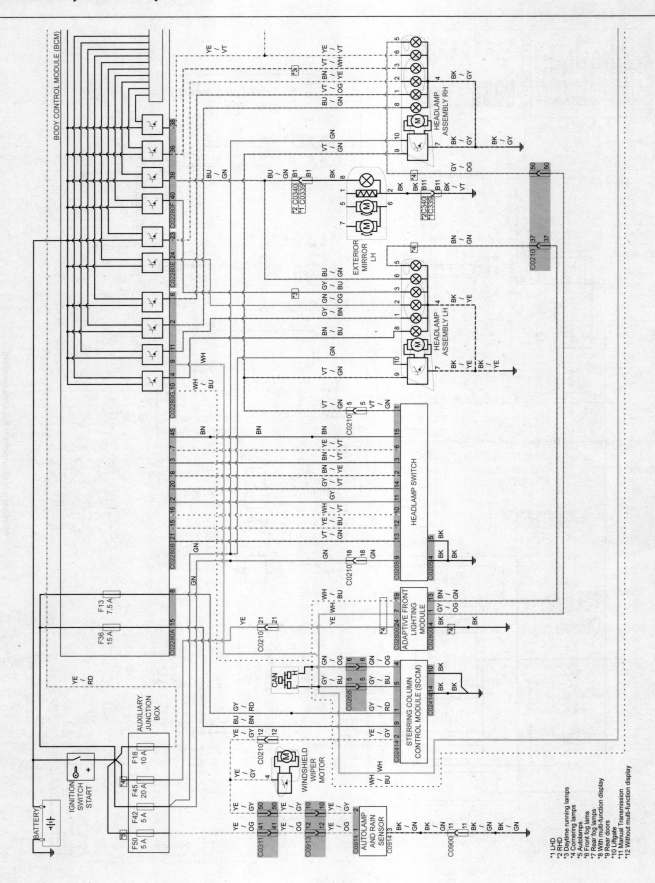

Exterior lighting - 2.0 litre models - Part 1

*1 LHD
*2 RHD
*3 Daytime running lamps
*4 Cornering lamps
*5 Autolamps
*6 Front fog lamps
*7 Rear fog lamps
*8 With multi-function display
*9 Rear doors
*10 Liftgate
*11 Manual Transmission
*12 Without multi-function display

Exterior lighting - 2.0 litre models - Part 2

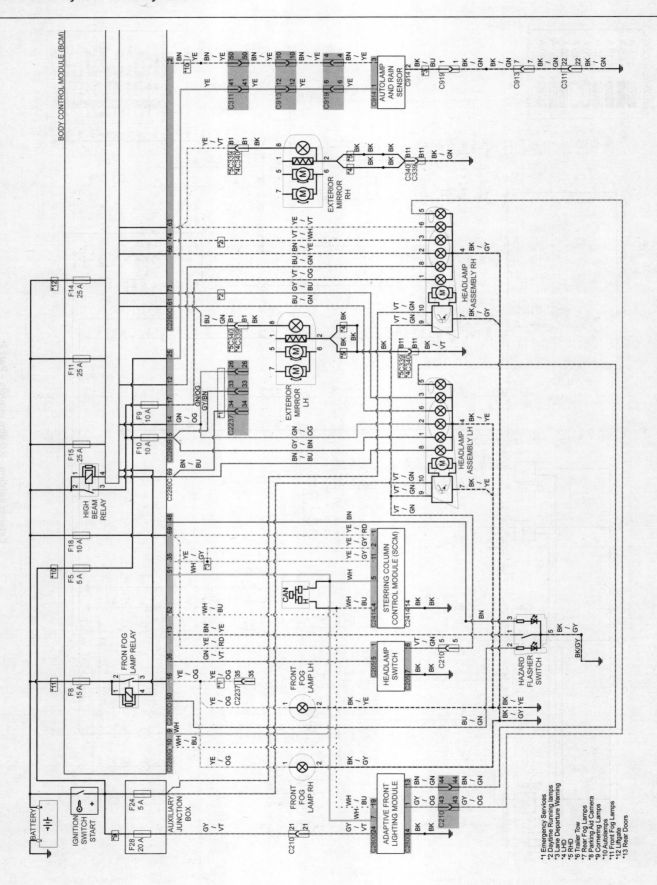

Exterior lighting - 2.2 litre models - Part 1

*1 Emergency Services
*2 Daytime Running lamps
*3 Lane Departure Warning
*4 LHD
*5 RHD
*6 Trailer Tow
*7 Rear Fog Lamps
*8 Parking Aid Camera
*9 Cornering Lamps
*10 Autolamps
*11 Liftgate
*12 Front Fog Lamps
*13 Rear Doors

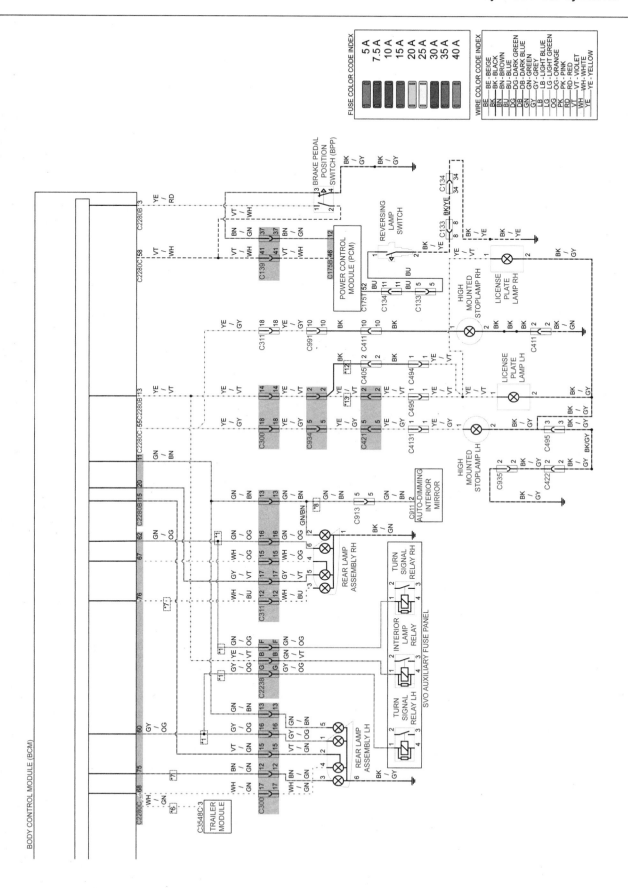

Exterior lighting - 2.2 litre models - Part 2

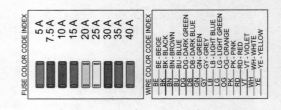

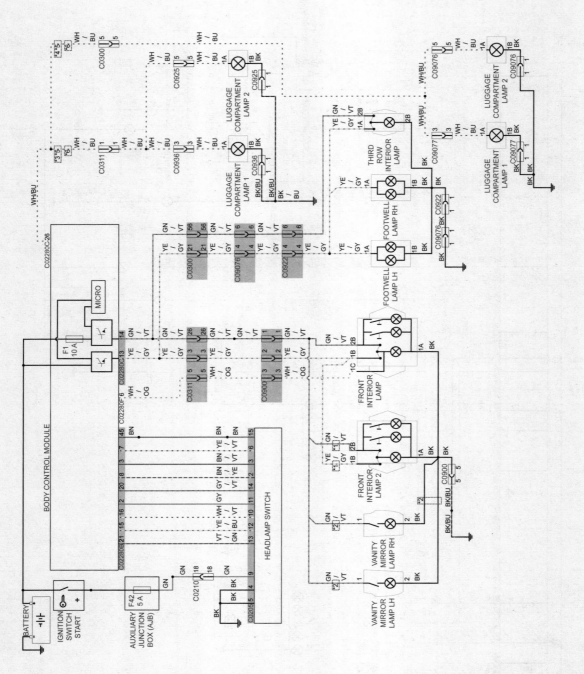

Interior lighting - 2.0 litre models

*1 Dome lamp 2
*2 Vanity mirrors
*3 LHD
*4 RHD
*5 Without Led
*6 With Led

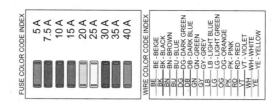

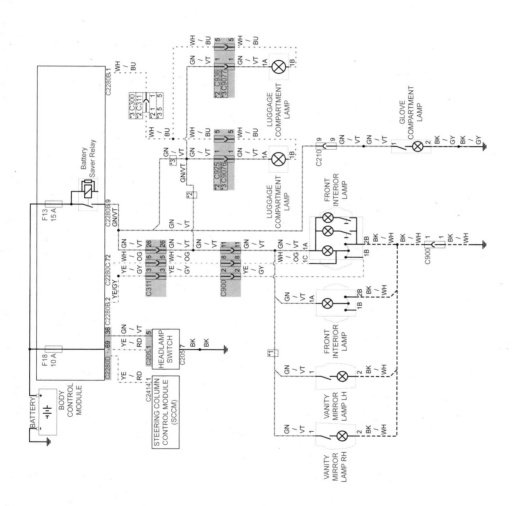

Interior lighting - early 2.2 litre models

*1 Illuminated Vanity Mirrors
*2 LHD
*3 RHD

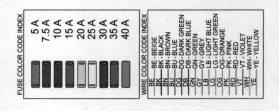

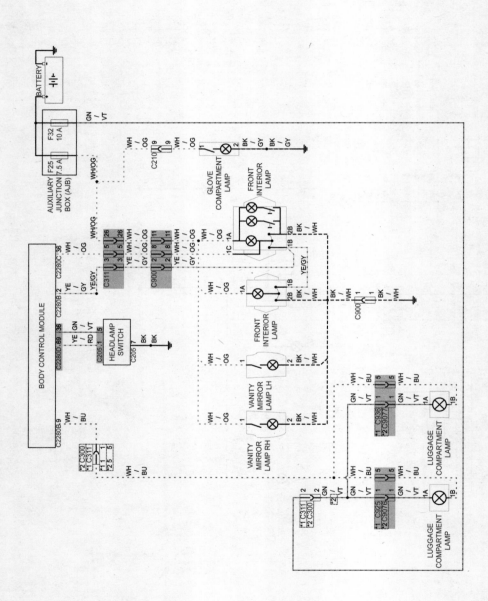

Interior lighting - later 2.2 litre models

*1 LHD
*2 RHD

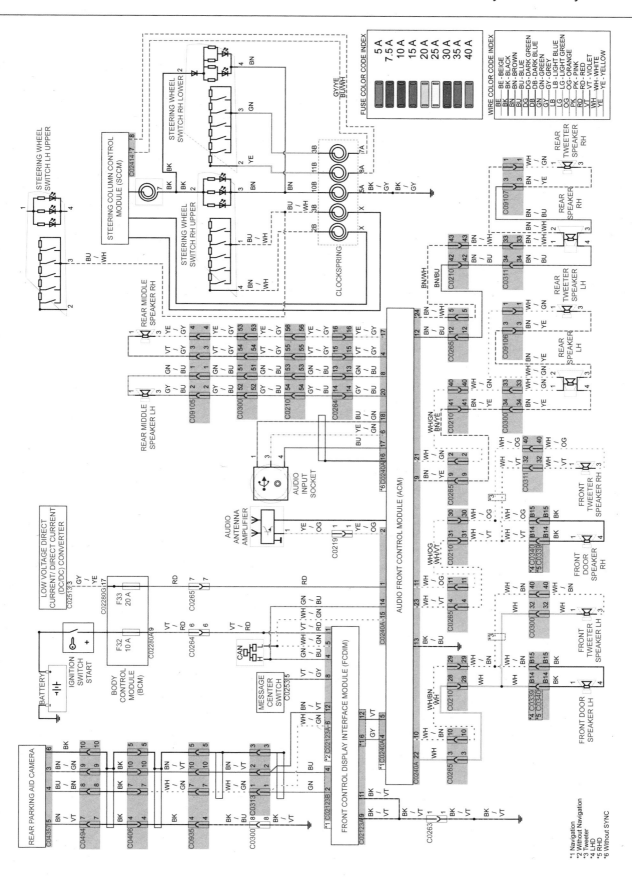

Sound system - 2.0 litre models with Multi-function display

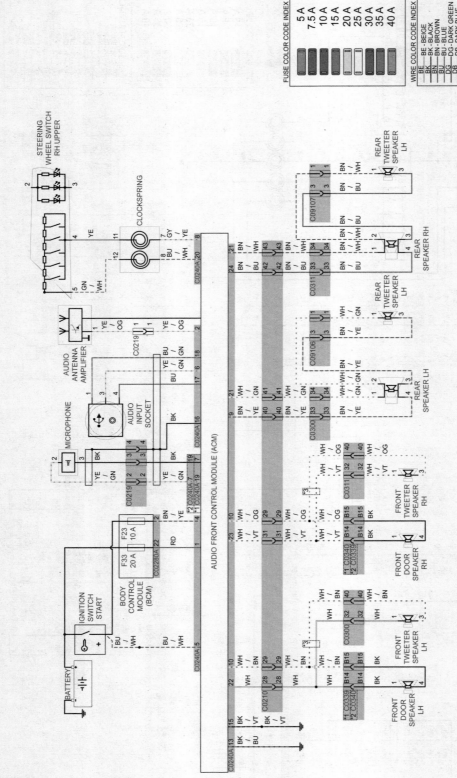

Sound system - 2.0 litre models without Multi-function display

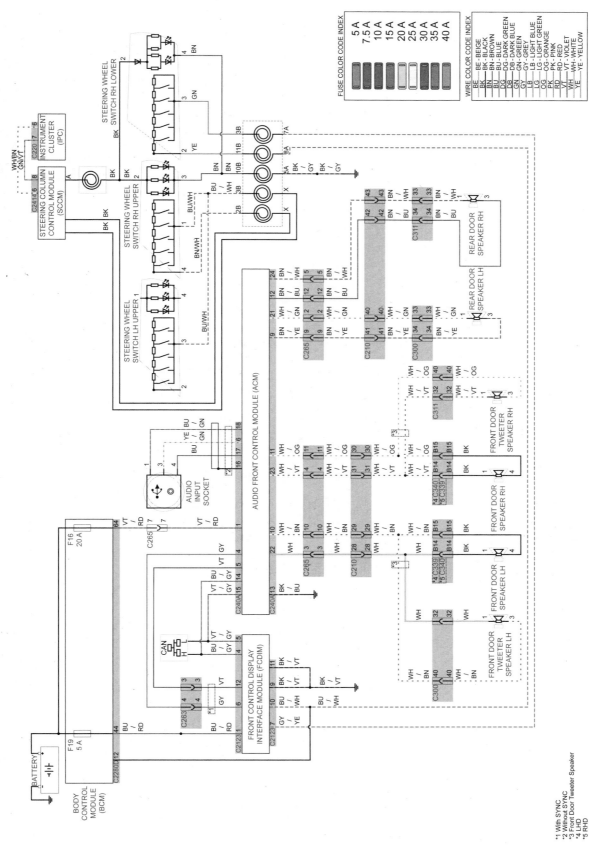

Sound system - 2.2 litre models with Multi-function display

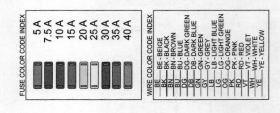

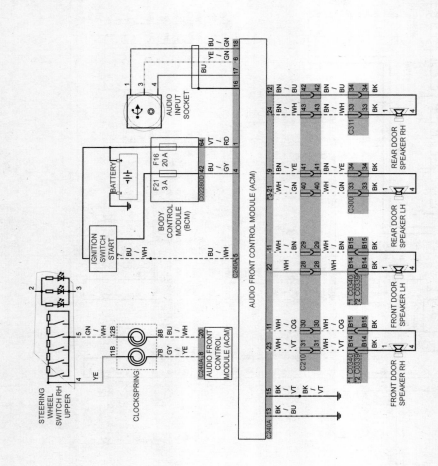

Sound system - 2.2 litre models without Multi-function display

*1 LHD
*2 RHD
*3 Rear Door Speaker

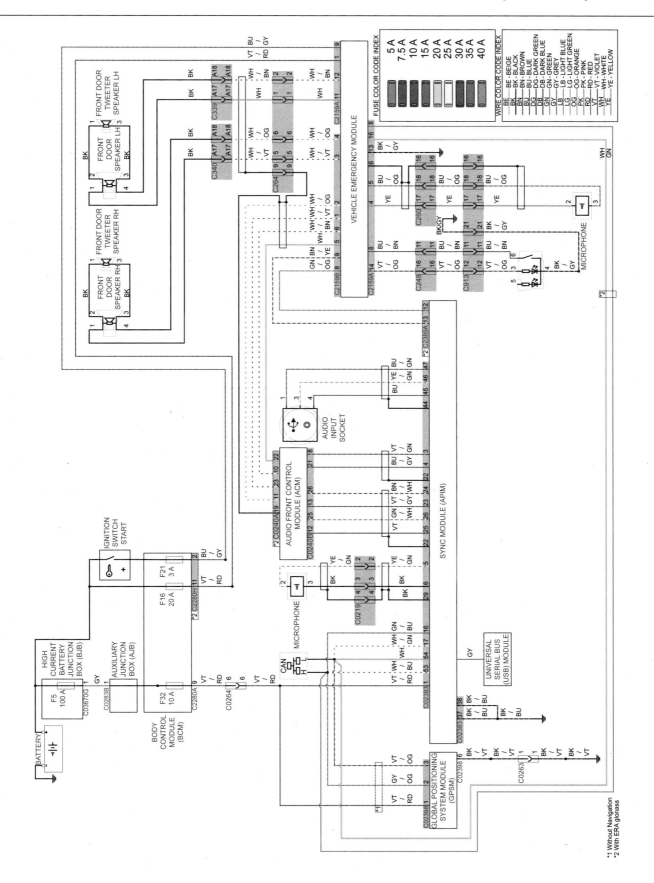

Sound system - SYNC, ERA Glonass

*1 Without Navigation
*2 With ERA glonass

Notes

Dimensions and weights

Note: *All figures are approximate, and may vary according to model. Refer to manufacturer's data for exact figures.*

Dimensions

Overall length (Van and Bus without rear step):
    Short wheelbase. . . . . 4972 mm
    Long wheelbase . . . . 5339 mm
Overall width (excluding door mirrors):
    Van and Bus . . . . 1986 mm
Overall height (unladen):
    Van and Bus:
        Low roof . . . . 1979 to 2016 mm
        High roof . . . . 2280 to 2385 mm

Weights

Kerb weight . . . . *Refer to information contained on the vehicle identification plate*

Length (distance)

Inches (in)	x 25.4	= Millimetres (mm)	x 0.0394	= Inches (in)
Feet (ft)	x 0.305	= Metres (m)	x 3.281	= Feet (ft)
Miles	x 1.609	= Kilometres (km)	x 0.621	= Miles

Volume (capacity)

Cubic inches (cu in; in³)	x 16.387	= Cubic centimetres (cc; cm³)	x 0.061	= Cubic inches (cu in; in³)
Imperial pints (Imp pt)	x 0.568	= Litres (l)	x 1.76	= Imperial pints (Imp pt)
Imperial quarts (Imp qt)	x 1.137	= Litres (l)	x 0.88	= Imperial quarts (Imp qt)
Imperial quarts (Imp qt)	x 1.201	= US quarts (US qt)	x 0.833	= Imperial quarts (Imp qt)
US quarts (US qt)	x 0.946	= Litres (l)	x 1.057	= US quarts (US qt)
Imperial gallons (Imp gal)	x 4.546	= Litres (l)	x 0.22	= Imperial gallons (Imp gal)
Imperial gallons (Imp gal)	x 1.201	= US gallons (US gal)	x 0.833	= Imperial gallons (Imp gal)
US gallons (US gal)	x 3.785	= Litres (l)	x 0.264	= US gallons (US gal)

Mass (weight)

Ounces (oz)	x 28.35	= Grams (g)	x 0.035	= Ounces (oz)
Pounds (lb)	x 0.454	= Kilograms (kg)	x 2.205	= Pounds (lb)

Force

Ounces-force (ozf; oz)	x 0.278	= Newtons (N)	x 3.6	= Ounces-force (ozf; oz)
Pounds-force (lbf; lb)	x 4.448	= Newtons (N)	x 0.225	= Pounds-force (lbf; lb)
Newtons (N)	x 0.1	= Kilograms-force (kgf; kg)	x 9.81	= Newtons (N)

Pressure

Pounds-force per square inch (psi; lbf/in²; lb/in²)	x 0.070	= Kilograms-force per square centimetre (kgf/cm²; kg/cm²)	x 14.223	= Pounds-force per square inch (psi; lbf/in²; lb/in²)
Pounds-force per square inch (psi; lbf/in²; lb/in²)	x 0.068	= Atmospheres (atm)	x 14.696	= Pounds-force per square inch (psi; lbf/in²; lb/in²)
Pounds-force per square inch (psi; lbf/in²; lb/in²)	x 0.069	= Bars	x 14.5	= Pounds-force per square inch (psi; lbf/in²; lb/in²)
Pounds-force per square inch (psi; lbf/in²; lb/in²)	x 6.895	= Kilopascals (kPa)	x 0.145	= Pounds-force per square inch (psi; lbf/in²; lb/in²)
Kilopascals (kPa)	x 0.01	= Kilograms-force per square centimetre (kgf/cm²; kg/cm²)	x 98.1	= Kilopascals (kPa)
Millibar (mbar)	x 100	= Pascals (Pa)	x 0.01	= Millibar (mbar)
Millibar (mbar)	x 0.0145	= Pounds-force per square inch (psi; lbf/in²; lb/in²)	x 68.947	= Millibar (mbar)
Millibar (mbar)	x 0.75	= Millimetres of mercury (mmHg)	x 1.333	= Millibar (mbar)
Millibar (mbar)	x 0.401	= Inches of water (inH₂O)	x 2.491	= Millibar (mbar)
Millimetres of mercury (mmHg)	x 0.535	= Inches of water (inH₂O)	x 1.868	= Millimetres of mercury (mmHg)
Inches of water (inH₂O)	x 0.036	= Pounds-force per square inch (psi; lbf/in²; lb/in²)	x 27.68	= Inches of water (inH₂O)

Torque (moment of force)

Pounds-force inches (lbf in; lb in)	x 1.152	= Kilograms-force centimetre (kgf cm; kg cm)	x 0.868	= Pounds-force inches (lbf in; lb in)
Pounds-force inches (lbf in; lb in)	x 0.113	= Newton metres (Nm)	x 8.85	= Pounds-force inches (lbf in; lb in)
Pounds-force inches (lbf in; lb in)	x 0.083	= Pounds-force feet (lbf ft; lb ft)	x 12	= Pounds-force inches (lbf in; lb in)
Pounds-force feet (lbf ft; lb ft)	x 0.138	= Kilograms-force metres (kgf m; kg m)	x 7.233	= Pounds-force feet (lbf ft; lb ft)
Pounds-force feet (lbf ft; lb ft)	x 1.356	= Newton metres (Nm)	x 0.738	= Pounds-force feet (lbf ft; lb ft)
Newton metres (Nm)	x 0.102	= Kilograms-force metres (kgf m; kg m)	x 9.804	= Newton metres (Nm)

Power

Horsepower (hp)	x 745.7	= Watts (W)	x 0.0013	= Horsepower (hp)

Velocity (speed)

Miles per hour (miles/hr; mph)	x 1.609	= Kilometres per hour (km/hr; kph)	x 0.621	= Miles per hour (miles/hr; mph)

Fuel consumption*

Miles per gallon, Imperial (mpg)	x 0.354	= Kilometres per litre (km/l)	x 2.825	= Miles per gallon, Imperial (mpg)
Miles per gallon, US (mpg)	x 0.425	= Kilometres per litre (km/l)	x 2.352	= Miles per gallon, US (mpg)

Temperature

Degrees Fahrenheit = (°C x 1.8) + 32   Degrees Celsius (Degrees Centigrade; °C) = (°F - 32) x 0.56

It is common practice to convert from miles per gallon (mpg) to litres/100 kilometres (l/100km), where mpg x l/100 km = 282

Spare parts are available from many sources, including maker's appointed garages, accessory shops, and motor factors. To be sure of obtaining the correct parts, it will sometimes be necessary to quote the vehicle identification number. If possible, it can also be useful to take the old parts along for positive identification. Items such as starter motors and alternators may be available under a service exchange scheme – any parts returned should be clean.

Our advice regarding spare parts is as follows.

Officially appointed garages

This is the best source of parts which are peculiar to your vehicle, and which are not otherwise generally available (eg, badges, interior trim, certain body panels, etc). Make sure you store the receipt(s) safely in case a warranty claim has to be made.

Accessory shops

These are very good places to buy materials and components needed for the maintenance of your vehicle (oil, air and fuel filters, light bulbs, drivebelts, greases, brake pads/shoes, touch-up paint, etc). Components of this nature sold by a reputable shop are usually of the same standard as those used by the vehicle manufacturer.

Besides components, these shops also sell tools and general accessories, usually have convenient opening hours, charge lower prices, and can often be found close to home. Some accessory shops have parts counters where components needed for almost any repair job can be purchased or ordered.

Motor factors

Good factors will stock all the more important components which wear out comparatively quickly, and can sometimes supply individual components needed for the overhaul of a larger assembly (eg, brake seals and hydraulic parts, bearing shells, pistons, valves). They may also handle work such as cylinder block reboring, crankshaft regrinding, etc.

Tyre and exhaust specialists

These outlets may be independent, or members of a local or national chain. They frequently offer competitive prices when compared with a main dealer or local garage, but it will pay to obtain several quotes before making a decision. When researching prices, also ask what extras may be added – for instance fitting a new valve and balancing the wheel are both commonly charged on top of the price of a new tyre.

Other sources

Beware of parts or materials obtained from market stalls, car boot sales or similar outlets. Such items are not invariably sub-standard, but there is little chance of compensation if they do prove unsatisfactory. In the case of safety-critical components such as brake pads, there is the risk not only of financial loss, but also of an accident causing injury or death.

Second-hand components or assemblies obtained from a car breaker can be a good buy in some circumstances, but this sort of purchase is best made by the experienced DIY mechanic.

Vehicle identification

Modifications are a continuing and unpublicised process in vehicle manufacture, quite apart from major model changes. Spare parts manuals and lists are compiled upon a numerical basis, the individual vehicle identification numbers being essential to correct identification of the component required.

When ordering spare parts, always give as much information as possible. Quote the vehicle type, year of manufacture and vehicle identification and/or engine numbers as appropriate.

The vehicle identification plate is attached to the front door pillar on the passenger's side and includes the Vehicle Identification Number (VIN), engine code, vehicle weight information and paint and trim colour codes. The VIN is also stamped on a tag on the facia, so that it can be seen through the bottom of the windscreen (see illustrations).

The engine number is stamped on a horizontal flat located on the cylinder block (see illustration).

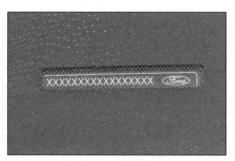

The vehicle identification plate is attached to the front door pillar on the passenger's side...

...and the VIN is also visible at the bottom of the windscreen

The engine number is stamped on a horizontal flat located on the cylinder block

General repair procedures

Whenever servicing, repair or overhaul work is carried out on the car or its components, observe the following procedures and instructions. This will assist in carrying out the operation efficiently and to a professional standard of workmanship.

Joint mating faces and gaskets

When separating components at their mating faces, never insert screwdrivers or similar implements into the joint between the faces in order to prise them apart. This can cause severe damage which results in oil leaks, coolant leaks, etc upon reassembly. Separation is usually achieved by tapping along the joint with a soft-faced hammer in order to break the seal. However, note that this method may not be suitable where dowels are used for component location.

Where a gasket is used between the mating faces of two components, a new one must be fitted on reassembly; fit it dry unless otherwise stated in the repair procedure. Make sure that the mating faces are clean and dry, with all traces of old gasket removed. When cleaning a joint face, use a tool which is unlikely to score or damage the face, and remove any burrs or nicks with an oilstone or fine file.

Make sure that tapped holes are cleaned with a pipe cleaner, and keep them free of jointing compound, if this is being used, unless specifically instructed otherwise.

Ensure that all orifices, channels or pipes are clear, and blow through them, preferably using compressed air.

Oil seals

Oil seals can be removed by levering them out with a wide flat-bladed screwdriver or similar implement. Alternatively, a number of self-tapping screws may be screwed into the seal, and these used as a purchase for pliers or some similar device in order to pull the seal free.

Whenever an oil seal is removed from its working location, either individually or as part of an assembly, it should be renewed.

The very fine sealing lip of the seal is easily damaged, and will not seal if the surface it contacts is not completely clean and free from scratches, nicks or grooves. If the original sealing surface of the component cannot be restored, and the manufacturer has not made provision for slight relocation of the seal relative to the sealing surface, the component should be renewed.

Protect the lips of the seal from any surface which may damage them in the course of fitting. Use tape or a conical sleeve where possible. Where indicated, lubricate the seal lips with oil before fitting and, on dual-lipped seals, fill the space between the lips with grease.

Unless otherwise stated, oil seals must be fitted with their sealing lips toward the lubricant to be sealed.

Use a tubular drift or block of wood of the appropriate size to install the seal and, if the seal housing is shouldered, drive the seal down to the shoulder. If the seal housing is unshouldered, the seal should be fitted with its face flush with the housing top face (unless otherwise instructed).

Screw threads and fastenings

Seized nuts, bolts and screws are quite a common occurrence where corrosion has set in, and the use of penetrating oil or releasing fluid will often overcome this problem if the offending item is soaked for a while before attempting to release it. The use of an impact driver may also provide a means of releasing such stubborn fastening devices, when used in conjunction with the appropriate screwdriver bit or socket. If none of these methods works, it may be necessary to resort to the careful application of heat, or the use of a hacksaw or nut splitter device. Before resorting to extreme methods, check that you are not dealing with a left-hand thread!

Studs are usually removed by locking two nuts together on the threaded part, and then using a spanner on the lower nut to unscrew the stud. Studs or bolts which have broken off below the surface of the component in which they are mounted can sometimes be removed using a stud extractor.

Always ensure that a blind tapped hole is completely free from oil, grease, water or other fluid before installing the bolt or stud. Failure to do this could cause the housing to crack due to the hydraulic action of the bolt or stud as it is screwed in.

For some screw fastenings, notably cylinder head bolts or nuts, torque wrench settings are no longer specified for the latter stages of tightening, "angle-tightening" being called up instead. Typically, a fairly low torque wrench setting will be applied to the bolts/nuts in the correct sequence, followed by one or more stages of tightening through specified angles.

When checking or retightening a nut or bolt to a specified torque setting, slacken the nut or bolt by a quarter of a turn, and then retighten to the specified setting. However, this should not be attempted where angular tightening has been used.

Locknuts, locktabs and washers

Any fastening which will rotate against a component or housing during tightening should always have a washer between it and the relevant component or housing.

Spring or split washers should always be renewed when they are used to lock a critical component such as a big-end bearing retaining bolt or nut. Locktabs which are folded over to retain a nut or bolt should always be renewed.

Self-locking nuts can be re-used in non-critical areas, providing resistance can be felt when the locking portion passes over the bolt or stud thread. However, it should be noted that self-locking stiffnuts tend to lose their effectiveness after long periods of use, and should then be renewed as a matter of course.

Split pins must always be replaced with new ones of the correct size for the hole.

When thread-locking compound is found on the threads of a fastener which is to be re-used, it should be cleaned off with a wire brush and solvent, and fresh compound applied on reassembly.

Special tools

Some repair procedures in this manual entail the use of special tools such as a press, two or three-legged pullers, spring compressors, etc. Wherever possible, suitable readily-available alternatives to the manufacturer's special tools are described, and are shown in use. In some instances, where no alternative is possible, it has been necessary to resort to the use of a manufacturer's tool, and this has been done for reasons of safety as well as the efficient completion of the repair operation. Unless you are highly-skilled and have a thorough understanding of the procedures described, never attempt to bypass the use of any special tool when the procedure described specifies its use. Not only is there a very great risk of personal injury, but expensive damage could be caused to the components involved.

Environmental considerations

When disposing of used engine oil, brake fluid, antifreeze, etc, give due consideration to any detrimental environmental effects. Do not, for instance, pour any of the above liquids down drains into the general sewage system, or onto the ground to soak away, as this is likely to pollute your local environment. Many local council refuse tips provide a facility for waste oil disposal, as do some garages. You can find your nearest disposal point by calling the Environment Agency on 03708 506 506 or by visiting www.oilbankline.org.uk.

Note: It is illegal and anti-social to dump oil down the drain. To find the location of your local oil recycling bank, call 03708 506 506 or visit www.oilbankline.org.uk.

The jack supplied with the vehicle tool kit (located in an aperture beneath the driver's seat) should only be used for changing roadwheels – see *Wheel changing* at the front of this manual. Ensure the jack head is correctly engaged before attempting to raise the vehicle. When carrying out any other kind of work, raise the vehicle using a hydraulic jack, and always supplement the jack with axle stands positioned under the vehicle jacking points.

When jacking up the vehicle with a trolley jack, position the jack head under one of the jacking points. **Do not** jack the vehicle under the sump or any of the steering or suspension components. Supplement the jack using axle stands **(see illustration)**.

⚠ *Warning: Neaver work under, around, or near a raised vehicle, unless it is adequately supported in at least two places.*

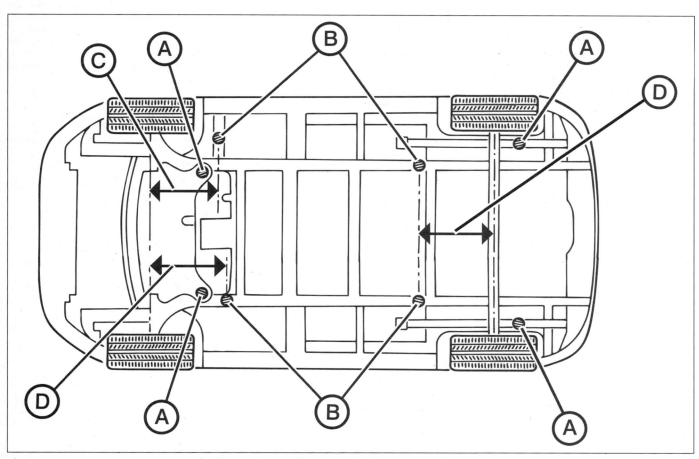

Jacking and supporting points for Van and derivative models

A Trolley/workshop jack lifting points	C 500 mm
B Ramp arms and axle stands	D 700 mm

Introduction

A selection of good tools is a fundamental requirement for anyone contemplating the maintenance and repair of a motor vehicle. For the owner who does not possess any, their purchase will prove a considerable expense, offsetting some of the savings made by doing-it-yourself. However, provided that the tools purchased meet the relevant national safety standards and are of good quality, they will last for many years and prove an extremely worthwhile investment.

To help the average owner to decide which tools are needed to carry out the various tasks detailed in this manual, we have compiled three lists of tools under the following headings: *Maintenance and minor repair*, *Repair and overhaul*, and *Special*. Newcomers to practical mechanics should start off with the *Maintenance and minor repair* tool kit, and confine themselves to the simpler jobs around the vehicle. Then, as confidence and experience grow, more difficult tasks can be undertaken, with extra tools being purchased as, and when, they are needed. In this way, a *Maintenance and minor repair* tool kit can be built up into a *Repair and overhaul* tool kit over a considerable period of time, without any major cash outlays. The experienced do-it-yourselfer will have a tool kit good enough for most repair and overhaul procedures, and will add tools from the *Special* category when it is felt that the expense is justified by the amount of use to which these tools will be put.

Maintenance and minor repair tool kit

The tools given in this list should be considered as a minimum requirement if routine maintenance, servicing and minor repair operations are to be undertaken. We recommend the purchase of combination spanners (ring one end, open-ended the other); although more expensive than open-ended ones, they do give the advantages of both types of spanner.

☐ *Combination spanners:*
  Metric - 8 to 19 mm inclusive
☐ *Adjustable spanner - 35 mm jaw (approx.)*
☐ *Spark plug spanner (with rubber insert) - petrol models*
☐ *Spark plug gap adjustment tool - petrol models*
☐ *Set of feeler gauges*
☐ *Brake bleed nipple spanner*
☐ *Screwdrivers:*
  Flat blade - 100 mm long x 6 mm dia
  Cross blade - 100 mm long x 6 mm dia
  Torx - various sizes (not all vehicles)
☐ *Combination pliers*
☐ *Hacksaw (junior)*
☐ *Tyre pump*
☐ *Tyre pressure gauge*
☐ *Oil can*
☐ *Oil filter removal tool (if applicable)*
☐ *Fine emery cloth*
☐ *Wire brush (small)*
☐ *Funnel (medium size)*
☐ *Sump drain plug key (not all vehicles)*

Repair and overhaul tool kit

These tools are virtually essential for anyone undertaking any major repairs to a motor vehicle, and are additional to those given in the *Maintenance and minor repair* list. Included in this list is a comprehensive set of sockets. Although these are expensive, they will be found invaluable as they are so versatile - particularly if various drives are included in the set. We recommend the half-inch square-drive type, as this can be used with most proprietary torque wrenches.

The tools in this list will sometimes need to be supplemented by tools from the *Special* list:

☐ *Sockets to cover range in previous list (including Torx sockets)*
☐ *Reversible ratchet drive (for use with sockets)*
☐ *Extension piece, 250 mm (for use with sockets)*
☐ *Universal joint (for use with sockets)*
☐ *Flexible handle or sliding T "breaker bar" (for use with sockets)*
☐ *Torque wrench (for use with sockets)*
☐ *Self-locking grips*
☐ *Ball pein hammer*
☐ *Soft-faced mallet (plastic or rubber)*
☐ *Screwdrivers:*
  Flat blade - long & sturdy, short (chubby), and narrow (electrician's) types
  Cross blade – long & sturdy, and short (chubby) types
☐ *Pliers:*
  Long-nosed
  Side cutters (electrician's)
  Circlip (internal and external)
☐ *Cold chisel - 25 mm*
☐ *Scriber*
☐ *Scraper*
☐ *Centre-punch*
☐ *Pin punch*
☐ *Hacksaw*
☐ *Brake hose clamp*
☐ *Brake/clutch bleeding kit*
☐ *Selection of twist drills*
☐ *Steel rule/straight-edge*
☐ *Allen keys (inc. splined/Torx type)*
☐ *Selection of files*
☐ *Wire brush*
☐ *Axle stands*
☐ *Jack (strong trolley or hydraulic type)*
☐ *Light with extension lead*
☐ *Universal electrical multi-meter*

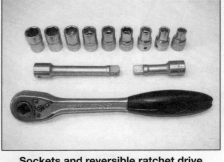
Sockets and reversible ratchet drive

Brake bleeding kit

Torx key, socket and bit

Hose clamp

Angular-tightening gauge

Special tools

The tools in this list are those which are not used regularly, are expensive to buy, or which need to be used in accordance with their manufacturers' instructions. Unless relatively difficult mechanical jobs are undertaken frequently, it will not be economic to buy many of these tools. Where this is the case, you could consider clubbing together with friends (or joining a motorists' club) to make a joint purchase, or borrowing the tools against a deposit from a local garage or tool hire specialist.

The following list contains only those tools and instruments freely available to the public, and not those special tools produced by the vehicle manufacturer specifically for its dealer network. You will find occasional references to these manufacturers' special tools in the text of this manual. Generally, an alternative method of doing the job without the vehicle manufacturers' special tool is given. However, sometimes there is no alternative to using them. Where this is the case and the relevant tool cannot be bought or borrowed, you will have to entrust the work to a dealer.

- [ ] Angular-tightening gauge
- [ ] Valve spring compressor
- [ ] Valve grinding tool
- [ ] Piston ring compressor
- [ ] Piston ring removal/installation tool
- [ ] Cylinder bore hone
- [ ] Balljoint separator
- [ ] Coil spring compressors (where applicable)
- [ ] Two/three-legged hub and bearing puller
- [ ] Impact screwdriver
- [ ] Micrometer and/or vernier calipers
- [ ] Dial gauge
- [ ] Tachometer
- [ ] Fault code reader
- [ ] Cylinder compression gauge
- [ ] Hand-operated vacuum pump and gauge
- [ ] Clutch plate alignment set
- [ ] Brake shoe steady spring cup removal tool
- [ ] Bush and bearing removal/installation set
- [ ] Stud extractors
- [ ] Tap and die set
- [ ] Lifting tackle

Buying tools

Reputable motor accessory shops and superstores often offer excellent quality tools at discount prices, so it pays to shop around.

Remember, you don't have to buy the most expensive items on the shelf, but it is always advisable to steer clear of the very cheap tools. Beware of 'bargains' offered on market stalls, on-line or at car boot sales. There are plenty of good tools around at reasonable prices, but always aim to purchase items which meet the relevant national safety standards. If in doubt, ask the proprietor or manager of the shop for advice before making a purchase.

Care and maintenance of tools

Having purchased a reasonable tool kit, it is necessary to keep the tools in a clean and serviceable condition. After use, always wipe off any dirt, grease and metal particles using a clean, dry cloth, before putting the tools away. Never leave them lying around after they have been used. A simple tool rack on the garage or workshop wall for items such as screwdrivers and pliers is a good idea. Store all normal spanners and sockets in a metal box. Any measuring instruments, gauges, meters, etc, must be carefully stored where they cannot be damaged or become rusty.

Take a little care when tools are used. Hammer heads inevitably become marked, and screwdrivers lose the keen edge on their blades from time to time. A little timely attention with emery cloth or a file will soon restore items like this to a good finish.

Working facilities

Not to be forgotten when discussing tools is the workshop itself. If anything more than routine maintenance is to be carried out, a suitable working area becomes essential.

It is appreciated that many an owner-mechanic is forced by circumstances to remove an engine or similar item without the benefit of a garage or workshop. Having done this, any repairs should always be done under the cover of a roof.

Wherever possible, any dismantling should be done on a clean, flat workbench or table at a suitable working height.

Any workbench needs a vice; one with a jaw opening of 100 mm is suitable for most jobs. As mentioned previously, some clean dry storage space is also required for tools, as well as for any lubricants, cleaning fluids, touch-up paints etc, which become necessary.

Another item which may be required, and which has a much more general usage, is an electric drill with a chuck capacity of at least 8 mm. This, together with a good range of twist drills, is virtually essential for fitting accessories.

Last, but not least, always keep a supply of old newspapers and clean, lint-free rags available, and try to keep any working area as clean as possible.

Micrometers

Dial test indicator ("dial gauge")

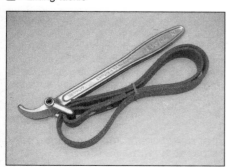
Oil filter removal tool (strap wrench type)

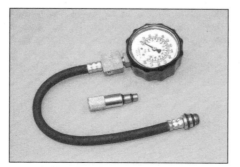
Compression tester

Bearing puller

This is a guide to getting your vehicle through the MOT test. Obviously it will not be possible to examine the vehicle to the same standard as the professional MOT tester. However, working through the following checks will enable you to identify any problem areas before submitting the vehicle for the test.

It has only been possible to summarise the test requirements here, based on the regulations in force at the time of printing. Test standards are becoming increasingly stringent, although there are some exemptions for older vehicles.

An assistant will be needed to help carry out some of these checks.

The checks have been sub-divided into four categories, as follows:

1 Checks carried out **FROM THE VEHICLE INTERIOR**

2 Checks carried out **WITH THE VEHICLE ON THE GROUND**

3 Checks carried out **WITH THE VEHICLE RAISED AND THE WHEELS FREE TO TURN**

4 Checks carried out on **YOUR VEHICLE'S EXHAUST EMISSION SYSTEM**

---

1 Checks carried out **FROM THE VEHICLE INTERIOR**

Handbrake (parking brake)

☐ Test the operation of the handbrake. Excessive travel (too many clicks) indicates incorrect brake or cable adjustment.
☐ Check that the handbrake cannot be released by tapping the lever sideways. Check the security of the lever mountings.

☐ If the parking brake is foot-operated, check that the pedal is secure and without excessive travel, and that the release mechanism operates correctly.
☐ Where applicable, test the operation of the electronic handbrake. The brake should engage and disengage without excessive delay. If the warning light does not extinguish, or a warning message is displayed when the brake is disengaged, this could indicate a fault which will need further investigation.

Footbrake

☐ Depress the brake pedal and check that it does not creep down to the floor, indicating a master cylinder fault. Release the pedal, wait a few seconds, then depress it again. If the pedal travels nearly to the floor before firm resistance is felt, brake adjustment or repair is necessary. If the pedal feels spongy, there is air in the hydraulic system which must be removed by bleeding.

☐ Check that the brake pedal is secure and in good condition. Check also for signs of fluid leaks on the pedal, floor or carpets, which would indicate failed seals in the brake master cylinder.
☐ Check the servo unit (when applicable) by operating the brake pedal several times, then keeping the pedal depressed and starting the engine. As the engine starts, the pedal will move down. If not, the vacuum hose or the servo itself may be faulty.

Steering wheel and column

☐ Examine the steering wheel for fractures or looseness of the hub, spokes or rim.
☐ Move the steering wheel from side to side and then up and down. Check that the steering wheel is not loose on the column, indicating wear or a loose retaining nut. Continue moving the steering wheel as before, but also turn it slightly from left to right.
☐ Check that the steering wheel is not loose on the column, and that there is no abnormal movement of the steering wheel, indicating wear in the column support bearings or couplings.

☐ Check that the ignition lock (where fitted) engages and disengages correctly.
☐ Steering column adjustment mechanisms (where fitted) must be able to lock the column securely in place with no play evident.

Windscreen, mirrors and sunvisor

☐ The windscreen must be free of cracks or other significant damage within the 'swept area' of the windscreen. This is the area swept by the windscreen wipers. A second test area, known as 'Zone A', is the part of the swept area 290 mm wide, centred on the steering wheel centre line. Any damage in Zone A that cannot be contained in a 10 mm diameter circle, or any damage in the remainder of the swept area that cannot be contained in a 40 mm diameter circle, may cause the vehicle to fail the test.

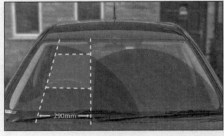

☐ Any items that may obscure the drivers view, such as stickers, sat-navs, anything hanging from the interior mirror, should be removed prior to the test.
☐ Vehicles registered after 1st August 1978 must have a drivers side mirror, and either an interior mirror, or a passenger's side mirror. Cameras (or indirect vision devices) may replace the mirrors, but they must function correctly.
☐ The driver's sunvisor must be capable of being stored in the "up" position.

Seat belts, seats and supplementary restraint systems (SRS)

Note: *The following checks are applicable to all seat belts, front and rear.*

☐ Examine the webbing of all the belts (including rear belts if fitted) for cuts, serious fraying or deterioration. Fasten and unfasten each belt to check the buckles. If applicable, check the retracting mechanism. Check the security of all seat belt mountings accessible from inside the vehicle, ensuring any height adjustable mountings lock securely in place.

☐ Where the seat belt is attached to a seat, the frame and mountings of the seat form part of the belt mountings, and are to be inspected as such.

☐ Any airbag, or SRS warning light must extinguish a few seconds after the ignition is switched on. Failure to do so indicates a fault which must be investigated.

☐ Seat belts with pre-tensioners, once activated, have a "flag" or similar showing on the seat belt stalk. This, in itself, is a reason for test failure.

☐ Check that the original airbag(s) is/are present, and not obviously defective.

☐ The seats themselves must be securely attached and the backrests must lock in the upright position. The driver's seat must also be able to slide forwards/rearwards, and lock in several positions.

Doors

☐ Both front doors must be able to be opened and closed from outside and inside, and must latch securely when closed.

☐ The rear doors must open from the outside.

☐ Examine all door hinges, catches and striker plates for missing, deteriorated, or insecure parts that could effect the opening and closing of the doors.

Speedometer

☐ The vehicle speedometer must be present, and appear operative. The figures on the speedometer must be legible, and illuminated when the lights are switched on.

2 Checks carried out WITH THE VEHICLE ON THE GROUND

Vehicle identification

☐ Number plates must be in good condition, secure and legible, with letters and numbers correctly spaced – spacing at (A) should be 33 mm and at (B) 11 mm. At the front, digits must be black on a white background and at the rear

black on a yellow background. Other background designs (such as honeycomb) are not permitted.

☐ The VIN plate and/or homologation plate must be permanently displayed and legible.

Electrical equipment

☐ Switch on the ignition and check the operation of the horn.

☐ Check the windscreen washers and wipers, examining the wiper blades; renew damaged or perished blades. The wiper blades must clear a large enough area of the windscreen to provide an 'adequate' view of the road, and be able to be parked in a position where they will not affect the drivers' view.

☐ On vehicles first used from 1st September 2009, the headlight washers (where fitted) must operate correctly.

☐ Check the operation of the stop-lights. This includes any lights that appear to be connected – Eg. high-level lights.

☐ Check the operation of the sidelights and number plate lights. The lenses and reflectors must be secure, clean and undamaged.

☐ Check the operation and alignment of the headlights. The headlight reflectors must not be tarnished and the lenses must be undamaged. Where plastic lenses are fitted, check they haven't deteriorated to the extent where they affect the light ouput or beam image. It's often possible to restore the plastic lens using a suitable polish or aftermarket treatment.

☐ Where HID or LED headlights are fitted, check the operation of the cleaning and self-levelling functions.

☐ The headlight main beam warning lamp must be functional.

☐ On vehicles first used from 1st March 2018, the daytime running lights (where fitted) must operate correctly.

☐ Switch on the ignition and check the operation of the direction indicators (including the instrument panel tell-tale) and the hazard warning lights. Operation of the sidelights and stop-lights must not affect the indicators – if it does, the cause is usually a bad earth at the rear light cluster. Indicators should flash at a rate of between 60 and 120 times per minute – faster or slower than this could indicate a fault with the flasher unit or a bad earth at one of the light units.

☐ The hazard warning lights must operate with the ignition on and off.

☐ Check the operation of the rear foglight(s), including the warning light on the instrument panel or in the switch. Note that the foglight

must be positioned in the centre or driver's side of the vehicle. If only the passenger's side illuminates, the test will fail.

☐ The warning lights must illuminate in accordance with the manufacturers' design (this includes any warning messages). For most vehicles, the ABS and other warning lights should illuminate when the ignition is switched on, and (if the system is operating properly) extinguish after a few seconds. Refer to the owner's handbook.

☐ On vehicles first used from 1st September 2009, the reversing lights must operate correctly when reverse gear is selected.

☐ Check the vehicle battery for security and leakage.

☐ Check the visible/accessible vehicle wiring is adequately supported, with no evidence of damage or deterioration that could result in a short-circuit.

Footbrake

☐ Examine the master cylinder, brake pipes and servo unit for leaks, loose mountings, corrosion or other damage. If ABS is fitted, this unit should also be examined for signs of leaks or corrosion.

☐ The fluid reservoir must be secure and the fluid level must be between the upper (A) and lower (B) markings.

☐ Check the fluid in the reservoir for signs of contamination.

☐ Inspect both front brake flexible hoses for cracks or deterioration of the rubber. Turn the steering from lock to lock, and ensure that the hoses do not contact the wheel, tyre, or any part of the steering or suspension mechanism. With the brake pedal firmly depressed, check the hoses for bulges or leaks under pressure.

Steering and suspension

☐ Have your assistant turn the steering wheel from side to side slightly, up to the point where the steering gear just begins to transmit this movement to the roadwheels. Check for excessive free play between the steering wheel and the steering gear, indicating wear or insecurity of the steering column joints, the column-to-steering gear coupling, or the steering gear itself. With a standard (380 mm diameter) steering wheel, there should be no more than 13 mm of free play for rack-and-pinion systems, and no more than 75 mm for non-rack-and-pinion designs.

☐ Have your assistant turn the steering

wheel more vigorously in each direction, so that the roadwheels just begin to turn. As this is done, examine all the steering joints, linkages, fittings and attachments. Renew any component that shows signs of wear or damage. On vehicles with hydraulic power steering, check the security and condition of the steering pump, drivebelt and hoses.

☐ Note that all movement checks on power steering systems are carried out with the engine running.

☐ Check that the vehicle is standing level, and at approximately the correct ride height.

Exhaust system

☐ Start the engine. With your assistant holding a rag over the tailpipe, check the entire system for leaks. Repair or renew leaking sections.

3 Checks carried out WITH THE VEHICLE RAISED AND THE WHEELS FREE TO TURN

Jack up the front and rear of the vehicle, and securely support it on axle stands. Position the stands clear of the suspension assemblies. Ensure that the wheels are clear of the ground and that the steering can be turned from lock to lock.

Steering mechanism

☐ Have your assistant turn the steering from lock to lock. Check that the steering turns smoothly, and that no part of the steering mechanism, including a wheel or tyre, fouls any brake hose or pipe or any part of the body structure.

☐ Examine the steering rack rubber gaiters for damage or insecurity of the retaining clips. If power steering is fitted, check for signs of damage or leakage of the fluid hoses, pipes or connections. Also check for excessive stiffness or binding of the steering, a missing split pin or locking device, or severe corrosion of the body structure within 30 cm of any steering component attachment point.

☐ Check the track rod end ball joint dust covers. Any covers that are missing, seriously damaged, deteriorated or insecure, may fail inspection.

Front and rear suspension and wheel bearings

☐ Starting at the front right-hand side, grasp the roadwheel at the 3 o'clock and 9 o'clock positions and rock gently but firmly. Check for free play or insecurity at the wheel bearings, suspension balljoints, or suspension mountings, pivots and attachments.

☐ Now grasp the wheel at the 12 o'clock and 6 o'clock positions and repeat the previous inspection. Spin the wheel, and check for roughness or tightness of the front wheel bearing.

☐ If excess free play is suspected at a component pivot point, this can be confirmed by using a large screwdriver or similar tool and levering between the mounting and the component attachment. This will confirm whether the wear is in the pivot bush, its retaining bolt, or in the mounting itself (the bolt holes can often become elongated).

☐ Carry out all the above checks at the other front wheel, and then at both rear wheels.

Springs and shock absorbers

☐ Examine the suspension struts (when applicable) for serious fluid leakage, corrosion, or damage to the casing. Also check the security of the mounting points.

☐ If coil springs are fitted, check that the spring ends locate in their seats, and that the spring is not corroded, cracked or broken.

☐ If leaf springs are fitted, check that all leaves are intact, that the axle is securely attached to each spring, and that there is no deterioration of the spring eye mountings, bushes, and shackles.

☐ The same general checks apply to vehicles fitted with other suspension types, such as torsion bars, hydraulic displacer units, etc. Ensure that all mountings and attachments are secure, that there are no signs of excessive wear, corrosion or damage, and (on hydraulic types) that there are no fluid leaks or damaged pipes.

☐ Check any suspension and anti-roll bar link ball joint dust covers. Any covers that are missing, seriously damaged, deteriorated or insecure, may fail inspection.

☐ Examine each shock absorber for signs of leakage, corrosion of the casing, missing, detached or worn pivots and/or rubber bushes.

Driveshafts (fwd vehicles only)

☐ Rotate each front wheel in turn and inspect the inner and outer joint gaiters for splits or damage. Also check that each driveshaft is straight and undamaged.

Braking system

☐ If possible without dismantling, check brake pad wear and disc condition. Ensure that the friction lining material has not worn excessively, (A) and that the discs are not fractured, pitted, scored or badly worn (B). As a general rule, if the friction material is less than 1.5 mm thick, the inspection will fail.

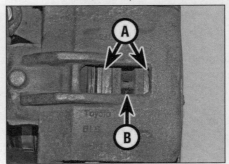

☐ Examine all the rigid brake pipes underneath the vehicle, and the flexible hose(s) at the rear. Look for corrosion, chafing or insecurity of the pipes, and for signs of bulging under pressure, chafing, splits or deterioration of the flexible hoses.

☐ Look for signs of fluid leaks at the brake calipers or on the brake backplates. Repair or renew leaking components.

☐ Slowly spin each wheel, while your assistant depresses and releases the footbrake. Ensure that each brake is operating and does not bind when the pedal is released.

□ Examine the handbrake mechanism, checking for frayed or broken cables, excessive corrosion, or wear or insecurity of the linkage. Check that the mechanism works on each relevant wheel, and releases fully, without binding.

□ Check the ABS sensors' wiring for signs of damage, deterioration or insecurity.
□ It is not possible to test brake efficiency without special equipment, but a road test can be carried out later to check that the vehicle pulls up in a straight line.

Fuel and exhaust systems

□ Inspect the fuel tank (including the filler cap), fuel pipes, hoses and unions. All components must be secure and free from leaks. Locking fuel caps must lock securely and the key must be provided for the MOT test.
□ Examine the exhaust system over its entire length, checking for any damaged, broken or missing mountings, security of the retaining clamps and rust or corrosion.

□ If the vehicle was originally equipped with a catalytic converter or particulate filter, one must be fitted.

Wheels and tyres

□ Examine the sidewalls and tread area of each tyre in turn. Check for cuts, tears, lumps, bulges, separation of the tread, and exposure of the ply or cord due to wear or damage. Check that the tyre bead is correctly seated on the wheel rim, that the valve is sound and properly seated, and that the wheel is not distorted or damaged.
□ Check that the tyres are of the correct size for the vehicle, that they are of the same size and type on each axle, and that the pressures are correct. The vehicle will fail the test if the tyres are obviously under-inflated.
□ Check the tyre tread depth. The legal minimum at the time of writing is 1.6 mm over the central three-quarters of the tread width. Abnormal tread wear may indicate incorrect front wheel alignment or wear in steering or suspension components.
□ Check that all wheel bolts/nuts are present.

□ If the spare wheel is fitted externally or in a separate carrier beneath the vehicle, check that mountings are secure and free of excessive corrosion.

Body corrosion

□ Check the condition of the entire vehicle structure for signs of corrosion in load-bearing areas. (These include chassis box sections, side sills, cross-members, pillars, and all suspension, steering, braking system and seat belt mountings and anchorages.) Any corrosion which has seriously reduced the thickness of a load-bearing area (or is within 30 cm of safety-related components such as steering or suspension) is likely to cause the vehicle to fail. In this case professional repairs are likely to be needed.
□ Damage or corrosion which causes sharp or otherwise dangerous edges to be exposed will also cause the vehicle to fail.

Towbars

□ Check the condition of mounting points (both beneath the vehicle and within boot/hatchback areas) for signs of corrosion, ensuring that all fixings are secure and not worn or damaged. There must be no excessive play in detachable tow ball arms or quick-release mechanisms.
□ Examine the security and condition of the towbar electrics socket. If the later 13-pin socket is fitted, the MOT tester will check its' wiring functions/connections are correct.

General leaks

□ The vehicle will fail the test if there is a fluid leak of any kind that poses an environmental risk.

4 Checks carried out on **YOUR VEHICLE'S EXHAUST EMISSION SYSTEM**

Petrol models

□ The engine should be warmed up, and running well (ignition system in good order, air filter element clean, etc).
□ Before testing, run the engine at around 2500 rpm for 20 seconds. Let the engine drop to idle, and watch for smoke from the exhaust. If the idle speed is too high, or if dense blue or black smoke emerges for more than 5 seconds, the vehicle will fail. Typically, blue smoke signifies oil burning (engine wear); black smoke means unburnt fuel (dirty air cleaner element, or other fuel system fault).
□ An exhaust gas analyser for measuring carbon monoxide (CO) and hydrocarbons (HC) is now needed. If one cannot be hired or borrowed, have a local garage perform the check.

CO emissions (mixture)

□ The MOT tester has access to the CO limits for all vehicles from 1st August 1992. The CO level is measured at idle speed, and at 'fast idle' (2500 to 3000 rpm). The following limits are given as a general guide:
  At idle speed – Less than 0.3% CO
  At 'fast idle' – Less than 0.2% CO
  Lambda reading – 0.97 to 1.03
□ If the CO level is too high, this may point to poor maintenance, a fuel injection system problem, faulty lambda (oxygen) sensor or catalytic converter. Try an injector cleaning treatment, and check the vehicle's ECU for fault codes.

HC emissions

□ The MOT tester has access to HC limits for all vehicles. The HC level is measured at 'fast idle' (2500 to 3000 rpm). The following limits are given as a general guide:
  At 'fast idle' – Less than 200 ppm
□ Excessive HC emissions are typically caused by oil being burnt (worn engine), or by a blocked crankcase ventilation system ('breather'). If the engine oil is old and thin, an oil change may help. If the engine is running badly, check the vehicle's ECU for fault codes.

Diesel models

□ If the vehicle was fitted with a DPF (Diesel Particulate Filter) when it left the factory, it will fail the test if the MOT tester can see smoke of any colour emitting from the exhaust, or finds evidence that the filter has been tampered with.
□ The only emission test for diesel engines is measuring exhaust smoke density, using a calibrated smoke meter.
□ This test involves accelerating the engine to its maximum unloaded speed a minimum of once, and a maximum of 6 times. With the smoke meter connected, the engine is accelerated quickly to its maximum speed. If the smoke level is at or below the limit specified, the vehicle will pass. If the level is more than the specified limit then two further accelerations are carried out, and an average of the readings calculated. If the vehicle is still over the limit, a further three accelerations are carried out, with the average of the last three calculated after each check.
Note: *On engines with a timing belt, it is VITAL that the belt is in good condition before the test is carried out.*

Vehicles registered after 1st July 2008
Smoke level must not exceed 1.5m-1 – Turbo-charged and non-Turbocharged engines

Vehicles registered before 1st July 2008
Smoke level must not exceed 2.5m-1 – Non-turbo vehicles
Smoke level must not exceed 3.0m-1 – Turbocharged vehicles:

□ If excess smoke is produced, try fitting a new air cleaner element, or using an injector cleaning treatment. If the engine is running badly, where applicable, check the vehicle's ECU for fault codes. Also check the vehicle's EGR system, where applicable. At high mileages, the injectors may require professional attention.

Engine

- [ ] Engine fails to rotate when attempting to start
- [ ] Engine rotates, but will not start
- [ ] Engine difficult to start when cold
- [ ] Engine difficult to start when hot
- [ ] Starter motor noisy or rough in engagement
- [ ] Engine starts, but stops immediately
- [ ] Engine idles erratically
- [ ] Engine misfires at idle speed
- [ ] Engine misfires throughout the driving speed range
- [ ] Engine hesitates on acceleration
- [ ] Engine stalls
- [ ] Engine lacks power
- [ ] Engine backfires
- [ ] Oil pressure warning light illuminated with engine running
- [ ] Engine runs-on after switching off
- [ ] Engine noises

Cooling system

- [ ] Overheating
- [ ] Overcooling
- [ ] External coolant leakage
- [ ] Internal coolant leakage
- [ ] Corrosion

Fuel and exhaust systems

- [ ] Excessive fuel consumption
- [ ] Fuel leakage and/or fuel odour
- [ ] Excessive noise or fumes from exhaust system

Clutch

- [ ] Pedal travels to floor – no pressure or very little resistance
- [ ] Clutch fails to disengage (unable to select gears)
- [ ] Clutch slips (engine speed increases, with no increase in vehicle speed)
- [ ] Judder as clutch is engaged
- [ ] Noise when depressing or releasing clutch pedal

Manual transmission

- [ ] Noisy in neutral with engine running
- [ ] Noisy in one particular gear
- [ ] Difficulty engaging gears
- [ ] Jumps out of gear
- [ ] Vibration
- [ ] Lubricant leaks

Driveshafts

- [ ] Clicking or knocking noise on turns (at slow speed on full-lock)
- [ ] Vibration when accelerating or decelerating

Rear axle

- [ ] Roughness or rumble from the rear of the vehicle (perhaps less with the handbrake slightly applied)

Braking system

- [ ] Vehicle pulls to one side under braking
- [ ] Noise (grinding or high-pitched squeal) when brakes applied
- [ ] Excessive brake pedal travel
- [ ] Brake pedal feels spongy when depressed
- [ ] Excessive brake pedal effort required to stop vehicle
- [ ] Judder felt through brake pedal or steering wheel when braking
- [ ] Brakes binding

Steering and suspension

- [ ] Vehicle pulls to one side
- [ ] Wheel wobble and vibration
- [ ] Excessive pitching and/or rolling around corners, or during braking
- [ ] Wandering or general instability
- [ ] Excessively-stiff steering
- [ ] Excessive play in steering
- [ ] Lack of power assistance
- [ ] Tyre wear excessive

Electrical system

- [ ] Battery will only hold a charge for a few days
- [ ] Ignition/no-charge warning light remains illuminated with engine running
- [ ] Ignition/no-charge warning light fails to come on
- [ ] Lights inoperative
- [ ] Instrument readings inaccurate or erratic
- [ ] Horn inoperative, or unsatisfactory in operation
- [ ] Windscreen wipers inoperative, or unsatisfactory in operation
- [ ] Windscreen washers inoperative, or unsatisfactory in operation
- [ ] Electric windows inoperative, or unsatisfactory in operation
- [ ] Central locking system inoperative, or unsatisfactory in operation

Introduction

The vehicle owner who does his or her own maintenance according to the recommended service schedules should not have to use this section of the manual very often. Modern component reliability is such that, provided those items subject to wear or deterioration are inspected or renewed at the specified intervals, sudden failure is comparatively rare. Faults do not usually just happen as a result of sudden failure, but develop over a period of time. Major mechanical failures in particular are usually preceded by characteristic symptoms over hundreds or even thousands of miles. Those components which do occasionally fail without warning are often small and easily carried in the vehicle.

With any fault-finding, the first step is to decide where to begin investigations. Sometimes this is obvious, but on other occasions, a little detective work will be necessary. The owner who makes half a dozen haphazard adjustments or replacements may be successful in curing a fault (or its symptoms), but will be none the wiser if the fault recurs, and ultimately may have spent more time and money than was necessary. A calm and logical approach will be found to be more satisfactory in the long run. Always take into account any warning signs or abnormalities that may have been noticed in the period preceding the fault – power loss, high or low gauge readings, unusual smells, etc – and remember that failure of components such as fuses may only be pointers to some underlying fault.

The pages which follow provide an easy-reference guide to the more common problems which may occur during the operation of the vehicle. These problems and their possible causes are grouped under headings denoting various components or systems, such as Engine, Cooling system, etc. The general Chapter which deals with the problem is also shown in brackets; refer to the relevant part of that Chapter for system-specific information. Whatever the fault, certain basic principles apply. These are as follows:

Verify the fault. This is simply a matter of being sure that you know what the symptoms are before starting work. This is particularly important if you are investigating a fault for someone else, who may not have described it very accurately.

Don't overlook the obvious. For example, if the vehicle won't start, is there fuel in the tank? (Don't take anyone else's word on this particular point, and don't trust the fuel gauge either!) If an electrical fault is indicated, look for loose or broken wires before digging out the test gear.

Cure the disease, not the symptom.

Substituting a flat battery with a fully-charged one will get you off the hard shoulder, but if the underlying cause is not attended to, the new battery will go the same way.

Don't take anything for granted. Particularly, don't forget that a 'new' component may itself be defective (especially if it's been rattling around in the boot for months), and don't leave components out of a fault diagnosis sequence just because they are new or recently-fitted. When you do finally diagnose a difficult fault, you'll probably realise that all the evidence was there from the start.

Consider what work, if any, has been carried out recently. Many faults arise through careless or hurried work. For instance, if any work has been performed under the bonnet, could some of the wiring have been dislodged or incorrectly routed, or a hose trapped? Have all the fasteners been properly tightened? Were new, genuine parts and new gaskets used? There is often a certain amount of detective work to be done in this case, as an apparently unrelated task can have far-reaching consequences.

Engine

Engine fails to rotate when attempting to start

- ☐ Battery terminal connections loose or corroded (see *Weekly checks*)
- ☐ Battery discharged or faulty (Chapter 5 Section 3)
- ☐ Broken, loose or disconnected wiring in the starting circuit (Chapter 5)
- ☐ Defective starter solenoid or ignition switch (Chapter 5 or 12)
- ☐ Defective starter motor (Chapter 5 Section 10)
- ☐ Starter pinion or flywheel ring gear teeth loose or broken (Chapter 5 Section 9)
- ☐ Engine earth strap broken or disconnected (Chapter 5)
- ☐ Engine suffering 'hydraulic lock' (eg from water drawn into the engine after traversing flooded roads, or from a serious internal coolant leak) – consult a main dealer for advice

Engine rotates, but will not start

- ☐ Fuel tank empty
- ☐ Battery discharged (engine rotates slowly) (Chapter 5 Section 3)
- ☐ Battery terminal connections loose or corroded (see *Weekly checks*)
- ☐ Immobiliser fault, or 'uncoded' ignition key being used (Chapter 12)
- ☐ Preheating system faulty (Chapter 5)
- ☐ Fuel injection/engine management system fault (Chapter 4A or Chapter 4B)
- ☐ Air in fuel system (Chapter 4A Section 4)
- ☐ Major mechanical failure (Chapter 2A or Chapter 2B)

Engine difficult to start when cold

- ☐ Battery discharged (Chapter 5 Section 3)
- ☐ Battery terminal connections loose or corroded (see *Weekly checks*)
- ☐ Preheating system faulty (Chapter 5)
- ☐ Fuel injection/engine management system fault (Chapter 4A or Chapter 4B)
- ☐ Wrong grade of engine oil used (see *Weekly checks* or Chapter 1)
- ☐ Low cylinder compression (Chapter 2A Section 2 or Chapter 2B Section 2)
- ☐ Air in fuel system (Chapter 4A Section 4)

Engine difficult to start when hot

- ☐ Air filter element dirty or clogged (Chapter 1 Section 27)
- ☐ Fuel injection/engine management system fault (Chapter 4A or Chapter 4B)
- ☐ Low cylinder compression (Chapter 2A Section 2 or Chapter 2B Section 2)
- ☐ Air in fuel system (Chapter 4A Section 4)

Starter motor noisy or excessively rough in engagement

- ☐ Starter pinion or flywheel ring gear teeth loose or broken (Chapter 2A or Chapter 2B or Chapter 5 Section 10)
- ☐ Starter motor mounting bolts loose or missing (Chapter 5 Section 10)
- ☐ Starter motor internal components worn or damaged (Chapter 5 Section 10)

Engine starts, but stops immediately

- ☐ Fuel injection/engine management system fault (Chapter 4A or Chapter 4B)

Engine idles erratically

- ☐ Air filter element clogged (Chapter 1 Section 27)
- ☐ Uneven or low cylinder compression (Chapter 2A Section 2 or Chapter 2B Section 2)
- ☐ Camshaft lobes worn (Chapter 2A Section 9 or Chapter 2B Section 9)
- ☐ Fuel injection/engine management system fault (Chapter 4A or Chapter 4B)
- ☐ Air in fuel system (Chapter 4A Section 4)

Engine misfires at idle speed

- ☐ Faulty injector(s) (Chapter 4A Section 12)
- ☐ Uneven or low cylinder compression (Chapter 2A Section 2 or Chapter 2B Section 2)
- ☐ Disconnected, leaking, or perished crankcase ventilation hoses (Chapter 4B)
- ☐ Fuel injection/engine management system fault (Chapter 4A or Chapter 4B)

Engine misfires throughout the driving speed range

- ☐ Fuel filter choked (Chapter 1 Section 12)
- ☐ Fuel tank vent blocked, or fuel pipes restricted (Chapter 4A)
- ☐ Faulty injector(s) (Chapter 4A Section 12)
- ☐ Uneven or low cylinder compression (Chapter 2A Section 2 or Chapter 2B Section 2)
- ☐ Blocked catalytic converter (Chapter 4A Section 19)
- ☐ Fuel injection/engine management system fault (Chapter 4A or Chapter 4B)
- ☐ Engine overheating (Chapter 3)

Engine hesitates on acceleration

- ☐ Faulty injector(s) (Chapter 4A Section 12)
- ☐ Fuel injection/engine management system fault (Chapter 4A or Chapter 4B)

Engine (continued)

Engine stalls

- [ ] Fuel filter choked (Chapter 1 Section 12)
- [ ] Fuel tank vent blocked, or fuel pipes restricted (Chapter 4A)
- [ ] Faulty injector(s) (Chapter 4A Section 12)
- [ ] Fuel injection/engine management system fault (Chapter 4A or Chapter 4B)

Engine lacks power

- [ ] Air filter element blocked (Chapter 1 Section 27)
- [ ] Fuel filter choked (Chapter 1 Section 12)
- [ ] Fuel pipes blocked or restricted (Chapter 4A)
- [ ] Engine overheating (Chapter 3)
- [ ] Accelerator pedal position sensor faulty (Chapter 4A Section 6)
- [ ] Faulty injector(s) (Chapter 4A Section 12)
- [ ] Uneven or low cylinder compression (Chapter 2A Section 2 or Chapter 2B Section 2)
- [ ] Fuel injection/engine management system fault (Chapter 4A or Chapter 4B)
- [ ] Blocked catalytic converter (Chapter 4A Section 19)
- [ ] Brakes binding (Chapter 1 or Chapter 9)
- [ ] Clutch slipping (Chapter 6)

Engine backfires

- [ ] Fuel injection/engine management system fault (Chapter 4A or Chapter 4B)
- [ ] Blocked catalytic converter (Chapter 4A Section 19)

Oil pressure warning light illuminated with engine running

- [ ] Low oil level, or incorrect oil grade (see Weekly checks)
- [ ] Faulty oil pressure warning light switch, or wiring damaged (Chapter 2A Section 13 or Chapter 2B Section 13)
- [ ] Worn engine bearings and/or oil pump (Chapter 2A, Chapter 2B, or Chapter 2C)
- [ ] High engine operating temperature (Chapter 3)
- [ ] Oil pump pressure relief valve defective (Chapter 2A Section 12 or Chapter 2B Section 12)
- [ ] Oil pump pick-up strainer clogged (Chapter 2A Section 12 or Chapter 2B Section 12)

Engine runs-on after switching off

- [ ] Excessive carbon build-up in engine (Chapter 2C Section 7)
- [ ] High engine operating temperature (Chapter 3)
- [ ] Fuel injection/engine management system fault (Chapter 4A or Chapter 4B)

Engine noises

Pre-ignition (pinking) or knocking during acceleration or under load

- [ ] Excessive carbon build-up in engine (Chapter 2C Section 7)
- [ ] Fuel injection/engine management system fault (Chapter 4A or Chapter 4B)
- [ ] Faulty injector(s) (Chapter 4A Section 12)

Whistling or wheezing noises

- [ ] Leaking exhaust manifold gasket or pipe-to-manifold joint (Chapter 4A)
- [ ] Leaking vacuum hose (Chapter 4A or Chapter 4B)
- [ ] Blowing cylinder head gasket (Chapter 2A Section 10 or Chapter 2B Section 10)
- [ ] Partially blocked or leaking crankcase ventilation system (Chapter 4B)

Tapping or rattling noises

- [ ] Worn valve gear or camshaft(s) (Chapter 2A or Chapter 2B)
- [ ] Worn or damaged dual-mass flywheel (Chapter 2A Section 16 or Chapter 2B Section 16)
- [ ] Ancillary component fault (coolant pump, alternator, etc) (Chapter 3, 5, etc)

Knocking or thumping noises

- [ ] Worn big-end bearings (regular heavy knocking, perhaps less under load) (Chapter 2C)
- [ ] Worn main bearings (rumbling and knocking, perhaps worsening under load) (Chapter 2C)
- [ ] Piston slap – most noticeable when cold, caused by piston/bore wear (Chapter 2C)
- [ ] Ancillary component fault (coolant pump, alternator, etc) (Chapter 3, 5, etc)
- [ ] Engine mountings worn or defective (Chapter 2A Section 17 or Chapter 2B Section 17)
- [ ] Front suspension or steering components worn (Chapter 10)

Cooling system

Overheating

- [ ] Insufficient coolant in system (see Weekly checks)
- [ ] Thermostat faulty (Chapter 3 Section 3)
- [ ] Radiator core blocked, or grille restricted (Chapter 3 Section 5)
- [ ] Cooling fan faulty (Chapter 3 Section 4)
- [ ] Inaccurate cylinder head temperature sensor (Chapter 4A Section 10)
- [ ] Airlock in cooling system (Chapter 1 or Chapter 3)
- [ ] Expansion tank pressure cap faulty (Chapter 1 or Chapter 3)
- [ ] Engine management system fault (Chapter 4A or Chapter 4B)

Overcooling

- [ ] Thermostat faulty (Chapter 3 Section 3)
- [ ] Inaccurate cylinder head temperature sensor (Chapter 4A Section 10)
- [ ] Cooling fan faulty (Chapter 3 Section 4)
- [ ] Engine management system fault (Chapter 4A or Chapter 4B)

External coolant leakage

- [ ] Deteriorated or damaged hoses or hose clips (Chapter 3 Section 2)
- [ ] Radiator core or heater matrix leaking (Chapter 3 Section 5)
- [ ] Expansion tank pressure cap faulty (Chapter 1 or Chapter 3)
- [ ] Coolant pump internal seal leaking (Chapter 3 Section 6)
- [ ] Coolant pump gasket leaking (Chapter 3 Section 6)
- [ ] Boiling due to overheating (Chapter 3)
- [ ] Cylinder block core plug leaking (Chapter 2C Section 11)

Internal coolant leakage

- [ ] Leaking cylinder head gasket (Chapter 2A Section 10 or Chapter 2B Section 10)
- [ ] Cracked cylinder head or cylinder block (Chapter 2C)

Corrosion

- [ ] Infrequent draining and flushing (Chapter 1 Section 32)
- [ ] Incorrect coolant mixture or inappropriate coolant type (Chapter 1 Section 32)

Fuel and exhaust systems

Excessive fuel consumption

- ☐ Air filter element dirty or clogged (Chapter 1 Section 27)
- ☐ Fuel injection system fault (Chapter 4A or Chapter 4B)
- ☐ Engine management system fault (Chapter 4A or Chapter 4B)
- ☐ Crankcase ventilation system blocked (Chapter 4B)
- ☐ Tyres under-inflated (see *Weekly checks*)
- ☐ Brakes binding (Chapter 1 or Chapter 9)
- ☐ Fuel leak, causing apparent high consumption (Chapter 1 or Chapter 4A or Chapter 4B)

Fuel leakage and/or fuel odour

- ☐ Damaged or corroded fuel tank, pipes or connections (Chapter 4A)

Excessive noise or fumes from exhaust system

- ☐ Leaking exhaust system or manifold joints (Chapter 1 Section 19 or Chapter 4A Section 19)
- ☐ Leaking, corroded or damaged silencers or pipe (Chapter 1 Section 19 or Chapter 4A Section 19)
- ☐ Broken mountings causing body or suspension contact (Chapter 1 Section 19 or Chapter 4A Section 19)

Clutch

Pedal travels to floor – no pressure or very little resistance

- ☐ Air in hydraulic system/faulty master or release/slave cylinder (Chapter 6)
- ☐ Faulty hydraulic release system (Chapter 6 Section 4)
- ☐ Faulty clutch release/slave cylinder (Chapter 6 Section 4)
- ☐ Broken diaphragm spring in clutch pressure plate (Chapter 6 Section 6)

Clutch fails to disengage (unable to select gears)

- ☐ Air in hydraulic system/faulty master or release/slave cylinder (Chapter 6)
- ☐ Faulty hydraulic release system (Chapter 6)
- ☐ Clutch disc sticking on transmission input shaft splines (Chapter 6 Section 6)
- ☐ Clutch disc sticking to flywheel or pressure plate (Chapter 6 Section 6)
- ☐ Faulty pressure plate assembly (Chapter 6 Section 6)

Clutch slips (engine speed increases, with no increase in vehicle speed)

- ☐ Faulty hydraulic release system (Chapter 6)
- ☐ Clutch disc linings excessively worn (Chapter 6 Section 6)
- ☐ Clutch disc linings contaminated with oil or grease (Chapter 6 Section 6)
- ☐ Faulty pressure plate or weak diaphragm spring (Chapter 6 Section 6)

Judder as clutch is engaged

- ☐ Clutch disc linings contaminated with oil or grease (Chapter 6 Section 6)
- ☐ Clutch disc linings excessively worn (Chapter 6 Section 6)
- ☐ Faulty or distorted pressure plate or diaphragm spring (Chapter 6 Section 6)
- ☐ Worn or loose engine or transmission mountings (Chapter 2A Section 17 or Chapter 2B Section 17)
- ☐ Clutch disc hub or transmission input shaft splines worn (Chapter 6 Section 6)

Noise when depressing or releasing clutch pedal

- ☐ Faulty clutch release/slave cylinder (Chapter 6 Section 4)
- ☐ Worn or dry clutch pedal bushes (Chapter 6 Section 5)
- ☐ Faulty pressure plate assembly (Chapter 6 Section 6)
- ☐ Pressure plate diaphragm spring broken (Chapter 6 Section 6)
- ☐ Broken clutch disc cushioning springs (Chapter 6 Section 6)

Manual transmission

Noisy in neutral with engine running

- ☐ Lack of oil (Chapter 1 Section 28)
- ☐ Input shaft bearings worn (noise apparent with clutch pedal released, but not when depressed) (Chapter 7)*
- ☐ Clutch release/slave cylinder faulty (noise apparent with clutch pedal depressed, possibly less when released) (Chapter 6 Section 4)

Noisy in one particular gear

- ☐ Worn, damaged or chipped gear teeth (Chapter 7) *

Difficulty engaging gears

- ☐ Clutch fault (Chapter 6)
- ☐ Worn, damaged, or poorly-adjusted gearchange (Chapter 7 Section 4)
- ☐ Lack of oil (Chapter 1 Section 28)
- ☐ Worn synchroniser units (Chapter 7) *

Jumps out of gear

- ☐ Worn, damaged, or poorly-adjusted gearchange (Chapter 7)
- ☐ Worn synchroniser units (Chapter 7) *
- ☐ Worn selector forks (Chapter 7) *

Vibration

- ☐ Lack of oil (Chapter 1 Section 28)
- ☐ Worn bearings (Chapter 7) *

Lubricant leaks

- ☐ Leaking driveshaft or selector shaft oil seal (Chapter 7)
- ☐ Leaking housing joint (Chapter 7) *
- ☐ Leaking input shaft oil seal (Chapter 7) *

Although the corrective action necessary to remedy the symptoms described is beyond the scope of the home mechanic, the above information should be helpful in isolating the cause of the condition, so that the owner can communicate clearly with a professional mechanic.

Driveshafts

Clicking or knocking noise on turns (at slow speed on full-lock)

☐ Worn outer constant velocity joint (Chapter 8 Section 6)
☐ Lack of constant velocity joint lubricant, possibly due to damaged gaiter (Chapter 8)

Vibration when accelerating or decelerating

☐ Worn inner constant velocity joint (Chapter 8 Section 6)
☐ Bent or distorted driveshaft (Chapter 8 Section 6)
☐ Worn intermediate shaft bearing (Chapter 8 Section 5)

Rear axle

Roughness or rumble from the rear of the vehicle (perhaps less with the handbrake slightly applied)

☐ Rear hub bearings worn (Chapter 8 Section 8)
☐ Loose rear spring U-bolts (Chapter 10 Section 12)
☐ Roadwheel nuts loose (Chapter 1 or Chapter 10)

Braking system

Vehicle pulls to one side under braking

Note: *Before assuming that a brake problem exists, make sure that the tyres are in good condition and correctly inflated, that the front wheel alignment is correct, and that the vehicle is not loaded with weight in an unequal manner. Apart from checking the condition of all pipe and hose connections, any faults occurring on the anti-lock braking system should be referred to a Ford dealer for diagnosis.*

☐ Worn, defective, damaged or contaminated brake pads on one side (Chapter 1 or Chapter 9)
☐ Seized or partially seized brake caliper (Chapter 1 or Chapter 9)
☐ A mixture of brake pad materials fitted between sides (Chapter 1 or Chapter 9)
☐ Brake caliper mounting bolts loose (Chapter 9)
☐ Worn or damaged steering or suspension components (Chapter 1 or Chapter 9)

Noise (grinding or high-pitched squeal) when brakes applied

☐ Brake pad/shoe friction lining material worn down to wear sensor or metal backing (Chapter 1 or Chapter 9)
☐ Excessive corrosion of brake disc (may be apparent after the vehicle has been standing for some time (Chapter 1 or Chapter 9)
☐ Foreign object (stone chipping, etc)
☐ trapped between brake disc and shield (Chapter 1 or Chapter 9)

Excessive brake pedal travel

☐ Faulty master cylinder (Chapter 9 Section 10)
☐ Air in hydraulic system (Chapter 9 Section 2)
☐ Faulty vacuum servo unit (Chapter 9 Section 12)
☐ Faulty vacuum pump (Chapter 9 Section 14)
☐ Disconnected, damaged or insecure brake servo vacuum hose (Chapter 9 Section 13)

Brake pedal feels spongy when depressed

☐ Air in hydraulic system (Chapter 9 Section 2)
☐ Deteriorated flexible rubber brake hoses (Chapter 1 Section 20 or Chapter 9 Section 3)
☐ Master cylinder mounting nuts loose (Chapter 9 Section 10)
☐ Faulty master cylinder (Chapter 9 Section 10)

Excessive brake pedal effort required to stop vehicle

☐ Faulty vacuum servo unit (Chapter 9 Section 12)
☐ Faulty vacuum pump (Chapter 9 Section 14)
☐ Disconnected, damaged or insecure brake servo vacuum hose (Chapter 9 Section 13)
☐ Primary or secondary hydraulic circuit failure (Chapter 9)
☐ Seized brake caliper (Chapter 9)
☐ Brake pads incorrectly fitted (Chapter 9)
☐ Incorrect grade of brake pads fitted (Chapter 9)
☐ Brake pad lnings contaminated (Chapter 1 or Chapter 9)

Judder felt through brake pedal or steering wheel when braking

Note: *Under heavy braking, vibration may be felt through the brake pedal. This is a normal feature of ABS operation and does not constitute a fault.*

☐ Excessive run-out or distortion of discs (Chapter 1 or Chapter 9)
☐ Brake pad linings worn (Chapter 1 or Chapter 9)
☐ Brake caliper mounting bolts loose (Chapter 9)
☐ Wear in suspension or steering components or mountings (Chapter 1 or Chapter 10)
☐ Front wheels out of balance (see *Weekly checks*)

Brakes binding

☐ Seized brake caliper (Chapter 9)
☐ Faulty master cylinder (Chapter 9 Section 10)

Suspension and steering

Vehicle pulls to one side

Note: *Before diagnosing suspension or steering faults, be sure that the trouble is not due to incorrect tyre pressures, mixtures of tyre types, or binding brakes.*
- [ ] Defective tyre (see *Weekly checks*)
- [ ] Excessive wear in suspension or steering components (Chapter 1 or Chapter 10)
- [ ] Incorrect front wheel alignment (Chapter 10 Section 24)
- [ ] Accident damage to steering or suspension components (Chapter 1 or Chapter 10)

Wheel wobble and vibration
- [ ] Front wheels out of balance (vibration felt mainly through the steering wheel) (see *Weekly checks*)
- [ ] Rear wheels out of balance (vibration felt throughout the vehicle) (see *Weekly checks*)
- [ ] Roadwheels damaged or distorted (see *Weekly checks*)
- [ ] Faulty or damaged tyre (see *Weekly checks*)
- [ ] Worn steering or suspension joints, bushes or components (Chapter 1 or Chapter 10)
- [ ] Wheel nuts loose (Chapter 1)

Excessive pitching and/or rolling around corners, or during braking
- [ ] Defective shock absorbers (Chapter 1 or Chapter 10)
- [ ] Broken or weak spring and/or suspension component (Chapter 1 or Chapter 10)
- [ ] Worn or damaged anti-roll bar or mountings (Chapter 1 or 10)

Wandering or general instability
- [ ] Incorrect front wheel alignment (Chapter 10 Section 24)
- [ ] Worn steering or suspension joints, bushes or components (Chapter 1 or Chapter 10)
- [ ] Roadwheels out of balance (see *Weekly checks*)
- [ ] Faulty or damaged tyre (see *Weekly checks*)
- [ ] Wheel nuts loose (Chapter 1)
- [ ] Defective shock absorbers (Chapter 1 or Chapter 10)
- [ ] Power steering system fault (Chapter 10)

Excessively-stiff steering
- [ ] Seized steering linkage balljoint or suspension balljoint (Chapter 1 or Chapter 10)
- [ ] Incorrect front wheel alignment (Chapter 10 Section 24)
- [ ] Steering rack damaged (Chapter 10 Section 18)
- [ ] Power steering system fault (Chapter 10)

Excessive play in steering
- [ ] Worn steering column/intermediate shaft joints (Chapter 10 Section 17)
- [ ] Worn track rod balljoints (Chapter 1 or Chapter 10)
- [ ] Worn steering rack (Chapter 10 Section 18)
- [ ] Worn steering or suspension joints, bushes or components (Chapter 1 or Chapter 10)

Lack of power assistance
- [ ] Broken power steering pump drivebelt (Chapter 1 Section 8)
- [ ] Power steering system fault (Chapter 10)
- [ ] Faulty steering rack (Chapter 10 Section 18)

Tyre wear excessive

Tyres worn on inside or outside edges
- [ ] Tyres under-inflated (wear on both edges) (see *Weekly checks*)
- [ ] Incorrect camber or castor angles (wear on one edge only) (Chapter 10 Section 24)
- [ ] Worn steering or suspension joints, bushes or components (Chapter 1 or Chapter 10)
- [ ] Excessively-hard cornering or braking
- [ ] Accident damage

Tyre treads exhibit feathered edges
- [ ] Incorrect toe-setting (Chapter 10 Section 24)

Tyres worn in centre of tread
- [ ] Tyres over-inflated (see *Weekly checks*)

Tyres worn on inside and outside edges
- [ ] Tyres under-inflated (see *Weekly checks*)

Tyres worn unevenly
- [ ] Tyres/wheels out of balance (see *Weekly checks*)
- [ ] Excessive wheel or tyre run-out
- [ ] Worn shock absorbers (Chapter 1 or Chapter 10)
- [ ] Faulty tyre (see *Weekly checks*)

Electrical system

Battery will not hold a charge for more than a few days

Note: *For problems associated with the starting system, refer to the faults listed under 'Engine' earlier in this Section.*
- [ ] Battery defective internally (Chapter 5 Section 3)
- [ ] Battery terminal connections loose or corroded (see *Weekly checks*)
- [ ] Auxiliary drivebelt worn or faulty automatic adjuster (Chapter 1 Section 8)
- [ ] Alternator not charging at correct output (Chapter 5 Section 5)
- [ ] Alternator or voltage regulator faulty (Chapter 5 Section 7)
- [ ] Short-circuit causing continual battery drain (Chapter 5 or Chapter 12)

Ignition/no-charge warning light remains illuminated with engine running
- [ ] Auxiliary drivebelt broken, worn, or faulty automatic adjuster (Chapter 1 Section 8)
- [ ] Internal fault in alternator or voltage regulator (Chapter 5 Section 5)
- [ ] Broken, disconnected, or loose wiring in charging circuit (Chapter 5 or Chapter 12)

Ignition/no-charge warning light fails to come on
- [ ] Faulty instrument cluster (Chapter 11 Section 27)
- [ ] Broken, disconnected, or loose wiring in warning light circuit (Chapter 5 or Chapter 12)
- [ ] Alternator faulty (Chapter 5 Section 5)

Electrical system (continued)

Lights inoperative

- [ ] Bulb blown (Chapter 12)
- [ ] Corrosion of bulb or bulbholder contacts (Chapter 12)
- [ ] Blown fuse (Chapter 12 Section 3)
- [ ] Faulty relay (Chapter 12 Section 3)
- [ ] Broken, loose, or disconnected wiring (Chapter 12)
- [ ] Faulty switch (Chapter 12 Section 5)

Instrument readings inaccurate or erratic

Fuel or temperature gauges give no reading

- [ ] Faulty gauge sender unit (Chapter 4A Section 10 or Chapter 4A Section 8)
- [ ] Wiring open-circuit (Chapter 12)
- [ ] Faulty instrument panel (Chapter 11 Section 27)

Fuel or temperature gauges give continuous maximum reading

- [ ] Faulty gauge sender unit (Chapter 4A Section 10 or Chapter 4A Section 8)
- [ ] Wiring short-circuit (Chapter 12)
- [ ] Faulty instrument panel (Chapter 11 Section 27)

Horn inoperative, or unsatisfactory in operation

Horn operates all the time

- [ ] Horn push either earthed or stuck down (Chapter 12)
- [ ] Horn cable-to-horn push earthed (Chapter 12)

Horn fails to operate

- [ ] Blown fuse (Chapter 12 Section 3)
- [ ] Cable or connections loose, broken or disconnected (Chapter 12)
- [ ] Faulty horn (Chapter 12 Section 13)

Horn emits intermittent or unsatisfactory sound

- [ ] Cable connections loose (Chapter 12)
- [ ] Horn mountings loose (Chapter 12 Section 13)
- [ ] Faulty horn (Chapter 12 Section 13)

Windscreen wipers inoperative, or unsatisfactory in operation

Wipers fail to operate, or operate very slowly

- [ ] Wiper blades stuck to screen, or linkage seized or binding (Chapter 12)
- [ ] Blown fuse (Chapter 12 Section 3)
- [ ] Battery discharged (Chapter 5 Section 3)
- [ ] Cable or connections loose, broken or disconnected (Chapter 12)
- [ ] Faulty relay (Chapter 12 Section 3)
- [ ] Faulty wiper motor (Chapter 12 Section 15)

Wiper blades sweep over too large or too small an area of the glass

- [ ] Wiper blades incorrectly fitted, or wrong size used (see *Weekly checks*)
- [ ] Wiper arms incorrectly positioned on spindles (Chapter 12 Section 14)
- [ ] Wiper motor mountings loose or insecure (Chapter 12 Section 15)

Wiper blades fail to clean the glass effectively

- [ ] Wiper blade rubbers dirty, worn or perished (see *Weekly checks*)
- [ ] Wiper blades incorrectly fitted, or wrong size used (see *Weekly checks*)
- [ ] Wiper arm tension springs broken, or arm pivots seized (Chapter 12 Section 14)
- [ ] Insufficient windscreen washer additive to adequately remove road film (see *Weekly checks*)

Windscreen washers inoperative, or unsatisfactory in operation

One or more washer jets inoperative

- [ ] Blocked washer jet (Chapter 12 Section 17)
- [ ] Disconnected, kinked or restricted fluid hose (Chapter 12 Section 17)
- [ ] Insufficient fluid in washer reservoir (see *Weekly checks*)

Washer pump fails to operate

- [ ] Broken or disconnected wiring or connections (Chapter 12)
- [ ] Blown fuse (Chapter 12 Section 3)
- [ ] Faulty washer switch (Chapter 12 Section 5)
- [ ] Faulty washer pump (Chapter 12 Section 17)

Washer pump runs for some time before fluid is emitted from jets

- [ ] Faulty one-way valve in fluid supply hose (Chapter 12)

Electric windows inoperative, or unsatisfactory in operation

Window glass will only move in one direction

- [ ] Faulty switch (Chapter 12 Section 5)

Window glass slow to move

- [ ] Battery discharged (Chapter 5 Section 5)
- [ ] Regulator seized or damaged, or in need of lubrication (Chapter 11 Section 18)
- [ ] Door internal components or trim fouling regulator (Chapter 11)
- [ ] Faulty motor (Chapter 11 Section 18)

Window glass fails to move

- [ ] Blown fuse (Chapter 12 Section 3)
- [ ] Faulty relay (Chapter 12 Section 3)
- [ ] Broken or disconnected wiring or connections (Chapter 12)
- [ ] Faulty motor (Chapter 11 Section 18)

Central locking system inoperative, or unsatisfactory in operation

Complete system failure

- [ ] Remote handset battery discharged, where applicable
- [ ] Blown fuse (Chapter 12 Section 3)
- [ ] Faulty relay (Chapter 12 Section 3)
- [ ] Broken or disconnected wiring or connections (Chapter 12)
- [ ] Faulty motor (Chapter 11)

Latch locks but will not unlock, or unlocks but will not lock

- [ ] Remote handset battery discharged, where applicable
- [ ] Faulty master switch (Chapter 12 Section 5)
- [ ] Broken or disconnected latch operating rods or levers (Chapter 11)
- [ ] Faulty relay (Chapter 12 Section 3)
- [ ] Faulty motor (Chapter 11)

One solenoid/motor fails to operate

- [ ] Broken or disconnected wiring or connections (Chapter 12)
- [ ] Faulty operating assembly (Chapter 11)
- [ ] Broken, binding or disconnected latch operating rods or levers (Chapter 11)
- [ ] Fault in door latch (Chapter 11)

Note: *References throughout this index are in the form* "**Chapter number**" • "**Page number**". *So, for example, 2C•15 refers to page 15 of Chapter 2C.*

Note: *References throughout this index are in the form* "**Chapter number**" • "**Page number**". *So, for example, 2C•15 refers to page 15 of Chapter 2C.*

*Note: References throughout this index are in the form "**Chapter number**" • "**Page number**". So, for example, 2C•15 refers to page 15 of Chapter 2C.*

Preserving Our Motoring Heritage

< *The Model J Duesenberg Derham Tourster. Only eight of these magnficent cars were ever built – this is the only example to be found outside the United States of America*

Almost every car you've ever loved, loathed or desired is gathered under one roof at the Haynes Motor Museum. Over 300 immaculately presented cars and motorbikes represent every aspect of our motoring heritage, from elegant reminders of bygone days, such as the superb Model J Duesenberg to curiosities like the bug-eyed BMW Isetta. There are also many old friends and flames. Perhaps you remember the 1959 Ford Popular that you did your courting in? The magnificent 'Red Collection' is a spectacle of classic sports cars including AC, Alfa Romeo, Austin Healey, Ferrari, Lamborghini, Maserati, MG, Riley, Porsche and Triumph.

A Perfect Day Out

Each and every vehicle at the Haynes Motor Museum has played its part in the history and culture of Motoring. Today, they make a wonderful spectacle and a great day out for all the family. Bring the kids, bring Mum and Dad, but above all bring your camera to capture those golden memories for ever. You will also find an impressive array of motoring memorabilia, a comfortable 70 seat video cinema and one of the most extensive transport book shops in Britain. The Pit Stop Cafe serves everything from a cup of tea to wholesome, home-made meals or, if you prefer, you can enjoy the large picnic area nestled in the beautiful rural surroundings of Somerset.

> *John Haynes O.B.E., Founder and Chairman of the museum at the wheel of a Haynes Light 12.*

< *Graham Hill's Lola Cosworth Formula 1 car next to a 1934 Riley Sports.*

The Museum is situated on the A359 Yeovil to Frome road at Sparkford, just off the A303 in Somerset. It is about 40 miles south of Bristol, and 25 minutes drive from the M5 intersection at Taunton.
Open 9.30am - 5.30pm (10.00am - 4.00pm Winter) 7 days a week, *except Christmas Day, Boxing Day and New Years Day*
Special rates available for schools, coach parties and outings Charitable Trust No. 292048